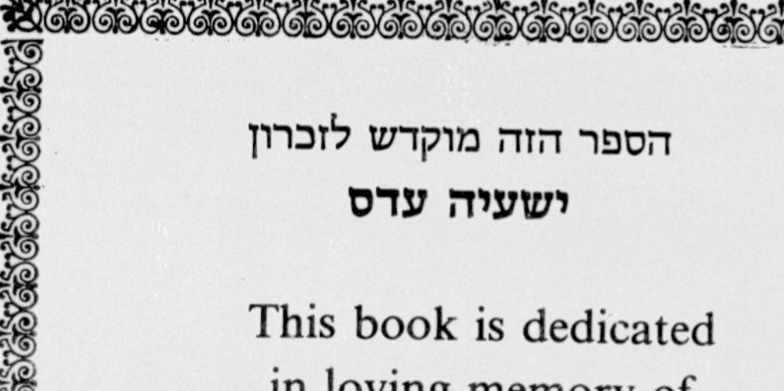

הספר הזה מוקדש לזכרון
ישעיה עדס

This book is dedicated
in loving memory of
STEPHEN ISAIAH ADES

A SOCIAL AND RELIGIOUS HISTORY OF THE JEWS

High Middle Ages, 500–1200: Volumes III–VIII

VOLUME III

HEIRS OF ROME AND PERSIA

A SOCIAL AND RELIGIOUS HISTORY OF THE JEWS

By SALO WITTMAYER BARON

Second Edition, Revised and Enlarged

High Middle Ages, 500–1200: Volumes III–VIII

VOLUME III

HEIRS OF ROME AND PERSIA

Columbia University Press
New York
The Jewish Publication Society of America
Philadelphia

LIBRARY OF CONGRESS CATALOG CARD NUMBER: 52-404

PRINTED IN THE UNITED STATES OF AMERICA
10 9 8 7

PREFACE

DURING the High Middle Ages the ancient Jewish heritage reached its full fruition. Still largely concentrated in the Eastern Mediterranean countries, but already developing new centers of life and learning under Western Islam, especially in Spain, the Jewish people fully utilized the opportunities given to it by its legal status as a self-governing "protected" minority. Despite innumerable external and internal difficulties it fostered and enriched its traditional socioreligious institutions, cultivated its time-honored ways of life by constantly adjusting them to the ever-changing environmental conditions, and maintained its world-wide cohesiveness and unity in the midst of growing diversity. At the same time it laid firm foundations for Jewish life among the young and backward but vigorous and rapidly expanding nations of Western Christendom.

By 1200 its world center of gravity had begun shifting to these Western lands. This transformation had profound effects on the political, socioeconomic, cultural, and even religious life of Jews, as well as their neighbors. It is planned, therefore, to devote the next section of this work to the period from 1200–1650, the era of Western Jewry's predominance, before the onset of Jewish emancipation.

Although generally adhering to the historical approach of the first two volumes, the author found it necessary to devote to the High Middle Ages, a period of but seven centuries (500–1200), much more space than he had to the treatment of the preceding two millennia. Several considerations imposed that decision.

The area of Jewish settlement was constantly expanding in both size and intensity. During the period here under review Jewish communities were found from Britain and France to China and Korea. Moreover, practically all of really known ancient Jewish history took place first in Palestine, than in Palestine and Hellenistic Egypt, and subsequently in Palestine and Babylonia. Our information about other Jewish communities and periods is largely limited to a few flashes of light pertaining to Egypt before the Exodus or the Elephantine colony, to the Babylonian Exile, and to the city of Rome as reflected in its subterranean inscriptions. During the High Middle Ages, on the other hand, we have much first-hand testimony concerning Jewish life under three major civilizations: the Islamic, the Byzantine, and the West European, in addition to small groups of Jews settled in India, China, and East Africa. While there was pervading uniformity in the Islamic attitude toward Jews and Judaism, there also existed important divergences among individual countries, especially Iraq, Iran, Syria and Palestine, Egypt, Morocco, Spain, and Sicily. This is even more true of Western Europe. Here the over-all controls of the Catholic Church encountered definite variations in France, Germany, England, Spain, or Italy. In fact, these very countries were often divided against themselves with respect to their Jewish policies, and were subjected to alternating fits of governmental toleration and exclusion, as well as of popular good will and hostility. Finally, the constant changes in Jewish destinies in the Byzantine Empire were complemented by the rise of new Jewish communities in the Slavonic countries and, for a time, in the Jewish kingdom of Khazaria. The foundations were then laid for the remarkable evolution of the great Jewish communities of Eastern Europe in modern times. Each of these civilizations naturally affected also Jewish internal life and thought, and received in turn many stimuli from its Jewish subjects.

Corresponding to that geographic and political diversity were the growing ramifications of the Jewish culture and religion, likewise attested by a richly available documentation. Even the great classical achievements of ancient Judaism now underwent important revisions and obtained their definitive formulations. The Bible, long canonized, achieved its final textual form only through the Masoretic schools in the ninth and tenth centuries. Many new Bible translations were added (for example, Saadiah's Arabic rendition), while the older versions, particularly the Aramaic Targumim, were carefully revised. At the same time new philological and rationalist approaches to Scripture created new schools of biblical exegesis, reaching unmatched heights in the commentaries of Saadiah, Rashi, and Ibn Ezra. The Talmud, in its Babylonian and to a lesser extent in its Palestinian form, was finally revised, committed to writing, and reinterpreted by the schools of Saboraim, geonim, and their successors. The contributions to Jewish jurisprudence and homiletics now proliferated into a vast array of commentaries, responsa, works on methodology, and codes, as well as a host of hermeneutic compilations. In fact, almost all the great midrashic works in use today, and the authoritative legal compendia of the geonim Alfasi and Maimonides, were composed in our period. Great creativity in the field of Jewish liturgy, including the compilation of the first Jewish prayer books by Amram and Saadiah, led to the emergence of a new Hebrew poetry, secular as well as sacred, which reached its postbiblical heights in the writings of Ibn Gabirol, Halevi, and Moses ibn Ezra. Novel approaches to Hebrew philology and lexicography opened new vistas on the ancient language and literature. The tenth to the twelfth centuries also represent the classical period of Jewish philosophy and science from Saadiah to Maimonides. These great intellectual achievements were coupled with an effervescence of religious creativity among the masses, finding an outlet in the strong sectarian and messianic movements during the early Muslim period and culminating in the permanent Karaite schism. All these endeavors left behind a rich and variegated literature which requires considerable attention in any comprehensive study of Jewish social and religious life.

Last but not least, one must take account of the relative paucity of scholarly syntheses in that field. Unlike the ancient period, for which we possess much secondary literature of high quality and recent vintage, Jewish history in the High Middle Ages has been treated only in a vast and ever-growing number of monographic studies published in many tongues all over the world. No comprehensive review has appeared in any language since the publication of Simon M. Dubnow's *Weltgeschichte des jüdischen Volkes* three decades ago. It so happens that even in Dubnow's work the High Middle Ages were not treated as fully as the later periods. In many respects we must go back almost a century to Heinrich Graetz's *Geschichte der Juden* for an adequate synthesis; adequate, of course, only for the time of its writing. The present author had to allot, therefore, sufficient space for the broad analysis of the most significant phases of that vital historic evolution.

The list of chapter titles of Volumes III–VIII (see p. xii) shows that Volumes III–V are devoted largely to an analysis of the political, socioeconomic and religious evolution. Volumes VI–VIII consist of a review of the main areas of Jewish intellectual creativity and its important contributions to human civilization. In all these surveys an effort was made to integrate the main lines of Jewish historical evolution with that of the surrounding cultures.

As in Volumes I–II, the bibliographical references included in text and notes omit subtitles, places and dates of publication, and some other relevant data which will be supplied in the comprehensive Bibliography in the final volume of the whole series. In the meantime, the reader ought to find the abbreviated entries here given sufficiently identifiable for all practical purposes. Once again a determined effort was made to assure their up-to-date character. Although far from exhaustive, these bibliographical references include all the more important publications in any language which had come to the writer's attention up to the end of 1956; a few entries of even later date were incorporated during the proofreading. While a prodigious amount of time and energy was expended on the verification of each quotation, here, too, a small fraction of all entries (less than one percent of the total) was unavailable in New York. As in the previous volumes it was felt that, if otherwise reliably recorded, such books and articles ought to be brought to the readers' attention. If at the time of the publication of the final Bibliography any of these entries should prove erroneous or still unavailable, these facts will be made clear, as in the first edition, and indicated by a dagger. Numerous cross references and the comprehensive Index at the end of Volume VIII should facilitate the quest for fuller bibliographical or factual information.

Our attempt to be consistent has encountered serious obstacles. Unlike other Hebrew names, most of those recorded in the Bible were quoted in their traditional English form and without diacritical marks; yet we followed the widely accepted example of Yehudah Halevi and spelled that first name regularly Yehudah, rather than

Judah. Less well known levites, however, appear under the customary form ha-Levi. Since the original sources themselves are inconsistent on this score, the patronymics of the Babylonian and Ashkenazic leaders were, as a rule, indicated through the Aramaic *bar;* all others through the Hebrew *ben*. However, the Babylonians David *ben* Zakkai or Samuel *ben* 'Ali have long been so designated in the literature, while Yehudah al-Barceloni is known as *bar* Barzillai and the Palestinian Simon *ben* Yaḥai is also frequently cited as *bar* Yaḥai.

The uniform transliteration of Hebrew titles of books or journals had to be suspended in cases where the title pages contain Western transliterations (for instance *Otzar ha-gaonim* or *Zion*). Hebrew, Aramaic, or Arabic consonants were usually distinguished by the necessary diacritical marks, but the *alif* sound was, as a rule, not further identified, and the distinction between long and short vowels emphasized only when it was thus given in the original texts. Names of authors are cited as they appear in their particular books or articles, despite changes in family or first names. Such changes, only occasionally indicated in the Notes, will be fully noted in the final Bibliography.

In this series, too, the effort was made not to trouble the reader to consult a mere reference to a source or sources at the end of the volume. Such brief references were, therefore, sometimes inserted in the text itself. More frequently all sources pertaining to an entire paragraph are cited in a single note; citations are followed by analyses of these sources and more detailed discussions, some of which have assumed the character of regular excursuses.

In conclusion, I wish to acknowledge with genuine pleasure my indebtedness to several co-workers. While working without any research assistants, I have been fortunate in having found competent secretaries in Mrs. Betty Berman, Mrs. Miriam Antler Brownstone, Mrs. Nina J. Lieberman and Mrs. Ida B. Perlmann, who conscientiously attended to the technical preparation of the manuscript in its successive stages. Miss Vergene Leverenz of the Columbia University Press has graciously edited the entire manuscript, and Miss Matilda L. Berg is preparing the comprehensive Index for Volumes III–VIII. Above all, I am again deeply indebted to my wife for her unstinting collaboration and encouragement during all the successive stages of writing, verification, and proofreading.

SALO W. BARON

Yifat Shalom
Canaan, Conn.
April 14, 1957

CONTENTS

XVI THE PREISLAMIC WORLD 3

AGE OF JUSTINIAN; GROWING DESPAIR; FINAL UPRISING; ITALY AND THE PAPACY; VISIGOTHIC SPAIN; "ONE NATION"; MEROVINGIAN FRANCE; THE LAST SASSANIANS; ANCIENT ARAB-JEWISH RELATIONS; ARABIAN PENINSULA; JEWISH KINGDOM; GATHERING STRENGTH.

XVII MOHAMMED AND THE CALIPHATE 75

PENINSULAR UNITY; CREATIVE SYNCRETISM; TOWARD WORLD CONQUEST; STIMULI OF THE CALIPHATE; JEWISH EXPANSION; BIOLOGICAL STRENGTH; THE FAR EAST AND AFRICA; RENAISSANCE OF ISLAM AND JUDAISM.

XVIII PROTECTED MINORITY 120

PERSONAL SECURITY; RELIGIOUS TOLERATION; NEW SYNAGOGUES; SOCIAL DISCRIMINATION; OFFICIALS AND COURTIERS; TAXATION; DELIMITED FREEDOMS.

XIX EASTERN EUROPE 173

BYZANTINE ERUPTIONS; LEGAL CONTINUITY; SLIGHT FISCAL CONTRIBUTIONS; CONVERSION OF KHAZARS; KHAZAR SYNCRETISM; AMONG SOUTHERN SLAVS AND MAGYARS; IN RUSSIA AND POLAND; NEW HORIZONS.

ABBREVIATIONS 225

NOTES 229

XVI, 229–61; XVII, 262–87; XVIII, 288–312; XIX, 313–40

A SOCIAL AND RELIGIOUS HISTORY OF THE JEWS: HIGH MIDDLE AGES

VOLUME III HEIRS OF ROME AND PERSIA
- XVI THE PREISLAMIC WORLD
- XVII MOHAMMED AND THE CALIPHATE
- XVIII PROTECTED MINORITY
- XIX EASTERN EUROPE

VOLUME IV MEETING OF EAST AND WEST
- XX WESTERN CHRISTENDOM
- XXI AGE OF CRUSADES
- XXII ECONOMIC TRANSFORMATIONS

VOLUME V RELIGIOUS CONTROLS AND DISSENSIONS
- XXIII COMMUNAL CONTROLS
- XXIV SOCIORELIGIOUS CONTROVERSIES
- XXV MESSIANISM AND SECTARIAN TRENDS
- XXVI KARAITE SCHISM

VOLUME VI LAWS, HOMILIES, AND THE BIBLE
- XXVII REIGN OF LAW
- XXVIII HOMILIES AND HISTORIES
- XXIX RESTUDY OF THE BIBLE

VOLUME VII HEBREW LANGUAGE AND LETTERS
- XXX LINGUISTIC RENASCENCE
- XXXI WORSHIP: UNITY AMIDST DIVERSITY
- XXXII POETRY AND BELLES-LETTRES
- XXXIII MAGIC AND MYSTICISM

VOLUME VIII PHILOSOPHY AND SCIENCE
- XXXIV FAITH AND REASON
- XXXV SCIENTIFIC EXPLORATION
- XXXVI MEDICAL SCIENCE AND PRACTICE
- INDEX TO VOLUMES III–VIII

HEIRS OF ROME AND PERSIA

XVI

THE PREISLAMIC WORLD

Withdrawing behind the rampart of talmudic law and religion, the Jewish people of the sixth century continued to pursue its historic career quietly, almost inarticulately. After the brilliant light—and shadows—emerging from the talmudic letters in both Palestine and Babylonia, Jewish life was now suddenly enveloped in a deep mist. The few flashes of light occasionally breaking through from the outside assumed a weird opaqueness from the general coloring of profound hostility in a world torn by sectarian strife and intolerance. Jews now experienced the bitter fate previously reserved for their own sectarian groups, such as the Samaritans or Sadducees; their history during the century and a half before Mohammed can no longer be reconstructed from their own records, but must painfully be pieced together, chiefly from stray data preserved by enemies. That most of these reports are concerned only with a few dramatic incidents and shed light only on either the political relations between Jews and Gentiles, or the laws issued by emperors and kings heaping ever new disabilities on the stubborn minority, lies in the very nature of these sources, in the main written by Christian ecclesiastics or jurists.

Nor could Judaism remain entirely unaffected by the general feeling of despondency and pessimism characteristic of that period of transition from the ancient to the medieval world. Both the Mishnah and the Babylonian Talmud were produced largely in an era of general well-being in Rome and Persia. Although Jews suffered increasingly from administrative oppression, their political and economic life reflected the general prosperity in a certain degree. The two empires began to decline, however, after the tannaitic age in Palestine, and in the generation following that of R. Ashi (died *ca.* 427) in Babylonia. Intensified discrimination against Jews, coupled with the widespread feeling that the end of the world was impending, likewise contributed to stifle Jewish economic and intellectual endeavor. Already in the second century, we recall, a Latin Spengler had spoken of the *senectus* of Roman civilization. Under these circumstances, it is truly astonishing that Hellenistic, Roman, and Persian pessimism, pagan and Christian alike, had so slightly affected that inveterate Jewish reliance in a better future which permeates all talmudic literature. When the downfall finally came, the Jews recoiled to await in their sheltered corner those better times which, they still confidently hoped, were soon to come.

Many new forces were at work, however; quietly gathering momentum, these prepared the Jews for the great historic role they were to play in the new era dawning upon mankind. The rapid spread of Islam in the century after its rise, the establishment of an enormous empire reaching from India and central Asia to Morocco and southern France, brought about a marvelous rejuvenation of these decaying countries. A new dynamic force transformed into a vast, flourishing realm most of the provinces of the Byzantine Empire, all of Persia, and many adjoining provinces of India, North Africa, and western Europe. The cultural and economic superiority of the Caliphate over its eastern and western neighbors, including Byzantium, was uncontested. The Jewish people, too, were quickened, and entered another great period of achievement. But first they had to suffer some of their greatest agonies under both Persia and Byzantium, and even amidst the newer civilizations slowly emerging from the smoldering ruins of Western Rome.

AGE OF JUSTINIAN

For a while it appeared as if the old Roman Empire, hereditary enemy of the Jewish people, were to be reestablished in its former glory. In his vigorous, though often confused and erratic, effort to stem its progressive disintegration and to reunite the long-lost western provinces with the essentially intact eastern half, Justinian encountered the resistance of many religious groups, including Jews. A "barbarian" by birth, a Latin by speech (he is said to have spoken Greek with a foreign accent all his life), and a despot by temperament, the emperor viewed his high office as a

God-given trust to introduce order into the prevailing chaos. He sought, particularly, to replace the theretofore tenuous balance between the warring political parties and religious sects by a stable political system and ideology. More than any of his predecessors he combined in his outlook the heritage of ancient Rome's "manifest destiny" with the missionary zeal of the Greek Orthodox Church, and sincerely believed in the divine right of his autocratic caesaropapist regime.

Jews were both a stumbling block to unity and a lightning rod absorbing some raging storms of sectarian controversy. In contemporary letters the term "Jew" often lost its ethnic-religious connotations and became a fighting word freely employed to designate any opposing ideology. It was bandied around, often with even less intrinsic justification than the terms "fascist," "imperialist," or "communist" today. Because he had stressed the human nature of Christ's body, Nestorius and his followers were called "Jews" even by emperors in their official correspondence. Twenty years after the deposition of Nestorius as Patriarch of Constantinople by the third ecumenical Council of Ephesus (431), another great Council, meeting in Chalcedon, tried to restore peace in the Eastern Church by adopting a compromise formula: "We confess one Jesus, Lord, only Son, whom we acknowledge *in* two natures." After the rejection of a more moderate version, "*of* two natures," this formula closely resembled that previously advocated by Pope Leo in Rome, and it soon became the official credo of the Greek Orthodox Church as well. The radical spokesmen of Monophysitism, on the other hand, dominant in Egypt and Syria, insisted on the exclusively divine nature of Christ and denounced the doctrine of two natures as an outright Jewish heterodoxy. They circulated a story that the Jews, upon learning of the newly adopted canon, mockingly petitioned Emperor Marcian: "For a long time we were regarded as descendants of those who crucified a God and not a man, but since the Synod of Chalcedon has met and demonstrated that they had crucified a man and not a God, we beg that we be forgiven for this offense, and that our synagogues be restored to us." The distinguished Patriarch Severus of Antioch now glibly lumped together Nestorians and Chalcedonians in his denunciation of "Jewish" heresies. When Severus was exiled in 519 his successor, Paul, a Chalcedonian, was generally surnamed "the Jew," and was driven out by his Monophysite flock.[1]

Antioch was, indeed, the storm center of the Empire. Inheriting the role formerly played by Alexandria, it now was the scene of endless street riots between the various religious sects and political parties, often masked behind the cloak of the "Green" and the "Blue" circus factions. Despite the tongue-lashing they had received from Antioch's most renowned "golden-mouthed" preacher, Jews mingled freely with the Christian population and often took part in these controversies. Curiously, they seem more frequently to have taken the side of the "Blues," largely representative of the Orthodox middle classes, than that of the mostly lower-class, pro-Monophysite "Greens." Sometimes they paid a high price for such abandonment of their wonted neutrality. On one occasion, we learn, the Antioch "Greens" destroyed the synagogue in neighboring Daphne, where the Antiochian Jews worshiped after their loss of the city synagogues through mob violence instigated by Simeon Stylites the Elder some two generations earlier (after 423). After this attack Emperor Zeno, who through his *Henoticon* of 484 had tried to appease the Monophysites and certainly had no desire to appear as a protector of Jews, real or alleged, exclaimed, "Why did they not burn the living Jews with the dead?" There is no way of telling what connection there was between that attack of the "Greens," which occurred in 489–90, and an alleged general uprising of Antiochian Jewry against the imperial power in 486, reported by the generally well-informed Byzantine chronicler, Malalas, writing about 550. Malalas may have confused these events with some riots he himself was to record under the reign of Anastasius in 507. Anastasius (491–518), who once publicly denounced the Nestorian patriarch of Constantinople, Macedonius, as "this Jew who is amongst us," must through some hostile act have provoked the real Jews of Antioch to an overt uprising. Perhaps it was this new bloodletting which so weakened the Antiochian community that it apparently played no role in the Persian raids of 529 and 540. Even the hostile chroniclers of the period fail to record any Jewish "disloyal" acts on these occasions. There is no doubt, however, that the Jewish remnant suffered severely from the city's nearly total devastation in 540, although no Jews are recorded among the captives carried away by the Persians to the New Antioch in Persia.[2]

Embarking upon the reconquest of the West, Justinian found it necessary to side with the "Jewish" Chalcedonians, whose doctrine agreed with that espoused by the Latin Church, even if it meant sacrificing the support of the Monophysite Egyptians and Syrians. He rode roughshod over the sensibilities of Empress Theodora, whose Monophysite sympathies he had allegedly promised before their marriage to respect. Little did he sense how much his policy of violent repression of the Eastern sectarian movements, reinforced by the semiconscious striving of the Egyptians and the Syrians for national self-preservation, was paving the way for the ultimate disintegration of the Eastern Empire. He was much more concerned with the immediate problem of captivating the benevolence of the western Catholics, and with the suppression of the western heresies. Arianism, especially among the North African Vandals, certainly appeared as a major obstacle. Of course, Arianism, teaching Christ's inferiority to God the Father, had long been viewed as a "Jewish" movement. One could readily argue that only complete elimination of professing Jews might remove a permanent source of heterodox infection from these threatened areas.

For this reason the western campaigns of Belisarius, Justinian's famous general, were characterized by outbursts of total intolerance in sharp deviation from the Empire's long-established policies. Remembering the sufferings of their ancestors during the last decades of the Western regime and deeply imbued by their own homilists with a deep distrust of the hereditary "kingdom of evil," Jews evidently joined the most stubborn resisters. Their last-ditch defense of Naples in 536 evoked the grudging admiration of the Byzantine historian, Procopius. They not only fought valiantly in the positions assigned to them, but had in part been responsible for persuading their fellow citizens to reject Belisarius' tempting offers to surrender. Evidently, North African Jews had proved no less intractable two years earlier. Their resistance must have appeared doubly dangerous, as their missionary successes among the Berber tribes secured for them strong allies among these turbulent neighbors, who were repeatedly to overrun the exposed province.

Hence came Belisarius' apparently gradual elimination of the Jewish community of the small but strategically important city of Borion, and the conversion into a church of its ancient synagogue, attributed by local legends to the days of King Solomon. More, the general, backed by imperial legislation, tried to impede any form of organized Jewish life in North Africa; he confiscated all synagogues and prohibited Jewish public worship in any form. This abrupt departure from the traditional toleration of synagogues may perhaps be explained by a local tradition. According to a martyrology, apparently composed in the fourth or fifth century, a Christian saint, Marciana, had allegedly been grievously insulted by Jews during Diocletian's persecutions of 304–5. Thereupon the martyr was said to have cursed the offenders, and predicted that their synagogue would burn down and never be rebuilt.[3]

Neither Belisarius nor Justinian, however, seems to have intended this outburst to be followed by any general outlawry of Judaism throughout the Empire. Although the emperor failed to reproduce in his code the significant general affirmation by Theodosius I that "the Jews' sect has not been prohibited by any law," the tenor of his entire legislation and administrative practice clearly reflected basic adherence to this principle. Apart from theological considerations, simple prudence often stayed the hand of persecutors. Many an imperial administrator must have thought along the lines of Emperor Arcadius, when in 400 he refused to permit the bishop of Gaza to destroy a pagan temple. "I know well," the emperor had stated, "that this town is full of idols; but it pays its taxes loyally and contributes much to the Treasury. If, suddenly, we terrorize these people, they will take to flight and we shall lose considerable revenues." Doubtless cognizant of the stream of Jewish refugees to Persia in the preceding centuries, the emperors had the less reason to encourage such a flight, as they must have realized how much the escape of thousands of "Jewish" Nestorians to the Sassanian Empire had strengthened the hand of that hereditary enemy of Rome. Certainly the presence of real Jews was far less threatening to the unity of empire. Even the outlawry of synagogue worship in North Africa was evidently intended as but a temporary punitive measure. To all intents and purposes it was abrogated ten years later by Justinian himself in his *Novella* 131, in which he merely renewed the old prohibition of erecting new synagogues and by implication allowed the maintenance of all existing structures, including those which may have survived the confiscation in the African province. That is undoubtedly why the earlier *Novella* was not considered part and parcel of the permanent legislation by later jurists.[4]

We must bear in mind, however, that, once despoiled of their synagogues for any length of time, Jews of any locality found it extremely difficult to replace them by new houses of worship because of the permanent outlawry of new structures. This may well have been the reason why the community of Alexandria, though it had doubtless successfully weathered the mob onslaught led by Cyril in 414 (who, incidentally, had used some of the same demagogic arguments which proved so effective against the local Jews in his subsequent major struggle against the "new Jew," Nestorius) had to get along for several generations without a public place of worship. This is evidently the meaning of the saying attributed by a later chronicler to the Coptic sect of Theodosians who allegedly decided to build a church in the Egyptian capital, "lest they be like the Jews." [5]

Nevertheless, the basic continuity in the Empire's general toleration of Judaism becomes doubly evident when one considers Justinian's contrasting treatment of the Samaritans. We shall see in another context how troublesome these sectarians, after their great religious revival under Baba Rabba, had become to the Byzantine administration. Justinian thought that he could settle the problem by a sleight of hand. By declaring the Samaritans a Christian rather than a Jewish sect, in 529 he removed from under their legal status whatever props had been lent them by their traditional toleration as adherents of the Jewish faith, long recognized as a *religio licita.* Not only was their temple on Gerizim to be permanently replaced by a church, but their synagogues were to be destroyed everywhere. In the subsequent legislation, too, their faith appears as merely part and parcel of the Christian heretical movements. While heresies were much too widespread throughout the empire and embraced too large and influential segments in the population to be placed under the sanction of capital punishment as they later were in Western laws, the very continuity of existence of the Samaritan denomination was now severely threatened.[6]

As before, the imperial masters were mainly concerned with the protection of the dominant faith against the inroads of Jews and Judaism. For this reason they readily approved of the various anti-Jewish canons adopted by Church councils, often convoked by themselves. Ironically, however, they allowed their general legislation to become deeply permeated with the spirit of canon law. They thus unwittingly injected many Jewish legal concepts into the ancient legal heritage of pagan Rome. Conversion of a Christian to the Jewish faith still was severely prohibited, though characteristically not punishable by death, but merely by exile and confiscation of property. On the other hand, to encourage conversion from Judaism, baptism of children with the consent of either parent was declared valid. The inheritance rights of converts were protected against discriminatory testamentary provisions by angry parents. Outright assaults on Jewish converts actually carried the extreme penalty. Intermarriage still was strictly prohibited, except in cases of previous conversion of the Jewish mate to Christianity. Of course, neither the Byzantine state nor Church was interested in racial origins. Even clerics and their sons could marry converted Jewesses, according to a canon adopted at the Council of Chalcedon.[7]

Jews could not legally erect new synagogues, but, at least outside the province of Africa, they were allowed to maintain their old houses of worship. There probably were innumerable bureaucratic chicaneries which made extremely awkward the maintenance of even older synagogues in a state of good repair. That is perhaps why an earthquake in Laodicaea caused the collapse of all synagogues while all churches survived, if we are to believe a contemporary report which bears the earmarks of a miracle tale. Undoubtedly synagogues suffered from extralegal expropriation at times, although we hear less frequently of mob violence on this score. On the other hand, many disabilities were doubtless mollified by such vested Christian interests as those of the Church of Amida and the usual *douceurs* offered to highly receptive Byzantine officials.[8]

More important, and in many ways entirely unprecedented, was Justinian's interference in inner Jewish religious and communal affairs. He evidently believed, with Theodosius II, in the therapeutic power of the law "to bring them [the Jews] back to sanity." Himself the author of three controversial tracts, he was a "theological amateur" (E. Schwartz), constantly awake also to the religious controversies among the sectarian groups. Without clearly spelling out the principle, reiterated by later medieval inquisitors, he arrogated to his caesaropapist office the power of defining the proper bounds of heterodoxy within the Jewish community as well. He, therefore, not only passed over in silence the ancient immunities granted by the older Roman laws to synagogue officials, but also futilely tried to safeguard the uniform observance of the orthodox Easter among his Christian subjects by forcing the Jews to postpone their Passover celebration until after the Christian holiday (543). More significantly, he believed that regulation of higher Jewish education might serve his centralizing and ecclesiastical aims equally as well as had his transfer of the famous law school from Beirut to Constantinople and his closing down of the still more renowned philosophic academy in Athens. The latter, incidentally, had included among its latest leading members, two Jews or Samaritans, Domninus and Marinus.[9]

In his much-debated *Novella* 146 enacted in 553, Justinian laid down the law concerning certain controversial subjects of the Jewish credo and ritual. That he was instigated to this extraordinary measure by the ever turbulent Jewish factions of Constantinople doubtless made imperial intervention doubly effective. Evidently but a small minority in that overcrowded metropolis which increasingly became the heart of the empire, Jews were quite early segregated in a quarter of their own established not by law but by mutual consent. Nevertheless they managed to make their voices heard in imperial circles. When Belisarius brought back from his western campaigns the seven-branched candelabrum and other Roman trophies from the Temple of Jerusalem—he had captured them from the Vandals who had taken them to Africa after their sack of Rome—a Jew predicted that the presence of these relics would bring bad luck to any locality other than Jerusalem. The superstitious emperor required only this hint to decide to transfer the sacred objects back to the Holy City. At times Constantinople Jewry even dared to stage riots of its own.[10]

In the prolix style so characteristic of his *Novellae,* in contrast to the succinct and pithy formulas taken over from the ancient legislators in his Digest and Code, Justinian informed Areobindas, and, through him, all provincial governors, of the complaints which had reached him from the Jewish community about a controversy raging in its ranks with respect to the reading of Scripture. While the Constantinople elders insisted upon the recitation of the weekly lesson in Hebrew only, a dissident group wished to follow such readings, or possibly even replace them entirely, by the recitation of a Greek version. This limited debate, with either party doubtless invoking older precedents, gave the emperor the opportunity to broaden the scope of his intervention.

> Wherever there is a Hebrew congregation [he decreed] those who wish it may, in their synagogues, read the sacred books to those who are present in Greek, or even Latin, or any other tongue. . . . Those who use Greek shall use the text of the seventy interpreters, which is the most accurate translation, . . . but that we may not seem to be forbidding all other texts we allow the use of that of Aquila, though he was not of their people, and his translation differs not slightly from that of the Septuagint.
>
> But the Mishnah, or as they call it the second tradition [*deuterosin*], we prohibit entirely. For it is not part of the sacred books, nor is it handed down by divine inspiration through the prophets, but the handiwork of man, speaking only of earthly things, and having nothing of the divine in it. . . .
>
> If any among them seek to introduce impious vanities, denying the resurrection and the judgment, or the work of God, or that angels are part of creation, we require them everywhere to be expelled forthwith; that no backslider raise his impious voice to contradict the evident purpose of God. Those who utter such sentiments shall be put to death and thereby the Jewish people shall be purged of the errors which they introduced.

Characteristically, Justinian put only the radical heresies under the sanction of the extreme penalty. Disobedience toward the other provisions of the *Novella* was to be punished less severely. For example, the Jewish "elders, *archipherekitai* and presbyters, and those called magistrates" who would dare to prevent the worshipers from reciting Scripture in translation, were threatened only with corporal punishment and the confiscation of their property. Nor did Justinian try to conceal his basically missionary aims. In his preamble he clearly stated that he expected the Jews not to confine themselves to the letter of Scripture, "but they should also devote their attention to those sacred prophecies that are hidden from them, and which announce the mighty Lord and Savior Jesus Christ." So important was this objective that the emperor was prepared to overlook his general diffidence toward translations which made him insist upon the exclusive validity of the official Latin and Greek versions of his Code. It is small wonder then, that, generally distrusting commentaries, the annexing of which to his Code he had forbidden in a special decree, he was doubly opposed to the Jewish "second Torah." [11]

Compared with this far-reaching infringement of Jewish religious autonomy, Justinian's renewal of the maxim that the Jewish community should control the market prices among Jews indicated that, despite the emperor's silence on this score, Judaism still was a *religio licita,* and that its adherents still enjoyed many rights refused to Christian heretics. Justinian and his legal advisers, headed by Trebonian, evidently exercised considerable restraint in changing the long-established legal status of the Jewish minority. They realized that the *modus vivendi* established by Theodosius II and his predecessors, which had proved sufficiently acceptable to both sides to obviate the necessity of any major legislation between 439 and 527, could not be disturbed without unbalancing the rather tenuous relationships. That is why they took over more than a score of provisions from the Theodosian Code, and incorporated them, with but minor modifications, into the new *Corpus.* True, even the omission of a single word could have serious juridical connotations. For example, by deleting the word *non* before *ad superstitionem eorum . . . pertinent* in the law of 398, Justinian's advisers clearly subjected Jewish religious affairs, too, to the jurisdiction of state courts. This intent was fully borne out by the emperor's far-reaching *Novella.* But such intentional, substantive alterations were relatively rare. If Trebonian and his collaborators omitted some thirty other regulations, the reason was more often technically legalistic (elimination of repetitions or outworn qualifications) than the reflection of intent to establish a new legal status.[12]

Omission of the general principle of Jewish toleration might have had serious consequences if the imperial administration had wished to extend its intolerant decrees from newly conquered Africa to the other provinces. Somewhat later, as we shall see, Byzantine emperors repeatedly made use of their legal prerogative of completely outlawing Judaism in their realm. Under Justinian, however, even the African prohibition extended outside Borion only to the domain of public worship. The emperor and his advisers doubtless knew how tenuous was the Christian faith of the relatively few and more easily controlled Samaritans, who had embraced Christianity under duress. Not long thereafter the author of the *Chronicon Paschale* bitterly commented that many of them "to the present day profess either religion. When they face strict governors, they publicly behave as Christians in a perfidious and misleading way. But, encouraged by the weakness and indulgence of avaricious governors, the Samaritans turn into as many haters of Christians and pretend as if they knew nothing about Christianity. By bribing the governors, they even consider it permissible to samaritize [publicly]." Clearly, with the vast extension of the Jewish dispersion and the constant changes in local law enforcement agents, close supervision of the orthodoxy of unwilling Jewish converts must have appeared utterly hopeless. That is probably why no Roman lawgiver of the period dared to classify a relapse of a Jewish convert to his ancestral faith as outright apostasy—a legal doctrine which was to play so much havoc with Jewish life under western Christendom. The Byzantine administration continued to encourage voluntary conversion, and, like its predecessors, tried to tempt pagan slaves of Jews to secure freedom through baptism. After the conquest of North Africa it made a special effort to persuade the Arian slaves there to turn Orthodox by promising them freedom, even if their Jewish masters were likewise to become Christian. To secure execution, Justinian exceptionally placed the operation of this law under the direct supervision of ecclesiastical authorities, and threatened lawbreakers with capital punishment. Elsewhere he was satisfied with the imposition of a heavy fine of thirty pounds, doubtless a reminiscence of the slave's valuation at thirty shekels in the Bible.[13]

GROWING DESPAIR

Despite Justinian's powerful and, on the whole, prosperous regime, the feeling that the end of an era, perhaps of the world, was approaching persisted among the Christians, and even more strongly among the Jews. The fall of Western Rome had left an indelible imprint on the Mediterranean peoples. St. Jerome was not alone in mourning "the mother of nations [which] had also become their tomb" and in viewing the destruction as a realization of the ancient apocalyptic visions of Daniel and the Sibylline poets. The restoration of Byzantine rule over parts of Italy by Belisarius' armies did not completely wipe out that impression. Christian chronology reinforced both the hopes for millennial redemption and the fears of the preceding disasters which, according to the old lore, were to accompany the appearance of the Antichrist. We shall see that, for reasons nurtured by Jewish messianic speculations, the Christian writers beginning with Julius Africanus (2d cent.) had placed the appearance of Jesus in the middle of the sixth millennium since the world's creation. Riding roughshod over Jewish objections, Christian experts merely argued as to whether the incarnation had taken place in 5492 *anno mundi*, according to the "Alexandrian," or in 5509 A.M. (since Heraclius 5508 A.M.), according to the "Byzantine" computation. In any case, the sixth millennium, and with it the duration of the world corresponding to the six days of Creation, was drawing to a close shortly before, or after, 500 C.E. Even though the crucial reign of Anastasius had passed without any major catastrophies and was soon followed by the "glorious" days of Justinian, neither the fervent messianic hopes, nor the deep apprehensions, had lost their force.[14]

While writers of the sixth century, learning from the mistakes of their predecessors, were less definitive concerning the actual date of the second coming of Christ, popular expectations received new nourishment from an extraordinary series of elementary disasters which befell the Byzantine world during the reign of Justinian. Apart from the appearance of a menacing comet, we are told by Barhebraeus on the basis of older sources, the sun darkened in 537 for eighteen months. During "that year," the Syrian chronicler added, "the fruits did not ripen, and the wine tasted like urine." In 544 there was a severe pestilence all over the empire, and many local inundations endangered especially the coastal areas of Phoenicia and Palestine. Time and again horror-stricken populations fled their houses during the recurrent earthquakes. One allegedly shook Constantinople for forty days. Nor were man-made disasters apt to contribute to the peace of mind of the masses. The picture drawn by the leading contemporary historian, Procopius, that "the whole earth was constantly drenched with human blood shed by both the Romans and practically all the barbarians," must have reinforced the feeling that such conditions could not last for ever.[15]

If the Christian masses viewed these awesome events as messianic portents, how much more prepared were the minds of harassed Jewry to see in them signs of approaching redemption. Certainly those Jews who viewed the remnants of the ancient 105-foot Colossus of Rhodes, further destroyed by an earthquake in the days of Athanasius—one of them allegedly was to acquire these remnants as scrap iron from the Arabs in 653—could readily translate this shameful end of a glorified symbol of Gentile might into a messianic foreboding. That is why large segments of the populace were ready to follow any messianic pretender. It is almost unbelievable how many of these false messiahs, whether genuine ecstatics or ruthless careerists, from Moses of Crete in the fifth to Serenus-Severus in the eighth century, found immediate acceptance among the masses and little overt opposition on the part of the more sophisticated leaders. The contemporary revival of Jewish apocalyptic literature likewise testifies to this sudden upsurge of messianic hopes. We shall see how many of the newly created aggadic midrashim, though speaking in a lofty timeless verbiage, may confidently be dated to that period, shortly before and after the rise of Islam. One such aggadic apocalypse, especially, bearing the name of Elijah (*Sefer Eliyahu* or *Pereq Eliyahu*) has plausibly been attributed to the days of the emperors Phokas (602–10) and Heraclius (610–41). Through the haze of their mystic phraseology one can still sense the intensity of their authors' conviction that the great prophet and ultimate harbinger of the Messiah of the house of David would soon appear.[16]

Sudden changes on the international scene added force to these extravagant hopes. Long inured to the idea, expressed by an ancient homilist, that God had divided the world between Christianity and Zoroastrianism (or later between Christianity and Islam) "only in order to preserve Israel," Jews shuddered at the thought of the Persian Empire crumbling before the onslaught of the Byzantine armies, or else becoming dependent on Byzantium in some other way. The sixth century had started with a thirty years' war (502–32) which, despite formal and informal truces, lasted through the reign of the "brothers" Justin and Kavadh I, and was not terminated until after Kavadh's death in 532. Justinian, to whom Kavadh had written in a characteristic letter, "Kavadh, king of kings and lord of the Eastern sun, to Flavius Justinian Caesar, lord of the Western moon," secured peace by the payment of regular tribute to the Eastern neighbor, so as to obtain a free hand for the reconquest of the Western Empire. However, the uneasy peace was often interrupted by raids of Persians or their Arab vassals, at times extending all the way to Antioch. It was against this background that Patriarch Severus informed Theodosius of Alexandria of his writing the letter "under the fear of the Jews." More significantly, if we are to believe the contemporary chronicler, Malalas, the Samaritans once sent a delegation to the king of Persia (Kavadh, or more likely Khosroe I), urging him to resume the war with Byzantium and allegedly promising to aid him with an auxiliary force.[17]

All such hopes seemed to be dashed when, in 562, Justinian concluded with Persia a peace treaty for fifty years. Although that treaty was broken within ten years by Justin II, who by his refusal to continue paying the tribute provoked Khosroe I to invade both Armenia and Cappadocia, the Persians were defeated and had to withdraw in 575. Fifteen years later Khosroe II, faced by an internal uprising led by Baḥram Tshubin, escaped to Byzantium and, with the aid of Emperor Maurice, his adoptive "father," reconquered his country. Until the end of Maurice's regime (602), the political entente between the two emperors, as well as domestic pressures, made any expectation of Persian help to the suffering Jews of the Byzantine Empire entirely illusory. In fact, when Maurice's relative, Domitian, entered Melitene in Armenia, he forced the Jews and Samaritans of that city, or perhaps the entire province, to accept Christianity. The Egyptian chronicler, John of Nikiu, to whom we owe this information, complained, however, of the insincerity of these new converts, as well as of Domitian's obstinacy in compelling the Christian clergy to admit them to ecclesiastical functions.[18]

FINAL UPRISING

By a sudden reversal, however, a new war started almost immediately after the assassination of Maurice in 602. Claiming that he felt obliged to avenge the death of his "father," Khosroe II resumed the hostilities. At first he merely sought to reconquer the territories voluntarily ceded in 592. But, encountering little Byzantine resistance, his armies gradually occupied all of western Asia and ultimately penetrated Egypt. They thus momentarily reestablished the boundaries of the ancient Achaemenid Empire. After the conquest of Chalcedon in 610, and again in 626 when they were aided by an Avar invasion of Byzantium's Balkan possessions from the north, Persian troops seriously threatened Constantinople, whose conquest might have ended Byzantine rule nine centuries before the Turkish occupation. Unused to major naval warfare, however, the Persians neglected to build up maritime support for their invasions. As often happened in history, naval power ultimately won out. Heraclius, who had fought ineffectively since his accession to the imperial throne in 610, transferred a sizable army to the eastern shores of the Black Sea and, with the aid of Caucasian tribes including the Khazars, attacked the Persian armies from their rear. After the loss of Ctesiphon, Khosroe's enlarged empire collapsed more speedily than it had been built up, and eventually (in 628) the king of kings himself lost his life at the hand of Persian assassins.

During that crucial quarter century (604–30) Jews took an active part in abetting the Persian campaigns. Their vivid expectations of the approaching redemption are well illustrated by the aforementioned Elijah Apocalypse. Quoting, as was customary, some of the recognized ancient authorities, the homilist betrayed his messianic objective through transparent allusions to the various names of the "last king of Persia." Apart from the traditional name, Armilus, the equivalent of the Antichrist in Christian terminology, that monarch was called Cyrus or Artaxerxes, an obvious reference to those Achaemenid kings who had helped rebuild the Second Commonwealth, or, even more specifically and definitively, *hakhasra* (in one version *Khosri*), to contemporary readers doubtless a clear enough reference to Khosroe II. That "last king" was to "go up to Rome for three years in succession." He also was to defeat three heroes descending from the sea to meet him—an allusion to the landing of Byzantine troops as long as the sea lanes were controlled by the western Empire, after the severance of land communications with Palestine and following the conquest of Chalcedon and Antioch—including a king "the lowest among kings, son of a slave girl [Phokas]." Of course, we must discount many reports about Jewish "treacheries" and "atrocities" in the Christian chronicles of that or a later period. But we need not doubt that Jews generally welcomed the Iranian invaders as liberators from the hostility and heavy yoke of Justinian's successors. In 610 they staged a sanguinary riot in Antioch, killed the patriarch, and so greatly weakened the city's defenses that it surrendered almost without resistance to the approaching Persians (611). Antiochian Jews thus avenged the patriarch's policy of repression which, ever since his return to the patriarchal see in 593, had also led to the massacre of Monophysites in Edessa and forced conversions of pagans. Jews had an additional score to settle for the humiliating punishment, meted out to their entire community for the transgression of a single coreligionist by Emperor Maurice in 592–93. Possibly in reprisal Phokas ordered his prefect Georgios forcibly to convert Jews not only in Antioch, but also in Palestine and Alexandria, though not in the European provinces (610).[19]

In 610, another chronicler reports, the 4,000 Jews inhabiting Tyre staged a rebellion and called to their assistance a Jewish force of 20,000 men assembled from Palestine, Damascus, and Cyprus. The latter island evidently now again embraced a sizable Jewish community in defiance of Trajan's sharp outlawry of Judaism half a millennium earlier, which decree had never been formally revoked. Whatever we think of the accuracy of the chronicler's figures, the city, forewarned, closed its gates and treated the local Jews as hostages. For every church outside its walls destroyed by the Jews, we are told, one hundred Jewish captives were executed, and their heads thrown across the walls to the besiegers. It seems true, in any case, that this strategically located natural fortress, as frequently before in its long and checkered history, withstood the Jewish siege and that its local Jewish community suffered severely.[20]

Palestine, understandably enough, was the main scene of Persian-Jewish collaboration. Far beyond its military and economic importance that province had lovingly been cultivated by Christian emperors ever since Constantine and his mother Helena. Its loss to "infidels" was now deeply mourned throughout the Christian world. Although apparently reduced to but 10–15 percent of the population, Palestinian Jews still were sufficiently numerous and concentrated, particularly in the northern districts, to make their weight felt in the country's affairs. Most of their thirty-one rural and twelve urban settlements recorded in that period were located in Galilee, on the military route leading from Damascus, which the Persians occupied in 611, to Palestine's provincial capital of Caesarea. The Jewish communities were effectively led by the Tiberian elders, whose intellectual prowess, buttressed by the prestige of the Davidic descent of the successors of Mar Zuṭra III, made up for the lack of imperial recognition since the abolition of the patriarchate. Some Jews had also long defied the imperial prohibition and settled in Jerusalem. They were sufficiently numerous in the Holy City for the local governor to force them to accept baptism *en masse* in 607, at a time when the storm was slowly gathering momentum.[21]

Like the Persians, the Jews owed their military successes to a large extent to the inner divisions in the Christian population. The old ecclesiastical rivalry between Jerusalem and Caesarea, to be sure, had given way to the former's recognized supremacy. Owing to the machinations of Bishop Juvenal in the era of the councils of Ephesus and Chalcedon, his see in Jerusalem was raised to a patriarchate, fifth in rank after those of Rome, Constantinople, Alexandria, and Antioch. Monophysitism, too, and other sectarian movements were far less widespread in the Holy Land than in Egypt or Syria. Nevertheless, the sharp theological controversies, nurtured by the frequent reversals of imperial policies, sharply divided also the Palestinians. Even the Orthodox of the Holy Land repudiated the new compromise formulas emanating from Constantinople and known in Christian theology as monenergism and monotheletism. Although economically the country benefited greatly from the inpouring of pilgrims and pious donations, Byzantine maladministration created conditions favorable to constant breaches of public order and even to organized highway robbery. Among the local gangsters was Jacob, son of Tanumas (Tanḥuma), who, after his forced conversion to Christianity, left behind an interesting controversial tract interspersed with autobiographical data. If we are to believe him, he constantly switched his allegiance from the "Blues" to the "Greens," so long as the internecine struggles between these parties gave him the opportunity of killing Christians.[22]

Hearing of the irresistible march of Persian troops, the Palestinian Jews were perfectly convinced that these were signs of the approaching Messiah. Already in the reign of Maurice a dream of the head of the academy in Tiberias about the Messiah's birth within eight years had found widespread credence. Unfortunately, Persia's military campaign in the Holy Land and the Jewish part therein have been described only on the basis of hostile Christian reports. The only Jewish source which seems to shed some light on the events during that final armed uprising of Palestinian Jewry against their Roman masters, the apocalyptic Book of Zerubbabel, was not only composed after the suppression of that revolt, but, by its very nature, it is too vague and obscure to enable us to reconstruct any significant details.[23]

At any rate it appears that the Jewish communities around Tiberias, led by the wealthy and learned Benjamin, opened the road for the Persian conquest of the administrative capital of Caesarea. When the Persians finally turned toward Jerusalem, the Jews seem to have obtained from them a formal promise that the city would be handed over to Jewish rule. After a twenty-day siege the Holy City surrendered (614). Following their old practice, the Persians deported some 37,000 Christian inhabitants led by Patriarch

Zechariah. As a symbol of their great victory they carried away the True Cross to Ctesiphon. The impression this booty made on all of Christendom may easily be gauged from the fact that only a few decades before the Frankish princess, Radegund, had "sent clerics into the East to procure wood of the True Cross." Many more thousand Christian captives were sold to the Jews, who allegedly slew all those who refused to adopt Judaism. More circumspectly, Eutychius spoke of "Jews together with the Persians killing innumerable Christians." That, however, Persians rather than Jews were responsible for the carnage appears evident from their failure to bury the corpses. This neglect, which gave the opportunity to a saintly Christian, Thomas, and his associates to perform their charitable burial in the cemetery of Mamilla, ran counter to accepted Jewish practice, which had long demanded the speedy burial even of executed criminals. But it accorded fully with the Zoroastrian reluctance to "defile" the earth by unclean corpses. So important was this issue even to Persian commanders of conquered provinces that, after his conquest of Armenian Iberia, Kavadh had expressly written a prohibition of burying the dead into the treaty of surrender. The Iberians' ensuing appeal for help in 527 had led, according to Procopius, to the outbreak of the Perso-Byzantine hostilities.[24]

Acting in accordance with a previous agreement, the Persian general, Romizanes, surnamed Shahrabaz (the Shah's wild boar), entrusted the Jews with the administration of the Holy City. An unnamed leader quickly assumed the name of Nehemiah; he seems even to have attempted the restoration of Jewish sacrificial worship. Many Jews undoubtedly saw in these events a repetition of the reestablishment of a Jewish commonwealth by Cyrus and Darius, and behaved as rulers of city and country. After three years the Persians realized, however, that the Jews expected from them more than they were willing to concede. On second thought they also must have felt that the aid extended to them by the small Jewish minority could not in the long run compensate them for the animosity of the Christian majority, sectarian as well as orthodox, whose loyalty toward Byzantium could otherwise be easily undermined. We do not know of the actual incident which led to the breach between the allies, but about 617 the Persians suddenly suppressed the Jewish regime in Jerusalem, forbade Jews to settle within a three-mile radius from the city, and deported a number of obstreperous leaders.[25]

Even more severe were the measures taken by the returning Byzantines in 629–30. Heraclius, to be sure, was statesmanlike enough to wish to pacify the restless Asiatic provinces, rather than to exacerbate the existing sectarian conflicts. When the Jews of the important fortress of Edessa continued to resist after the evacuation of the Persian troops, the emperor personally stayed the hand of his brother Theodorus, commander of the besieging army, and proclaimed amnesty for the Jewish resisters (628). Similarly, upon arrival in Tiberias, where he was lavishly entertained by Benjamin, he solemnly promised the Jews to let bygones be bygones. Doubtless familiar with the atrocity tales circulated by the Church, he considered them but the natural concomitant to the contemporary methods of warfare, this time operating in reverse. After his entry into Jerusalem, however, he yielded to the entreaties of the ecclesiastical leaders, whom he was seeking to placate also by retrieving the True Cross from the Persians. The Church proclaimed a special "fast of Heraclius" (celebrated for centuries thereafter in Coptic churches) to secure for the emperor expiation for the breach of his oath. This reversal opened the gate to formal prosecutions of individual Jews implicated in the previous attacks on Christians, as well as to mass lynchings.[26]

Thus ended the last attempt of Palestinian Jewry to secure political independence, or at least autonomy under Persian suzerainty, and perhaps also to rebuild the Temple of Jerusalem. The ensuing disillusionment led to the conversion of many Jews, including Benjamin. In the other provinces of the decaying empire, the repercussions seem to have been no less serious. We know very little about Egyptian Jewry of the period. But we get a glimpse of its feeling of frustration and the Christian missionary pressures as early as 622, when we learn that the entire community of 375 Jews of Tumai voluntarily accepted baptism.[27]

More far-reaching was the realization in imperial circles that the long downtrodden and apparently emasculated Jewish minority still was a cohesive and, militarily as well as politically, far from negligible entity. When immediately thereafter the Muslim Arabs appeared on the borders of both belligerent countries, sweeping away all organized resistance, Heraclius and his advisers became panicky. In 632–35 they tried to stem the tide by reestablishing religious uniformity throughout the empire by various monenergistic compromise formulas which they forced through in Armenia and Egypt. In collaboration with Pope Honorius, Heraclius even forbade his subjects to discuss theological issues. Only the Jews seemed to remain outside the now united church. At that time (632) the emperor decided to force all Jews, too, to accept baptism.

This was a fateful decision indeed. Ever since Cyril of Alexandria's mob action had forced most Jews out of the Egyptian metropolis, a few local attempts had been made, as we recall, to outlaw Judaism. But that action, or even the more formal legal prohibitions enacted with respect to Borion, Melitene, or Jerusalem, could not compare with such a universal and abrupt breach in the traditional coexistence of the two faiths established by the Christian Empire. This new method of settling the ancient Judeo-Christian controversy was to have immediate and far-reaching repercussions under western Christendom as well. Despite its evident failure in execution, it also served as a dramatic precedent to be followed by Heraclius' successors on the Byzantine throne and many western Christian potentates. It is small wonder, then, that at Heraclius' death in 641, the Jews of Constantinople actively participated in a street riot against his widow and son. According to a later but well-informed chronicler, on that occasion they stormed Christendom's leading cathedral.[28]

ITALY AND THE PAPACY

Otherwise, Byzantine influences on the Jews of western Europe were felt more indirectly. Of course, the Italian and Spanish territories incorporated into the Empire as a result of Belisarius' conquests, were subject to essentially the same laws as were the eastern provinces. For several generations the exarchate of Ravenna, on the Italian mainland, and the island of Sicily remained major outposts of Byzantine imperialism and Greek culture. Streams of Greek refugees, escaping the devastating invasions of the Balkans by Huns, Avars, and Slavs, helped restore all through southern

Italy the ancient traditions of Magna Grecia, fully justifying the medieval Hebrew designation of that region as "Italy of Greece." Elsewhere, however, Byzantine supremacy was purely nominal. Even if Theodoric (489–526) and Gregory I (590–604), both designated Great by admiring posterity, recognized the general overlordship of the Byzantine emperor (the pope only claimed precedence over the exarch of Ravenna), they successfully resisted the incursion of newly developing Byzantine patterns.

For many generations, therefore, the Theodosian Code, not that of Justinian, dominated the legal systems prevailing in the West. The barbarian invaders, although militarily victorious, recognized their own inferiority in numbers and civilization, and readily left the existing order as intact as possible. So long, especially, as the conquerors of Italy and Spain remained separated from the conquered majority by their Arian faith, they were satisfied with a general line of separation between the law of their own Teuton followers, and that of the mass of the "Roman" population, including Jews. If the law code promulgated by Theodosius II contained anti-Jewish provisions, these, too, were left unchanged. The new rulers felt the less prompted to upset the existing equilibrium, as they did not wish to antagonize further the Catholic majority by any favoritism shown to the relatively small Jewish communities. Our information about those Jewish settlements is almost entirely derived from occasional sketchy references in outside sources. But it appears that, largely concentrated in major urban areas which at that time still included a substantial number of landowners and tillers of the soil, they had suffered greater than average losses from the slaughter and pillage of the barbarian invasions. Even such services as they rendered in the defense of Naples against Belisarius went unrewarded.[29]

Yet slowly and imperceptibly a new world was arising from the ruins of ancient civilization. New legal concepts and institutions were gradually taking shape, which, reflecting the vast changes in socioeconomic and cultural life, were to determine the destinies of West European Jewry for centuries to come. Theodoric, for example, and still more his classically trained chancellor Cassiodorus, doubtless thought of merely renewing the law of 398 when they inserted into the so-called *Edictum Theoderici* a provision safeguarding Jewish judicial autonomy (after 512). But by giving it an equivocal formulation ("quos inter se jurgantes et suis viventes legibus eos judices habere necesse est, quos habent observantiae preceptores"), they reversed the main objective of the older decree. The ancient emperors, as we recollect, had intended to undermine the control of the Jewish communal authorities by declaring their courts as mere courts of arbitration. The king of the Ostrogoths, on the other hand, and his chancellor, to whose collection of state papers we owe most of our information concerning the events of the period, clearly wished to uphold the power of Jewish judges. There is no reference in their Edict to any prior consent of the parties, nor to any right of appeal from Jewish to general courts—the two main innovations of the law of 398. That Theodoric and his advisers probably were not even fully aware of that basic change, is doubly revealing. Precisely because the division of the country between Arian Teutons and Catholic Romans presupposed the operation of separate laws and judiciaries within the Christian population, the idea of Jewish judicial self-government, too, appeared perfectly natural. Here we already have the adumbration of the future medieval corporate divisions, so greatly promoted by the spread of Teuton legal concepts and feudal institutions.[30]

Not that the king or his advisers wished to preach religious freedom. In allowing the Jews of Genoa to repair their old dilapidated synagogue in accordance with the ancient provisions, Theodoric concluded: "Why do you seek what you ought to escape? We grant you the permission, but we believe to perform a laudable thing when we censure the wish of the misguided. [However,] we cannot order your faith, for no one can be forced to believe against his will." Here again Theodoric sounded a keynote of the regnant Christian view on Jews and Judaism, which, though frequently honored by its breach, was to be repeated by Thomas Aquinas and others. In his several recorded interventions in behalf of Jews the king was guided by the principle that, no matter how much they might be "known to err," they were entitled to the full protection of their established rights which "would be of service to the commonalty" (*pro servanda civilitate*).[31]

Of even greater importance for the future status of western Jewry were the parallel developments in canon law, especially as it was then being reshaped under the guidance of the Papacy. The fundamentals of the Church's attitude toward the Jews had long been laid down in the writings of the apostolic and patristic age and the enactments of universal and provincial councils, often formally approved by monarchs. However, with the emergence of the Papacy as a growingly independent power in Italian, and soon also in European, affairs, views expressed by individual popes in their homilies and writings, and decisions rendered by them in individual cases, often assumed the force of legal precedents and significantly enriched the ever growing body of canonical concepts and practices.

Personal relations likewise played a certain role. With the constant shrinkage in size of the city of Rome, the relations between Jews and Christians became more intimate. For this reason we need not be surprised to find Pope Gelasius, in the early days of Theodoric, recommending to another bishop a relative of one Telesinus, "apparently" a Jew, who had rendered him considerable services. Nor may we simply dismiss as a canard the report that, shortly before his death, Theodoric, too, employed a Jewish lawyer, Symmachus, in the preparation of a decree aimed at converting all Catholic into Arian churches. Only death allegedly prevented the king from issuing this intolerant decree. The anonymous chronicler may indeed have attempted to malign the memory of the sectarian king and, in order to underscore Theodoric's ill will, made him employ a Jew in carrying out a secret cabal, in which he could not have counted on the cooperation of such trusted Catholic advisers as Cassiodorus. It is significant, nevertheless, that the presence of such a Jewish counsellor at the royal court did not seem at all incredible to the rumor mongers of that time.[32]

Twenty-four or twenty-five letters written by Gregory the Great (of a total of 848 letters recovered from three early collections) dealt with the position of Jews in various Italian and French communities, and these exercised a particularly enduring influence. This physically weak and unworldly monk who, after reluctantly accepting election to the papal office, turned out to be one of the Church's greatest organizers and administrators, reiterated his views on the Jewish question with great vigor and conviction. Because a grateful posterity believed that every one of his statements was written under the inspiration of the Holy Ghost—later iconography often depicted the pope as listening to a dove transmitting supernatural messages—even his epistles dealing with momentary situations helped shape the thinking of canon jurists for many generations.[33]

In general the pope, like Theodoric, believed in maintaining the long-established Jewish status, since the Jews "are allowed to live in accordance with the Roman laws." He who combated all forms of paganism, Manichaeism, and Christian heresies to the death, and preached the use of force in converting heretics, vigorously denied the application of the same methods to Jews. Shortly after ascending the Papal See, Gregory learned from Roman Jewish travelers that their coreligionists in southern France had been forced to accept baptism. He immediately wrote to the bishops of Arles and Marseilles (June, 591), lauding the intention underlying that zealous performance.

> But unless that intention [he added] be accompanied by a corresponding influence of Holy Scripture, I fear that the act will bring no reward hereafter, and that the result in some cases will be the loss of the very souls we wish to save—which God forbid! For when anyone is led to the baptismal font, not by the sweetness of instruction, but by compulsion, if he returns to his former superstition he perishes the more grievously from the very cause which seemed to be for him the beginning of a new life. I therefore beg your Fraternity to preach frequently to these persons, and to appeal to them in such a manner that the kindness of the teacher more than anything else may make them desire to change their former mode of life.

On a later occasion Gregory made clear that he did not mind supporting such persuasion by worldly advantages. In October of 594 he advised the papal administrator of ecclesiastical property in Sicily to promise prospective Jewish converts a reduction in rent by one third, "or in such proportion as your Affection may think fit, so that the burden of the person converted may be lightened without the interests of the Church suffering too heavy a loss." The pope realized, of course, that persons baptized for such worldly reasons were not likely to become true Christians. But he comforted himself and his correspondent with the thought that in time the children and grandchildren of even insincere converts would grow up as loyal members of the Church. Rather inconsistently, however, he refused to apply the same argument in favor of forced conversions of Jews.[34]

A corollary of abstention from enforced conversions was permission for the Jews to practice their religion in their accustomed way. True, Gregory often reiterated the derogatory views of the Church on the "Jewish corruption" (*Judaica perditio*) and deprecated both the "silly" Jewish attacks on Christianity and the excessively literal Jewish interpretation of Scripture. Even more than other teachers of the Church he believed in the essential superiority of the allegorical interpretation over the simple "historical" exposition and the derivative "moral" lesson. In his lengthy homily, for example, on the meaning of the tables in the outer and inner courts of the Temple in Ezekiel's puzzling blueprint, he felt certain that those of the inner court symbolized the true Christian virtues of Faith, Love, Goodness, and Patience. Those of the outer court, however, were the place of the ordinary sacrifice, because they represented only the limited Jewish categories of Prophecy, Law, Circumcision, and Sacrificial Ritual. The contrast between that ordinary sacrifice and the burnt offering brought to the tables of the inner court likewise mirrored the difference between the Synagogue and the Church, for only the latter was permeated with the fire of the Holy Ghost. In another homily on Ezekiel, Gregory explained the story of Isaac's blessing in Genesis 27 as a mere adumbration of the future division between Jews and Gentile Christianity. By a characteristic inversion he saw in Esau the prototype of the Jewish people, while Jacob represented the Gentile nations, become elect through their faith in Jesus. Gregory could indulge in such flights of fancy the more readily as his inadequate linguistic training made him less prone to expatiate on the simple meaning of Scripture. Jewish adherence to that simple meaning, which he considered the cause of many heresies, annoyed him therefore doubly as but a mark of Jewish stubbornness.[35]

Nevertheless, once accepting the principle of toleration of Jews, Gregory felt that "since they are permitted to live in accordance with Roman law, it is but just that they should manage their own affairs as they think best, and let no man hinder them." For this reason, he argued in his letter to the bishop of Terracina in 591, it was wrong to deprive the Jews of opportunities for public worship simply because their prayers disturbed the Christian worshipers in a neighboring church. Gregory ordered that another building be assigned to the Terracina Jews where they might undisturbedly perform their services. Similarly, when seven years later he learned that the Jews of Palermo had lost their synagogue and hospitals to an overzealous bishop who, to prevent the restitution of these buildings, had speedily consecrated them into church property, Gregory ordered full indemnification to the Jewish community, as well as the physical restitution of all books and implements. This protection of Jewish religious institutions, while in keeping with the accepted Roman law, was particularly significant in Italy in so far as there the conflict between Saint Ambrose and the emperor over the illegal expropriation of the synagogue of Callinicum in 388 had helped create the illusion that the Church favored such mob action. That is why Theodoric had to intervene personally in both Rome and Ravenna against the ringleaders responsible for the destruction of synagogues, and why he had to issue the aforementioned protective decree for the Jews of Milan. The fact that Gregory now threw the whole weight of his revered personality and exalted office behind the old imperial law and, indirectly, disavowed the famous bishop of Milan whom he otherwise deeply admired and often imitated, contributed greatly to the reestablishment of that ancient compromise under which the European communities were enabled to carry on their accustomed religious worship.[36]

Another vital decision emanating from the papal chancery concerned the employment of Christian help by Jews. Of course, Gregory followed strictly the imperial prohibition of Jews' owning Christian slaves. He even went further than the accepted law of the Western Empire. Adhering to the more rigid regulations of the Eastern Empire and the Code of Justinian, he demanded instantaneous freedom for a pagan slave of a Jew who expressed a desire to turn Christian. He could not quite prevent such subterfuges as were employed by one Basil who, while himself remaining Jewish, turned over his Christian slaves to his sons previously baptized. Nor did the pope wish seriously to interfere with Jewish slave trade, which, even discounting the exaggerations by modern scholars, performed an economic function for many Christian lands. He accepted, therefore, Basil's excuse that a shipment of slaves from Gaul included a number of Christians by sheer oversight. The pope also drew the general distinction between permanent Jewish ownership and the temporary holding of slaves by dealers. In the latter case, the master could retain even a Christian slave for a period of forty days, and a pagan slave turned Christian for as long as three months. Only if after those periods of grace the Jewish trader failed to dispose of his explosive merchandise to a Christian purchaser, was he to lose possession. In this way Jewish slave trade could be made not only to accrue to the economic benefit of Christian countries, but also indirectly to bring into the Christian fold countless pagans from distant lands. Most vital was another distinction first drawn by Gregory. The prohibition of owning Christian slaves, the pope declared, did not apply to Jewish landlords wishing to employ Christian *coloni* on their lands. Since this form of share cropping was rapidly gaining ground, the papal decision was to facilitate greatly, at least for a time, continued Jewish landholdings in the increasingly hostile environment of feudal Europe.[37]

Gregory was utterly uncompromising, however, in all matters pertaining to the prestige and interests of the Church. In 602 he vigorously protested against those Christians in Rome who abstained from work on Saturday, following the patterns of "Jewish infidelity" (*Judaicam perfidiam*). He always extolled the number 8, rather than 7, because Sunday was the eighth day from the beginning of Creation. Perhaps harking back to Justinian's *Novella* 131, which had forbidden the Jews the acquisition of any property on which a church was located, the pope severely scolded all parties guilty of selling sacred vessels from the church of Venafro to a Jew (591). He also unhesitatingly ordered the removal of the Terracina synagogue to a more distant location, because of the disturbing Jewish *vox psallentium*. If familiar with Augustine's sermon on the prodigal son, he may have wished thus to underscore the inferiority of the Jewish faith, so movingly expressed by the Jewish spokesman in that sermon. "We observe the laws of our forefathers . . ." the Jew is said to have complained; "Now they [the Christians], holding our Scriptures, sing our psalms in the whole world, and offer their daily sacrifice [the mass]. But we have lost both our sacrifice and our Temple." On learning that a Sicilian Jew had "impiously" attracted many Christian worshipers to his newly erected altar for "blessed Elijah," the pope ordered the bishop to "inflict without delay the severest corporal punishment" on the culprit. Internationally, too, where his practical responsibilities were limited, he lauded the Spanish king, Reccared, for his anti-Jewish legislation, and vigorously protested to the Frankish monarchs Theodoric, Theodebert, and Brunichild against the practice of allowing Jews to own Christian slaves (599). In short, Gregory tried to uphold the traditional middle course of the Church's toleration of Jews in a status of legal and social inferiority, and to maintain the compromise solutions previously attained by the imperial legislation. He finally coined that famous sentence which was for centuries thereafter to sound the keynote of all papal-Jewish relations:

> Therefore, just as the Jews [*sicut illis, scil. Judaeis*] in their synagogues must not have the license to undertake anything beyond what the law permits them, so ought they not to suffer, contrary to justice and an equitable order, any prejudice and diminution in their rights.[38]

These middle-of-the-road policies were largely to persist in Rome and its environs. They were unable, however, to mitigate the severity of the storms which were to engulf the Jewish communities of western Europe in the decades following the death of the great pope. During the critical seventh century, Heraclius' final attempt to outlaw Judaism throughout his possessions found both predecessors and successors in the West. Not even Italy remained immune, papal warnings notwithstanding. The rapidly expanding Teuton Langobards, especially, though increasingly submissive to papal preachments and ultimately abandoning their Arian creed in favor of Catholicism, at times evinced complete lack of understanding for those fine compromises achieved by both the Roman and Canon jurists in dealing with the complexities of the Jewish question. A poem written in honor of the Council of Pavia in 698 referred rather briefly to a large-scale persecution which occurred in parts of the Langobard kingdom in 661. Perctarit, we are told here, son and successor of King Aripert, the first Catholic ruler of the Langobards, forced the Jews of his realm to adopt Christianity. Those who refused were exterminated at the point of the sword.[39]

As in most similar outbursts of intolerance, to be sure, many Jews survived, perhaps by paying lip service to Christianity. Their presence in northern Italy in later generations is well attested. It is also noteworthy that the important collection of Langobard laws, largely compiled in the seventh century, though never mentioning Jews expressly, was nevertheless greatly indebted to Jewish legal teachings. However, Perctarit's decree boded ill for the future of Jews even on the Appenine Peninsula which, because of the very survival there of ancient Roman institutions in fairly unbroken historical continuity and the steadying influences of the Papacy, was to prove more enduringly hospitable to the Jewish minority than any other West European country.[40]

VISIGOTHIC SPAIN

From another angle, the developments in Spain of the sixth and seventh centuries exerted an equally great influence on the later destinies of medieval Jewry. True, Spain was but a province of the Church, not its main center. The continuity of its historic evolution was sharply interrupted by the Muslim occupation. On the other hand, Spain's Jewish center was soon to overshadow those of Italy and any other European country, and its fate determined to a large extent the fate of world Jewry. The survival, therefore, of certain concepts and institutions of the Visigothic age, first in the non-Muslim corners of the country, and, after the gradual *reconquista,* in all of Spain and Portugal, was to have substantial bearing on the status of Jews under Christian domination. The repercussions of Visigothic enactments, moreover, made themselves immediately felt also in other countries. Many of these originated from discussions at the various Councils of Toledo, which served simultaneously as church synods and state diets. While in Spain proper the synodal canons required royal approval, outside the country they were to be cited for centuries thereafter as the considered opinions of leading churchmen, and hence also as major sources of universal canon law.

As in Italy, the Jews in Spain looked back on a rather long

historic evolution. We need not take at their face value the numerous traditions, kept alive throughout the Middle Ages, concerning the Jewish settlement on the Peninsula in remote antiquity, even in the days of King Solomon. The inextinguishable memories of Phoenician-Carthaginian control over Spanish Tartessus could the more readily be associated with the ancient Israelitic navigators to Tarshish, as a great many descendants of the Phoenician colonizers seem to have joined the Jewish faith in the Graeco-Roman period. Now under the reign of increasingly fanatical Christian rulers, Spanish, as well as other European, Jews evinced a special interest in these ancient traditions. If they only succeeded, they believed, in persuading their Christian neighbors that their particular ancestors had left Palestine long before the beginning of the Christian era, they personally would not have to share the accursed fate of descendants of the original "Christ killers." For this reason such an obviously spurious inscription as that found in Murviedro on an alleged tombstone of Adoniram, King Solomon's commander, was often ardently accepted as genuine even by scholars of more critical mind. Less credence was given to a letter purportedly written by the Jews of Toledo about 30 C.E. to their Palestinian coreligionists, pleading against the crucifixion of Jesus. But wholly disregarding legendary records of this kind, there are sufficiently reliable sources to attest to the existence of well developed Spanish Jewish settlements in the third century, and probably much earlier. From that century dates, indeed, the first authentic Spanish Jewish inscription commemorating the death of a little girl, Annia (or Junia) Salomonula, aged one year, four months, and one day. It was found in Adra (the ancient Abdera) in the province of Almeria.[41]

We do not know how many Jews lived on the Iberian Peninsula during the period of transition from Roman to "barbarian" rule. But if we judge from the later conditions in Muslim Spain, they must have been concentrated from time immemorial in certain cities and districts, while being spread more thinly over most of the country. The thirteenth-century author, Menaḥem ben Aaron ibn Zeraḥ, claimed, with more enthusiasm than historical accuracy, that "the entire township [of Lucena] consists of Jews who, according to tradition, are descendants of early exiles from Jerusalem who had settled there and built the town." Precisely because Christianity made its first advances through the established Jewish communities, it was doubly important for the ecclesiastical leaders to keep the two groups apart, socially as well as religiously. That is why one of the main preoccupations of the Council of Elvira, meeting about 300 C.E. when Christians still were but a persecuted minority, was to prevent too close social relations between the two denominations. Despite such conciliar decisions, Jews remained a fully integrated group in the Iberian population long after the majority had adopted Christianity. This very integration, combined with the full retention of Jewish identity, made the Jewish question more "burning" in Spain than elsewhere, when the later Visigothic rulers undertook to merge the theretofore disparate ethnic and religious groups into a homogeneous nation.[42]

None of that hostility was discernible in the early period of Visigothic rule. So long as the newcomers here, too, belonged to the Arian sect and were distinct both ethnically and religiously from the Catholic majority, so long did the monarchs respect the accepted Jewish status within the "Roman" population. Even before Theodoric, Alaric II tried to summarize the existing law, largely based on the Theodosian Code, in a briefer manual of his own. In his *Lex Romana Visigothorum* of 506, which restated the laws governing his Roman subjects by eliminating repetitions, contradictions, and many obsolete provisions (it was therefore aptly designated as the *Breviarium Alarici*), he reduced the provisions dealing with Jews from fifty-three in the older code to a mere ten. But he included also three other regulations, borrowed from Theodosius II's *Novella* of 439 and the "Sentences" of the jurist Paulus. Most of the laws suppressed in Alaric's condensation evidently appeared superfluous under the then existing conditions. For example, the provisions relating to the Palestinian patriarchate and its *aurum coronarium,* or those dealing with the Alexandrian Jewish guild of shipowners, had no meaning for sixth-century Spain. Even the more significant omission of any reference to the Jewish control over communal markets, the privileges of rabbis, or the right of baptized Jews to revert to their former faith, need not have been the result of any anti-Jewish animus. Our knowledge of the Spanish Jewish communities of the period is so limited that we cannot even assert whether there was any separate class of rabbis, or whether the community had ever effectively controlled prices. Nor did relapsed converts as yet constitute the major problem they were to become in the seventh century. In fact, the Catholic church council meeting at Agde in 506 merely sought to prevent such relapses by insisting that all prospective converts first undergo a thorough training in Christian fundamentals during a catechumenate of eight months. This provision soon became an integral part of universal canon law.[43]

This basic reaffirmation of the existing legal status seems to have remained intact for the following eighty years. Alaric's successors probably issued some additional detailed regulations, or rendered specific decisions in individual cases, but their enactments were passed over in silence in the later legal compilations permeated with a strong anti-Jewish spirit.

"ONE NATION"

The great turning point came with the conversion of the royal house to Catholicism—a major step toward making the Visigothic kingdom "one nation," as it was hailed by Archbishop Leander, the leading churchman of the period. Not long after his accession to the throne in 586 and his conversion in 587, Reccared issued a constitution concerning Jews. Although conceived in an anti-Jewish vein, it must have appeared too mild to most of his successors. They included, therefore, in the later *Leges Visigothorum*, only the provision that no Jew might purchase or acquire by gift a Christian slave under the sanction of the latter's immediate emancipation. Should the Jewish owner circumcise his slave, all his other property would be confiscated. This law went further not only than the somewhat equivocal *Breviarium*, but also than the related decision of the Third Council of Toledo, meeting under Reccared's leadership in 589. Here the only penalty for circumcision was the loss of the slave. Unable to stem the practice of mixed marriages, moreover, and apparently realizing the inefficacy of the severe penalties imposed on such unions by both the Theodosian and Alarician codes, which had treated them on a par with adultery, the Council, on the king's recommendation, merely demanded that the offspring be raised in the Christian faith. Doubtless the other provisions of Reccared's "Constitution" resembled his radical departure from the accepted law concerning slave ownership. That is why the Jews tried to bribe the king into revoking that law. Reccared resisted, however, calling forth the aforementioned congratulatory message by Gregory the Great of 599.[44]

Reccared's laws set the stage for a century of legislative vagaries. In fits alternating between total exclusion of Jews from the realm and attempts at achieving some form of peaceful coexistence, kings and councils produced an agonizing succession of laws, their modifications, revocations, and reenactments, the like of which was rarely recorded in mankind's legislative annals. Our understanding of these confusing cross currents is further aggravated by the nearly total absence of nonlegal sources, which might throw light on the extent to which these laws were practically applied, and on their underlying social and political motivations. Matters are further complicated by the frequent differences between these royal enactments and the more or less synchronous decisions of the respective Toledan Councils (from the fourth to the eighteenth), as a rule promulgated with royal approval. It is not surprising therefore, that, despite all efforts of distinguished jurists, historians, and theologians, our knowledge of that crucial evolution has not progressed much beyond what has been known half a century, even a century, ago when the major texts had become available.[45]

One of the unexplained shifts in Visigothic policy came at the beginning of the reign of Sisebut (612–20). This monarch commanded a higher degree of education than most of his predecessors. He even dabbled in theological problems on his own, and enjoyed the guidance of no lesser a savant than Isidore of Seville. However, he evidently reacted emotionally, rather than intellectually, to the difficulties of the Jewish question as it had developed since the days of Reccared. From the outset, moreover, he was engaged in the liberation of the Peninsula from Byzantine domination, and ultimately he succeeded in reducing the emperor's possessions to a tiny district around Ossonoba. He doubtless realized that his success was largely owing to the serious difficulties besetting the Empire, then locked in its deathly combat with Khosroe II. Keeping his ear attuned to all the news arriving from the East, he must have heard endless rumors about the Byzantine Jews' "betrayal" to the Persians and, worse, about their attacks on Christians. The stories about Jewish massacres of the Christian inhabitants of Antioch and, later, of Jerusalem, greatly exaggerated by contemporary chroniclers, must have reached the western shores of the Mediterranean in a still more inflated fashion. Sisebut seems to have set his mind on eliminating once and for all the Jewish minority.[46]

In the first year of his reign, Sisebut merely tried to tackle anew the never-ending difficulties with Jewish slaveholdings and mixed marriages. He renewed the decision of the Third Toledan Council concerning the obligatory Christian allegiance of all children of mixed unions, and extended the prohibition of slave ownership even to the employment by Jews of Christian *coloni* and free domestic servants. The latter provision, evidently justified in the king's mind by dangers accruing to the orthodoxy of such employees from contacts with socially superior Jews, set a significant precedent which was to embitter Judeo-Christian relations throughout the Middle Ages and early modern times, indeed down to the Nuremberg laws of 1935.

Before long Sisebut despaired, however, of his ability to enforce these decrees in the face of a noncooperative Christian public. In his law concerning Christian slaves he himself had to extend three or four months of grace for their Jewish owners to dispose of a merchandise which, according to legal theory in force for several generations, they had no business of possessing altogether. He also had to nullify all special authorizations, apparently issued to Jewish slaveholders by civil and ecclesiastical authorities. Soon thereafter he specifically threatened with severe penalties those Christians who would assist Jews in their constant evasions. Finally losing patience, he tried peremptorily to settle the problem by issuing, in 613, a decree forcing the Jews of Spain to accept baptism —the first such decree affecting an entire Christian country. Nor did he apparently leave them the melancholy choice of departing from the country, although a great many refugees seem to have succeeded in reaching more hospitable lands. Sisebut's extremism antagonized not only the numerous friends of Jews, but even churchmen and the king's collaborators, such as Isidore of Seville, who publicly condemned conversions against the converts' will. On the other hand, this last of the Western Church Fathers, and under his leadership the Fourth Toledan Council of 633, decided that even such involuntary converts, once baptized, had no right to relapse to their former creed. "For it is known," they argued, "that they [the converts] have partaken of the divine sacraments, and received the grace of baptism." Their desertion, therefore, of the Christian faith might make the latter appear "vile and contemptible." [47]

Thus began a century of Jewish martyrdom which, in many essentials, anticipated the well-known tragedy of Spanish Jewry eight centuries later (1391–1492). As on that and many other occasions, the mass conversion of Jews, rather than leading to the immediate absorption of the new converts by the majority, created still another easily identifiable group of "converted Jews." No longer formally members of the Jewish faith and hence no longer subject to the existing anti-Jewish restrictions, these converts were, as a rule, regarded neither by themselves nor by their neighbors as full-fledged Christians. To the end of the Visigothic regime the laws continued to refer, almost in the same breath, to "Jews, baptized and non-baptized." In fact, in many cases the term *Judaei,* without any adjective, clearly related to converts, while in many other instances the intent of the legislator was left obscure, whether consciously or unwittingly. The very coexistence of the two types of "Jews" on the Peninsula made relapse relatively easy for the converts and nurtured undying suspicions of their orthodoxy.[48]

Kings came and went, but the Jewish problem seemed to persist forever. The sheer survival of a professing Jewish community in the face of reiterated outlawry cannot easily be explained. Despite constant changes in the succession to the Visigothic throne, many kings coming to power in overt opposition to the policies of their predecessors or even as outright usurpers, there is no record of any formal revocation of Sisebut's intolerant decree. Not even the king's solemn curse on any of his successors who would dare abrogate it was ever expunged from the record; under propitious circumstances it could be invoked by any intolerant ruler. If the sixteenth-century Jewish chronicler, Joseph ha-Kohen, reports that Sisebut's successor, the mild and tolerant Swinthila (621–31), "recalled the

Jews banished previously, and many returned to their Lord at that time," this very formulation bears the earmarks of later medieval practice. The new regime doubtless merely closed its eyes to the violations of existing prohibitions, and tolerated both the return of Jewish exiles from France and elsewhere, and the public profession of Judaism by persons baptized under the previous regime. But the law remained on the statute books, and could readily be enforced by Swinthila's successors, as well as by the respective Councils of Toledo, which, after a lapse of forty-four years, began meeting again with increasing frequency and self-assertion.[49]

International as well as domestic tensions added to the growing sense of insecurity among the ruling classes of the Spanish state and church. In 632 Mohammed died, leaving behind a united Arabia and a people bent on establishing another universal religious empire. The successes of the Muslim armies in the following few years opened up before the Christian world vistas of an unprecedented catastrophe. We shall see that the letter allegedly addressed to the western monarchs by Emperor Heraclius was but a popular dramatization of that widespread panic. But Heraclius' authentic decree of forced conversion of Jews in his own Empire undoubtedly made a deep impression also on the Spaniards.

Nor is there any doubt about the authenticity of a letter of Pope Honorius I, urging the Spanish Church to take more stringent measures against the false converts. The text of that letter, apparently written but a few months before the pope's death, has not been preserved. But we may deduce from the reply by Braulio, the highly revered bishop of Saragossa, that Honorius betrayed on this score an extraordinary anxiety, which squared neither with his *doctrina potens,* extolled on his epitaph, nor his generally moderate approach to Church discipline. It is explainable only by that general state of hysteria in the Christian world. Although Spain was still too far removed from the battlegrounds of the 630's, the apprehensions of its rulers were heightened by the country's easy-going acceptance of treason. "Under the Visigothic monarchy," rightly comments Dom H. Leclercq, "the state of conspiracy seems to have become chronic." Had not Athanagild invited the Byzan tines into the country in 554? Half a century earlier the pretender Gesalich had relied on Vandal assistance, while now Sisenand came to power with the aid of the Franks, to whom he had allegedly promised a precious gold chalice from the spoils of Solomon's Temple. The future Pope Gregory I extolled Hermenegild, who had raised the flag of revolt against his own father, and looked for assistance to Spain's Byzantine foes. Loyalty to one's class and, even more, to one's faith so far exceeded at that time one's loyalty to the country, that treason in behalf of these superior loyalties was usually taken for granted. In 633, in fact, the Third Toledan Council had to adopt stringent resolutions against bishops who entered into secret negotiations with foreign powers and clerics who took up arms against their own fatherland. In 681 King Wamba complained of the numerous nobles and clergy on the frontiers who, on some flimsy excuse, failed to defend the country against the foreign aggressors. The king threatened such traitors with servitude. How then could Jews, downtrodden and persecuted for nearly half a century, be trusted to avoid foreign contacts for the purpose of sheer self-preservation? [50]

It is small wonder, then, that the Fourth and Sixth Councils (633 and 638) indulged in a veritable orgy of regulations concerning the new converts, culminating in the provision that "baptized Jews must have no intercourse with the unbaptized." The Sixth Council, finally, with royal approval, sweepingly decreed that in all future times no one but a Catholic might be allowed to live in the realm, and that any future ruler breaking that law should be placed under a ban (*sit anathema*) and devoured by eternal fire. Nevertheless, Jews continued to live in Spain, and fifteen years later (653), Recceswinth opened the Eighth Toledan Council with a hysterical speech: "I denounce the life and mores of the Jews, whose contagious pestilence pollutes the lands of my realm. For after the omnipotent God had radically extirpated all heresies from this region, this sacrilegious shame [*dedecus*] alone has remained." The king pledged himself either, through his devotion, to bring the Jews back to the correct road, or else to destroy them with his vengeance.[51]

Among the various experiments to make the new Christians adhere to the narrow path of orthodoxy were written agreements, in which each convert solemnly pledged himself to abjure unequivocally his former beliefs and practices and to become an observant Catholic. In the first recorded *placitum* of this kind, issued under Chintila (636–39), the converts promised also to supervise all members of their households, and to suppress any deviation by stoning the perpetrator, "so that the sacrilege shall be punished by his death." Another lengthy pledge was inserted by Recceswinth into the new law code, the *Liber judicum* or *Leges Visigothorum,* which replaced the old *Breviarium* in 654, incidentally removing whatever legal safeguards had still been left for professing Jews. This compact reads, in part:

> To our most merciful and serene lord Recceswinth the king, from all of us the Jews of Toledo and Spain, who have witnessed or signed below. . . . We therefore freely and voluntarily make these promises to your greater glory, on behalf both of ourselves and our wives and children, through this our Declaration, undertaking for the future not to become involved in any Jewish rites or obnoxious customs nor to enter any accursed association with Jews who remain unbaptized. We shall not follow our habit of contracting incestuous unions or practicing fornication with our own relatives to the sixth degree. We shall not under any circumstance, either ourselves, our children, or our descendants, choose wives from our own stock, but in the case of both sexes we will always link ourselves in matrimony with Christians. We shall not practice carnal circumcision, or celebrate the Passover, the Sabbaths, or the other feast days in accordance with the Jewish ritual. Nor shall we keep to our old habit of discriminating in matters of food.

While an exception was made in the case of pork which the convert could refuse as unpalatable to him, he must not abhor any food prepared with bacon and similar ingredients. As a penalty for breaking their pledge the converts accepted death by burning or stoning—curiously harking back to Old Testament methods of execution, rather than those generally practiced among the Visigoths or medieval Jews. Only if the king should, in his grace, prefer to spare their lives, he might give them away as slaves to Christian masters.[52]

By this involuntary consent the Jews evidently did not confer any new right on the king, since relapse after baptism had long been considered a capital crime. More important in practice was the royal prerogative, here reiterated, to sell culprits into slavery and to appropriate all their possessions. Confiscation was, indeed, a frequent method of increasing the royal domain, and of enabling the kings to reward their followers. Perhaps most significant in this context was the phrase about giving the Jews away into perpetual slavery (*perpetuae subjectae servituti*), a phrase which, later repeated in the context of Egica's punitive action by the Seventeenth Toledan Council (canon 8 in Mansi's *Collectio*, XII, 102), was to play a significant role in the subsequent development of Jewish "serfdom."

Placing the burden of supervision on the Church, the kings beginning with Sisenand (631–36), tried to suppress Judaizing tendencies among the converts by a variety of police measures. The Fourth Council of Toledo had already resolved, as we recollect, to remove children of suspect converts and hand them over to true Christians for education. Under Erwig (Euric, 680–87), who initiated his reign with the preparation of a collection of twenty-eight anti-Jewish laws, all converts were told to spend both Jewish and Christian holidays in the company of priests who would supervise their profaning the Jewish, and properly observing the Church festivals. No convert could set out on a journey without providing himself with an exit permit from his parish priest. Wherever he came, he had to register with the local priest, who had to certify in his papers the time of his arrival and departure, as well as his intervening good behavior. Erwig also enjoined the clergy tirelessly to lecture to these ever suspect parishioners. Under Egica (687–702), finally, every business transaction between a convert and a professing Christian had to begin with a demonstration of conformity, like the recitation of the Lord's Prayer and the consumption of a dish of pork. As if such methods could resolve the state of Babel-like confusion throughout the country, of which the Eleventh Toledan Council had so bitterly complained five years previously! It was this approach to totalitarian controls, without the means of a totalitarian state, which inspired Montesquieu's oft-cited condemnation of the Visigothic laws as "puerile, ridiculous, and foolish: they attain not their end; they are stuffed with rhetoric and void of sense, frivolous in the substance, and bombastic in the style." [53]

Montesquieu's harsh judgment may not have been justified in regard to the entire system of Visigothic laws, especially as compared with other contemporary systems. Modern legal historians are, for the most part, prepared to condone even the introductory section of the *Leges Visigothorum* which tried, with an overdose of rhetoric, to define the legal philosophy on which the code was based. But there is no question that, in its Jewish sections, it is not only deficient in clarity and marred by constant repetitions, but also often vitiated by overt contradictions. Its general efficacy was also seriously undermined by the weakness of the monarchy which alone might have enforced it. While the seventh-century kings fared better than their predecessors, ten of whom had been assassinated, they were always in danger of being deposed by a successful armed rebellion or palace intrigue (this happened indeed to Swinthila, Tulga, and Wamba). Of little avail were hysterical appeals like Erwig's before the Twelfth Toledan Council. "With tears in my eyes," the king exclaimed, "I implore the venerable assembly to apply all its zeal to the purification of the country of the leprosy of the [Jewish] corruption. I call on you, Arise, Arise, and destroy the hold of the culprits . . . and above all eradicate with its roots the Jewish pest which constantly comes to the fore in a new form of insanity." Such exhortations may have induced the Councils to pass the requested resolutions, but they were far from ensuring actual enforcement.

Before long the kings themselves realized that even the Church was not an altogether reliable police organ. Apart from certain reservations which many churchmen, cognizant of the ancient traditions of limited toleration of Jews, must have had against many extreme measures—the more radical anti-Jewish canons of the Toledan Councils seem to have been enacted under royal prompting rather than on purely ecclesiastical initiative—many priests, even bishops, were accessible to Jewish bribery. Corruption became increasingly rampant under that tottering regime, made doubly impotent by the ever recurrent conflicts among classes and provinces. It took the great refinements of the inquisitorial procedures developed in centuries of constant strife with heretical movements to work out any kind of close supervision of insincere converts. Even then the centuries-long underground persistence of Marranism on the Iberian Peninsula revealed how far those measures fell short of perfection. In Visigothic Spain the very will was often lacking among both the ecclesiastical and civil authorities. To combat this lackadaisical attitude, Erwig threatened any negligent priest with excommunication of three months and a fine of a pound of gold (if the priest was too poor, the fine was converted into an additional excommunication of three months), and ordered each bishop to watch the behavior of other bishops and, if need be, denounce it to the authorities. The king actually envisaged the possibility of a concerted sabotage on the part of the Spanish episcopate. Similarly unreliable were the nobles and judges, who evidently were the more accessible to Jewish *douceurs,* as they had little heart for enforcing what obviously were unpopular royal whims. Nor were Erwig's injunctions that the converts spy on one another any more effective.[54]

In desperation Egica finally decided to attack what he considered the ultimate source of effective Jewish resistance: Jewish economic power. At this late date Jews still owned much land and cultivated it with the aid of slaves, thereby provoking the polemical *Liber Responsionum,* by Saint Julian, Archbishop of Toledo, himself a descendant of Jews previously converted. In cooperation with the Sixteenth Council of Toledo (693) under the presidency of Julian's successor and admiring biographer, Felix, Egica decreed that Jews should immediately turn over to the Treasury all slaves, buildings, and agricultural and other property ever acquired by them from Christian owners. By making such property available at low prices to churchmen and nobles, he hoped to enlist their whole-hearted cooperation. Similarly, to gain the support of Christian merchants, he forbade the Jews to engage in the export and import business, and allowed them to trade within the realm only among themselves. A year later, at the Seventeenth Council, the king submitted evidence of an attempted Jewish conspiracy with their North African coreligionists. Thereupon, the Council, with royal approval, resolved to declare all Jews as slaves of those Christian masters who would assume the obligation of supervising their orthodox mode of living. All Jewish children from the age of seven were to be removed from parental control, educated in true Christian homes or monasteries, and later married to persons of non-Jewish descent. By this same resolution all Jewish property was to be confiscated. Only the Jews of Septimania, who were apparently economically and strategically indispensable, were exempted from this law.[55]

Even this utter ruthlessness did not resolve the problem for the Spanish monarchy. Much of this extremism was undoubtedly the result of the mass frenzy spreading through Christian countries as a consequence of the spectacle of the irresistible expansion of Islam in the eastern Mediterranean and, soon also, in neighboring North Africa. But, if the loyalty of both the professing and converted Jews, in the face of that looming conflict, appeared dubious, violent repression and hysterical denunciation were certainly not the most effective methods of patriotic indoctrination. In their utter desperation, Jews were indeed likely to take the side of whatever regime seemed to promise them some respite. According to Archbishop Julian, whose ardent orthodoxy, though intermingled with much political opportunism, showed that not all descendants of converts remained permanently unassimilated, the Jews sided with Hilderic, governor of Nîmes, in his revolt against King Wamba (672–80). If we are to believe this Jew-baiting chronicler, the eminent general, Duke Paul, sent to suppress the revolt, became a Judaizer and went over to the enemy. In reprisal Wamba allegedly expelled the Jews from Narbonne, which, however, did not prevent them from being treated as indispensable by Egica two decades later.[56]

Egica, in turn, may have had good reasons for complaining that some Jews conspired with their coreligionists in Morocco to deliver Spain to the Moors. By their very nature such conspiracies, however, could have been manipulated only by a small number of individuals. Such considerations, of course, did not impede Egica's punitive legislation against all Jews. But selling a great many of them into slavery, and forcing many others to flee, part of them undoubtedly to the Moors, did not improve matters. A day of reckoning was soon to come. At that time the whole structure of the Visigothic state and society collapsed with unexpected suddenness. This downfall was accelerated, as we shall see, by the presence in the country of a desperate minority which hailed the small Moorish army as liberators from an unbearable yoke.

MEROVINGIAN FRANCE

Interdependence of Jewish fate in various countries came to the fore even among the sparse and isolated Jewish communities of the Frankish kingdom. The intolerant acts of Sisebut and his successors served as an example to be followed by fanatical Christians in neighboring lands, and they helped to spread everywhere aspersions against Jewish behavior and its allegedly adverse influence on the Christian population. The medieval mind, being prone to accept rumors and unverified accusations, especially if these were disseminated by respected writers and preachers, the royal and conciliar rhetoric against Jews in neighboring Spain could not fail to make an impression. More directly, the arrival in various French cities of thousands of refugees from Septimania or across the Pyrenees made the presence of Jews more conspicuous, and doubtless injected a new factor of instability into the existing Judeo-Christian relations. The reunification of the Frankish possessions by Clothar II in 613, the very year of Sisebut's decree, subjected the Jews to the control of a single administration and broadened the scope of anti-Jewish agitation among both the clergy and the laity. Not that there had been no previous outcroppings of verbal and activist intolerance. But the sharpness of the conflicts leading up to Dagobert's attempted suppression of Judaism in 633 was felt, even by contemporaries, to have been largely a reflection of world developments.[57]

The presence of Jews in Roman and Frankish Gaul for several centuries before Dagobert is proved by sparse but incontestable evidence. Here, too, we may discount some such medieval legends as that in which three crewless ships filled with Jewish captives from the Roman war of 66–70 had providentially drifted to the harbors of Arles, Lyons, and Bordeaux. While not completely severing the link between French Jewry and the "deicides" of Golgotha, this legend helped explain to later generations the existence of Jewish settlements in the country reaching back to immemorial antiquity. The banishment of Archelaus to Vienne in 6 C.E., and of Herod Antipas to Lyons thirty-three years later, fully attested by Josephus, must have brought into the country a considerable retinue of Palestinian Jews who unwittingly laid the foundations for Jewish, and indirectly also, for Christian, community life north of the Pyrenees.[58]

Here, too, the inextinguishable memories of Phoenician colonization in southern France must have been reinforced by tombstones and other vestiges of ancient civilization which gave free reign to popular imagination. A few tombstone inscriptions commemorating deceased Jews in Gaul from the period before Charlemagne have survived to the present day. The oldest definitely datable inscription is that now preserved in the Narbonne Museum and dedicated to the memory of three siblings, aged between nine and thirty years, who died in the second year of Egica's reign (688), probably from one of the then frequent pestilences. Were it not for the Hebrew formula, "Peace unto Israel," and the initial symbol of a five-branched candelabrum (the Narbonne Jews seem to have taken seriously the rabbinic discouragement of too close emulation of the Temple's seven-branched candlestick) we would never have guessed from the wholly Latin names of the three deceased persons, their father, and grandfather, or the honorific designation of each of the latter as *dominus,* that they were Jews. Many other such inscriptions, whether located in plots specially set aside for Jewish cemeteries, or placed in the midst of Christian graveyards during the early tolerant period, must have reminded onlookers of the Jews' old roots in the country.[59]

Although the extant epigraphic sources in Gaul are almost as old and as numerous as those relating to the Jews of Spain, there is little doubt that the Jewish population in the Frankish realm was smaller and less important than the communities south of the border. On the whole, Jews seem to have followed here the Roman legions, whether as members of Rome's armed forces, or as purveyors and merchants. In the eyes of Gauls and Teutons they appeared as but another variety of "Romans." An organized Jewish community existed even in Cologne, a remote Roman outpost on the Rhine. The very existence of such a community would have escaped the attention of later generations, had it not been for Constantine's conversion to Christianity and the need he felt to issue two decrees addressed to Cologne's Jewish leaders. Fortunately also for later historians, if not for the Jews then living, these laws became part and parcel of the imperial legislation and, therefore, were incorporated in the Theodosian Code.[60]

Because of that association with the Roman military and bureaucratic apparatus, most Jews undoubtedly settled in the administrative centers established along the main strategic and trade routes. They also seem to have clung to them longer than the non-Jews. While the political instability and fiscal pressures of the declining empire forced many inhabitants out of the cities and contributed greatly to the rise of an increasingly self-sufficient manorial system, proportionately more Jews seem to have braved the Roman tax collector and stayed on in those larger centers which offered them greater educational and religious opportunities. Although, as we shall see, there were also numerous Jewish landowners and tillers of the soil, many more turned to mercantile occupations in which they could put to good use their contacts with Jews of other lands, and their general familiarity with the more advanced cultures of the eastern Mediterranean. The same factors which favored the Christian-Syrian international trader in all western lands, operated also, though to a lesser extent, in gradually shifting the Jewish economy's center of gravity to mercantile endeavors. They also brought ever new Jewish settlers into the backward European societies emerging from the disaster of the barbarian migrations.[61]

Paucity in numbers, close social relations with the Christian population, and apparently also the absence of any pronounced outward distinctions, explain the relative calmness with which the Jewish question was treated in Gaul, at least until the days of Dagobert. As in Spain, the Jews seem long to have been viewed as but part and parcel of the conquered "Roman" population. In large portions of France, then still under Visigothic rule, the *Breviarium,* issued by Alaric II from his residence in Toulouse, specifically maintained that status. In the east a similar system prevailed under the analogous *Lex Romana Burgundionum.* Here, however, the *Lex Burgundionum* addressed to the Germanic rulers provided for sharp penalties for Jews assaulting Christians. Such assault and battery was to be punished by the loss of a hand (or a fine of 75 solidi): in the case of a priest by death and confiscation of property. Even in the parts of Gaul dominated by the Catholic Franks, where Clovis' conversion to Catholicism (in 498–99, or slightly later) had more speedily eliminated the cleavage between the newcomers and the older settlers, the Jews were evidently allowed to pursue for a time their traditional mode of living. To be sure, the legal order, or rather disorder, prevailing in that period left much room for arbitrary decisions by monarchs, bishops, and nobles. The constant subdivisions of the country through inheritance, and the repeated restoration of its unity through war and intrigues, likewise added greatly to the insecurity of all groups, and particularly of a defenseless minority like the Jews. But barring some exceptional incidents, which alone are as a rule recorded in the sources, life proceeded along customary lines inherited from the prebarbarian regime.[62]

Even the various church councils meeting in France during the sixth century evinced more concern for the protection of their Christian flocks against "insidious" Jewish propaganda than for restrictions of Jewish rights as such. Time and again they passed resolutions against mixed marriages, evidently quite frequent in the Merovingian period (Second and Third Councils of Orléans of 533 and 538). The smallness of the Jewish population and the likely preponderance of males among the immigrants from Visigothic Spain and elsewhere must have greatly narrowed the choice of Jews wishing to establish families, making them more than usually exogamous. Beginning with the early Council of Vannes, Brittany (465), harking back to the still earlier Council of Elvira, the French ecclesiastical leaders also tried to restrict conviviality of Jews with the clergy, and later with all Christians (Epaon, Burgundy, in 517; Third Orléans in 538; First Mâcon in 581; Clichy in 626). Here the additional argument was frequently heard that the Church's prestige must suffer when Christians consumed Jewish dishes, while Jews treated Christian food as ritually impure. This prohibition was often extended to other forms of social intercourse, particularly during holidays. Some councils (Third Orléans and Mâcon) specifically forbade Jews to mix with Christians during the period of highest tension from Holy Thursday through Easter, "since we live under the domination of Catho-

lic kings" (538). In part this provision, also enacted in a royal decree of Childebert I, perhaps merely in confirmation of the Orléans canon, doubtless was a wise precaution to prevent undesirable incidents during a weekend annually devoted to an elaborate description of Christ's passion and the Jewish role therein.[63]

Several councils fulminated against the practice of entrusting Jews with judgeships and administrative posts (Clermont of 535 and Mâcon). The Fifth Council of Paris 614, the largest of all gatherings of Merovingian bishops, actually demanded that any Jew given military or civil authority over Christians should be forced to accept baptism for himself and his family (essentially repeated by the Council of Clichy). Most frequent were complaints about Jewish control over Christian slaves. Many resolutions were adopted, demanding severe penalties especially for the attempted conversion or circumcision of such slaves (Third Orléans, Fourth Orléans of 541; Mâcon, Clichy, and Châlon sur Saône, the latter held sometime between 647 and 654). As a rule, however, Jewish slaveowners did not simply lose their property, but were paid some sort of indemnity.[64]

None of these postulates was strikingly new. In essence they demanded only what had long been accepted canon doctrine and, for the most part, also conceded to the Church by Roman legislation. The fact that the councils found it necessary to reiterate these demands is a clear indication of their ineffectiveness in the new society, then still in its formative stages. Even in religious matters Frankish Christianity had not departed from Jewish customs and traditions to the same extent as had the Eastern Churches. The houses of worship of the two faiths differed, of course, in their respective sizes, and through the presence or absence of crosses. But otherwise none showed the elaborate imagery, whose display in the East was soon to erupt in the great iconoclastic controversy. The Third and Fourth Councils of Orléans took issue with the practice of consuming meat of animals killed by other beasts, doubtless a source of meat supply frequent enough among hunters, and demanded other forms of ritualistic abstinence reminiscent of the seven prohibitions enacted by talmudic law for all children of Noah. In ordinary times Jews seem to have got along well with all classes of the population. Even a bishop, Cautinus of Clermont (about 551–71), is accused by Gregory of Tours of being neither pious nor versed in letters. "With the Jews to whose influence he submitted, he was on familiar terms, not for their conversion, which should have been his care as a good shepherd, but to buy of them precious objects. He was easily flattered, and they gave him gross adulation. Then they sold him the things at a higher price than they were worth." No one seems to have resented it if Jews accompanied funeral cortèges of revered bishops, like Hilary or Caesarius of Arles, by forming special groups of mourners singing Hebrew psalms. Even the anti-Jewish Chilperic I had in his employ, in 581–82, a Jewish court jeweler, Priscus.[65]

Priscus' experiences at the royal court showed, however, the precariousness of Jewish status. Before long the king, trying to persuade his Jewish agent to adopt Christianity, staged a religious disputation between the Jewish merchant and himself as well as Gregory of Tours, a most learned Christian theologian and experienced debater. Remarkably, the Jewish jeweler held his ground and, according to Gregory's own admission, the disputation ended without decision. "This wretch felt not remorse, so as to believe, but held his peace." After a while the king, a half-educated despot called by Gregory "the Nero and Herod of our time," lost his patience and forced a number of Jews to be baptized, personally serving as their godfather. Priscus, still resisting, was thrown into prison and murdered by Phatir, one of these recent converts. Although extending pardon to the chief assassin, the king condemned his accomplices to death, while Phatir himself, after an escape to Burgundy, was killed there a few days later by Priscus' blood-feuding relatives. This story told with much picturesque detail by Gregory, reveals both the conversionist pressures under which the Jews lived in Paris and other French areas, and their strong and self-assertive resistance.[66]

A public display of such resistance, however, often embroiled an entire Jewish community in serious difficulties. Several years before these events in Paris (in 576), Bishop Avitus of Clermont, after long and persistent urging, succeeded in persuading one Jew to submit to conversion. A month later the new convert, marching in a church procession, was attacked by a former coreligionist who threw at him a bowl of rancid oil. The infuriated mob, dissuaded by the bishop from lynching the assailant, turned on the local synagogue and leveled it to the ground. The bishop finally placed before the entire community the alternative of either accepting baptism or leaving the city. According to Gregory, more than five hundred Jews were baptized—doubtless a gross exaggeration —while the rest sought refuge in Marseilles. They were not too safe even there, however, and in 597, as we recall, Pope Gregory the Great was obliged to protest vigorously against forced conversions in both the Marseilles and Arles dioceses. In the meantime the synagogue of Orléans suffered a similar fate. According to Roman precedents, however, the Jewish community expected the government to force the culprits to indemnify it for the losses sustained, or in some other way to enable it to rebuild its house of worship. Hopes surged high when, after Chilperic's assassination in 584, King Gontram, highly praised by Gregory of Tours for his fairness and sense of justice, arrived in the city. Gregory thus describes the welcome extended to the king by the whole city:

> Here was heard the tongue of the Syrians, there that of the Latins, there, again, even that of Jews, all harshly mingling in various acclamations as the crowds shouted: "Long live the king! and may his dominion endure over the peoples throughout uncounted years!" The Jews, who seemed to share in these greetings, kept crying: "Let all peoples adore thee and bow the knee, and be in subjection under thee." But all they effected was that after Mass, when the king sat at table, he said: "Woe to the race of Jews, ever evil and faithless and crafty of heart. They acclaimed me this day with praise and flattery, protesting that all peoples should adore me as their lord, simply in the hope that I might order the rebuilding, at public cost, of their synagogue, which the Christians some time ago destroyed. The Lord forbiddeth any such deed, and I will never do it." [67]

These occasional incidents boded ill for any period of emergency. Rumblings of popular discontent seem to have multiplied after the arrival of several thousand Jewish refugees from Sisebut's persecution, although, deprived as we are of a colorful guide like Gregory of Tours, we lack direct documentation. Some twenty years after Sisebut, the Merovingian king Dagobert followed his example and decreed that all Jews must accept baptism or leave the country. The impetus to this extreme act came here, too, from the events in the East. We may discount the legend that Dagobert was prompted by a letter from Emperor Heraclius, informing him of a dream, or an augury based upon astrological computations, that a circumcised people (namely, the Arabs) would endanger the very existence of Christendom. But there is no reason to doubt either the fact of such a diplomatic exchange, or the general anti-Jewish reaction in the face of the unprecedented Persian, and later Arab, victories. Dagobert's decree certainly was in line with the experiences of the forced convert Jacob in North Africa in 634, and the intolerant canon adopted by the Spanish and Septimanian churchmen foregathered at the Sixth Council of Toledo in 638. Perhaps to underscore the international character of the new wave of intolerance, that council was presided over not by an archbishop of Seville or Toledo, but by one from Narbonne.[68]

THE LAST SASSANIANS

From these western countries, whose importance for Jewish history was to unfold in the following centuries, we must return east to the main center of pre-Islamic Jewish life, Sassanian Persia. Although no longer the scene of that great intellectual activity which in the preceding generations had brought forth the monumental achievement of the Babylonian Talmud, the Euphrates Valley and the other provinces of the Sassanian empire still harbored many populous and affluent Jewish settlements, which in the aggregate may possibly have equaled the Jewish population in the rest of the world. Regrettably, however, with the completion of the Talmud, our main sources of information stemming from the Jewish academies themselves are reduced to a few faint echoes preserved in the editorial notes of the final redactors of the Talmud, the so-called Saboraim (Reasoners). We also possess many homiletic utterances of uncertain date and provenance, some of which probably originated in that period. Nor are the Persian sources sufficiently numerous or particularly informative. Even in so far as they are reflected through Byzantine contemporaries (for instance, Agathias Scholasticus, who evidently had at his disposal some Persian archives) or Muslim successors, they rarely mention Jews.

Perhaps this silence may be largely attributed to the fact that, at least externally, there was little change in the status of the Jewish minority. All the fundamental decisions had been made in the first generations after the establishment of the Persian Empire under Ardashir I and Shapur I. These arrangements survived, as we recall, even the major crisis of the transformation of the Roman Empire, Persia's hereditary enemy, into a Christian country, whose expansive religion reinforced its imperial ambitions.

True, the fifth century had ended on a threatening note: the successive execution of two exilarchs. The anti-Jewish riots in Isfahan, under Peroz (459–84), sparked by uncontrolled rumors of the murder of two Zoroastrian priests by Jews, demonstrated from another angle the insecurity of Jewish life in the face of royal or popular whims. On this occasion that ancient Jewish community (the city itself was allegedly founded by Palestinian exiles in the days of Nebukadrezzar), in which, according to a geonic source, Rab had wished to found his academy, suffered severely. Half of the Jewish population, we are told, was executed by the king, and the children forcibly brought up as Zoroastrians (472). Not long thereafter the Mazdakite movement, temporarily enjoying royal support, doubtless affected to some extent the religious minorities, too. However, the general status of the Jews seems to have remained unaltered. Much has been made, in both the almost exclusively anti-Mazdakite sources and modern investigations, of the Mazdakite preachment of the community of women, as well as of goods. However, one must not overlook the Mazdakite insistence on the woman's free consent. In the case of the Zoroastrian majority, this actually meant betterment of status for the women, since, according to the previous laws, any man had been entitled to give away to another his wife for free use, temporary or permanent, without the wife's approval. Probably few Jewish or Christian women assented to such promiscuity which, in their community, would not only expose them to public contumely, but also deprive them of all the legal safeguards for their married state. With their utopian brand of communism, moreover, Zaradusht, the founder, and Mazdak, the main propagator of the movement, hoped to achieve their aims without the use of force. They specifically prohibited killing for religious, or any other reasons, which must have further reduced the pressure on the religious minorities wishing to pursue their accustomed ways of living. Nor is there any evidence that Kavadh I (488–531), even in the early stages of his support of the Mazdakite movement, had gone beyond the distribution of the property of some of the nobles. Apparently he never tried to enforce the community of women even among the Persians. The large-scale riots of the liberated peasantry and attacks on the noble estates probably affected Jews more by the anarchy they generated than by direct victimization of Jewish landowners.[69]

Whatever difficulties the Jews encountered during the long reign of Kavadh did not arise because of their Jewishness. In fact, we are told that, on one occasion, the king asked his Byzantine foes for a truce in the campaign so as to enable the Jewish combatants freely to observe their Passover festival. The long-established Jewish status evidently remained unimpaired also during the remainder of the Sassanian regime, especially under Khosroe I (who served as coregent from 513, and as sole "king of kings" from 531 until his death in 579), Hormizd IV (579–90), and Khosroe II (590–628). The first Khosroe, one of the greatest Persian rulers known as Anushirvan (Anoshake-Ravan, or Of the Immortal Soul), was also given the attribute "Just" by a grateful posterity. While often as cruel as any other Persian king in his domestic and foreign conflicts and known, in particular, for his ruthless destruction of Antioch in 540, he was prepared to protect the religious rights of his Jewish and Christian subjects. His fiscal reforms probably also accrued to the ultimate benefit of the religious minorities. By imposing a uniform head and land tax on the entire population, excepting the privileged three upper estates, the king distributed the burden somewhat more equitably. Probably Jews and Christians still contributed more than their proportionate share to the Treasury. But it is likely that the discrepancy was no longer as glaring as when the Zoroastrians, perhaps then fewer in number, were largely exempt from direct payments to the government, though not to their oppressive landlords. By thus broadening greatly the tax base, Khosroe enabled his successors to increase the state's fiscal revenue to some $170 million in 607. By 626 the state's reserve grew to some $460 million, notwithstanding the protracted and long-successful western campaign of Khosroe II along the Mediterranean shores. Rather than increasing the pressure on Christians and Jews, as is often assumed, the fiscal reform of Khosroe I must have limited to some extent the arbitrary methods of tax gathering among the minorities as well.[70]

Evidently, Jews outside the Persian Empire did not consider Khosroe an anti-Jewish monarch. On one occasion, we are told by Theophanes, the Samaritans of Palestine sent to him a delegation trying to persuade him to desist from an intended peace treaty with Justinian. The Samaritans offered, together with the Jews, to furnish a contingent of 50,000 men to the Persian army. Although the date of these negotiations is uncertain and the continuator of Malalas actually ascribed them to Kavadh, the general strategic situation seems to presuppose a sufficient proximity of Persian troops for this Samaritan-Jewish aid to be effective in any way. Only Khosroe's campaign of 540, which had brought Persian troops to northern Syria, seems to have created such an opportunity.[71]

Obviously, the sectarian controversies in the Byzantine Empire contributed to the internecine strife in Persia among the Christian sects, as well as between Christians and Jews. Rather than cooperating in the face of the common danger, these minority groups often neutralized one another's forces by mutual recrimination, even outright hostilities. An Eastern Christian chronicler knew of no greater praise that he could bestow on Bishop Rabbula of Edessa (411–35), than reporting that the bishop had eliminated from his diocese all Jews, Arians, Marcionites, Manichaeans, and various gnostic groups, including one bearing the noteworthy name of Sadduceans.

Contemporary martyrologies were likewise filled with anti-Jewish recriminations. We are told, for example, that Jews joined the Persian magi in trying to reconvert a Persian girl, Shirin, who at the age of eighteen had embraced Christianity—a capital crime under the laws of Persia. In contrast thereto the official Persian policy stood out as a shining example of religious toleration. Khosroe's son and successor, Hormizd, reputedly countered the tirades of his fanatical Zoroastrian councilors with this eloquent declaration:

> Just as our royal throne cannot be supported solely by its front legs without its legs in the rear, so could our government not subsist and

remain assured if we provoked against us the revolt of the Christians and the adherents of other religions who do not share our faith. Stop attacking the Christians, therefore, but rather with great zeal perform good works. In this way the Christians and the adherents of the other religions will observe them. They will praise you and feel attracted toward your faith.[72]

Hormizd's death, followed by a long civil war, and Khosroe II's subsequent reign belong to the stormiest periods of Near Eastern Jewish history. They revealed both the insecurity of Jewish life in a rapidly changing world, and the power and tenacity of the Jewish communities under Persia and Byzantium. To speak of the sixth century as a period of exhaustion of the Jewish people was justified only at a time when Jewish history was equated with the history of Jewish letters, and it was assumed (erroneously) that the so-called Saboraic period was one of nearly complete intellectual stagnation.

From the outset Khosroe II faced strong opposition. After the assassination of Hormizd, apparently accomplished with Khosroe's connivance, the victorious general who had led the revolt, Baḥram Tshubin, succeeded in ousting the young king and taking his place. Only the support of a Byzantine army reestablished Khosroe on the throne in Ctesiphon. For about a year (590–91), however, Baḥram held sway over all Persian provinces. The Jews had the less reason to oppose him, as they could expect little consideration from a ruler supported by their Byzantine oppressors. Had not, largely for the same reason, the Nestorian *catholicos,* Ishoyabh, refused to accompany Khosroe into his Byzantine exile, and subsequently to go out to meet him upon his return at the head of the Byzantine troops? Not surprisingly, the Jews had to pay a high price for betting on the wrong pretender. We recall the fate of the Jewish community of Melitene in Armenia, forced to accept baptism by the revengeful conquerors. On arrival at the gates of New Antioch, a suburb of Ctesiphon largely populated by Christian captives of 540, the Persian general Mhebodh appealed to the inhabitants in the name of Christianity and persuaded them to deliver to him Baḥram's partisans. On the sixth day, we are informed by the nearly contemporary chronicler, Theophylactus Simocatta, Christians staged a regular anti-Jewish *pogrom* in Maḥoza, another component city of the Persian capital. This massacre inspired the chronicler to a diatribe, characteristic of the prevailing attitude of the Near Eastern Christians toward their Jewish neighbors. Jews had settled in Persian lands, Theophylactus declared, after the burning of their Temple by Vespasian.

Here they acquired great riches. Hence [!] they were easily disposed to staging seditious movements and inflaming the Persian peoples with the love of innovations. This is namely a perverse nation, cultivating a minimum of loyalty; desirous of tumults, tyrannical and forgetful of friendships; fanatical and envious; because of hatred it condones nothing and is irreconcilable.

In this way the Byzantine conquest and Persian reconquest of Ctesiphon led to the destruction of the ancient Jewish community of Maḥoza, which, though sometimes condemned by the ancient rabbis because of its materialism, had for a time served as the seat of an important academy and apparently also of the exilarchate.[73]

As soon as peace was reestablished, however, and Khosroe felt secure on his throne (in 591), he seems to have pursued a policy of pacification. He who outdid even his predecessors in the grandiloquence of his self-praise and called himself "an immortal man among the gods, and an illustrious god among men," did not indulge in petty, useless revenge. At least we possess no record of any further reprisals against the Jews. The academies of Sura and Pumbedita were allowed to continue their activities. After 602 the great Perso-Byzantine war found not only the Persian Jews, but also those of Palestine and other Byzantine provinces allied for a time with the Persian invaders.

We recall how quickly the Jews' messianic hopes were dashed, and how many grievances they had against their Persian allies. Those living in the interior of Persia were less deeply affected by these sudden changes in the fortunes of war. But in the embattled areas, they often felt the heel of the conqueror. After a futile defense of Edessa following its evacuation by Persian troops, the Jewish warriors were saved from bloody vengeance only by the chance appearance of one of their refugees before Heraclius himself. Many Edessene Jews, moreover, seem to have taken a hint from the emperor, and sought refuge among the neighboring Arab tribes. All Persian Jews were also able to observe from close range the influence of Khosroe's favorite Christian wife, Shirin (in a harem reputed to number three thousand wives and concubines), and of his fiscal agent, Yazed. Without suffering from any immediate new disabilities, they, too, must have become seriously concerned about these endless shifts and the general instability in their lives. However, they were not alone in this feeling of despondency over the deterioration in the political and social life of their country. Even a good Persian like Burzoe, Khosroe's chief medical officer, noted in his autobiography that, "our age, having become old and decrepit, may have a clear appearance, but in reality it is deeply disturbed." While praising the king to the sky, he emphasized that there was a complete reversal of all values, and that "domination has been transferred from the capable to the unfit. It is as if the world, drunken with joy, would say: I have concealed all that is good, and brought forth all that is bad." There was more than mere literary flourish in these protestations. Evidently large segments of the non-Jewish population, too, looked forward to some major cataclysm which would put an end to that state of uninterrupted crisis.[74]

ANCIENT ARAB–JEWISH RELATIONS

Such a cataclysmic change was soon to come in the shape of the Arab conquest of Persia. The last king, Yazdegerd III, was assassinated in exile in 651. From that time the new world factor, the Arabs, began to affect deeply the destinies of the whole Jewish people.

In the seventh century Arab-Jewish relations already had a long history behind them. When Mohammed appeared as the prophet of a new religion, he found before him an Arab world, extending from the Yemen to Syria and Mesopotamia, densely interspersed with Jewish settlements, where ancient traditions, reaching back to the times before the separation of the Semitic nations, had been kept alive through steady contact. The spread of the Nabatean Arabs into southern and eastern Palestine and Babylonia had made the Arab a familiar figure in the Jewish mass settlements, just as the penetration of Jewish refugees, soldiers, and merchants into the

Arabian Peninsula helped to acquaint even the remotest Bedouin tribesmen with "the people of the book."

Even leaving aside the now discredited theory of Midianite influences on the "nomadic ideals" of the Mosaic religion, there is no reason to doubt the immemorial ties which linked the ancient Israelites with their immediate southern neighbors. In fact, the first fully datable event of Israelitic history, the battle of Karkara (853–852 B.C.E.), involved among Aram's allies both King Ahab of Samaria and King Jindibu, the Arabian, with his 1,000 camels. Arab kings, mentioned by Jeremiah, began playing a greater role in the destinies of Palestine during the Second Commonwealth, as their regime had displaced that of Edomites in Petra, and had begun fanning out into Transjordan. The books of Ezra and Nehemiah and the works of Josephus are filled with references to petty Arab rulers, the Jewish historian no longer being able to distinguish them from the ancient Ammonites.[75]

In one of its periodic revivals Transjordan, in particular, entered under Nabatean-Roman domination a period of economic and cultural prosperity, which, despite temporary relapses, was to last to the end of the first millennium. Rome's incorporation of Arabia into the imperial structure shortly after the fall of Jerusalem (105 C.E.) further intensified the contacts between the two peoples. About 358, finally, the entire area between the Red Sea and the Mediterranean was united with Palestine, probably for Christian as well as for administrative reasons, and thenceforth appeared in the records as the province of *Palaestina Tertia.* No less intensive were the interrelations between the Jews and their Arab neighbors in that vast no man's land which was allowed to persist in the Syrian desert as a buffer between Rome and Persia. Jewish communities existed particularly under the Lakhmids, Arab vassal princes of Sassanian Persia who, from the third century on, dominated a large area close to the great centers of Jewish life and learning in Babylonia. In the very Lakhmid capital, Ḥira, under King Imru al-Qais (whose extant epitaph dated 328 C.E. is a remarkable specimen of early Arabic epigraphy), R. Hamnuna presided over an important Jewish academy of learning.[76]

That the relations were not always friendly, lay in the nature of such expansive movements. In Palestine much energy had to be expended by the local rulers from Jehoram to the Herodians and, in the fourth century, by the Samaritan leader, Babba Raba, to keep off Arab invaders, while the Assyrians, Persians, and Romans used these local animosities to their own advantage. In Babylonia, too, the great city of Nehardea was so frequently exposed to raids by roving Arabs that R. Naḥman specifically exempted the local Jews from the prohibition of carrying weapons on Sabbath ('Erubin 45a). When earlier in the third century Palmyra-Tadmor, that Arab jewel of the desert, saved Imperial Rome by checking the triumphant march of Shapur I at a critical juncture, Babylonian Jewry had to part with the high messianic hopes aroused by the first successes of the Persian army. It was only a step from blaming the Palmyrenes for this failure to accusing them of having participated in the destruction of the Second, or even of the First Temple, and to R. Kahana's irate exclamation, "Israel is going to proclaim a festival on the day of Tadmor's destruction" (see the interesting debate in Yebamot 17a).

On the other hand, the Jewish legend ascribing to the sons of that oasis a descent from Solomon's slaves, captive Jewesses or Jewish bastards, reflects Babylonian Jewry's consciousness of the strange blood ties uniting it with this offshoot of the Arabian race. Among these Aramaic-speaking Arabs themselves a legend spread, and was later recorded by Muslim writers, that the city of Tadmor —which incidentally is mentioned in a cuneiform tablet before 1000 B.C.E.—had been built by *jinns* (demons) for Solomon. This was a hostile version of the biblical report that Solomon had "built Tadmor in the wilderness." Other legends (recorded by Malalas), claimed that Solomon had thus wished to commemorate David's victory over Goliath, and that during his campaign against Jerusalem, Nebukadrezzar first had to destroy Tadmor then occupied by a Jewish garrison. More significant historically is, as we recall, the great role played by Jews in that crossroad of caravan routes during the era of her great commercial prosperity in the second and third centuries. Although the vast majority of Palmyrenes had remained pagans, they dedicated more inscriptions to the "highest" god (*Hypsistos*) than to any other deity. The city suffered severely after the defeat of her overambitious Queen

Zenobia, but many Jews continued to live and prosper there. As late as 1240 a French traveler, Rabbi Jacob, was shown there "a tower of David and very great and wondrous buildings built by the 'Anaqim [biblical giants] and . . . the tomb of Joel, the son of Pethuel." [77]

Similarly, although Josephus is completely silent on this aspect of the problem, the temporary rise of a Jewish principality in the vicinity of Nehardea under the brothers Asinaeus and Anilaeus in the days of Tiberius (*Antt.* XVIII.9.1–9. 310–79), was doubtless facilitated by the disorganized conditions in that area concomitant with the infiltration of wandering Bedouins. In fact, the Jewish historian's consciously romanticizing description of this episode leaves one with the impression that the Parthian administration at that time toyed with the idea of creating, at its western borders, a Jewish vassal principality of the kind later entrusted by the Sassanian kings to the Lakhmids. One wished that our sources were also more articulate about the interrelations, if any, between the new Arab arrivals and the converted Jewish dynasty of Adiabene or, later, between the short-lived Jewish state built by Mar Zuṭra II and its Lakhmid neighbors.

ARABIAN PENINSULA

Mixtures of Jewish and Arab strains were still more pronounced in the Arabian mother country. Many centuries before Mohammed, Jews, partly of Jewish and partly of native stock, began to settle all over the Peninsula. We may leave in abeyance the question raised by widespread Arab legends connecting the first Jewish settlers with Moses' alleged banishment of some of his disobedient followers during his war with Amalek (an evident confusion with the subsequent conflict between Samuel and Saul over Agag the Amalekite), and with David's reputed military exploits in the vicinity of Medina. More serious is Torrey's attractive, though as yet unproved, theory concerning the settlement of Jews in Teima in the days of Nabonidus. More recently recovered sources have confirmed the fact that the last king of Chaldea, a friend of Jews, had taken up residence in this northern Arabian oasis. From there he sent, for example, an Arab official, Temuda, to collect a large quantity of silver from Erech. The Babylonian Sin (moon) worship had penetrated at that time even into southern Arabia. There is nothing intrinsically wrong with the suggestion that Nabonidus may have been preceded in Teima by Jewish refugees from the wars of Nebukadrezzar and by other foot-loose exiles who, as we know, were roaming in those years all over the Near East from Elephantine to Assyria in quest of new forms of Jewish living.[78]

More definite is Josephus' report about Herod's 500 Jewish soldiers accompanying Aelius Gallus' ill-fated expedition to southern Arabia in 25–24 B.C.E. This contingent, like that of the Nabateans, was probably used to facilitate the expedition through its knowledge of roads and its contacts with the local population, rather than merely to augment Roman manpower. Be this as it may, the tombstone inscriptions of a Shubeit "Yehudaya" erected in Al-Ḥijr in 42 C.E. (or possibly 45 B.C.E.), that of one Simon in 307 (incidentally, the latest Nabatean inscription as yet discovered), and a number of inscribed *grafitti* are indubitable remnants of pre-Islamic Arab-Jewish life. That afterwards, up to the sixth century, the Jewish tribes altogether dominated Yathrib (Medina), has become clear through more recent investigations. Among some twenty Jewish tribes mentioned in later Arabic literature stand out the Aramaic-sounding Banu Zaghura. More important were the Banu Nadhir, Banu Quraiẓa and Banu Qainuqa', who, between them, occupied at one time fifty-nine strongholds and practically the entire fertile countryside. It was probably owing to these Jewish settlers that the city's ancient Egyptian name, Yathrib (Athribis), also recorded in Greek sources, was changed to the Hebrew-Aramaic Medina (city). Similarly Khaibar, another focal center of Jewish life in northern Arabia located some 60 miles north of Medina, may have owed its name to an adaptation of the Hebrew term, *ḥeber* (association, here possibly league of communities), or some derivative of *kabir* (strong) as intimated by Yaqut. Other Jewish settlements, evidenced by more or less verifiable inscriptions or later traditions, included Dedan, Al-Ḥijr, Teima, Ablaq, central Arabian Yamama, Ta'if, and, possibly, Mecca. Some Jews, perhaps moving southward from Babylonia, also established themselves along the Arabian shores of the Persian Gulf, particularly Bahrein, famed in recent years for its great oil resources. In short, Werner Caskel is not guilty of an overstatement when he calls the Jews the main representatives of Nabatean culture in Hejaz after 300 C.E. Citing two Nabatean inscriptions, he declares, "These are the beginnings of the Jewish population, which later occupied all the oases in the northwest including Medinah." [79]

Flourishing settlements of this type irresistibly attracted the Bedouins from all over the Peninsula. Much as the latter glorified their freedom and independence from the sedentary ways of life, sooner or later they began viewing such agriculturally prosperous oases not only as fit objects for raids, but ultimately also as enviable sources of economic security. By slow infiltration several Arab tribes drifted into Medina and its vicinity, and were hospitably received by the Jewish farmers. By the sixth century, these new arrivals, steadily reinforced from the south and unified under an able leader, Malik ibn Ajlan, eventually prevailed over their hosts. Nevertheless, Mohammed still found vigorous Jewish tribes in and around that center of northern Arabia, possibly constituting the majority of the settled population. Of course, they were not all of Jewish extraction. In large part they were descended from Arab proselytes, as indicated, for example, in the remarkable story of the Banu Hishna in Teima. These arrivals "were prevented by the Jews," says Al-Bakri, "from entering their fort as long as they professed another religion, and only when they embraced Judaism were they admitted" (*K. Mu'jām, Das geographische Wörterbuch,* ed. by F. Wüstenfeld, I, 21).

The early history of Jews in the prosperous districts of southern Arabia is likewise shrouded in darkness. Solomon's trade relations with Ophir (Ẓafar?) and his legendary connections with the Queen of Sheba merely show how far back Jewish acquaintance with the great civilization of Ḥimyara extended. But the first reliable historical record of the entry of Jews into the South seems to be Josephus' narrative of the Jewish soldiers who had shared Aelius Gallus' disaster.

At any rate, we hear afterwards from a Christian writer (Philostorgius) that when the missionary Theophilus arrived in Ḥimyara about the middle of the fourth century, he found there "not a small number of Jews," whose "accustomed fraud and malice" he had to silence. He and his imperial backers obviously resented, for political as well as religious reasons, the extensive Jewish proselytizing. At that time the campaigns of Shapur II had threatened to disrupt all land routes connecting Rome and Constantinople with the Far East. To salvage the empire's life line to India, as well as to build up a system of Roman satellite states as a permanent threat to Persia's flank, Constantius embarked upon a policy of converting to Christianity the far-flung Arab settlements and their Ethiopian neighbors. More immediately successful in Ethiopia, where Egyptian influences combined with the presence of old Jewish communities had long paved the way for Christianity, his and his successors' missionary efforts led to the conversion of the northern Ghassanids and the establishment of Christian communities in Najran and elsewhere on the Peninsula proper.[80]

Nonetheless, Judaism continued to gain even more ground. In a fifth-century inscription one Sahir, probably a convert, wrote, "Blessed and praised be the name of the Merciful, who is in Heaven, and Israel and its God, the Lord of Judah." Sahir also gave to one of his sons the good Jewish name, Meir. The impact of Judaism is also reflected by the monument erected by a powerful ruler in 449–50 and inscribed to a monotheistic Baal, "the Lord of Heaven and Earth," suggesting vestiges of the ancient Israelitic popular religion. Another inscription, recently recovered, speaks of a dedication to "the Lord, Him of Heaven, the greatest. . . ." Of a dozen other overtly monotheistic inscriptions thus far uncovered, only two refer to Jesus and the Trinity, and both seem to have been left behind by foreign administrators. Absence of pagan formulations, even where such were in order, from numerous other inscriptions, attests at least to a strong negative influence of both Jews and Christians.[81]

JEWISH KINGDOM

More certain is the full adoption of Judaism by Dhu Nuwas (after 516). This Jewish king may have borne also the name of Marthad-ilan Aḥsan and been the son or some other close relative of Ma'd-Karib Ya'fur, who is designated in an inscription of 516 as "King of Saba and Dhu-Raidan, and Ḥadhramaut, and Yamnat, and their Arabs of Taud and Tihanat." The latter, and perhaps some of his ancestors, may already have professed Judaism of sorts. The political background of this conversion, namely the effort of these kings to erect through Judaism a dam against advancing Christianity, as well as Christian Abyssinia's punitive expedition to check this assertion of independence, indicates the complexity of the situation in which these ancestors of Yemenite Jewry found themselves, even before the rise of Islam. We need not take too literally the atrocity stories about Dhu Nuwas' treacherous extermination of the Christian community in Najran. Such stories could well serve as an excuse for Abyssinian intervention, preparations for which had been observed in the Abyssinian capital by Cosmas the Indicopleustes "at the beginning of Justin's reign," that is, even before the first rumors of the attack on Najran could possibly have reached Africa. In fact, Dhu Nuwas' attack on the Christians of Najran and other communities seems to have taken place after 523, in the interval between two Abyssinian invasions. He may merely have retaliated for acts of treason committed by local Christians during the first invasion. Atrocity tales could also help to cover up treaty-breaking by the Abyssinians themselves, as well as serving the purposes of Christian mission on a par with other martyrologies. The fact that the various Eastern churches have commemorated the martyrdom of their Najran coreligionists on different dates (October 2, 20, 24, November 22, or December 31) seems to indicate that some probably minor local persecution was exaggerated into a large-scale suppression of all Christianity in the southern kingdom. Much of that martyrology is also written in a traditional, by then almost stereotype vein, as when a nine-year-old Christian girl was reputed to have spat in Dhu Nuwas' face and exclaimed, "May thy mouth be closed, Jew, killer of his Lord." [82]

More significant are the international implications of this clash between the two monotheistic religions. According to Simeon of Beth Arsham, Bishop of the Persians, from whose letter we have just quoted, "those Jews who are in Tiberias send priests of theirs year by year and season by season to stir up commotion against the Christian people of the Ḥimyarites" (some such connections with Tiberias are, indeed, attested by a remarkable third-century inscription and monogram of a Ḥimyarite Jewish elder, Menaḥem, discovered in the cemetery of Beth She'arim). Simeon also reported that while on a diplomatic mission in Ḥira, he saw a messenger of the king of Ḥimyara to the Lakhmid king, Mundhir, bearing a letter which ended in the following exhortation:

> These things have we written to your Majesty, that you may rejoice that we have not left a Christian, not one, in this land of ours, and that you also may act likewise, that all the Christians who are in your dominions you may make followers of your religion, as we have done in our dominion; but as for the Jews who are in your dominion that you be their helper in everything, and whatever is needed in your dominion in return for this, send to us that we may dispatch it to you.

Whatever one thinks of the authenticity of this message, there is no doubt about the use Simeon made of this alleged letter to stir up Christian public opinion in Egypt, Syria, Cappadocia, Cilicia, and Edessa. He tried to bring about both Byzantine armed intervention in Ḥimyara and the treatment of imperial Jewry as hostages for the good behavior of its southern coreligionists.[83]

Very likely Dhu Nuwas was the leader of a liberation movement from Abyssinian supremacy. He sought to secure assistance from the related pro-Persian Lakhmids, and possibly from Persia herself. But his entry into the arena of international power politics ended in dismal failure. The Christian Abyssinians and Ghassanids (who often staged raids into the Jewish settlements of northern Arabia) could count on the whole-hearted support of Byzantium. In fact, Justin I, and, at his request, Patriarch Timothy III (IV) of Alexandria, urged the Abyssinian King Elesboas (Kaleb Ella Asbaha) to intervene in Yemen against "the abominable and lawless Jew." The Empire supplied the necessary ships for the transport of the Abyssinian troops to southern Arabia (523–25). At the same time the Jewish king received little more than verbal encouragement from the Sassanian king, Kavadh I. True, Persia had a genuine interest in staving off Christian hegemony over the Arabian Peninsula. But having no expectation of establishing there the Zoroastrian state religion, which had few missionary successes outside the imperial borders, the Persian rulers often wavered between helping the native pagans to maintain their heathen religions and encouraging them to adopt either Judaism or Nestorian Christianity. The latter sect feared the expansion of Orthodox Byzantium almost as much as did the Jews. At that particular moment (523–25), moreover, the Sassanian empire was still recuperating from the internal anarchy generated by the Mazdakite movement, which a quarter century before had induced Kavadh I to call to his assistance the Huns from Central Asia.

Another remarkable Jewish political enterprise thus ended in failure. But its repercussions must have dramatized Jewish teachings and observances before the whole Arab population on the Peninsula and in its border lands. It was associated in the minds of many liberty-loving Ḥimyarites with the idea of resistance to Abyssinian domination, which they succeeded in shaking off after half a century. According to Arab traditions, the leader of the new liberation movement, Saif Dhu Yazan, was a descendant of Dhu Nuwas and likewise a professing Jew. Curiously Saif ventured to appeal to the Byzantine emperor for aid against the Abyssinians—Byzantium had every reason to resent Abyssinia's noncooperation in her recurrent conflicts with Persia—but was rebuked, because "you are Jews, while the Ethiopians are Christians." His appeal to Persia proved more successful, and brought a Persian expeditionary force. But the result was merely the exchange of one foreign oppressor for another. Nor was the involvement of Persian Jewry on the side of Baḥram against Khosroe II helpful to its southern coreligionists. Nevertheless, Ḥimyarite Jews, whether of Jewish or Arab extraction, weathered the harsh Abyssinian regime, just as their descendants were to weather many later persecutions down to modern times. As is well known, in recent decades decimated Yemenite Jewry continued to play a significant role in its own country, while greatly contributing to the building up of the Jewish homeland in Palestine.[84]

Jews living among the northern Arabs likewise suffered serious political reverses. Following a Persian occupation of the island of Yotabe in the Gulf of Aqaba in 473, Jewish merchants established there a semiautonomous colony engaged in the Red Sea trade. Their autonomy seems to have been respected by Emperor Anastasius when he recaptured the island in 498, although the Jewish community could not prevent the loan of seven Byzantine merchant vessels stationed in that island for the Abyssinian expedition against their coreligionists of Himyara. Before long Justinian, perhaps finding that his subjects could carry on the island's international trade without the intensive cooperation of Jews, withdrew the latter's autonomous status (about 535). Nor was the Jewish position in the Arab buffer states altogether secure. Especially when at the end of the century the Lakhmid king, Nu'man III, deeply impressed by Maurice's victorious alliance with Khosroe II, was formally converted to Christianity, the old and important Jewish communities of that entire border area must have felt seriously threatened. This danger passed, however, when Nu'man was captured by Khosroe II in 602, at the beginning of the Persian campaign against Byzantium, and his kingdom was converted into a Persian province.[85]

While these dramatic changes were taking place at the two extremes of the Arab ethnological area, Jews living in northern Arabia continued to cultivate their particular blend of Arab-Jewish culture. As in many other areas, they served as leaven to stir up the long-quiescent life of their neighbors. The Jews of Yathrib, Khaibar, and Teima, particularly, seem to have pioneered in introducing advanced methods of irrigation and cultivation of the soil. They also developed new arts and crafts from metal work to dyeing and the production of fine jewelry, and taught the neighboring tribes more advanced methods of exchanging goods and money. Most of the agricultural terms and names of implements recorded in pre-Islamic Arabic poetry or the Qur'an are borrowed from their Aramaic speech. Arab traditions themselves ascribe to them the introduction of the honey bee and many new fruits, including the date. The palm tree, long glorified in Palestinian letters as a symbol of Judaism, now became the object of adulation in Arabic poetry as well. A Jewess was reputed to have brought the first vine to Ta'if near Mecca, an area later proverbial for its fine viticulture.[86]

By their irrigation system, the observance of certain dietary rules, and especially by building their castles on hills rather than in the fever-invested valleys, the Jews pioneered also in fighting the theretofore deadly contagious diseases. So impressed were their neighbors that, on one occasion, an Arab woman who had lost several children vowed to bring up as Jews all her future offspring. These castles also helped them to stave off Bedouin *razzias* (this term for raids is actually a European loan word from the language of Arab nomads), and to introduce constant refinements in the amenities of their life, which appeared as the acme of luxury in their primitive environment. Jews must also have significantly contributed to the urban settlements. We need not go the whole length of Sidney Smith's assertion that "there were thriving cities in Arabia, old foundations as civilized as any in Syria or Iraq, and perhaps as large, apart from Antioch and Madaim [Ctesiphon]" (*BSOAS,* XVI, 467), and yet admit the presence of a sizable urban population, engaged in trade and industry. In short, during the few generations of Jewish control, the focal northern areas were raised almost to the high level of the southern civilization, which had long earned for Ḥimyara and its vicinity the Roman designation of *Arabia Felix*. As soon as the Jews were all but eliminated from northern Arabia by Mohammed's sword, the whole countryside relapsed into its former backwardness.

No less significant was Jewish cultural pioneering. Being a "people of the book," as Mohammed was to call them as well as the Christians, the Jews of Yathrib and Khaibar had fairly broad intellectual interests. Along with the art of writing, they consciously or unwittingly communicated to their neighbors certain rudiments of their religious and ethical outlook. Always captivated by effective story telling, Arabs used to foregather in Jewish and Christian inns, and over a glass of wine listen to the recitation of the exploits of one or another biblical hero. These stories need not have clung too closely to the biblical narratives, but were often adorned with all the embroideries of the later Aggadah, or the creations of the story teller's own fertile imagination. In the minds of the Arab listeners and, sometimes, of the Jews themselves, these old and new ingredients soon blended into an indistinguishable whole. Much more than the few merchant-travelers from Mecca or Ḥimyara, the Jewish settlers thus kept alive the links between the ancient Arabian traditions and the more advanced intellectual heritage of the Syro-Palestinian and Babylonian centers.

Besides the Jews there were numerous Christians and, doubtless also, Judeo-Christian sectarians of all kinds. In addition one could find, as Muqaddasi observed, "Manichaeans and atheists among the tribe of Quraish, Mazdakites and Mazdeans [Zoroastrians] among that of Tamim." The Jews themselves were apparently familiar with Scripture and some parts of the midrashic literature, but they had few direct intellectual contacts with the centers of Jewish life in Babylonia and Palestine. The several distinguished poets among them evidently were much more Arabian than Jewish, in so far as can be gleaned from a total of some two hundred stanzas which have come down to us. The Medinese poet, Ka'b ibn al-Ashraf, for instance, son of a Jew and an Arab woman, spent years of his youth among the Bedouin tribes studying the Arabic language, where it was at its purest. Another Jewish poet, Samau'al ibn 'Adiyah, sang in his famous poem of liberty, "We are men of the sword, and when we draw it we exterminate our enemies." Such a martial exclamation would have sounded rather strange to most posttalmudic Jews in other countries. Even an ancient Israelitic psalmist would, at least, have praised God as the real victor. But Samau'al, the knightly lord of Al-Ablaq near Teima, whose name soon became proverbial for faithfulness in the whole Arab world, was typical of the warlike, yet economically fairly advanced, Jewish settlers of the Peninsula.[87]

GATHERING STRENGTH

Jewish poets were not limited to the Arab lands or speech. We shall see that, contrary to long-held views, the sixth and seventh centuries belong to the richest period of creativity in the realm of Hebrew liturgical poetry. It was during those four generations between the conclusion of the Babylonian Talmud and the rise of Islam that synagogue services were not only organized with a certain measure of finality, but were also enriched with works of great beauty and inwardness. Bible learning likewise continued to make quiet but significant progress. The recension of the scriptural text in all its smallest minutiae engaged the attention of generation after generation of painstaking scholars, and ultimately produced the grandiose structure of Masorah. The Bible was also popularized among the Aramaic-speaking masses by the recension of old, and the addition of new, Aramaic translations of various scriptural books. The homiletical outpourings of rabbis continued unabated, and the sustained effort of compiling and reviewing the ever growing aggadic heritage was now begun in earnest. Several important midrashic collections, as we shall see, have properly been ascribed by their modern investigators to the century before and that after the rise of Islam. Foundations were laid for still other works of this kind, which emerged into the light of day a century or two later. Nor was the halakhic achievement of talmudic Jewry left uncultivated. Apart from the work of the saboraic schools on the text of the Talmud itself, considerable effort was expended on the continued interpretation of the innumerable legal traditions handed down orally at the academies and cultivated locally in many communities under the guise of customs.

Even observers who are inclined to limit the range of Jewish history to the Jewish people's contributions to learning and culture can no longer, therefore, pass over slightingly the so-called saboraic period. They must admit that, however overtly inarticulate, the first posttalmudic generations were effectively continuing the creative work of their forefathers and extended it into ever new areas. They may not have been the ones to reap the full harvest. But they certainly helped to sow fertile seeds, as well as to gather and preserve the harvests of earlier generations in a fashion making them a vital link in the entire history of Jewish culture.

Socially and politically, too, they revealed an astounding vigor. Placed between the crushing millstones of two hostile empires, they showed enough virility and tenacity to defy all external pressures, and even to play a significant role in the unceasing imperial conflicts of the age. However exaggerated may be the reports by antagonistic writers, the fact that, after centuries of oppressive rule and popular hostility, the Jews of Antioch were strong enough to stage repeated revolts and allegedly even to attack the Christian majority, should give pause to any student of human affairs. Similarly, their active participation in the Perso-Byzantine war under Khosroe II, and their seizure of and three-year reign in the Holy City, from which they had been kept out by an imperial decree during the preceding half millennium, could only have come from a people which, in the face of extreme adversity, had preserved its indomitable faith in the future.

At the same time the Jews had begun laying foundations for new communities in lands with a drab and uninviting appearance, but with untold possibilities. In western and central Europe, particularly, these were the centuries of slow germination, out of which was ultimately to emerge the remarkable structure of medieval Western Jewry. Here, too, Jews revealed some unsuspected powers of resistance. After a century of intermittent but vigorous efforts by the combined powers of the Visigothic state and church to suppress the Jewish minority, the latter emerged as a powerful ally of the Moorish invaders. In the Arab heartland, too, Jewry celebrated a great, though short-lived, victory in the conversion of Dhu Nuwas and his tribesmen. For a while it appeared as if the entire Peninsula were to turn Jewish. If, owing to the military intervention of neighboring powers, this largely unconscious and unorganized missionary enterprise came to naught, Jews had injected enough of their restless quest of religious values into the tribes of both the Peninsula and the borderlands between Persia and Byzantium to help prepare the ground for a new effervescence of religious and cultural creativity.

XVII

MOHAMMED AND THE CALIPHATE

AGAINST this background of turmoil in the entire Western world, the Byzantine Empire's sudden loss, after a firm hold of six and a half centuries, of almost all its Asiatic provinces and Egypt, its equally sudden recapture of them, and its penetration to the very heartland of Sassanian power, we may understand the meteoric rise of the new religious civilization called Islam. The deep yearning of the masses for peace and security, the growing conviction of the intellectual leaders that the end of an era was approaching, the bitter sectarian strife—all prepared the ground for some such fresh start at rebuilding and unification.

The Qur'an may only tangentially refer to these international developments. "The Greeks are overcome," reads the beginning of surah 30, "in the nighest parts of the land; but after being overcome they shall overcome in a few years; . . . and in that day the believers shall rejoice in the help of God." This surah was written in Mecca, some time before 622; that is, before the tide in the Perso-Byzantine war had begun to turn in the Greeks' favor. Mohammed, who as a merchant-traveler had often traversed the Arabic-speaking border lands between the two empires, was certainly aware of these great historic events. Increasingly drifting toward a monotheistic creed, he genuinely hoped for a victory of the Christian empire over dualistic Persia. But he must also have seen in this struggle of titans a sign of an approaching new era. A political realist, he comprehended the rare opportunity offered to his attempt at unification of the Arabian Peninsula by the deep preoccupation of the two powerful rivals in their struggle for survival. This preoccupation made it possible for him to establish there a new religion without any immediate outside intervention, such as had put an end to Dhu Nuwas' kindred undertaking.

PENINSULAR UNITY

During his lifetime, the new prophet, or, as he liked to call himself, the Messenger, concentrated on the conversion of the various Arab tribes scattered over the vast territories of Arabia. Here Jews, Christians, and the syncretistic sectarians among them provided the substratum for his new religious preachment. Alfred Jeremias's remark, however, that "the whole Islamic movement was created . . . by apostasizing Judeo-Christian sectarians," is an overstatement justified only, if at all, when one reviews the situation in all of western Asia and North Africa, rather than in Arabia proper. The Messenger, arising among the Arabs, evidently expected help from the culturally more advanced Jewish farmers and merchants. Whether Mohammed's purported saying that, if ten Jews were to accept his message, all the Jews would soon be converted, is authentic or not, it is beyond doubt that he made considerable efforts to find support among the Jews, especially in Medina. But, even though he actually found more than "ten Jewish companions" and later married the Jewess, Ṣafiya, daughter and bride of two of his Jewish victims, the overwhelming majority met his missionary zeal with skepticism or, what pained him more, with ridicule. Ka'b ibn al-Ashraf was assassinated in the dark by Mohammed's henchmen for daring to compose a dirge on the death in battle of many of his Meccan opponents. Seeing his hopes of converting the Jews vanish, the Messenger became their harshest enemy. Ultimately, tradition ascribed to him the last injunction, "Let no two religions be left in the [Arabian] Peninsula." Although clearly spurious, this saying explained to later generations of Muslims why he and his first successors, Abu Bakr and 'Umar I, annihilated the Jewish settlements in northern Arabia and showed by many enactments their extreme animus toward the "people of the book." [1]

We need not expatiate here on the thrice-told tale of the gradual deterioration of the relationships between Mohammed and the Jews. Suffice it to say that in the many years preceding his religious ministry Mohammed had ample opportunity to meet both Jews and Christians in his native Mecca. Although the Jewish community was rather small, Jewish traders being discouraged from settling there by the native merchants and moneylenders, it had a cemetery and, according to later traditions, a street of its own. Its leaders must have been intellectually superior not only to the pagan majority, but also to the local Christian community, largely recruited from Abyssinian slaves. Mohammed doubtless encountered many other Jews, including some scholars, on his numerous journeys as head of caravans dispatched by his wealthy wife Khadijah. While still in Mecca he rhapsodized on the ancient period when "we (speaking in the name of God) did bring the children of Israel the Book and judgment and prophecy, and we provided them with good things, and preferred them above the worlds." In his so-called second Meccan period he still confidently spoke of the "learned men [*'ulama*] of the children of Israel" who affirmed his divine message.[2]

After his momentous exodus (*hejira*) to Medina, however, Mohammed ran into serious difficulties with the local Jewish tribes. First admitted hospitably and even supported as an ally in his war against the opposing Meccan faction (we possess a fairly authentic record of the mutually agreed constitution), he antagonized the Jews by his ever more insistent claims to being the "seal" of all prophecy. The Medinese Jews had long been accustomed to look down upon their illiterate pagan neighbors. They could not help viewing the *ummi* (uneducated) prophet as an arrogant pretender. Mohammed, on his part, could not understand why, always claiming to be a light unto the nations, Jews should be so hostile to him for trying more effectively to expound their monotheistic doctrine.[3]

In Medina the Messenger doubtless observed also the upsurge of Jewish messianic hopes, nurtured by the great international upheavals, and the bitter conflicts between Jews and Christians in neighboring Palestine since 614. Reiterated Muslim traditions, to be sure, about individual Jews foretelling, shortly before Mohammed's birth, the imminent arrival of their Messiah, are clear borrowings of motifs long popularized by the Gospel narratives. But there are many other indications of strong messianic trends among the Arabian Jews of that period. These served both as powerful stimuli to Mohammed's prophetic calling, and as deep irritants to his followers over the Jewish refusal to recognize in him the awaited redeemer. The pagan tribes, on the other hand, may well have feared that, by accepting Mohammed as their long-foretold leader, the Jews would gain rapid ascendancy and conquer the entire Peninsula, which indeed they might have achieved.[4]

Evidently the Jewish tribesmen and their leaders underestimated the extraordinary capacity of the "madman," as they were to call him in their later writings. Appealing to the religious, as well as nationalistic, yearnings of his countrymen, the Messenger found an increasing number of devoted fanatical followers, while the opposition lacked unity and a forward-looking program. Not realizing the ultimate threat to their faith and ethnically predisposed to listen to Mohammed's call to Arab unity, the Christian Arabs on the Peninsula offered no resistance whatsoever. Their leading community of Najran soon came to terms with the unifier of northern Arabia, and was the first to assume the obligation to pay a regular capitation tax as a price for Muslim protection. In a Medinese surah Mohammed himself contrasted the "strongest Jewish enmity against those who believe" with the Christians' sympathetic attitude, which he ascribed to their priests and monks, "and because they are not proud." The pagan Arabs, whether sedentary in and around Medina, or Bedouin in the vicinity of Khaibar, at critical moments deserted their Jewish allies.[5]

Mohammed played his game shrewdly. He often succeeded in undermining a threatening hostile alliance by exploiting the mutual animosities among its members. Sooner or later the Jews were abandoned by their allies, and left to fight the war by themselves. Perhaps they were too naïve and took too seriously the appeal to fidelity by Shuraiḥ ibn 'Amran, one of their poets of the day. A descendant of the proverbially faithful Samau'al, the new lord of the castle of Ablaq, advised everyone fraternizing with his neighbors to "drink from their cups—even if they drink deadly poison." Nor were the Jews internally united. Even their enemies were struck by the deep cleavages in their midst, only occasionally bridged over by such manifestations of Jewish solidarity as the regular communal ransom of Jewish captives. Mohammed, who cited these internal Jewish divisions also as a theological proof of their stiff-necked rejection of prophecy, made excellent use of these enmities to dispose of the Jewish tribes one by one.[6]

The upshot was that the Banu-Qainuqa' were first beleaguered, and then, after their honorable surrender, told to leave Medina with their possessions (624 C.E.). The Banu-Nadhir followed suit two years later. Most tragic was the end of the Banu Quraiẓa, who were betrayed by their Arab companions. After a mock trial by the latter's chief, all males of the tribe were condemned to death unless they changed their faith. Remarkably, only three or four weak-kneed men chose apostasy, while all the remaining Jews, estimated at between 600 and 750, after a night spent in study, suffered martyrdom. They died unsung by their fellow Jews, and only recently did "the last of the sons of Quraiẓa," become the subject of a great poem by Saul Tchernichovsky. While a few early Arab poets paid deserved homage to the Banu Quraiẓa's great valor in battle and fortitude in death, later Arab historians tried to blacken their memory, so as to exculpate the cruel vindictiveness of the Messenger and his associates.[7]

After his conquest of Medina, Mohammed turned on the Jews of Khaibar and the other northern settlements. Despite the treachery of their Arab allies, the Khaibar Jews, some 3,000 strong, fiercely resisted the onslaught and secured a "negotiated" peace. They had theretofore, in order to secure tranquillity for their peaceful exploits, voluntarily delivered a part of their crops to their Bedouin neighbors. This practice, far from being considered at that time a sign of political weakness, was freely indulged in also by the great Byzantine and Persian empires to secure peace from many unruly neighboring tribes. It was far less expensive than keeping permanent garrisons to stave off raids. By arranging with Mohammed to pay him half of their annual produce, the Khaibar Jews may have thought that they had merely exchanged one recipient for another. Little did they realize that they thereby established a precedent which, together with that set by the Christian communities of Aila and Najran, was to affect deeply the fate of all religious minorities under Islam.

Mohammed concluded similar treaties with the Jews of Fadak, Teima, Maqna, and other communities from the Red Sea to the Persian Gulf. Typical of many such agreements is the treaty with the Jews of Maqna, signed by Mohammed's son-in-law 'Ali shortly before the Messenger's death in 632. It read in part:

When this communication will reach you, you will live securely and enjoy the protection of Allah and his Messenger. You shall suffer from no act of injustice or hostility, for Allah's Messenger takes you under his protection against anything he combats for his own sake. To Allah's Messenger belong your fine cloth, all your slaves, horses, and arms, except what he or his representative may forego. Thereafter you shall pay a quarter of the produce of your palm trees, your fishing, and the spinning of your women. In return you shall be free of all tribute [*ḥaraj*] and forced labor. If you listen and are obedient, Allah's Messenger will be in duty bound to honor him who will deserve it and to forgive him who will sin. To the believers and Muslims it shall be said: He who behaves well toward the people of Maqna shall reap a good reward; he who treats them badly shall receive the wages of his sins. No one shall have authority over you except a man from your own midst, or one from the clan of Allah's Messenger.

Even more liberal treaties were doubtless concluded with the southern communities, although we possess only the record of such an agreement with Christian Najran. In his letter to the Ḥimyarite kings, Mohammed made it perfectly clear, according to Ibn Isḥaq, that "he who holds fast to his religion, Jew or Christian, is not to be turned from it. He must pay the poll tax—for every adult, male or female, free or slave, one full dinar." To be sure, these treaties were frequently observed in their breach. 'Umar I, as we shall see, did not hesitate to expel the Jews from Khaibar within a few years after the Messenger's death. But small Jewish settlements persisted for many centuries in northern Arabia, while Yemenite Jewry seems to have emerged fairly intact from the crisis engendered by the rise of Islam.[8]

CREATIVE SYNCRETISM

While these political and military developments on the Arabian Peninsula wove the pattern of the subsequent legal status of "infidels" under Muslim domination, the decisions made by the Messenger and his associates in the religious sphere were even more definitive and far-reaching. From the very beginning Mohammed tried to persuade the Jews that he was only renewing the faith which "was in the books of yore—the books of Abraham and Moses." In describing his vision of the nineteen angels, "guardians of the fire," he emphasized their task so "that those who have been given the Book and the believers may not doubt." [9]

These Meccan surahs show that Mohammed at that time knew the Jewish Scriptures only from hearsay and through the mirror of their current homiletical reinterpretation. In fact, already then he used the Aramaic loan word *darusa* in the meaning of a searching study of Scripture (68:37). Although boasting of the pure Arabic of the Qur'an (16:105) in contrast to the "barbarous" speech of his mentor (most likely Jewish)—an assertion which was to play a vital role in the subsequent evolution of linguistic studies—he could not help borrowing from the Jews a number of other Hebrew or Aramaic phrases. The Jews of Mecca and Medina hardly spoke an Arabic dialect of the kind of Yiddish or Ladino, but they must have used a variety of Hebraic names and abstract terms, particularly from the domain of their religious life and literature. The Arabic language of that time, though highly developed for poetic uses, was still extremely inadequate for the rendering of abstract, philosophic, or theological ideas. Discussing religious problems a Jew of Hejaz or the Yemen doubtless unconsciously used many Hebrewisms in his Arabic speech, just as, conversely, half a millennium later the Ibn Tibbons expressed philosophic ideas in a Hebrew style permeated with Arabic forms.

According to an early tradition, Mohammed, upon entry into Medina, heard that the Jews were fasting their *ashurah* (tenth day of Tishre or Day of Atonement) in memory of their victory over Pharaoh (!). He decided, therefore, to adopt this holiday in commemoration of his own victories. This tradition, however garbled, underscores correctly the confusion in Mohammed's mind with respect to the meaning of Jewish rituals, as well as his willingness to accept many of them, in order to gain the support of the "people of the book." For this purpose he also directed his followers to pray in the direction (*qibla*) of Jerusalem, the seat of the "remote Mosque," to which he had allegedly made his miraculous night journey (*isra'*) before his ascent to the seventh heaven. He also tirelessly emphasized that he was in direct line of prophecy from Abraham (mentioned in 25 surahs) and Moses (in 34 surahs) to Jesus (in 11 surahs), and generally stressed the similarities of his doctrine with the ethical monotheism of Jews and Christians. He seems to have known far less about Zoroastrian teachings, although some of the Babylonian-Persian angelology and demonology, such as the spirits of Ḥarut and Marut, seeped down to him through Jewish and Christian channels. We have no evidence for the penetration of any form of Manichaeism into the Arabian Peninsula. But Mohammed certainly wished to draw, on a different plane, a synthesis of all the great Western faiths and to establish on their foundations a universal religion—an attempt for which Mani had suffered death some three and a half centuries before him. In addition, the Messenger tried to synthesize these teachings with certain native traditions, especially those relating to Hud, and other historical or legendary ancient prophets of Ḥadhramaut.[10]

Mohammed preached to a responsive audience. Whether or not they were in any way acquainted with the specific contents of the Bible, many thoughtful Arabs were familiar, as Arthur Jeffery has pointed out, "with a definite theory as to the nature of Scripture, a theory which had grown up in the Jewish community and had already before Mohammed's time passed from them to other communities." In this and many other ways the Jews had created on the Peninsula a climate of opinion which made possible an immediate response of the masses, even where no direct borrowing by Mohammed can be documented by chapter or verse. The Messenger's own familiarity with a written Bible appears extremely dubious. True, writing was not then as uncommon throughout the Peninsula as was long assumed. The presence of numerous inscriptions, including a trilingual one in Greek, Syriac, and Arabic dating from 512, clearly indicates that some Arabs knew how to read and write. Merchants, in particular, seem often to have recorded their transactions in writing, and to have indulged in occasional correspondence. There are also indications that both Jews and Christians had at their disposal a limited supply of scriptural and liturgical texts. A gospel version circulating in Medina later in the seventh century may have been based on an Aramaic text prepared by Christian missionaries for use amongst Syro-Palestinian Jews converted during the recurrent outbursts of intolerance in the days of Justinian and his immediate successors.[11]

Nevertheless Mohammed probably derived most of his information about the Bible from oral communications of Jewish and Christian acquaintances. He seems to have listened eagerly to such reports, and his knowledge of the biblical narratives constantly improved during the three phases of his activity in Mecca, still more during his sojourn in Medina. Of course, unable to check the texts directly, he could never distinguish clearly between the biblical record as such and the numerous accretions from the Jewish Aggadah, patristic legend, or sectarian interpretation. His informants themselves probably were unable to separate clearly the original biblical core from the subsequent hermeneutic elaborations.[12]

When the overwhelming majority of Jews and many Christians repudiated his message, Mohammed turned sharply against both faiths. He used against them some of the very arguments accumulated in their own age-old religious controversies. Although we know nothing about disputations between Jews and Christians in northern Arabia, some fundamental mutual objections had already become an integral part of their respective traditions, and these must often have been repeated, especially by Christian missionaries. The sharp, sanguinary clashes between the two religions in both Palestine and southern Arabia must also have produced further rationalizations, elements of which doubtless percolated into Hejaz. Involved in protracted warfare against the Jewish tribes, Mohammed understandably attacked Judaism more sharply than Christianity. He could readily accept Jesus and Mary, considering the former (whose very name Isa he might have learned from a Jewish persiflage) as a Jewish prophet, and badly confusing the latter with Miriam, the sister of Moses and Aaron. But, with the Jews, he sharply repudiated the Trinitarian dogma (curiously considering Mary a member of the Trinity), and pointedly rejected the sonship of Christ: "Say, Allah is One! Allah the Eternal! He begets not and is not begotten! Nor is there like unto Him any one!" (Qur'an 112).

At the same time the Messenger took over some Christian arguments against Jewish law and the Jewish interpretation of Scripture. Even pre-Islamic Arabs were amazed by the strict Jewish observance of the Sabbath and the ritual food requirements. They could not understand, in particular, why Jews should spurn the meat of camels, prized highly by them as both a daily necessity and a great delicacy. Mohammed adhered to the Sabbath without complete abstention from work, but shifted it to Friday in memory of his first entry into Medina, and thus differentiated between the Muslims and both Jews and Christians.

The Messenger rejected, however, most of the Jewish ceremonial law, ultimately claiming, with some Christian apologists, that the latter had been but a penalty for Israel's sins: "And for the injustice of those who are Jews have we forbidden them good things which we had made lawful for them." Borrowing a Hebrew simile, he spoke derogatorily of "the likeness of those who were charged with the law and then bore it not, [which] is as the likeness of an ass bearing books." Not that Mohammed was in any way an antinomian. On the contrary, law was to play as great a role in the entire fabric of Islam, as it did in Judaism, for both religions constantly stressed deeds even more than beliefs. But, in order to separate his followers more clearly from the recalcitrant Jews, Mohammed altered even those laws which he accepted. While stressing the Jewish type of worship, content and form of prayers, ablutions, and other rituals, he altered them sufficiently to draw a sharp line of demarcation. For the three Jewish daily services, for example, he later substituted five, whether or not he had heard of the five Jewish holiday services and a similar number practiced among the Zoroastrians. Of fundamental importance was also Mohammed's abrupt change, during his last pilgrimage, of the traditional system of intercalating an additional month roughly every three years, taken over by the pagan Arabs from Jews. By introducing a straight lunar year, instead of the prevailing Jewish solilunar system, he foreshortened the Muslim year to one of 354 days, causing the holidays to occur at different seasons, and producing the well-known divergences between the Muslim and Western calendars.[13]

Unavoidably this controversy, too, entered the realm of history. Before long Mohammed felt impelled to distinguish, though not with full consistency, between his contemporaries, the Jews (*Yahud*), and the biblical children of Israel (*Banu Isra'il*). He accused the former's ancestors of falsifying the text and meaning of Scripture. Ultimately he suspected all Jews and their way of handling documents. A later tradition reported, "Zaid ibn Thabit said: The Apostle of Allah ordered me to learn for him the Jewish method of writing, saying to me: 'I do not trust a Jew at my writing.' And not half a month passed before I learned it. I used to write to the Jews for him, and when they wrote to him, I would read their letters." Like the Christian apologists he often invoked the biblical record of the chastisement of Jews for their evil ways and, particularly, for their constant rejection of God's messengers. He sharply attacked their way of interpreting the Bible in support of their Oral Law, which he considered a mere perversion of "the words from their places." The Jews were, in his opinion, but a "sect who twist their tongues concerning the Book, that ye may reckon it to be from the Book, but it is not from the Book." One is readily reminded of the stereotype accusation of the Jews' "absurd interpretations" of Scripture taken over into Justinian's *Novella* 146 from a long succession of Christian apologists.[14]

Mohammed also contended that the Jews had an exaggerated estimate of their scholars, whom they idolized as the Christians idolized their monks. In fact, possibly having in mind a dubious tradition (reflected in IV Ezra 14:9, 14), he exclaimed, "The Jews say Ezra ['Uzair] is the son of God; and the Christians say that the Messiah is the son of God; that is what they say with their mouths, imitating the sayings of those who misbelieved before—God fight them! how they lie!" (Qur'an 9:30–32). That is why it was his duty, he felt, to restore the original revelation to its pristine purity.

Although always feeling a deep kinship to Moses, the great founder of both a religion and a nation, Mohammed, on becoming more fully acquainted in Medina with the relationship between Abraham and Ishmael, the Arabs' purported ancestor, turned to the first patriarch as to the main source of his inspiration. It was Abraham's readiness to sacrifice Isaac which symbolized at its highest a believer's complete surrender to the divine will—the very meaning of the term, "Islam," and the core of its faith. He claimed that Abraham, by destroying the idols and writing the first sacred book (here he accepted a widespread Jewish legend), had been the first Muslim, long before the Judaism of Moses or the Christianity of Jesus. "Abraham was not a Jew, nor yet a Christian. . . . Verily the people most worthy of Abraham are those who follow him and his prophets, and those who believe." To justify his nationalistic return to the pagan worship at the Ka'ba stone in Mecca, he claimed that it was founded by Abraham and Ishmael who were ordered by God to "cleanse My house for those who make the circuit, for those who pay devotions there." Curiously, despite these nationalistic leanings, he did not dare to elevate Ishmael above the other patriarchs, but merely summed up his general demand that the true believers declare

> We believe in God, and what has been revealed to thee, and what was revealed to Abraham and Ishmael, and Isaac, and Jacob, and the tribes, and what was given to Moses, and Jesus, and the prophets from their Lord,—we will make no distinction between any of them—and we are unto Him resigned. Whosoever craves other than Islam for a religion, it shall surely not be accepted from him, and he shall, in the next world, be of those who lose.[15]

TOWARD WORLD CONQUEST

Unbelievers were not to lose out completely in this world, however. The agreements signed by Mohammed with the Jews and Christians, amplified by many authentic, as well as spurious, sayings transmitted in his name in oral tradition (*ḥadith*), established the general principle that adherents of monotheistic faiths (including Zoroastrians) should be allowed to live under Muslim domination.

The events of the first decade after Mohammed's death shook the world. In 634 the Messenger's second "successor" (caliph), 'Umar I, embarked on a career of world conquest unprecedented since the days of Alexander. Within a few years his armies overran most of the Byzantine and Persian empires. Perhaps to establish a more secure base for his ambitious operations, 'Umar expelled the Jews of Khaibar, the largest and most intact non-Muslim group still remaining in northern Arabia. He considered this objective sufficiently important to break, for its sake, the express safeguards included in the treaty between Mohammed and the Khaibar community. The caliph was soon too preoccupied elsewhere, however, to pay concentrated attention to the execution of his decree. Khaibar Jewry seems to have bent its head before the onrushing wave, and lifted it again when the storm subsided. Its remnants persisted there to the tenth century and beyond.[16]

More significant was the Jewish encounter with the Arab armies outside the Peninsula. Even before Mohammed's death, we are told by Arab historians, the Messenger had transplanted many surrendering Jewish tribesmen from Medina to Edrei in Transjordan. Many more undoubtedly fled from Arabia and joined their brethren in neighboring Palestine, despite the unsettled conditions in that country during the Perso-Byzantine war. According to Al-Bukhari, 'Umar deported some Khaibar Jews to Jericho. A son of the slain Khaibar leader Al-Ḥarith was said to have nurtured all his life a deep nostalgia for this North Arabian homeland, but he staunchly resisted conversion to Islam because he did not wish to cast aspersion on his father's martyrdom in behalf of Judaism. When the Arab hosts now began spreading northward, they encountered a first focus of resistance in the city of Gaza, then occupied by a strong Byzantine garrison under the command of the provincial governor, Sergius. At that time Gaza embraced a substantial Jewish settlement, in fact the most important community in Judaea. Jews seem to have fought alongside the Byzantines in the ensuing battle, which ended in Sergius' defeat. Having paid a severe penalty for siding with the Persian invaders, they doubtless viewed a display of pro-Byzantine sentiments now as the better part of wisdom.[17]

From their side, the Arabs tried to captivate the benevolence of the far more numerous Christian sectarians, whose hatred of Jews and Judaism was no less intense than that of their Orthodox coreligionists. For this reason, on entering Jerusalem in 638, 'Umar accepted from the surrendering Christians, headed by the implacable Patriarch Sophronius, the condition that Jews would not be permitted to settle in the Holy City. The Christian population was still smarting under the recollection of the short-lived Jewish regime during the Persian occupation (614–17). The caliph himself, on the other hand, may have wished to perpetuate the physical separation of the Jews from the city which had already begun to be viewed by the Muslims, too, as a "holy city," in fact, as the third in holiness after Mecca and Medina. Before long the Arabs started to call it *Bet ha-maqdis* and, later more briefly, *Al-Quds* (the Holy One, from the Hebrew *Bet ha-miqdash,* or Temple). Many a native or resident of Jerusalem was to bear the distinguishing surname of Al-Maqdisi or Al-Muqaddasi. This glorification was soon extended to the entire "Holy Land." Palestine and its holy places became even more focal in Islam's world outlook a few decades later, as a result of the 'Umayyad dynasty's propaganda in behalf of the seat of its power in and around Damascus. The founder of that dynasty, Mu'awiya, symbolically assumed the office of caliph in a solemn ceremony at Jerusalem. Especially in periods of strained political or dynastic relations between the central government and the local powers in Mecca and Medina, it was vitally important for the former to be able to divert the streams of eager pilgrims to Palestine and its "holy" metropolis. The city of David proved a particular godsend to 'Abd al-Malik (685–705), and again to Al-Muqtadir (908–32) during the Qarmatian revolt. Both caliphs had an urgent interest in keeping the masses of pilgrims away from the direct influence of their North Arabian enemies.[18]

Sooner or later, however, 'Umar and his lieutenants had to conspire with the Jewish "fifth column" within the Byzantine Empire. True, the Palestinian Jews had been too weakened by the bloodletting during the preceding Byzantine reconquest, and too disillusioned by the Persian betrayal, to repeat their organized armed intervention of twenty years before. Nor was the news about the treatment of Jews by Mohammed, brought by refugees settling on both banks of the Jordan, very encouraging. Nevertheless, the Arabs found ready helpers among local Jews. According to Baladhuri, a Jew named Yusuf (Joseph) led the besiegers of Caesarea to a subterranean passage through which they captured the city after a difficult seven-year (more likely seven-month) siege.[19]

Penetrating northeast through the Arab borderlands into Babylonia and the Iranian Plateau, 'Umar's armies found the Persian empire in a state of dissolution after the sudden reversal in its martial fortunes against Byzantium, the ensuing civil war, and the quick succession of numerous "kings of kings." Jews and Nestorians, particularly, must have welcomed the invaders as liberators from both religious oppression and socioeconomic anarchy. The onrushing Arabs, on their part, began leaning heavily on these minorities in maintaining the continuity of public and private life. From that time, evidently, date the various Arab privileges, entrusting the leadership over these minorities to their own governmentally supervised organs, the Nestorian *catholicos,* and the Jewish prince of captivity. Of course, these ecclesiastical heads had long enjoyed many immunities and imperial recognition under the Sassanian regime. But by formalizing anew the status of Catholicos Ishoyabh, and Exilarch Bustanai (Ḥaninai), 'Umar's generals secured for the new regime influential supporters among the two most populous and activist minorities.

It is impossible to reconstruct the details of that transition through the maze of later legends. But it seems certain that Bustanai became an important adviser of the new rulers. In recognition, he was given from among the booty a Persian princess, Dara-Izdadwar, "King Khosroe's daughter." Treated as a prisoner of war, she became technically Bustanai's slave and, according to Jewish law, had to be manumitted before her master was allowed to marry her. Apparently no record of such a manumission was entered into the exilarchic archives. Hence after Bustanai's death his older sons from Jewish wives treated the princess's children as slaves. Even later the legitimacy of Bustanai's progeny from the princess, who came to power in the middle of the eighth century and occupied the exilarchic office for many generations, became the subject of extended controversy. At first, however, many Jews must have felt flattered by this union between their leader and the Sassanian dynasty. For centuries past, the royal family had been separated even from Zoroastrian commoners by an impenetrable wall of rigid court etiquette. This feeling of exaltation doubtless was heightened when 'Ali, the fourth caliph and glorified hero of the Shi'ite sect, gave to his son Ḥusain another Persian princess, the daughter of the last "king of kings" Yazdegerd III, and possibly Dara's sister.[20]

Nor did the Babylonian Jews seem to resent the transplantation into their midst of coreligionists from Arabia. Some of the survivors of the holocaust, especially from among the Jews of Khaibar, were directed by 'Umar toward the new Arab encampments in southern Babylonia, particularly Kufa. This military camp speedily developed into a major center of both trade and learning. The Jewish community, too, growing by leaps and bounds, contributed greatly to the city's intellectual and economic evolution. Before long the Jews believed that Kufa had been the scene of their very early settlement in the days of the Babylonian Exile. For centuries thereafter visitors were shown remains of the tomb of King Jeconiah, allegedly buried there after his death at Nebukadrezzar's court. In the twelfth century, at any rate, Benjamin found there an elaborate mausoleum adorned by a dome, doubtless similar to those crowning many Muslim mosques. Of even greater significance was the Jewish community in the rivaling intellectual, as well as commercial, center of Baṣra.[21]

Turning westward, the Arabs entered Egypt. Begun as a small raid with puny forces, the invasion encountered little resistance and proved successful beyond all expectations. Before accepting the surrender of Alexandria, whose magnificence overawed them, the conquerors repudiated the Christian patriarch's demand that Jews be excluded from settlement in the city. Despite Bishop Cyril's formal, though highly irregular, expulsion of Jews in 414, the Arabs allegedly still found there "40,000 poll tax paying Jews"—an evident exaggeration. Thus ended another critical episode in the millennial struggle between the city of Alexandria and its Jewish community, in which the successive Byzantine administrations (excepting that of Theodosius II but including that of Heraclius) had rather successfully restrained more intolerant outbursts on the part of both the mob and the municipal authorities.[22]

Arab expansion through the rest of North Africa proceeded more slowly, but it, too, was accomplished before the end of the seventh century. The Jewish role in these conquests is obscure, although persistent traditions among the Muslims of Morocco seem to bear out the fact that as many cities were evacuated by their Greek masters, Jews from Egypt and Syria moved in. A later Arab historian also informs us that, after the new important center of Kairuwan was founded in 670, messengers were sent to Egypt to secure the emigration of a thousand Coptic or Jewish families to the new city. This close Arab-Jewish collaboration broke down, however, when Arab might started to reach out beyond the densely settled northern areas into the vast stretches occupied by backward Berber tribes. We recall that, as a result of Justinian's intolerant policies, many Jews had sought refuge among the Berber tribesmen. Some of these seem to have been converted to Judaism during the sixth century, despite certain distorted anti-Jewish traditions inherited from Carthaginian times. Since Carthage had been founded by the Phoenician branch of the ancient Canaanites, Jew-baiters from time immemorial had claimed for some of these tribes descent from the Canaanite natives of Palestine dislodged by Joshua's conquest.[23]

Cherishing their freedom, some Berbers were no more ready now to submit to Arab rule than they had been to surrender meekly to the arms of Belisarius and his successors. Even more than the Byzantines, moreover, the Arabs were bent upon converting these war-like tribes to their own faith. Not surprisingly they had to overcome some Jewish resistance, giving rise to the story, embellished by many legends, of a coalition of Berber tribes led by a Jewish "priestess," Dahya (or Dehiyya) bint Tatit al-Kahina—a medieval version of the ancient prophetess Deborah. According to Ibn Khaldun this priestess lived 127 years and, with the aid of her three sons, governed the tribe of the Jeraua for 65 years. One may legitimately question most of the details, but the basic historical kernel of that story appears the less dubious, as women soothsayers and tribal leaders in war and peace had long been known and poetically extolled even among the pre-Islamic Arabs. However, all resistance proved futile. Like her predecessor, Qusila, the Kahina suffered from the disunity of the confederation of Berber tribes under her command, the great attraction of the belligerent religion of Islam, and the prospect of booty in ever new lands. Her troops went down in defeat, apparently in 701, and the overwhelming majority of descendants of these fighting tribesmen joined the ranks of Islam's mightiest and most ardent warriors.[24]

It was, in fact, largely a Berber-Muslim enterprise which soon thereafter led to the speedy overthrow of the Visigothic kingdom, and the occupation of Spain and southern France by the Muslims (711–12). From the standpoint of the Great Caliphate this was decidedly a minor undertaking, initiated by a subordinate officer, Ṭariq, and concluded by Morocco's governor Musa ibn Nuṣair. Only because of that relatively minor expenditure of effort, combined with sharp internal dissensions among the invaders, was the Arab expansion stopped after about two decades in the battle at Tours and Poitiers (732). The paucity of Arab forces, on the other hand, made the invaders dependent on Jewish assistance there even more than elsewhere.

Whatever truth there may be in the previous allegations of conspiracies hatched by Spanish Jews with their coreligionists in North Africa, the Visigothic Jews actively collaborated with the invaders after their arrival in the country. The persistent reports of Arab chroniclers show that, to relieve the shortage of their fighting men, the conquerors entrusted the garrisoning of such important cities as Elvira, Seville, or Cordova to the Jews, while pushing on in hot pursuit of the fleeing Visigoths. This could not be done, one chronicler informs us, in Malaga, which had no Jews and the Christian inhabitants had all left the city. The gates to the capital of Toledo were opened by Jews at a time when the Christians were assembled in their churches on Palm Sunday, although the attack was not unexpected and the Visigothic grandees, including the archbishop, had fled the city—the archbishop all the way to Rome. Such active revenge of decimated Spanish Jewry on their Visigothic oppressors need not be doubted. But we must, of course, discount many legendary accretions, gross exaggerations by later Christian chroniclers, as well as apologetic denials by such later Jewish historians as Joseph ha-Kohen, who wrote long after the tide had already turned back in favor of the Christian reconquest.[25]

All through these decades of military and economic successes, the Arab ruling classes learned quickly from the superior culture of the conquered populations. They integrated, however, these new ingredients into the fabric of Islam in an indistinguishable blend of the old and the new. Much of that synthesis, particularly in the religious and legal domains, was facilitated by the evolution of the *ḥadith* (tradition). Here many authentic sayings of the Messenger and his companions were modified and adjusted to fit the requirements of the new age, while many others were added through a process of often unconscious fabrication. In this way Islam was again able to absorb many Jewish, as well as Christian and Zoroastrian, teachings and legal concepts. Especially such Muslims of Jewish descent as Ka'b al-Aḥbar (or rather Al-Ḥabr, the rabbi), allegedly of Yemenite origin, deeply influenced the *ḥadith* in this its formative stage. Even today it is next to impossible to segregate fully those Jewish doctrines or practices which had entered Islam in pre-Mohammedan Arabia or in the days of the Messenger, from those incorporated in the oral traditions during the first century after the *hejira*. For that turbulent and highly creative epoch had left behind but few reliable contemporary records.[26]

The Jewish people of the period was not much more articulate. In order to perceive some Jewish intellectual reactions to the rise of the new faith and empire, we must have recourse to a few aggadic writings, chiefly of an apocalyptic nature, with their studied ambiguities and general uncertainties of dating. An outstanding example is the apocalyptic midrash *Nistarot de-R. Shimeon bar Yoḥai* (The Mysteries of R. Simon bar Yoḥai), apparently written in part during the days of the Arab conquest of Palestine. This visionary author saw in 'Umar "a lover of Israel who repaired their breaches" and reported that the angel, Meṭaṭron, had long comforted R. Simon, "Do not fear, son of man. The Holy One, blessed be He, is only bringing the kingdom of Ishmael in order to help you [the Jews] from the wicked one." Another homilist in his "Chapters," attributed to R. Eliezer, extolled the similarity of the basic belief in one God in Judaism and Islam. He pointed out that "of all the seventy nations that the Holy One, blessed be He, created in His world" He placed his name, El, only on Israel and Ishmael.[27]

STIMULI OF THE CALIPHATE

New realities soon enforced a complete reorientation. Once the Arab armies had conquered vast stretches of land inhabited by millions of Christians, Zoroastrians, and Jews, the new rulers had to tolerate these large populations to a degree far exceeding the intentions of the Messenger and his companions. In fact, the Islam of the ninth and tenth centuries was in many ways a different religion from that formulated in the Qur'an by the first lawgiver. Neither the Greek Hellenistic, now largely Christianized, culture, nor the achievements of the equally Christian Syrians, nor those of the Persians and Jews, could be wiped out by the military conquests of the primitive Arabs. All these civilizations soon reasserted them selves under a new guise. The Caliphate, in its ninth-century period of glory, resembled the Roman and the Persian Empires much more than it did the primitive Arab tribes of the preislamic period. The new religion was, to be sure, nourished by these early Arab sources. But in the higher walks of life, in economic structure, state organization, social life of the growing urban centers, and even in religious and cultural formulations, the influences of the Greek and Christian and, even more, of the Persian civilizations, finally made of Islam a world religion, attempting to become a universal religion.

Despite the reverses suffered in subsequent ages, despite the decline of its political and economic power, that religion now counts among its adherents about one sixth of the world's population. To this very day it is the most successful missionary faith, especially among primitive tribes of Africa and southeastern Asia. As late as 1689 a Moroccan sultan, Mula Ismael, officially invited King James II of England to join the community of Islam (H. De Castries in *RHR,* XLVII, 175). Today Muslim propaganda extends to England and America, testifying to the enormous tenacity of the Muslim hope of converting the West to the universal religion of Mohammed. Indeed, the recent awakening of the Orient, the pan-Islamic movement, and the developments in Egypt and Pakistan open entirely new vistas for the future of the Muslim world and its religion.

Judaism shared in the great development during the first centuries of achievement and affluence. Unlike the Christian religion, this new creed did not arise within Jewry. Although the Jewish, as well as the Christian, influences upon Mohammed and his early disciples were very strong, and although throughout the following centuries many additional Jewish elements were absorbed by the new faith, the founder and the great teachers were not of Jewish stock. It was, therefore, from the beginning, a struggle between strangers, rather than an internecine strife among brethren.

Mohammed's religion was from the outset a political movement. Unlike Jesus, the pacifist Galilean who rejected both state and nationality, Mohammed, the son of overcrowded, expansive Arabia, regarded the state as the chief instrumentality for carrying out his religious program, if not as a supreme aim in itself. Also unlike

Paul, who merely founded a church, 'Umar I was a "commander of the faithful" and one of the greatest empire builders in history. Islam, representing the state principle, became very dangerous to the Christian and Zoroastrian state religions. Its principal division of the earth between the *dar al-Islam* (world of Islam) and the *dar al-ḥarb* (world of the sword) not only singled out every neighboring non-Muslim country as a fit object for conquest, but also nurtured the ever lingering suspicions against the fidelity of Christian subjects. No such cloud hovered over the Jewish *dhimmis* (people of the covenant), despite the occasional outbursts of their messianic enthusiasm. In general Islam was, therefore, less inimical to Judaism, the religion of an ethnic group which continued to live, so to speak, on a different plane. Subjection rather than conversion was the watchword of the conquering armies. And the Jews had for a long time been subjected to foreign masters.

From the beginning, moreover, a sharp dichotomy arose between the interests of Islam as a religion and those of the new Islamic state, which, in a somewhat inverse way, operated to the detriment of the Jewish denominational aspirations, but largely accrued to the benefit of individual Jews. This dichotomy became manifest already in the days of 'Umar, and found expression in several of his letters to his commanding generals. In an epistle, for example (much quoted and hence often distorted in the subsequent traditions), to Ṣa'd ibn Abu Waqqaṣ following the conquest of Iraq, the second caliph vigorously protested against the demands of the conquering troops that all the captured lands be distributed among them.

At the receipt of this letter ['Umar ordered], examine the horses and [other movable] property which the troops had brought to the camp, and distribute them among the Muslims present. But leave the lands and the rivers to those who put them to use, so that the produce may be allocated to the Muslims. For if you were to divide them among those who are around you, there would remain nothing for those who would come after them. Originally, I have given you the order, before opening hostilities to appeal to those against whom you march to convert themselves. He who, before any attack, submits to your appeal is thenceforth counted among the Muslims, and has the same rights and the same duties as they; he has his share in Islam. On the other hand, he who was not converted until after a show of futile resistance, is to be counted among the faithful, but his property has devolved to the adherents of Islam by virtue of the offer of protection which the latter had made to him before his conversion.

More significantly, those who resisted conversion altogether were likewise to retain their landed property, and only pay a tax to the faithful. Taking a clue from Mohammed's arrangement with the Jews of Khaibar, 'Umar instructed his lieutenants to introduce a land tax, in addition to the capitation tax enjoined by the Messenger for the monotheists. Neither of these taxes was new as far as the Jews were concerned. Under both Persia and Byzantium they had long been inured to parting with a percentage of their crops and to paying poll taxes. In the actual administration of the *kharaj* (a variant of the talmudic-Sassanian *kharga*), as we shall see, the Persian patterns were followed rather closely.[28]

In the first rush undoubtedly many Jews likewise yielded to that appeal of total tax immunity and accepted conversion. But being inured to discriminatory taxation for many centuries, they must have felt the lure less acutely than their fellow landowners, large and small, among the Christian majority in Byzantium or the Zoroastrians in Persia. In fact, in the long run the new fiscal order helped sustain the Jewish communal cohesiveness. Apart from the general trend toward holding the entire community responsible for the state revenue from its members, there was a gradual relaxation in the conversionist pressures, inasmuch as each conversion of a Jew to Islam involved the loss of a taxpayer to the state. Many a worldly Muslim governor, feeling the pinch in his private purse, was therefore more than ready to apply the dictum ascribed by tradition to Mohammed himself: "If they do accept Islam, it is well; if not, they remain [as they are]; Islam is wide enough" (Al-Zuhri ibn Sa'd's *K. aṭ-Ṭabakat* [*Biographien Muhammeds*], VI, 109 f.).

Apart from satisfying, without totally yielding to, the craving for booty among their followers—one of the main propelling forces in that memorable expansive movement—'Umar and his associates also had to pay heed to the anxiety of their fellow tribesmen to assert their superiority over the conquered populations. The old Bedouin disdain for all urban and agricultural civilizations, never fully shared by those Meccan merchants who had known the neighboring lands from direct observation, quickly gave way to a recognition of the economic and intellectual values prevailing in Iraq, Syria or Egypt. It was doubly necessary, therefore, to buttress the self-esteem of the Arab conquerors by some outward signs of superiority.

Hence there gradually arose those overt distinctions in dress and other walks of social life which came to be included in the so-called "Covenant of 'Umar." The details of these discriminatory provisions will be analyzed in the next chapter. Suffice it to say here that, rather than being part and parcel of 'Umar's treaty with the Christian community of Jerusalem of 637–38 as is claimed by persistent Muslim traditions, this array of discriminatory provisions against the *dhimmis* represented a slow accumulation of customs and local ordinances, extending over the entire first century of Islam. In fact, so long as the Muslims were but an insignificant minority in the Great Caliphate, it would have been far simpler to elevate *them* from the mass of the conquered population by distinguished attire. But there is reason to believe that the name of 'Umar was not unjustly associated with this "covenant," inasmuch as some such marks of outward inferiority doubtless met with the approval of the great empire builder. But it seems to have been another 'Umar (II) who reigned during the turbulent years at the end of the first Muslim century (717–20), who compiled these laws into a single decree and lent them their finishing touches. Apart from personal piety, the determining factor in that caliph's ultraorthodox policy was the general feeling of disappointment among the Muslim masses about the Arab failure to capture Constantinople in 717, and the widespread feeling that the end of the world was rapidly approaching. We shall see that among the Jews, too, strong repercussions were felt to these messianic expectations. Led by 'Umar II, the orthodox Muslim circles reacted vigorously against the previous laxity and worldliness at the 'Umayyad court of Damascus, and the conquerors' excessive fraternization with unbelievers. Greater segregation of the faithful from the infidels now became the watchword of the age.[29]

If Islam thus proved narrow and bigoted with respect to members of other denominations, it almost always was "wide enough" not to discriminate among persons of diverse racial or ethnic origin. In fact, its inherent preachment of racial equality has always been an integral part of its great religious appeal to the underdeveloped peoples in Asia and Africa. True, racialist debates could not be completely silenced among the vast array of nationalities and linguistic groups included within the empire. While writers of Arab descent extolled the virtues of their tribal ancestors, the beauty of their brown complexion, and the richness and flexibility of their language, they were confronted by many detractors of Arab preeminence among the proud descendants of ancient Persians, or the Ibero-Roman-Visigothic Spaniards. In the East, sectarians like Ibn Jaḥiẓ tried to rationalize the religious disparity by emphasizing ethnic diversity, while in Spain the anti-Arab arguments of an Ibn Garcia seemed to add justification to the establishment of an independent caliphate in Cordova. The non-Arab writers stressed above all the great historic achievements of the ancient Persian and Graeco-Roman civilizations at a time when the Arabs still were but "shepherds of itchy camels." Either party, however, conceded the blood affinity of the offspring of Ishmael and Isaac, as well as the great historic significance of ancient Israel. In Yehudah Halevi, therefore, these racial apologists readily found their full-fledged Jewish counterpart.[30]

In practice, however, these debates had little influence on either the Muslim mission or state policies. When in 665 a detachment of 5,000 Slavonic mercenaries of Byzantium went over to the Arabs, they were readily resettled in Syria, from which many "Greeks" had fled. Later, Agapius of Menbidj informs us that one of Caliph Al-Manṣur's commanders, returning from an expedition to Armenia, transplanted to Syria many Armenians and Alans (*K. al-'Unvan,* II, 276). Certainly, the army, that mainstay of the early Caliphate, served as an effective "melting-pot" for the diverse racial and ethnic groups. Some of the caliphs themselves were sons of slave girls or free women recruited for their fathers' harems from all over the empire and beyond. They thus symbolized the fusion of all races and peoples within the spiritual and political cauldron of the total religious "surrender" to Allah and his Messenger on earth. For this reason, the ethnic issue never seriously complicated the Muslim-Jewish relations, at least not until the rise of the modern Zionist and pan-Arab movements.

JEWISH EXPANSION

Given the assurance of a fairly quiet evolution, Jews and Judaism now entered a new period of great physical and intellectual expansion. Unlike the Persian religion, which entirely disintegrated, since practically the whole nation became converted to the new faith; unlike the Christian peoples, who, having spent their forces in their perennial sectarian struggles under Byzantine domination, now largely gave up their inherited creed, the Jews gained in strength under Islam. Not only in Babylonia, their national and religious center during the last pre-Islamic centuries, but in Persia and in Palestine, in Egypt and all the rest of North Africa, in Spain and in many adjacent countries, the Jews increased in number and influence, duplicating in a way the experience of the Second Commonwealth.

Babylonia in general remained the populous and wealthy country of old. Just as the Persians, soon after the conquest, began glorifying that province as the "heart of the Iran" and founded there their capital of Ctesiphon, so the caliphs also felt the lure of the Fertile Crescent. Before long a new capital of a still vaster empire was erected there, Baghdad. It is very likely that among the 500,000 Babylonians, said to have been subjected to the capitation tax by 'Umar I (Ibn Khurdadhbah), a strong minority, if not the majority, was Jewish. Not only does the Talmud frequently discuss the legal import of a Jewish majority in Babylonian cities, but this fact is confirmed for Sura in the days of Saadiah by the report of a visiting Arab medical commission. Also the Syriac name of Mosul, Ḥesna Ebraya (Hebrew castle, frequently called Ashshur by the Jews themselves), undoubtedly had some factual basis. Therefore, the number of 90,000 Jews who under the leadership of Isaac, head of the academy of Firuz Shabur, are said to have welcomed 'Ali on his arrival in Babylonia, may not be greatly exaggerated. Afterwards with the increasing conversion of the other inhabitants to Islam, the Jews became the most influential minority in the province.[31]

Baghdad, the new capital, from its foundation as the "city of salvation" by Caliph Al-Manṣur in 763–66, attracted many Jewish settlers. In fact, it was the Jewish mathematician and astrologer,

Masha'allah, who together with An-Naubakht, a Persian astronomer, drew up the measurements for the new metropolis. The Aramaic name Al-Karkḥ (Karka) of the district in which a Jewish quarter was located, may have been derived from an earlier Jewish community there, whose existence is attested by the Talmud and other sources. After all the city as a whole still bore its old Persian designation of *Bagh-dad,* or "God's gift" to men. Identified in Hebrew letters with ancient Babel (*ha-Babli* becoming synonymous with *al-Baghdadi*), it embraced in its two Jewish quarters a large and affluent Jewish community.

Jews were also found in other sections of the metropolis which, according to the dependable thirteenth-century geographer Yaqut, had 6,000 streets in the west and 4,000 streets on the east side, within a perimeter of nearly twenty miles. The ratio of Jews hardly ever exceeded 2 percent of the population, which early in the tenth century allegedly amounted to some 2,000,000. (For comparison with contemporary Europe, it suffices to state that Angevin England in the twelfth century apparently had a population of no more than 1,500,000.) That the percentage of Jews was not much higher was probably due to intolerant outbursts of caliphs, who sometimes resented the presence of numerous "infidels" in the metropolis. Al-Ma'mun, for instance, the "liberal" ruler of the ninth century, once arrested 2,800 "unbelievers" and ordered the expulsion of a great many Jews, "the most corrupt people." Nevertheless, even after the city's sharp decline during the tenth century as a result of a catastrophic succession of civil wars, famines, and conflagrations, Benjamin of Tudela about 1168 still found in it some 40,000 Jews, maintaining twenty-eight synagogues and ten academies of learning. If at the time of the Mongolian conquest in 1258 a contemporary Arab writer reported the presence there of 36,000 Jewish poll tax payers owning but sixteen synagogues, this discrepancy may have resulted entirely from the preference of many Jews to pray in smaller semiprivate houses of worship, which may readily have escaped an outsider's attention.[32]

In Palestine, Jewry, oppressed and decimated by the last Byzantine rulers, recuperated in a short time to such an extent that it could attempt to wrest the hegemony over the Jewish world from the Babylonian geonim. Notwithstanding the desire of the Christians to keep the Jews out of Jerusalem in continuation of the Hadrianic prohibition, the Jewish community there grew by leaps and bounds. Neither its vengeful destruction by Heraclius' returning army in 628, nor 'Umar's pledge of 638 to keep Jews out of the Holy City, prevented the latter from gaining access to the very Temple area. A later report of unknown date, preserved in a Cambridge Genizah fragment, tells us about negotiations allegedly conducted by the Jews with 'Umar, as well as with the Christian patriarch of the Holy City. Under the caliph's pressure, the Christians are said to have first consented to the admission of fifty Jewish families. The Jews demanded a minimum of two hundred. Thereupon 'Umar decreed that seventy families be allowed to settle. The reason for the caliph's benevolence is explained in another, equally garbled, account of the tenth or eleventh century. In a typical letter of solicitation, addressed to the communities of the dispersion, the Jerusalem elders described the difficult situation in their community, owing in particular to the severe fiscal exactions, and the hostility of the Gentile population.

It was God's will [they reminisced] to make us find favor before the Ishmaelite kingdom at the time of its conquest of the Holy Land from the hands of Edom [Byzantium]. When they [the Arabs] came to Jerusalem, there were with them men from among the children of Israel who showed them the place of the Temple. This group has lived among them [the Arabs] from that time to the present. The Jews have agreed to a compact, whereby they would cleanse the Temple from all refuse. [In return] they would be allowed to pray at its gates, with no interference. They also bought Mount Olivet. . . . This is the place at which we worship on holidays, facing the Lord's Temple [especially] on *Hosha'nah* [*rabbah,* the seventh day of the Feast of Tabernacles]. There we bless the whole house of Israel, each country and its communities, with its elders and patrons. Every one who remembers Jerusalem and bears it in mind [with a contribution] is mentioned in the prayers and benedictions.[33]

The Jerusalem elders failed to indicate how these new residents had squared it with their conscience to perform services for the Mosque of the Rock, even in return for both freedom from poll taxes and the opportunity to worship at the only remnant of the Herodian Temple, the so-called Wailing Wall. In any case this Wall and the other reminders of ancient holiness soon attracted an increasing number of "Mourners for Zion," both Rabbanite and Karaite, who, subsidized by donations from many Jewish communities, substantially increased Jerusalem's permanent Jewish population. To be sure, Salmon ben Yeruḥim, a tenth-century Karaite, complained of the ill-treatment of Jews by both the Muslim authorities and the Christian population. In the eyes of an Arab observer, however, like Muqaddasi, himself a resident of Jerusalem and Salmon's younger contemporary, Jews shared with the Christians control over the city, whose architecture and way of life he greatly extolled. Despite occasional setbacks, as during the military upheavals of 1029, 1042 and 1071, the Jewish community of Jerusalem still existed, though in a greatly reduced state, until the conquering Crusaders mercilessly destroyed it in 1099.[34]

A similar fate befell many other Palestinian communities. Tiberias, which in unbroken historic continuity had maintained its leadership over the Galilean and indeed all Palestinian settlements throughout the Byzantine period, now had to part with its great rabbinic academy, which transferred its seat to Jerusalem. But until the tenth century the northern community continued to hold undisputed sway in the fields of Hebrew poetry, exegesis, and linguistic studies. Even its general run of citizens is supposed to have preserved the knowledge of the Hebrew language and the purity of its pronunciation far above any other Palestinian locality, according to the famous grammarian, Jonah ibn Janaḥ. Gaza, too, lost its status as the foremost community of Judaea, but it remained a center of learning and well-developed community life. Haifa, Ascalon, and many other cities likewise received an influx of new settlers and embraced growingly important Jewish communities. The Jews of the "fortress of Haifa," apparently an independent administrative unit, were to fight bravely on the side of the Muslims against the Crusaders. There arose also the new and important community of Ramleh. Founded by Caliph Sulaiman in 716, the city became not only the caliph's temporary residence, but also the permanent administrative capital of Palestine. It attracted a great many new inhabitants from many lands. Among its cosmopolitan population one could readily distinguish Jews from as far away as Babylonia and Persia, Morocco and Spain. There were also numerous Karaites and Samaritans. The Jewish heads of the Jerusalem community often visited Ramleh on communal business, the Jerusalem academy actually finding it convenient to station there one of its highest officials as a sort of permanent envoy to the provincial governor.[35]

Naturally enough, the coexistence in a small country of members of various Jewish, Christian, and Muslim denominations, each of which believed itself to possess special claims to the land's sanctity, created frequent tensions. Even within the Jewish community there was constant strife, while there was no end of bickering between it and its Karaite counterparts. On the whole, however, the relationships between the members of the three faiths were far more friendly than appears from the reports of ecclesiastical writers more interested in recording (and exaggerating) dramatic events than daily occurrences. To this category belongs, for example, Theophanes' story about the Jewish part in the removal of crosses in Jerusalem during the building of the Mosque of 'Umar, which supposedly led to the subsequent general prohibition of carrying crosses at public processions. The same chronicler also tells us of Emir 'Abd Allah's destruction of Christian sacred vessels in Palestine in 749, and his persuading some Jews to purchase them, while Yaḥya of Antioch describes at some length an alleged joint attack by Jews and Muslims on the Church of the Holy Sepulcher and the Zion Church in May of 966. On the other hand, a newly recovered inscription in Khirbet Mafjar shows that Christian laborers (and even clerics) could collaborate with a Jewish worker and the Muslim administration in peacefully erecting a palace under Caliph Hisham (724–43). Racially too, it may be remembered, only a relatively small segment of the population descended from the invaders under 'Umar or the Nabatean and other Arabs who had infiltrated the Holy Land at an earlier period. The majority of both Muslims and Christians were the progeny of that vast mixture of ethnic strains which had characterized the First and Second Jewish Commonwealths and was enriched by further admixtures from the other provinces of Rome and Byzantium.[36]

Syrian communities likewise felt the vitalizing effects of the new dynamic forces. The evacuation of Christians by the Byzantine navy, especially from some coastal cities, opened the gate to the influx of new Jewish settlers. Baladhuri informs us that in Tripolis, which was completely deserted by its Christian inhabitants, Mu'awiya settled a large number of Jews, "and it is they who live in that harbor to the present day." Rejuvenated Tyre, rebuilt at a slight distance from its ancient Phoenician locale, likewise received a great influx of Jews, some coming from as far away as Morocco and Spain. Its community, which included shipowners, glass manufacturers, and dyers, was in constant interrelation with the communities of Palestine, and was frequently counted by the Jerusalem authorities as an integral part of the Holy Land. After the Seljuk occupations of Jerusalem in 1071, the Jerusalem academy itself removed to Tyre, where it flourished for about a quarter century, until the city's occupation by the Crusaders. There also was a congregation of the Babylonian rite, in addition to some Karaites and Samaritans. Even after the havoc played by the Western invasion, Benjamin still found there some 400 Jews, while the French (?) traveler, Jacob, messenger of Yeḥiel of Paris (1238–44), spoke of its fine and beautiful synagogue. Damascus, the capital of the 'Umayyad Caliphate, once again became an important center of Jewish life and learning. It ultimately harbored both a *nasi* and a *gaon,* styled, respectively, the "head of the men of Palestine" and the "head of the academy of Palestine." In Petaḥiah's day it allegedly had a Jewish population of 10,000, although several years earlier Benjamin reported there the presence of only 3,000 Jews (possibly Jewish taxpayers). To the northeast ancient Palmyra retained much of its former glory. In that jewel of the desert Benjamin noticed with amazement the presence of 2,000 warlike Jews, who took an active part in their city's battles against both the Turks and the Crusaders.[37]

Among the younger communities, Aleppo assumed such importance that, in one of his letters, the Palestinian leader, Solomon ben Yehudah, singled out "our brethren, the Jews living in Palestine, Egypt, Damascus, and Ṣobah [Aleppo]" as special objects of prayers on Passover. The community preceded the rise of Islam. Although its synagogue inscription allegedly dated in 342 was really placed there in 833, there is sound archaeological evidence showing that the Great Synagogue had existed there not later than the fifth century, and may indeed have been founded a century earlier. There also existed another synagogue, whose remains excavated by French archaeologists date back to the sixth century. The Jews themselves were perfectly convinced of their community's antiquity. They explained to Petaḥiah the city's Hebrew name, Ḥaleb, by the fact that "on the mountain was the flock of Abraham our father . . . whence he was accustomed to hand milk [*ḥalab*] to the poor." One of their three synagogues was named after Moses. Nevertheless the era of its great prosperity and intellectual achievement came only after the expansion of Islam. On the other hand, the formerly large and affluent community of Antioch lost its position of leadership among Syrian Jews, just as the city at large had become but a shadow of its former self. We hear also relatively little about such ancient Jewish communities as those of Sidon, Byblos, or Beirut.[38]

In Egypt, too, Jewry regained much of its former glory. Speedily recovering from the oppression of the expiring Byzantine regime which, shortly before its end, had led to wholesale conversion of the small Jewish community of Tumai, Egyptian Jewry increased in numbers as well as in economic and intellectual strength. It received a considerable influx of Jews from the more populous Asiatic communities. As early as 750, we learn from a chance document, the community of Fusṭaṭ, which had arisen on the site of the former Muslim army camp, was headed by a Baghdad Jew (I. Abrahams in *JQR,* [o.s.] XVII, 426–30). Of course reference was here made to the then rather small provincial community of Baghdad some twelve years before it became the imperial capital.

Soon the two communities of Fusṭaṭ-Cairo and Baghdad outstripped all other Jewish centers, just as the cities in which they were located overshadowed all other Muslim metropolises. In the eleventh century, we have reasons to believe, Fusṭaṭ-Cairo outranked even Baghdad as the largest city in the world of Islam. Under the rule of the Faṭimid caliphs especially, whose conquest of Egypt and Palestine in 969 seems to have been promoted by Jews and Jewish converts to Islam, Egypt became a great center of science and Jewish learning. The Egyptian Jewish communities were strong enough to weather a severe crisis under Caliph Al-Hakim (1012–20) without permanent damage. This relative prosperity outlasted the downfall of the Faṭimids in 1171, and their replacement by the Seljuk regime, headed by the celebrated Saladin.

All through that period the community of Fusṭaṭ exercised an influence far transcending the boundaries of Egypt, and it served as a focal link between all Eastern and Western Jewries. Hence the great importance of its documentary depository, the Genizah, from which have emerged not only valuable local records but also numerous transcripts of important communications sent from Babylonia and Palestine to Fusṭaṭ, to be forwarded to their respective ultimate destinations. Fusṭaṭ's commercial and intellectual relations extended from India to Spain. It reached the acme of its fame in the days of its most illustrious citizen, Maimonides. Benjamin found there some 7,000 Jewish families, including 200 forming an "Italian" congregation. Alexandria, harboring a Jewish population of 3,000 families in Benjamin's days, now definitely ranked second to Cairo, but it still was a major emporium of international trade. Owing to its geographic position on the eastern Mediterranean, it was frequently called upon to perform the great charitable function of redeeming Jewish captives taken by Muslim raiders from Byzantine and other ships. Since these services often transcended its financial resources, it had to request aid from the community of Fusṭaṭ. Hence came the several letters of solicitation included in the latter's Genizah. There also existed Jewish shrines of immemorial antiquity in various parts of the country. The small community of Damwah, near Fusṭaṭ, possessed what Maqrizi was to call the most important synagogue in Egypt. The structure itself had allegedly been erected forty years after the fall of Jerusalem on the very spot where Moses had prayed after his interviews with Pharaoh. Because of that reputed association the synagogue became a major center of pilgrimages from all over Egypt both on Adar 7, the accepted date of Moses' death, and on the Festival of Weeks, which commemorates the divine revelation of the Torah to him. We also have the records of a number of other important communities all through the Nile valley.[39]

In their westward expansion, as we recall, the Arabs encountered numerous and long-established Jewish communities in central and western Africa as well as in Spain, southern France, and, ultimately, also southern Italy. The enmity toward the conquerors of the Berber tribes and their Jewish leaders subsided quickly enough, and by the end of the first Muslim century the majority of these unruly tribesmen were won over to Islam. In fact, the ethnic antagonisms between the Muslim Berbers and the Arabs became a permanent factor to be reckoned with in Morocco, Spain, and Sicily. The Jews, too, as we shall see, were to be affected by these conflicts, both favorably and adversely.

In Kairuwan and the province of Ifriqiya, the famous heir of the ancient Carthaginian-Semitic civilization, the Jews, reinforced by numerous arrivals from Egypt and Palestine, had a fully developed community life at the time of the Faṭimid rise to power (909). In fact, probably owing to the collaboration of some Jews in the subsequent Faṭimid campaigns in Egypt and western Asia, the enemies of the new dynasty asserted that it had much Jewish blood in its veins. This imputation was the more serious as the royal family prided itself on the purity of its descent from Mohammed's daughter Faṭimah, and thus justified its rejection of the "upstart" 'Abbasid caliphate. During the tenth century the city of Kairuwan, glorified by the Arabs as one of the four gates to Paradise, embraced a large and prosperous Jewish community. The latter soon felt strong enough to throw off the tutelage of the eastern academies, and, utilizing the arrival of the deposed exilarch Mar 'Uqba (about 912), it treated him with all the amenities appropriate to an actually reigning prince of captivity. Mar 'Uqba's arrival thus symbolized the growing independence of the west almost as effectively, if less dramatically, as had among the Muslims the landing of the 'Umayyad scion, 'Abd ar-Raḥman I, in Spain a century and a half earlier. While still voluntarily supporting the Babylonian academies, the "men of Kairuwan" were led by eminent scholars of their own, who corresponded with the Babylonian geonim on terms of equality. Their relations with their Muslim fellow citizens, too, were as a rule quite satisfactory. Describing, for instance, the erection of the great mosque in Kairuwan in 955–56, an Arab chronicler emphasized that it was built on Jewish land acquired by a "good" purchase without fraud.[40]

There also were Jewish settlements in neighboring Tripolitania, although the absence of sources makes it impossible to ascertain whether these communities had maintained some measure of historic continuity from the days of ancient Cyrenaica. They have left behind, however, few literary sources, and even their funeral inscriptions, if we may take a clue from a tombstone erected in 963 (published by D. Cazès in *REJ*, XX, 78), were utterly simple and inarticulate.

Morocco, on the other hand, rather than turning east, looked northward to Spain, which it had conquered for Islam and whose tottering Muslim regimes of the eleventh and twelfth centuries it often had to reinforce with its own manpower and military resources. At times ruled by the same monarchs, the two countries evinced a certain community of destiny, which was even more pronounced in Jewish life. Here Fez, the newly founded capital of the Shi'ite Idriside dynasty, became from its inception (808) a major center of Jewish culture. Numerous Jews were resettled there by the new rulers in a quarter of their own, in return for a pledge to pay an annual capitation tax of 30,000 dinars. Among Fez's residents were some of the most illustrious Jewish scholars and writers of the tenth and early eleventh centuries. Jews also lived in Marrakesh (founded in 1062) and in many of the older communities under the successive dynasties of Aghlabids, Zirids, and Almoravids. Moroccan Jewry's relatively speedy decline thereafter is attributed to the general deterioration in the political and economic conditions in the country and to the endless civil wars. During one such temporary occupation of Fez (in 1032–33) by the rebel Abu'l Kamal Tamim, we are told, 6,000 Jews were massacred, while many of their women were carried away into captivity. The Jewish community was further reduced, but not obliterated, by the rise of the extremely intolerant Almohade regime in 1146.[41]

The Almohades, as we shall see, inflicted permanent wounds on Spanish Jewry, which in the preceding two centuries had lived through its renowned "golden age." Reversing the trend under the last Visigothic kings, Spanish Jewry, together with its extensions in the Balearic Islands and the Provence, steadily grew in numbers and affluence. Unlike Morocco, Spain had no independent Berber-Jewish tribes who would seek to maintain their freedom against the Arab invaders and later become involved in the internecine tribal warfare among the Muslims. Some Spanish cities now became predominantly Jewish. Contemporary realities often obscured the historical recollection, and many Jews, as well as Gentiles, genuinely believed that the first and, for a time, only settlers of Seville had been Jews. The well-informed geographer, Al-Idrisi called Tarragona a "city of Jews." The important community of Lucena was exhorted by the gaon, R. Naṭronai bar Hilai of Sura (853–58), to do certain things, "since there is no Gentile living among you at all." Granada, too, was long called in Arabic *Ighranatat al-yahud* (Jewish Granada), because, Al-Ḥimyari explained, "the first inhabitants who had settled there were Jews." Quite similar, though on a far lesser scale, were the conditions of the rapidly expanding Jewish communities in Sicily and parts of southern Italy during the Saracen regime there in varying periods from the ninth to the eleventh centuries.[42]

No less pronounced was the eastward expansion. In Persia itself, which soon became one of the political and cultural foci of the Caliphate, the Jews evolved new cultural centers surpassing in intensity of religious feeling most Jewries of the western provinces. A "Jew town" (*Yehudiya*) existed in the vicinity of Isfahan, and another in that of Balkh. The former loomed so large in Muslim eyes that many believed that the Dajjal (the Muslim counterpart to Antichrist) would appear there, rather than in Kufa or Khorasan. The Isfahan Jewish quarter had evidently long been established, the sources differing only as to whether this happened under Shapur II, or under Yazdegerd I and his Jewish wife. Nevertheless local Jewish legends, believed also by some Arabs, dated the origin of the Jewish community back to the days of the First Exile. Although suffering from a severe persecution under Peroz Shapur in 472, the community seems to have recuperated quite speedily. Under Islam it became a major center of economic and cultural enterprise. According to Yaqut, even the noblest Muslim families in the city were the descendants of either Jews or weavers, two classes of the population which shared the contempt of Arab grandees everywhere. More generally, Muqaddasi found in Fars more Zoroastrians than Jews, but the latter outnumbered the Christians there as well as in Jibal and Khorasan. The latter province had, indeed, a great many Jews. According to a report which reached Moses ibn Ezra in Spain, there were 40,000 Jewish taxpayers in the capital of Khorasan and another 40,000 in its provincial communities. Not much more reliably Benjamin reported, evidently from hearsay, that even distant Samarkand had a Jewish population of 50,000 (or 30,000). It is small wonder, then, that from Isfahan, Nahawend, and Balkh also came some of the most influential Jewish religious reformers of the eighth and ninth centuries.[43]

Another heresiarch, Musa al-Zafrani, though born in Baghdad, settled in the then Armenian city of Tiflis, giving rise to the Jewish sect of "Tiflisites." The rest of Armenia likewise had Jewish settlements, some reaching back to remote antiquity. Persistence of animal sacrifices was denounced there as a "Jewish" custom as late as the eleventh century. Like their non-Jewish neighbors, these communities often suffered from the geographic position of their country between Byzantium and Islam, just as their ancestors had suffered from the constant proximity of the Roman and Sassanian armies. In fact, Moses of Khorene, the same Armenian historian who ascribed Jewish origin to his country's leading family of the Bagratids, also reported a large-scale Jewish deportation from Armenia to Isfahan by Shapur II. Armenia likewise was a frequent battle ground between the Caliphate and the Khazars, who were to play such a remarkable, though only transient, role in Jewish history. On the other hand, a Hebrew inscription found in Afghanistan revealed the presence there of Jews in the twelfth century. In short, within a few centuries after the rise of Islam the vast expanses of the Caliphate were dotted with large, affluent, and intellectually alert Jewish communities.[44]

BIOLOGICAL STRENGTH

This marvelous expansion of the Jewish people during the first centuries of Islam seems to have been owing to natural and social factors, rather than missionary successes. To secure an appreciable number of proselytes among the Muslims was out of the question, as apostasy from Islam was outlawed as a capital crime. Not even Christians or Parsees were permitted to become Jews or vice versa, toleration being extended only for adherence to an inherited creed. Moreover, Jewish proselytizing among the other religious minorities could proceed only very slowly in the face of the tremendous attraction of the new religion upon oriental minds and the many immediate advantages it offered to a convert. Indeed, proselytes are rarely spoken of in the vast mass of legal decisions of contemporary rabbis. Even one Abu al-Khair "al-ger," mentioned in an Egyptian tax list, may not have been a proselyte at all, or else may have been a convert from Christianity or even paganism.[45]

The major accretions to the Jewish community, therefore, could come from the outside only via the institution of slavery. It is, indeed, to be assumed that some of the slaves of Jews, who, according to Jewish law, had to be circumcised and made to observe many ritualistic requirements while living in the Jewish household, continued to adhere to Judaism after their manumission. But, as we shall see, Jews held slaves for purposes of resale as well as for use in domestic service. The number of freedmen joining the Jewish community probably was even smaller than it had been in ancient times. Concubinage with female slaves, on the other hand, a major social factor in the Islamic civilization, was severely frowned upon by the rabbis. True, there must have been more breaches of that law than are reflected in the sources. Stories like that described in a geonic responsum (by Sherira, probably jointly with his son Hai) must have occurred from time to time. A Jew, we are told, was suspected of intercourse with his wife's Christian slave, who became pregnant and bore a son. He brought the child to the synagogue to have him circumcised. But the congregation decided that the boy could not be circumcised until the mother testified whose son he was (*Sha'are ṣedeq,* III, 15, fol. 25a). However, numerically such additions to the Jewish populations must always have been very small.

Jewry's growth is doubly remarkable, therefore, as it also had to replace losses incurred in the mass conversions of Jews to Islam, especially in the first decades after the *hejira* and during the fitful suppression of both Judaism and Christianity in Al-Ḥakim's Egypt and Palestine, and in Almohade Spain and Morocco. The dissolution of social ties in the decadent Byzantine and Persian empires, followed by the onrush of enthusiastic and self-sacrificing "believers" in the new faith, seems to have impressed some Jews and particularly Jewish women. The posttalmudic *Sefer ha-Ma'asim li-bene Ereṣ Yisrael* (Book of Palestinian Halakhic Practice) reflects not only a considerable loosening of sex morality among the Jews of that period, but also mentions punitive measures to be taken against women, who, after using a lot of cosmetics, visited houses of idols. One of the few legal enactments attributed to a teacher of the seventh century, R. Raba, concerns the obstreperous woman (*moredet*), who evidently repudiated the authority of both her husband and the community at large. Sherira Gaon speaks of women who, with the aid of Gentiles, had at that time forced their husbands to give them writs of divorce, while a still later source ascribes that pro-feminist reform more specifically to the year 962 Sel. era (650–51 C.E.). In later generations, too, the strong assimilationist trends in Muslim society and the economic and political pressures produced enough conversions to induce the rabbis to change the existing law and to allow a convert's Jewish wife immediately to collect her marriage settlement. Maimonides, who reports uniform agreement in this matter among Jewish leaders of East and West, adds, "And such cases happen daily with us." [46]

We are not told by any of the contemporary writers how many Jews adopted Islam during the short span of Al-Ḥakim's persecution, nor how many of those made use, in 1020, of the permission to return to their former faith. But we can hardly doubt that the Jewish community suffered on this occasion some irretrievable losses. The same is true on a much larger scale of the forced conversions during the robust Almohade regime, which also doubtless enjoyed far greater cooperation on the part of its fanatical bureaucracy. Although, according to Maimonides, at first mere lip service seemed to satisfy the authorities, one need not be surprised if many Jews took the easier road of conforming with the governmental decrees. Many of their descendants certainly remained Muslims even after the storm had subsided. Maimonides' contemporary, Samau'al ibn Yaḥya al-Maghribi, himself a Jewish convert to Islam, stated with evident exaggeration that most of the Karaites in his day had found their way to the Muslim faith. Since there had been relatively few Karaites in the countries dominated by the Almohades, he must have had mainly eastern Karaites in mind. Nevertheless, it appears that from the eighth century on most conversions were individual and sufficiently sporadic not to interfere seriously with the increase of Jewish population. Even direct references to individual converts became relatively scarce despite the far greater abundance of sources.[47]

What was the size of the Jewish population during the first seven centuries of Islam? The only statement one may confidently make is that the large majority of the Jewish people lived in countries under Muslim domination throughout that period. Apart from Benjamin and, to a lesser extent, Petaḥiah, none of the contemporaries ventured to offer even "guestimates" for large areas. Since no regular censuses were taken by either the Muslim or the Christian governments of that time, the contemporaries themselves could not possibly answer such a query with any degree of assurance. Few, moreover, were at all interested in ascertaining these facts, our two travelers being laudable exceptions. At best, government officials and Jewish communal leaders evinced interest in the total number of poll tax payers in any locality or district. In many areas undoubtedly this was the only information available, and it was given to an interested visitor like Benjamin. That is why his figures on the smaller, if not better organized, Western and Byzantine communities are relatively moderate. In so far as they represent taxpayers, they must be multiplied at least five times to secure estimates of the general population, in view of the numerous exemptions from that tax in Muslim law. Of course, the practice here varied in ratio to changing fiscal needs, and the rapacity or efficiency of the respective tax collecting agencies. In many areas, on the other hand, Benjamin was undoubtedly given estimates for the total Jewish population, in part derived from other less reliable computations. At times, especially in the less orderly but densely populated eastern communities, he had to accept wild guesses offered him by local citizens, especially if his own sojourn was too brief to allow for his independent evaluation of such data. We must therefore discount some of his estimates as totally unreliable.

At the same time his figures are incomplete in so far as he did not visit all communities, not even all important ones; nor did he supply population data for all those through which he had passed. That is why his sum total, amounting to well over half a million for the Jewish population under the rule of eastern Islam (a superficial count of 512,532 depends on the acceptance of certain manuscript variants), probably still is a gross underestimate. The true global figure, it appears, may have been double that size or higher. One must also add Benjamin's numerous Jewish contemporaries, professing their religion in secret, in the countries under Almohade domination, and, of course, the Jewries under Christendom, the Far East, and East Africa. It is probably not too far-fetched an assumption, therefore, that the total Jewish population at the end of the twelfth century approximated some 2,000,000. If true, this figure may actually have been somewhat exceeded at the height of the East's prosperity two centuries earlier, but it certainly remained far behind the large Jewish population before the second fall of Jerusalem.[48]

THE FAR EAST AND AFRICA

Under the impetus of the great expansion of Islam and the opening up of vast new commercial opportunities, many Jews and Christians, as well as Muslims, penetrated in increasing numbers the lands lying on the periphery of the Great Caliphate. Of course, outside the Muslim and Christian countries, Jews were subjected to lesser conversionist pressures, while the Jewish mission itself could be much more successful. That, for instance, the Jews of India made use of the new opportunities for their religious propaganda, is proved by the existence of thousands of colored Jews in Cochin even today. At the same time, India appears to have absorbed a steady influx of Jews from the Caliphate, since it was a popular saying in Sura in the days of Saadiah that "everyone who goes to India gets rich." This adage is partially confirmed in a letter of a North African Jew of 1149. Here the writer informed his closely knit, though widely dispersed, family of the wealth which he had amassed in India, and which he wished to share with them. At the same time Jews also played a significant role in the early transmission of Indian science to the Arab world and, through it, to the Western countries as well.[49]

In 1020 or earlier (750 or possibly 476) Yusuf Rabban secured from the Rajah a privilege recorded on copper plates still extant. Signed by five princes and the commander of the army, the decree provided that "to Isuppu Irabban, prince of Ansuvannam [in Cranganore], and to his descendants . . . Ansuvannam (is) an hereditary estate as long as the world and the moon exist." Yusuf's family should also be entitled to ride on elephants, or be carried in litters, preceded by trumpets, so that the lower castes might withdraw from its path. Two centuries later Maimonides' brother, David, lost his life in a shipwreck while on a business trip to India. In the thirteenth century an Indian Jew wrote to his correspondent in Cairo about his frequent "journeys from Malabar to Ceylon but his goods are the whole year in Aden." He did not visit Aden that year, but a friend, Sheikh Joseph ibn Abulmana, went there and was likely to spend some time in Egypt as well. A much later Muslim source, narrating events of the sixteenth century, even accused the Jews there of having "made a great many Mohammedans to drink the cup of martyrdom." In short, the colored Jewish community of Cochin, of the self-styled Bene-Israel which spread to Bombay and other Indian cities, probably antedates Islam. At the outset it must have included a substantial kernel of Jewish immigrants from the West. Most of the later "white" Jews, however, had undoubtedly come during Islam's penetration of that vast subcontinent.[50]

Similarly Jews may have entered the important Chinese silk trade already under the Han dynasty at the beginning of the Christian era. They may also have paved the way for the spread of both Christianity and Islam in that great empire. But there is no doubt that the intensity of new contacts established by Muslim travelers and merchants added stimulus to Jewish immigration as well. Ibn Zaid al-Ḥasan, a ninth-century traveler, already mentions Jews among those massacred during riots at Khanfu. Sulaiman, an Andalusian Jew (?), supposedly visited China during the second quarter of that century and was hospitably received there by Hebrew-speaking Jews. In 941–43 a Muslim traveler, Abu Dulaf, came to a tribe Tübat (probably Tibet, or more specifically the oasis of Hotan, which had belonged to Tibet), where he found a large city built of cane, and inhabited also by Muslims, Jews, Christians, Magians, and Hindus. He also found Jews in neighboring Bahi (Bai or Pima?). From that time on these exotic communities frequently attracted the attention of European travelers and missionaries. Benjamin of Tudela evinced some interest in them, although he evidently knew little about their location and activities even from hearsay.[51]

Benjamin had little more information about African Jewry

south of Egypt. All he had to say about the large Jewish community of Abyssinia, the so-called Falashas, was that they included many successful warriors and that they were in contact with Aden. In fact, Abyssinia practically disappeared from Jewish and, to some extent, also from world history after its sixth-century expeditions to southern Arabia. Even its own sources became very sparse until the thirteenth century.

It is small wonder, therefore, that we know even less about the Jews settled further south along the east coast of Africa, although the Caliphate and its successor states maintained commercial relations with them that were far more intensive than those of their Phoenician or Greek predecessors. Even before the foundation of Kilwa (about 975) Arabs seem to have rediscovered the ancient gold mines which had once been vigorously exploited there by Egyptians and Phoenicians. Whenever Jews settled in that area, reaching it either through Ethiopia or by sea from the Gulf of Aden, their imagination may well have been kindled by the sight of remnants of such ancient Phoenician mines as were discovered in 1924 south of Lake Tanganyika. They readily remembered the biblical story of King Solomon's expeditions to Ophir. Whether we identify Ophir with Fura or Yufi behind the Sofala coast in Africa, as some modern scholars have, or prefer to look for it somewhere along the western coast of India, the memory of these Phoenician-Israelitic expeditions sufficed to give rise, and subsequently to lend great credence, to such traditions of the early arrival there of the ancient Israelitic tribe of Dan, as recorded by Eldad the "Danite." This nexus is by no means controverted by Eldad's failure to refer to Ophir and his reiterated identification of his homeland with the region behind the river Pishon. Apparently accepting the Midrash's and Saadiah's translation of Pishon by Nile, he could indeed look toward "the whole land of Havilah, where there is gold," which that river encompassed (Gen. 2:11), in the vicinity of the sources of the Nile in east-central Africa. In Benjamin's even vaguer terminology, "Havilah" included also Abyssinia.[52]

Much depends on how much credence we are willing to lend to the narratives of Eldad, the most illustrious Jewish native of that region, whose stories startled his listeners already in ninth-century

Kairuwan and other contemporary communities. His own life story, as it can be pieced together from these tales, sheds a weird light on the little known Jewish communities from Tanganyika to the Persian Gulf. Evidently he first came in touch with the main centers of Jewish life on a visit to Egypt which seems to have aroused in him a deep curiosity about the whereabouts of the rest of Jewry. Here he doubtless also became conscious of the implications of his family tradition that he was a descendant of the ancient tribe of Dan, one of the "lost" Ten Tribes. Not long after his return to his native country he embarked, therefore, on a more ambitious journey, apparently in order to pursue the traces of the other lost tribes. Claiming that, according to local traditions, his warlike ancestors had departed from Palestine soon after Solomon's death because they refused to participate in the northern rebellion against the house of David, he contended that after the fall of Samaria their independent Jewish principality attracted the exiled tribes of Naphtali, Gad, and Asher. He believed that descendants of all four tribes still were settled on both sides of the Gulf of Aden. To reach the remnants of the other tribes, Eldad set sail with a Jewish companion on the Indian Ocean. After capture by Negro cannibals, his miraculous rescue by an invading army, and his ransom by a coreligionist for thirty-two gold pieces, he reached the Persian Gulf. Here resided, in his opinion, remnants of the tribes of Reuben, Issachar, and Zebulun. The remaining three tribes were allegedly divided between the mountains of the Arabian Peninsula (Ephraim and part of Manasseh) and Khazaria (Simeon and the rest of Manasseh). Eldad did not claim to have visited all these tribes, but there is no question about his extensive travels, which had brought him to Babylonia, North Africa, and probably also Spain.[53]

RENAISSANCE OF ISLAM AND JUDAISM

As long as Western historians contemplated the rise of the new Muslim civilization from the exclusive focus of West European realities, the transformation in the fabric of political, economic, and cultural life brought about by the expansion of Islam seemed well-nigh miraculous. Their ancestors of the twelfth century had viewed with profound amazement the populousness and wealth, the cultural amenities and scientific achievements of the Muslim world, suddenly become familiar to them through direct observation during the era of Crusades. Modern students, too, were long unable to suppress their sense of wonder at the new life which seemed so suddenly to have sprung from long-decaying, indeed doomed, civilizations. This "provincial" approach has given way in recent decades to a more judicious interpretation of the underlying, slow, and long-range historic processes, and the realization that what had happened was more an intrinsic acceleration than a total reversal of the previous evolution. Owing to the significant progress in Byzantine, Syriac, Persian, and Indian studies, it became possible to comprehend more fully the basic strains of the preceding developments, which needed but to be tied together into a single multicolored line. The Arab expansion provided that unifying force. By introducing a single linguistic medium, in speech and in writing, from India to southern France, and by establishing certain basically similar institutions and approaches derived from a noteworthy synthesis of these manifold local variations, the Caliphate and its successor states were able to release a powerful stream which absorbed into itself and commingled with all these ancient tributaries. Curiously, it was the Persians, formerly the least articulate members of the new community, who now supplied some of the most important leaders in government and culture.

Without making a totally new start, Jews too were greatly quickened. Here too, appearances, largely based upon chance records of historical developments in a generally inarticulate era, were decidedly misleading. Some of these records were but accidentally preserved by generations which, moving on to different planes of cultural endeavor, lost interest in the earlier efforts. We recall how amazingly vigorous had been the superficially downtrodden Jewries of the last pre-Islamic century. True, for reasons largely beyond their control, they had missed their first real opportunity to reestablish their own Palestinian commonwealth under Persian overlordship, reminiscent of the days of Cyrus and Darius. Because of their, by then, traditional lack of enthusiasm for proselytizing, they also failed to concentrate on the great adventure, so auspiciously begun by Dhu Nuwas and the Yathrib clans, of converting to Judaism the Arab tribes with their untold pent-up energies. But, internally secure and unwaveringly believing in their ultimate messianic future, their majority refused to join the new universal faith. They merely made their peace with it.

Linguistically they accepted Arabic in lieu of their former Aramaic speech, in use mainly in their old cultural centers of Palestine, Syria, and Babylonia, and even here not fully understood by the Christian majority speaking and writing in the Syriac dialect. The new Arabic idiom unlocked for them the gates to nearly the entire *oikumene,* or at least that major part of it which really mattered. Now they could not only communicate with their non-Jewish neighbors throughout the vast expanses of Islam, but they also had a more ready access to their own coreligionists in many of the formerly Greek- or Latin-speaking Byzantine provinces, the interior of the Sassanian Empire, and beyond it.

Jews realized, and even their enemies admitted it, that they had stood at the cradle of the new civilization, that their religion had in many ways been the matrix of the new faith and of the regnant system of ethics and behavior. From the beginning they had also played a most important role in the shaping of the new society. After a while they too lost the relative inarticulateness into which they had sunk during the preceding two centuries. Many Jewish communities outside the old Palestino-Babylonian center now came to life. The Iranian Plateau, especially, began supplying Jewish men of vision and courage who searched for new religious truths, if need be even by raising the flag of sectarian revolt. Egyptian Jewry, after almost a millennium of silence, regained its voice. In the personalities of one of its emigrés, Saadiah, and one of its adoptive members, Maimonides, it was able to contribute two grand masters to medieval Jewry. West of Egypt, in Kairuwan and Morocco, in Spain, southern France, and Italy, the Jewish communities suddenly awakened for the first time, and, to the superficial onlooker, without much preparation quickly reached the acme of their achievement in their "golden age." In short, the Jewries of the *dar al-Islam* (world of Islam), together with the masses of other non-Muslim subjects helping shape the new world order, now achieved a novel equilibrium under their much-improved socio-political and economic status.

XVIII

PROTECTED MINORITY

JEWS had no difficulty in speedily regaining their equilibrium, since their new status did not materially differ from their formal position under either Persia or Byzantium. In fact, the new regime increasingly fell back upon the existing constitutional and administrative patterns in the conquered territories. Under the 'Umayyad dynasty residing in Damascus, the bureaucracy, largely recruited from converted Syrians and other Byzantine provincials, needed but relatively minor adjustments to carry on under the new regime. In the Caliphate's eastern provinces, too, Al-Hajjaj and his successors, left in command with little interference from the central government, successfully adjusted the Persian governmental machinery to the new requirements. The transfer of the capital to Baghdad in 762 merely symbolized the shift of the center of gravity to the formerly Sassanian provinces. The new civil service, even more gigantic and powerful than before, was now predominantly nurtured from the manpower of the eastern areas.

Confronted by millions of non-Muslim subjects, the new 'Umayyad administrators found that the traditional status of the Jewish minority in Byzantium and Persia could readily serve as a model for the new legislation concerning these religious dissenters. The old combination of a basic general toleration with severe discrimination in detail appealed particularly to those new rulers whose profession of the new monotheistic faith often betrayed the intolerant characteristics of Constantine and his successors. The treatment of the Byzantine Christian sectarians, on the other hand, was far less helpful. It revealed an undesirable, and in the long run untenable, contrast between total suppression in theory and extralegal, grudging toleration in practice. Nor were any major legislative adjustments required later, under the 'Abbasids, when Persian precedents carried greater weight, since the former position of the Jewish, as well as the Nestorian, minority in the Sassanian empire had differed in specific application rather than in principle from the Jewish status under the Christian Roman Empire. Understandably, the former Christian majority in the Byzantine Empire, and that of Zoroastrians in Persia, had tremendous difficulties in adjusting to the new minority status. Untold thousands, indeed, quickly gave up and rejoined the majority, now Muslim. But the Jews calmly viewed their new status as essentially but a continuation, on a somewhat improved plane, of their traditional way of life. They could, in fact, convey some lessons of their own centuries-old experience to the new administration, as well as to their fellow citizens of the other minority creeds. This extraordinary situation helps explain the tremendous impact, legal as well as religious, of Judaism on the Muslim *sha'riyah* (the equivalent of the Jewish *halakhah*) in its vital formative stages.[1]

PERSONAL SECURITY

Happy was Jewry in the dispersion when it had no political history of its own, at least not the type of history conventionally described by its historians in terms of persecutions and bloodshed. In the first centuries of Islam, enjoying a considerable measure of personal security and, as a rule, holding aloof from the raging political conflicts and intrigues, Jews rarely figured in contemporary accounts. Compared with the pogroms and massacres which, especially after 1096, began to fill one sanguinary page after another in the Jewish annals in western lands, the Jewish communities of the Great Caliphate and its successor states enjoyed an enviable measure of security of life and limb. Nor were they exposed, with two major exceptions limited in scope and duration, to those sudden withdrawals of religious toleration, expulsions, and enforced conversions, which were to mar much of medieval Jewish history in Christian Europe.

Of course, together with the other citizens, Jews suffered from the general insecurity engendered by wars, foreign and civil, and the recurrent periods of anarchy. Perhaps because of their greater political and economic vulnerability, they suffered proportionately more than the Muslim masses. At the transition, for example, from 'Umayyad to 'Abbasid rule in 133 A.H. (751), Agapius tells us, many Christians and Jews perished during the three-hour sack of Damascus by 'Abd Allah ibn 'Ali's troops. When at the dissolution of the 'Abbasid Caliphate in the tenth century looting by the country's own soldiers became commonplace, Sherira Gaon could legitimately complain that "robbers and thieves are quite common in our districts, both on the roads and in the cities." We also recall that even Abu'l Kamal Tamim's unsuccessful rebellion in Morocco, in 1032–33, cost several thousand Jewish lives. Under such circumstances no one could feel quite secure, not even the caliph himself. Of the first four caliphs, only one, Abu Bakr, died a natural death after a reign of but two years. 'Umar, 'Uthman and 'Ali all fell victim to murderous political and religious opponents. During the first half of the tenth century Al-Muqtadir (908–32) and Ar-Radhi (934–40) were assassinated by rebels, while Al-Qahir (932–34), Al-Muttaqi (940–44) and Al-Mustakfi (944–46) were deposed and blinded. Deprived of all their possessions, they were forced to live on charity.[2]

Nor were street riots altogether rare. Some of these were directed against Jews. A contemporary chronicler describes at great length, though with more verbosity than specific detail, what happened to Fusṭaṭ Jewry under the reign of the intolerant Faṭimid caliph, Al-Ḥakim (December 31, 1011, and the following days). For unspecified reasons the mob fell upon a large number of Jews returning from a funeral, and brought about the imprisonment of twenty-three Jewish elders, who were to be executed on the following day. These events allegedly had repercussions all over Egypt, and the Jews of the entire country felt threatened. However, even Al-Ḥakim (996–1021) objected to such mob action, and he liberated the prisoners. Since the chronicler himself is silent on this score—perhaps he expressed himself more fully in the missing portions of his "Scroll"—we must assume that the populace got excited over something touching it very deeply, such as an alleged blasphemy against Mohammed, or some other religious crime. This doubtless was the import of the following trial, at which supposedly only four unreliable witnesses, from among some two hundred Muslims present, were ready to testify for the prosecution. Street riots of this kind, on a major or minor scale, were undoubtedly more frequent than is indicated by the extant sources. They clearly reflect the tenuous nature of the usually amicable Muslim-Jewish relations, and the proneness of the Muslim masses to heed demagogic appeals in the name of religion. But one should bear in mind similar disturbances among the Muslims themselves. Sectarian or juridical controversies often kindled the spark. Whenever the Shi'ites built a mosque, "there was tumult and riot. In 323/935 the Malikites assaulted Shafi'ite pedestrians in the streets." Finally Shi'ites in Baghdad and elsewhere welcomed the pagan Mongols as liberators.[3]

Such outbreaks of intolerance were doubly serious when they accompanied a major political transformation. We shall see that a large-scale massacre, connected with a rebellion against the Jewish master of Granada, Joseph ben Samuel ibn Nagrela, spelled permanent disaster to that glorious Jewish community. The riots in Fusṭaṭ, coming at a time when the Christian minority was already subjected to severe persecutions, also presaged a period of great calamity for the Jews of the Faṭimid empire. Although Caliph Al-Ḥakim released the accused Jews, causing the contemporary Hebrew chronicler to shower him with praise (he was to be paid nearly divine homage by a contemporary prophet Darazi and his sect of Druzes down to the present time), his somewhat deranged mind perceived deep suspicion that Jews, as well as Christians, were using their houses of worship for the public vilification of Islam. According to a Jewish legend, recorded by the seventeenth-century chronicler Joseph Sambari, Al-Ḥakim on one of his nightly journeys overheard Jews reciting the Passover Haggadah. He took umbrage at the latter's vindictive passages relating to the king of ancient Egypt, which he mistakenly referred to himself. His first reaction apparently was a desire to expel all Jews and Christians from his domains. But he changed his mind when shown the Qur'anic passages and Mohammed's treaties with the *dhimmis,* promising them permanent religious toleration. In lieu of total outlawry he issued a number of humiliating decrees affecting Jewish and Christian badges, and either destroyed or converted into mosques their synagogues and churches. Untold thousands of Copts and Jews are said to have converted themselves to Islam. However, some eight years later (in 1020) the caliph changed his mind again, and allowed many of the unwilling converts to revert to their former faith (according to Maqrizi no less than 6,000 Copts availed themselves of that opportunity). He also restored some of the churches and synagogues to their owners, and allowed the rebuilding of others.[4]

Although Al-Ḥakim's infringement on the principle of religious toleration thus proved to be but short-lived and apparently left few permanent scars on the minority communities, it pointed up the precariousness of their status and their great dependence on the rulers' faithful adherence to the authoritative sources of early Islam. Everyone knew, however, that these sources lent themselves to divergent interpretation. With the rapid development of juristic techniques, promoted by the sharp dialectics cultivated at the various Muslim schools of jurisprudence, one could interpret into the Qur'an and *ḥadith* a great many contemporary biases. At times it sufficed to fabricate some new tradition which could entirely defeat the original purposes of almost any enactment.

At the beginning of the twelfth century a Muslim jurist in Cordova claimed to have found in Ibn Masarra's papers a tradition, soon widely accepted in Morocco and Spain, that Mohammed's original decrees of toleration of Jews had been limited to a period of five hundred years from the *hejira.* If by that time the expected Jewish Messiah were not to arrive, the Jews were supposed to give up their religion and join the ranks of Islam. That time limit expired, of course, in 1107. On this basis Yusuf ibn Tashfin, the Almoravid ruler of Morocco and conqueror of most of Spain, demanded from the Jews speedy conversion (1005). However, Lucena Jewry's gifts and the moderating influence of the prudent Cordova *qadhi,* Ibn Ḥamdin, averted that calamity.[5]

That spurious "tradition" never went into oblivion, however. Four decades later most of North Africa and Spain came under the domination of the ruthless sect of Almohades which, preaching the extreme "unity" of God (hence their designation of *al-muwaḥḥidun*), sought to suppress all opposing points of view among both the Muslims and the religious minorities. In 1146 'Abd al-Mu'min, disciple and successor of Ibn Tumart and the real builder of the Almohade empire, allegedly addressed the assembled Jews and Christians of the Moroccan capital, Fez, as follows:

> Have you not denied the mission of our prophet Mohammed, and refused to believe that he was the Messenger promised in your Scrip-

ture? You have stated that the Messiah will come only to confirm your law and strengthen your faith. . . . Your ancestors have asserted, however, that this Messiah would appear no later than after five hundred years [since the advent of Mohammed]. Now this half millennium has passed long ago, and no messenger nor prophet has arisen among you. We must not allow you to persevere in your error; nor do we desire any of your tribute. You have only the choice of Islam or death.

This declaration sounded the keynote for a religious persecution of Jews and Christians from Tripolitania to Spain, unflinchingly enforced for several decades. At times greedy generals and administrators utilized this decree for self-enrichment. If we are to believe an evidently biased Christian chronicler, the Almohades in some localities killed Christians and Jews "who had lived there from ancient times, and appropriated their wives, houses. and fortunes." [6]

Fortunately for the Jews and Christians, the early Almohades did not insist upon the performance of any specific Muslim rituals on the part of these enforced converts. They were satisfied with a verbal affirmation of the belief in Mohammed as God's Messenger. Maimonides, himself a victim of the Almohade persecution at the age of thirteen when Al-Mu'min's troops occupied his native Cordova, observed that the authorities "knew perfectly well that we do not believe that confession, and whosoever recites it does so only to save himself from the king." Some Jewish leaders uncompromisingly objected even to such lip service, and demanded cheerful acceptance of religious martyrdom, especially since there was the danger that the children would ultimately become genuine converts to Islam. More moderate opinion, however, held by Maimonides and his father, pointed out the unprecedented nature of that pure lip service. While eulogizing the relatively few martyrs, who were prepared to suffer death rather than recite the required formula, they merely advised early departure to more hospitable shores. This was, indeed the course pursued by Maimun's own family, which ultimately reached more tolerant Egypt. We must also bear in mind that this Almohade outlawry of the former "protected" faiths was dictated by imperial considerations as much as by religious fanaticism. Placed on the defensive by the Christian crusaders who had already recaptured a large part of the Peninsula, these Muslim rulers tried to stem the tide by enforcing religious and cultural uniformity among their subjects. Only so can we explain the contrast between their continued intolerance in Spain and the employment by Ya'qub al-Manṣur himself of Spanish Mozarabs (Christian Moors) in his bodyguard and his permission for them to erect churches in the less exposed Morocco (about 1170). Evidently Maimonides' family, too, had emigrated from Spain to North Africa, because it could practice there its Jewish rites much more freely.[7]

Al-Manṣur, however, soon saw himself forced to enact several new restrictions on these recent converts, and to distinguish them more sharply from the older Muslims. Once again the mass conversion of Jews, in this case also of Christians, did not lead to their speedy amalgamation with the majority, but merely created a new distinct group within the population. These converts were neither *dhimmis* nor regular believers in the dominant faith. If we may believe Ibn 'Aqnin, another victim of the Almohade persecution who succeeded in escaping to the East, many of them were denounced to the government by ill-wishers. Such denunciations often resulted in the execution of the accused, the confiscation of their property, and the appropriation by the state of their women and children. Even Ibn 'Aqnin admitted, however, that more frequently the judges, to safeguard the honor of the Muslim judiciary, found flaws in the testimony of witnesses and discharged the defendants.

In time the government despaired of assimilating this recalcitrant minority by ordinary means. Taking out a leaf, therefore, from similar experiences of the Jewish minority under earlier persecutions, it began removing children from under the control of their neo-Muslim parents, and giving them for proper religious training to reliable persons of old Muslim stock. To reduce the former's resistance, it also repeated Egica's experiment, and prohibited all commerce to converts, thereby greatly reducing the economic opportunities of their upper classes. It also forbade them to own slaves, both in order to increase that economic pressure and to counteract any possible conversionist efforts on their part. Finally, it tried to segregate them more sharply than ever before in separate quarters, and made them wear a different, very somber, indeed ludicrous, attire. The general tenor of that legislation is so similar to that enacted against Jews during the last century of Visigothic rule, that one wonders whether it was the mere result of similarly felt needs. The old Visigothic code (the *Liber Judicum*) still was in force in the Christian parts of the Peninsula, and many of its provisions were also applied by the autonomous Mozarab communities in both the Muslim and the Christian states. In his privilege of 1101 for the Mozarabs of Toledo, Alfonso VI specifically provided that their litigations be decided in accordance with the *Liber Judicum*. It is therefore not too venturesome to suggest that one or another of the converted Mozarab jurists had suggested these enactments to the Almohade rulers.[8]

Of course, if the Almohades' purpose was to secure complete amalgamation of these groups with the Muslim majority and thus to set up a religiously united front against the attacking Crusaders, they failed miserably. 'Abd al-Mu'min's exhortations of 1149 to the delegation from Cordova to increase the number of true Almohade believers were nullified when, some ten years later, he himself began drawing the distinction between the "original" Almohades, those who joined the faith after 1130, and the newcomers after the battle of Oran in 1145. The subsequent legal differentiation and external segregation of "converts" likewise fostered, rather than hindered, the preservation of these minority groups. According to Ibn 'Aqnin, many neo-Muslims, conscious of the inefficacy of their formal conversion, now reverted to their earlier faith. They did it either in utmost secrecy, or by seeking refuge in other lands. The upshot was that, rather than strengthening the Muslim hold on the country, this entire legislation merely played into hands of the Christian conquerors. Reversing their role during the Arab conquest, Spanish Jews were now prepared to welcome with open arms the Christian *reconquista*.

RELIGIOUS TOLERATION

Almohade extremism and, to a lesser extent, Al-Ḥakim's frantic quest for total religious conformity, were but exceptions proving the general rule that, under Islam, the Jews resided in their respective countries as of right, and not merely on temporary suffrance. This general policy of toleration was, in part, a continuation of long-established procedures under the Sassanian Empire and, in part, the effect of mutual adaptation of the original Muslim minority and the *dhimmi* majorities during the period of the first conquests.

All generalizations, to be sure, concerning the status of *dhimmis* under early Islam are somewhat hazardous, because none of the great Arab jurists ever took the trouble of writing a comprehensive and authoritative treatise on the subject. Only in the later Middle Ages did one or another Muslim sage answer some specific legal inquiries with a more general review of the legal rights and duties of infidels. Of this type were the valuable *fatwas* by Ibn al-Wasiti, Ibn an-Naqqash, and the more biased Ibn 'Ubayya. Jewish and Christian jurists were even less articulate. Their writings abound with references to incidents mirroral of the legal inferiority of their coreligionists. They and their confreres of other literary genres often were quite outspoken in voicing grievances against discriminatory laws and practices, particularly in the realm of taxation. But none of them ever composed a juridical monograph on the general legal position of their coreligionists in the Muslim world. Of course, this subject matter was really a branch of Muslim law, and not of Jewish law. No matter how seriously Jews were prepared to take the ancient adage of the law of the kingdom being also part of Jewish law, an analysis of the regulations and administrative practices in this field could not be written in terms of an halakhic treatise of the type then being made popular by the geonim Saadiah and Hai.

More fundamental is the difficulty inherent in the legal sources themselves. Modern and medieval jurists alike were largely limited to innumerable decrees issued by caliphs or governors, but often speedily revoked or modified; acute, but often contradictory, observations of contemporary scholars on certain particular aspects; and precedent-making decisions by individual judges in specific cases. It seems that the Caliphate as such never attempted clearly to define the position of the religious minorities, and even in the period of greatest Muslim power and affluence much was left to arbitrary decisions of provincial governors. With the subsequent dissolution of the empire into its constituent parts, the discrepancies between regions and successive rulers became so great that the basic uniformity of Islam's attitude toward minority creeds was easily obscured. Nevertheless certain basic principles have long been rightly recognized as underlying the often chaotic variations in detail. These principles were based on numerous utterances by Mohammed, spurious as well as authentic, and successive enactments of the first caliphs, as well as on the force of customs, which were found by the Muslim conquerors in the occupied territories, or else gradually evolved under their regime. In time the rapid expansion of Islam brought Muslims into contact with many countries and civilizations. A method had to be worked out for Muslims settling in foreign lands, especially India, China, and Khazaria, to maintain their way of life and, wherever possible, their autonomous communities. In many ways the treatment of non-Muslim minorities in the Caliphate helped shape the "capitulations" under which Muslims tried to live in the more hospitable foreign lands.[9]

At the outset we are confronted with the vexing problem of the so-called Covenant of 'Umar (*Aḥd 'Umar*), supposedly proclaimed by 'Umar after his conquest of Jerusalem, as the fundamental law for his nonconforming subjects. Muslim juristic tradition has not preserved even a single reliable text of that document. The purported texts differ widely in verbiage and in a great many details. One of the shortest is given in an alleged letter by 'Umar I, citing the following declaration of surrendering Christians to him:

> When you came to us we asked of you safety for our lives, our families, our property, and the people of our religion on these conditions: to pay tribute out of hand and be humiliated; not to hinder any Muslim from stopping in our churches by night or day, to entertain him there three days and give him food there and open to him their doors; to beat the *nākūs* [wooden cymbals summoning worshipers to prayers] only gently in them and not raise our voices in them in chanting; not to shelter there, nor in any of our houses, a spy of your enemies; not to build a church, convent, hermitage, or cell, nor repair those that are dilapidated, nor assemble in any that is in a Muslim quarter, nor in their presence; not to display idolatry nor invite to it, nor show a cross on our churches, nor in any of the roads or markets of the Muslims; not to learn the Koran nor teach it to our children; not to prevent any of our relatives from turning Muslim if he wish it; to cut our hair in front; to tie the *zunnar* [wrap] round our waists; to keep our religion; not to resemble the Muslims in dress, appearance,

saddles, the engraving on our seals (that we should engrave them in Arabic); not to use their *kunyas* [the Arabic "Ibn" or "Abu"]; to honor and respect them, to stand up for them when we meet together; to guide them in their ways and goings; not to make our houses higher (than theirs); not to keep weapons or swords, nor wear them in a town or on a journey in Muslim lands; not to sell wine or display it; not to light fires with our dead in a road where Muslims dwell, nor to raise our voices at their (our?) funerals, nor bring them near Muslims; not to strike a Muslim; not to keep slaves who have been the property of Muslims. We impose these terms on ourselves and our coreligionists; he who rejects them has no protection.

Needless to say that some of these provisions, such as those relating to crosses and icons ("idolatry"), had no bearing on Jews. But all the others applied to them, too, with minor modifications. The concluding sentence sounded particularly ominous, inasmuch as a person failing to live up to the conditions here enumerated became an outlaw to whom any judge might refuse the elementary safeguards for life and property inherent in the public order of the country.[10]

In this way there emerged under the Islamic regime an intermediary world between the *dar al-Islam,* consisting of true believers, and the *dar al-ḥarb,* the world of unbelievers, whose conversion to Islam, if need be by force, was to be a permanent major preoccupation of the Muslim world. The term sometimes used in Muslim jurisprudence was the *dar as-sulḥ* (world of allies), that is the world of such non-Muslims to whom toleration had been extended by treaty. They were to be allowed to profess their religion, provided they fulfilled the original conditions laid down in that treaty. In accordance with the Messenger's wishes, such treaties were to be concluded only with monotheists, including Sabians and Zoroastrians. No toleration at all was to be extended to heathen peoples. Even with respect to the Sabians doubts were raised as late as 933, some jurists contending that they could be murdered in cold blood. Their representatives, especially from their still intellectually very alert community of Ḥarran, had to spend considerable sums in securing a favorable decision from the government. Before long the facts of life overruled this narrow legal theory, and at least in India many "heathens" were allowed to practice their own rites undisturbedly, although their position in legal theory always remained a notch below that of the monotheists.[11]

Formal treaties were frequently supplemented by oral or written statements, authentic or spurious, attributed by tradition to 'Umar, or even to the Messenger himself. 'Umar is supposed to have declared in his testament: "I recommend to your care the *dhimmis*, for they enjoy the protection of the Prophet; see that the agreement with them is kept, and that no greater burdens than they can carry are laid upon them." More broadly, he was supposed to have ordered his followers "not to let yourselves or any other to do wrong to the protected peoples." One need not doubt the authenticity of some such utterances, nor of the general tenor of the various treaties concluded with the surrendering unbelievers, although many details were doubtless inserted later into the original texts in the light of the intervening experience. The "Covenant of 'Umar" represented, therefore, the authentic spirit and intentions of the second caliph, but the phrasing and specific provisions reflect an accumulation of practices which evolved in the course of the first century of Islam. They may well have been formally summarized by 'Umar II, whose authorship was subsequently confounded with that of the great conqueror.[12]

The main safeguards for the *dhimmis* consisted in the security extended by the law of the country to their persons, property, and religious observance, provided they remained adherents of their inherited creed. Conversions from one minority faith to another were severely discouraged. Ghazzali rationalized this fact by quoting a *ḥadith* which attributed to Mohammed the saying, "Everyone who is born is born with a sound nature; it is his parents who make him a Jew or a Christian or a Magian." Religious toleration was, indeed, the crux of all these rights. Because many fanatical Muslims were tempted to violate it, it had to be buttressed by strict orders attributed to Mohammed himself. Such an impressive utterance, for example, as that ascribed to him by Baladhuri, "If one oppresses a man bound to us by covenant and charges him with more than he can do, I am the one to overcome him by arguments [on the Day of Judgment]," although frequently lost sight of by his successors, remained a guiding principle. In fact no lesser a Muslim theologian than Ghazzali grudgingly pointed to the Jew "and the steadfastness of his faith, which can be shaken neither by threats, intimidation or insults, nor by persuasion, logical demonstration or proof." Forcible conversion to Islam, often performed *en masse* on vanquished populations such as the Berbers, was none the less declared a capital crime when applied to individuals. Indeed, in Turkey a law to this effect existed as late as the beginning of the twentieth century. Even the blanket outlawry of Judaism and Christianity by the Almohades in Spain and North Africa was generic rather than individual.[13]

Minorities were not only tolerated, but, in some areas, they enjoyed almost full equality before the law, both civil and criminal. The dominant schools of the Ḥanafites and Hanbalites required, for example, the same amount of blood money from the murderer of an "unbeliever" as from the murderer of a Muslim. Only the adherents of Malik and Shafi'i wished to see such a fine reduced to one half or one third. While some jurists argued for greater leniency in the case of manslaughter, and the majority insisted that no Muslim should ever be executed for the murder of an "infidel," they all agreed on severely punishing such criminals. Supernatural sanctions were added, as in the saying attributed to the Prophet himself; "He who slays a person attached to him by treaty [*dhimmi*] will not smell the scent of paradise even if that scent should be noticeable at a distance of a forty-years' journey." [14]

In the religious sphere proper there was sharper discrimination. Not only was apostasy from Islam punishable by death—conversion to Islam was, of course, encouraged and total conversion of mankind expected at the end of days—but mere blasphemy of Mohammed by a *dhimmi* was made a capital crime, as it also was in the case of a professing Muslim. Even here repentance, rather than destruction, was the chief aim. According to a *ḥadith,* the Messenger himself had insisted that a relapsed convert be summoned three times and given the opportunity to repent. Only if he persisted should he be put to death. The procedure outlined by 'Umar II, when he was told that a converted Jew had relapsed to his former faith, is fairly typical. "Invite him to accept Islam," the caliph ordered, "if he returns, let him go free. If he refuses, fetch a plank and make him lie on it, then repeat your appeal; if he still refuses, tie him to it, put a spear at his heart, and then ask him again. If he returns to Islam, let him go free; if he refuses, kill him." Not surprisingly the Jew yielded to this persuasive argument. There is no indication of how many times such backsliding could be practiced with impunity, if interrupted by formal "repentance." Remarkably, cursing the ruler was more ruthlessly punished. Forced converts were often given express permission to return to Judaism or Christianity, for instance by the repentant Al-Ḥakim in 1020. Nor were spokesmen of the "protected" religions prevented from defending their faiths against verbal or written attacks by Muslim debaters. The Jewish polemical and apologetical literature, often quite outspoken in its critique of Muslim fundamentals, seems to have enjoyed wide circulation without any overt hindrance by the authorities. At times Jews were even accused of meddling in purely Muslim religious controversies. A riot was staged in Baghdad in 1027 because some Jews allegedly had taken the part of the Shi'ites.[15]

Before the invention of printing, to be sure, any kind of censorship of literary output was necessarily restricted. The government could only retaliate after the event either by punishing the author, by destroying his book, or both. In extreme cases, like that of the famous mystic Hallaj in 922, the author's execution could be considered a sufficient warning for future culprits. However, we know from the entire history of crime that punishment, however drastic, has never served as an ultimate deterrent. More frequently books were burned and, as in Hallaj's case, banished from the book trade. This fate befell in Spain not only such radical works as those of Averroës, but even the books of a leading orthodox theologian like Ghazzali. In Baghdad, on one occasion, some purely astronomic works by 'Abd as-Salam were devoured by a public bonfire (1192). However, the effectiveness of such action evidently depended on the number of copies already in circulation. It could be totally nullified by the willingness of author or copyists to court the authorities' displeasure by continued reproduction of the condemned works. Most significantly, we have no record of the burning of any Jewish books by the Muslim authorities. We shall see that quite a few Jewish polemical works against the dominant faith were allowed to circulate, without causing immediate reprisals from the Muslim administration. Internally, too, the burning of Jewish books by Jewish communal organs, although at times advocated by authors, seems to have been extremely rare. Not a single reliable record of such a public performance under medieval Islam has come down to us. The mere fact that such an "obnoxious" book as that of Ḥivi al-Balkhi could, as we shall see, enjoy wide circulation for more than half a century, indicates a certain measure of forbearance, or impotence, on the part of the communal organs, which had no parallel in the Christian Middle Ages.

NEW SYNAGOGUES

Governmental, as well as popular, intolerance could play far greater havoc with the construction of synagogues. From the Byzantine Empire the Arab conquerors inherited the drive to exclusive possession of large and ornate houses of worship. After the Empire's administrative consolidation under 'Abd al-Malik (685–705) the previous austerity of Muslim worship was abandoned in favor of services in such magnificent structures as the Mosque of the Rock in Jerusalem, or the Grand Mosque in the imperial capital of Damascus. The caliph and his advisers thus hoped to impress upon the millions of their Christian subjects the permanence and grandeur of the new regime. From that time on the Muslim authorities also tried to hold the number and size of synagogues and churches to a minimum. Since, however, in the first century after the *hejira* the vast majority prayed in non-Muslim holy places and, at times, during a city's surrender special protection of churches or Parsee sanctuaries had been expressly stipulated by treaty, the burden of tradition weighed heavily in favor of toleration. There was ample room left, however, for casuistic debates in the schools of jurisprudence and arbitrary actions by rulers or populace.

On the whole, the principle was often reiterated that Jews must not build new synagogues, but might keep old ones in a state of repair. Both rules were largely observed in the breach. On the one hand, many new synagogues sprang up not only in older communities, but even in such localities as Kufa, which came into being as an Arab camp. In Fusṭaṭ, which had originated in a similar way, the Jews dared to display a synagogue inscription dating its foundation in 336 Sel. era (24–25 C.E.). With more justice Maqrizi claimed that "no one denies that all the synagogues of Cairo which we have named were built under Muslim rule." Even in Baghdad, which had had a Jewish community long before its elevation by Al-Manṣur, the twenty-eight synagogues functioning in Benjamin's time were "new" buildings. Indeed, sometimes the fact of their erection in Muslim times was adduced by *dhimmi* pleaders as evidence that there was no truth in the purported prohibition. On the other hand, not only Al-Ḥakim, but also such "reasonable" monarchs as Harun ar-Rashid or Mutawakkil, numerous local potentates, or an enraged populace, often razed to the ground structures which had long antedated Islam. Nor was the restoration or even repair of synagogues a simple routine matter. As late as 1837 a permit to rebuild a synagogue was issued by the Turkish Sultan only after lengthy hearings and the production of a written responsum by the ecclesiastical head of Islam. The Jews were allowed to restore their place of worship "under the condition that it would not exceed its former size by even a palm or finger in length, height or width." [16]

Perhaps the most serious aspect of the existing legal confusion was the permanent state of insecurity affecting Jewish control over the synagogues. No one could foretell at which time the opinion of some extreme Malikite jurist might prevail, and all synagogues, as well as churches and fire temples, would be outlawed throughout the empire or in one or another locality. In the later Middle Ages some jurists began arguing that Jews, not having been among the defenders during the original conquest or, for instance, during Saladin's reconquest of Jerusalem in 1187, possessed no treaty rights whatsoever and hence were not allowed to have synagogues at all. This was, in fact, the burden of Ibn 'Ubayyah's treatise of 1474, which tried to justify the wanton destruction of a synagogue in the Holy City. Often acts committed by Christians or Zoroastrians affected deeply the Jewish houses of worship, and vice versa. For example, the district governor of Ḥarran once noticed from his lofty palace some new white buildings. When told that these were new churches, and that the Muslim populace was greatly aroused by the Christian advances, he instantly ordered the destruction of all new synagogues, as well as churches. Only after the damage was done did he repent and allow the gradual rebuilding of these structures (814). At times the Jewish communal elders themselves overplayed their hand. In 1199, we are told, the synagogue worshipers of Madaïn (formerly Ctesiphon) were often disturbed by the sonorous calls to prayer in a neighboring mosque. Apparently unable to persuade the muezzin to tone down his summons, they secured redress from the local authorities. Thereupon a delegation was sent to Baghdad by the Muslim population. At first received coolly and even thrown into jail by officials, these delegates finally succeeded in inciting the zeal of a large congregation assembled for Friday services at the castle mosque. Despite the intervention of soldiers, the mob staged a regular anti-Jewish riot, plundered many Jewish shops, and destroyed the synagogue at the Basasiri gate. Ultimately the caliph yielded, and ordered the conversion of the Madaïn synagogue into a mosque.[17]

To make the possession of some synagogues more secure, the Jews often claimed that these particular buildings had been erected long before the rise of Islam. Hence the numerous legends, sometimes fortified by purported epigraphic evidence, concerning the original establishment of such houses of worship as those in Aleppo, Kufa, Fusṭaṭ, and Damwah. Often the location of a synagogue was associated with the tomb of an ancient and revered prophet, like Ezekiel or Ezra. To be sure, Bukhari recorded a tradition which had attributed to Mohammed the exclamation, "May God destroy the Jews who had taken the tombs of their prophets for houses of worship." But this alleged saying seems to have had few repercussions in the subsequent Muslim debates. To avoid complications, Jewish leaders seemed more than usually willing to acquire an old church and to convert it into a synagogue. Being an old *dhimmi* structure, it evidently could more readily be defended against the accusation of being a "new" house of worship. Such a case is recorded in Egypt, where the Jews purchased from the Monophysite patriarch Michael a church in Fusṭaṭ, as well as some church property in Alexandria and herds of camels belonging to a monastery. This transaction greatly chagrined the later Christian chronicler, Abu Saliḥ (?), although he admitted that the patriarch had to dispose of that property to pay a large tribute to the exacting Aḥmad ibn Tulun (868–84).[18]

Although from the standpoint of law and administrative practice sharing the same fate, Jews and Christians rarely evinced a spirit of cooperation and mutual helpfulness in the face of these recurrent crises. On one occasion, we are told by a rather prejudiced Christian chronicler (Yaḥya ibn Sa'id), Jews actually participated in the burning of St. Mary's Church in Ascalon (937; cited in *Sefer ha-Yishub,* II, 4). But this tale is too strictly in line with the Church's traditional accusations of Jewish involvement in anti-Christian persecutions to merit full credence.

Cemeteries were less frequently the subject of controversy. Yet an ambitious builder like Ibn Tulun did not hesitate, while erecting the new Katai quarter in Cairo (about 870), to plough up the Jewish and Christian "houses of eternity." Mutawakkil (847–61) decreed that the tombs of infidels be clearly distinguished from those of Muslims. Here, too, vast opportunities were offered for administrative chicaneries, particularly when some new burial ground had to be established. At times such permits were written in crude and vulgar terms to underscore the petitioners' inferiority. Although we have no pertinent records from the Great Caliphate, we may again take a clue from nineteenth-century Turkey, which maintained the old relationships in unbroken historic continuity. A magazine correspondent of 1921 found in the possession of a reputable Istanbul family three letters of authorization addressed in the early 1800's to Greek Orthodox, Armenian, and Jewish officials, respectively. The one handed to the rabbi in 1824 allegedly concluded, "The venerable Chéry authorizes thee, traitorous Rabbi, to find somewhere a latrine, which you will fill by throwing into it his stinking carcass." [19]

Ibn Tulun's drastic step seems to have been quite exceptional, however. The *weli* worship was too deeply ingrained in the Near Eastern peoples, for them to treat lightly burial places even of unbelievers. It may be noted that during the Cairo riots of 1011–12, the mob did not invade the Jewish cemetery, but awaited the mourners' return before it proceeded to attack them. That is why cemeteries figure so infrequently in the records of tense Muslim-Christian-Jewish relations. On the other hand, there occurred cases of cemetery vandalism in connection with warlike moves. During the early conquests, particularly, the Muslims seem to have desecrated many existing cemeteries, whether because of strategic necessity, or from sheer exuberance. There certainly was a grain of truth in the oft-cited apocalytic prediction attributed to "R. Eliezer," which claimed that among the fifteen innovations introduced by the reign of Ishmael would be that the Arabs "would convert cemeteries into sheep pastures and dumps." Subsequently, too, difficulties with the Muslim administration in securing permission for the acquisition of new or the enlargement of old cemeteries may have been responsible for the Palestinian practice of using old graves for the burial of new corpses, a practice censured by Hai Gaon. Nor was the ingenuity of the Muslim bureaucracy at a loss to devise a variety of fiscal and other chicaneries with respect to funerals of members of the minority faiths.[20]

Near Eastern insistence on prestige at times went to ludicrous lengths. In the Arab case, pride and haughtiness, long cultivated among the Bedouins, were reinforced by the rulers' sense of inferiority toward the age-old civilizations north and west of Arabia, and by the general political theory differentiating between the leisurely "aristocratic" conquerors and the plebeian masses of unbelievers. Ninth-century caliphs first emulated the old Byzantine regulations by insisting that no building be allowed to exceed in height the local mosque. Before long they demanded that Jewish and Christian private houses, too, be built lower than neighboring dwellings of Muslims. Neither were such houses safe, if for some reason (perhaps because of loud praying in them as in Christian countries) they annoyed officials of a neighboring mosque. This seems to be the import of the complaint voiced by one Nissim of Qaṭiyah, a trading post in Sinai on the caravan route from Cairo to Damascus. Nissim reported to his Egyptian correspondent "that the house which is here [in] Qaṭiyah has been torn down, all of it; and [that] they have brought accusations that it was near to the mosque." [21]

Legal discrimination of this kind, though sometimes annoying and always lurking in the background, affected Jewish life only to a minor extent. That is why the Jewish literature of the period, far from restrained in voicing grievances about fiscal oppression and the frequent miscarriage of justice, is so remarkably silent about the discriminatory measures affecting synagogues and other buildings. In contrast to Christians, who, accustomed at least in larger cities to worship in imposing edifices, bitterly resented the loss of some famous churches, the flourishing Jewish communities of the Caliphate continued unperturbedly to worship God in synagogues often larger and more ornate than they had ever possessed. In practice, moreover, many of these and other laws were rarely carried out, and influential Jews or Christians frequently found means of evading them. So corrupt did the bureaucracy of the Caliphate become, that in 917 a special Secret Profits Bureau was established to recapture some of the bounty for the state treasury.

SOCIAL DISCRIMINATION

As in the case of private houses, Muslim legislation sought generally to demonstrate the social superiority of the true believers over the *dhimmis.* Buttressed by the genuine desire of the ruling classes to separate themselves from the plebeian masses in an otherwise fairly egalitarian society, such social discrimination was relatively rigid. True, the laws concerning the special colors by which garments of "unbelievers" were to be distinguished from those worn by Muslims were frequently ignored. But their reiteration through the ages must have further lowered the social esteem of "infidels." The twelfth-century Sevillan writer, Ibn 'Abdun, expressly called these distinctive colors worn by the unbelieving "crew of Satan" (Qur'an 58:20) a "mark of their ignominy." At times these attempts assumed ridiculous forms. Mutawakkil's decree of 849–50, as recorded by Ṭabari, reads like a codification of impulsive, consciously derogatory reprisals rather than of calmly considered permanent regulations. The "protected peoples" were supposed

> to wear honey-colored robes and girdles. They were to ride on saddles with wooden stirrups; on the back of their saddles they were to affix two globes. Those who wore tall conical hats were to affix two buttons on them, and the hats themselves were to be of a different color from those worn by Muslims. They were to affix on a prominent part of the clothes of their slaves two patches, which were to contrast in color with any clothes that were showing; one of the patches to be in front and the other behind, and each to be the size of four fingers and the color of honey. If any [of such non-believers] wore a turban, it was to be of the color of honey; such of their women as went out of doors were not

to appear in public except dressed in a honey-colored outer wrapper. He also commanded that their slaves were compelled to wear plain girdles [of the kind ordinarily worn by the "protected" peoples], and were forbidden to wear the embroidered belts donned by free Muslims. He also commanded that the newer buildings amongst their places of worship were to be demolished, that a tenth of their dwellings was to be seized; where there was sufficient room in the churches or synagogues, they were to be turned into mosques; otherwise the space they had occupied was to be left vacant. He further commanded that wooden figures of devils were to be affixed with nails to the doors of their dwellings, in order to distinguish them from the houses of Muslims. Moreover, he forbade the employment of non-believers in any ministry or in any office of the government in which they would be in authority over Muslims; he also forbade their children to be taught in Muslim schools, nor was any Muslim to teach them, nor were they [the Christians] to display a cross on Palm Sunday, nor were they [the Jews] to cry out their *Shema'* ["Hear, O Israel," etc.]. Lastly he commanded that their graves were to be level with the ground in order not to resemble the graves of the Muslims [R. Levy's English translation in *A Baghdad Chronicle,* pp. 104 f.].

Five years later, perhaps in connection with a revolt in Emesa in which Jews and Christians seem to have been seriously implicated (hence the purported destruction of all the city's synagogues and churches after its suppression), Mutawakkil sharpened further his discriminatory decrees. According to Ṭabari, in two ordinances issued one month apart, he insisted that the *dhimmis* be made to wear two honey-colored *durra'a* (flowing overcoats) over their tunics—apparently also in hot summer days—and that they abstain from employing even packhorses for transportation. Particularly the somewhat deranged Faṭimid caliph, Ḥakim, whose disease was euphemistically termed "melancholia," carried the application of distinguishing marks to absurd extremes. He imposed upon the Christians the duty of wearing a cross with arms two feet long and a finger wide, while the Jews were ordered to carry around their necks balls weighing at least five pounds, in commemoration of the calf's head which their ancestors had once worshiped. According to later writers, the Jewish wooden block was to be carved into a bovine form, the better to remind the Jews of the Golden Calf. Hakim also chose black as the distinguishing color for all "infidels," perhaps in overt opposition to the express 'Abbasid prohibition of black garments for *dhimmis*. Attire of this color has been worn by most Egyptian Copts ever since. In Baghdad in the days of Al-Muqtadir (1075–94), reported the near-contemporary proselyte Obadiah the Norman, Vizier Abu Shuja prescribed

> that each male Jew should wear a yellow badge on his headgear. . . . In addition each Jew had to have a stamp of lead of the weight of a silver dinar [?] hang from his neck, on which the word *dhimmi* was inscribed symbolizing the Jews' subjection to the tax. He [the vizier] also forced them to wear girdles round their waists. On women he likewise imposed two distinguishing marks: the shoes worn by each woman had to be one red, and one black. She also had to carry either on her neck or attached to her shoe a small brass bell, announcing [her movements] so as the more effectively to segregate Jewish from Gentile women. He also appointed cruel Gentile men and women to oppress Jews, male and female, and to heap upon them all manner of curse, shame and contumely. And the Gentiles used to ridicule Jews, the mob and children often assaulting Jews in all the streets of Baghdad.

The Almohade Al-Manṣur, finally, made the Jews wear "dark blue garments with sleeves reaching down to their feet, and vile skull-caps covering their ears." [22]

Such extravagances could only discredit the whole institution, which hardly was fully established in accordance with the law. Ḥakim, who had originally wished forcibly to convert the entire non-Muslim population, was bound to revoke his humiliating decrees after eight years. The prohibition of riding on horseback might have led to occasional riots (for instance, in Baghdad in 885) against a Christian or a Jewish violator. It seems, however, that the grandees of the minorities seldom refrained from appearing in public in this dignified posture. Nor did a Byzantine arrival in eleventh-century Tyre encounter any difficulty in disposing there of some Byzantine clothing he had brought with him, in order to finance his journey to Jerusalem. During the same period a Kairuwanese Jewish visitor in the Holy City complained in a letter to his home that everyone was wearing shabby clothes "because the land belongs to poor country folk who own no stores." Well-to-do Jews rarely abstained even from publicly displaying costly jewelry and garments. Although generally in line with existing mores, indeed expected from wealthy Muslims, such conspicuous display by "infidels" often created bitter resentment among the Muslim masses.[23]

On the other hand, the Byzantine exclusion of Jews from bathing in rivers and other public places together with Christians, proclaimed as a universal canon of the Church by the great Trullan Council of 692, was never fully emulated under Islam. Puritanical 'Umar II tried to keep all women out of public baths. Even Ḥakim merely demanded that, while bathing, Christians carry their cumbersome crosses around their necks or, according to another version, wear bells announcing their approach from a distance. Only in 1400 were the Jews and Christians of Cairo formally excluded from public baths. The far more universal practice is reflected in Ghazzali's mere advice to Muslim women not to expose their bodies to *dhimmi* women. It was perfectly feasible, therefore, for Morocco's Idrisite ruler, Yaḥya ibn Yaḥya (after 860), to surprise a Jewish bathing beauty and fall in love with her at first sight.[24]

Naturally enough, the segregation of religious groups was at its height in family relationships. Muslim and Christian, as well as Jewish law, more or less strictly prohibited intermarriage, even the more liberal schools in Islam allowing only the marriage of a Muslim man with a non-Muslim girl before her conversion to Islam. Malik was opposed even to such marriages, while everybody agreed that if a *dhimmi* married a Muslim woman with her parents' consent all principals were to be severely punished. To encourage conversion, a converted Jewess or Christian was assured speedy divorce. If her husband was away on a long journey she did not have to await his return, but could immediately marry a Muslim. At the same time, in order to uphold Muslim morality, the law punished a Muslim's illicit relations with an unmarried *dhimmi* woman more severely than adultery among unbelievers. As a rule, however, the latter were handed over to their respective religious authorities. Mohammed's alleged order to stone two Jews convicted of adultery probably involved non-Jewish women. Nor did the Muslim administration force *dhimmi* women to wear veils as did the "believers." Veiled Jewesses must have rarely been seen in the eastern streets, notwithstanding Solomon ibn Parḥon's sweeping assertion in the middle of the twelfth century that "it is a custom in Palestine, Babylonia and Spain that all women cover their faces with a veil." [25]

Jewish leadership did not object to Mohammed's severity. On the contrary, it did everything in its power to stem such interfaith relationships, which, if widely indulged, would have threatened to submerge the Jewish minority in the world of Islam. In fact, with his flair for biological explanations, Jaḥiẓ attributed the lack of interest in philosophic speculation among his Jewish contemporaries (ninth century) to both their disparagement of philosophy as unbelief and their refusal to intermarry. In his opinion, constant inbreeding had deprived the Jewish race of high mental qualities as well as of a sound physique. It appears that, while free sexual relationships between Muslims and Christians were quite frequent in the erotically minded Orient, the rabbis kept them out of Jewish life with much greater efficacy. Lynching on the spot, still encouraged in the talmudic age and declared to be a meritorious deed even in the Maimonidean Code, could hardly be carried out under the more orderly conditions of early Muslim rule. Maimonides himself, there and in his Commentary on the Mishnah, succinctly stated that "we do not advise" such popular violence. But the rabbis imposed very heavy religious penances upon every transgressor. An ordinance, presumably enacted by Babylonian geonim, though preserved only by a later medieval author, stated that such a sinner "should fast forty-nine days . . . regard himself as excommunicated and be flogged every evening forty times." After finishing the forty-nine full fast days of twenty-four hours each, "he should leave his residence for a whole year, and during the days of his exile he should fast every Monday and Thursday." [26]

Intermarriage, as well as conversion, created a host of problems in civil law, especially in the realm of inheritance. Generally, Muslim law, true to its recognition of the religious minorities, considered the latter's communities as enjoying the right of eminent domain over the property of their members. Hence the transfer of assets from one community to another was to be impeded as far as possible.

Already Mohammed had taught, according to Al-Bukhari, that Muslims might not inherit from infidels, nor infidels from Muslims. Later jurisprudence expanded that doctrine. Certainly, a Muslim was not allowed to bequeath any of his property to an infidel by will. A *zindiq* (man without religion) could neither inherit nor bequeath any inheritance. A Muslim convert to another faith forfeited all his property rights. Only the property he had accumulated before his conversion went to his relatives, according to Abu Ḥanifa, while his earnings after conversion were to be confiscated. Shafi'i, as usual more rigid, insisted on the indiscriminate confiscation of all his property. More remarkably, 'Umar I is said to have refused the inheritance rights of a Muslim to the estate of a childless aunt who had married a Jew. In general *dhimmi* children converted to Islam lost the right to inherit their parents' property, just as, conversely, the father of a converted girl forfeited his right to give her away in marriage. Some jurists even conceded that, upon conversion, a protected subject gave up his own property, which immediately reverted to his own community.[27]

This liberality can be understood only in the light of the state's fiscal interest in the preservation of the property belonging to the protected communities because of their collective responsibility for the total amount of taxes due to the government. It certainly contrasted sharply with the strenuous efforts of the Christian Roman Empire and its successor states to safeguard the inheritance rights of converts to Christianity even against their parents' will. Jewish law, too, was quite one-sided. On the one hand, it tried to deprive apostates of their inheritance rights. On the other hand, a geonic responsum stated succinctly that "a Jew whose father apostasized, inherits his property. . . . Even when an ordinary Gentile dies, his proselyte son inherits his estate." Needless to say that, lacking political power, the Jews could not always enforce such regulations. But, living under constant fiscal pressure, they tried jealously to husband all their resources.[28]

A somewhat similar dichotomy existed also with respect to private dwellings. At no time did the Muslim administration establish formally segregated quarters for the different faiths, but the custom of religious and ethnic, and even mere social and economic groups preferentially to live together in streets of their own, had from time immemorial, lent a special tinge to most Near Eastern cities. The Muslims themselves, hailing from different regions, often at variance with one another in dialects and customs, usually preferred to settle in quarters predominantly inhabited by people of their own kind. Soon after its foundation, for example, Fez boasted of a Kairuwanese and an Andalusian quarter, each with a splendid mosque of its own. There also was a Jewish quarter in the northern section of the city, large enough to accommodate taxpayers obliged, as we recall, to deliver annually 30,000 dinars. More remarkably, there existed even a distinct group of Zoroastrians. Such predominantly homogeneous quarters were simply taken for granted, and no one bothered clearly to define their legal implications. Behind this voluntary separation often lurked persistent nationalist sentiments which were not wholly overcome by the overriding religious and cultural unity of the Islamic civilization. In the early decisive periods of Muslim conquests, moreover, enforced territorial segregation of the respective denominations would have been tantamount to locking up the Muslim masters in ghettos of their own. Legally, Christians and Jews were allowed therefore, as a rule, to settle wherever they pleased. Idrisi's report that a beautiful Moroccan village (Aghmat Ailan) was inhabited exclusively by Jews, and that the Almoravid 'Ali ibn Yusuf forbade them to visit his Moroccan possessions except on daytime business, was exceptional even under the conditions of Almoravid intolerance. There were many Jewish residences outside the two Baghdad quarters in which they formed a major segment of the population, just as there existed churches and monasteries in various sections of the imperial capital. For this very reason Muslim jurists were gravely concerned lest a church or synagogue exceed in height the neighboring mosque, and that even Muslim private houses not be dwarfed by those of their unbelieving neighbors.[29]

Jews, on the other hand, for social as well as ritualistic reasons, preferred to keep Gentiles away from their self-selected quarters. Ever since talmudic times they had suspected both the sexual ethics and the peaceful behavior of most of their Gentile neighbors. There certainly was more reason in their suspicions than in the Muslim tradition, reported by Jaḥiẓ, that "a Jew is never alone with a Muslim without plotting to kill him." Rabbinic law considered it, therefore, a serious transgression on the part of a Jewish owner to sell or rent his property in the Jewish quarter to a non-Jew. It granted to any Jewish houseowner in the vicinity the right of preemption, because he could refuse to have a "lion" as a neighbor. In his reply to an inquiry from Kairuwan, a ninth-century Babylonian gaon succinctly taught, "A Jewish houseowner must not rent his house to a Gentile for living quarters. This prohibition applies not only to a powerful and evil Gentile, who might do harm to the Jew, but also to one who is not known for his violence. For we have the general rule that the average Gentile is violent." More remarkably, Muslim law, too, conceded the right of preemption to the *dhimmi,* and not the Muslim, partner in a house owned jointly by them. This right of preemption was upheld by later Jewish jurists even at a time when the progress of economic freedom in the semicapitalistic economy of the Great Caliphate had made all such restrictions on the free sale of urban property extremely cumbersome. Maimonides, who generally favored some relaxation of these ancient restrictions, nevertheless permitted the sale of a Jewish house to a Gentile only when he was informed that the owner needed the money badly for his livelihood, and that no Jewish purchasers were available.[30]

This "narrow-mindedness" of the Jewish leaders, and its acceptance, however qualified, by the Muslim authorities, reflected the Jewish reaction to the existing powerful assimilatory pressures and the fiscal interests of the Muslim state in conserving the severely taxed *dhimmi* property. Always bent upon upholding Muslim prestige, Malik did not approve even of a Muslim renting land from an unbeliever in return for a share in the crop. But a *dhimmi* was allowed to serve as a sharecropper to a Muslim landowner. Other jurists, however, saw no reason for that distinction. In twelfth-century Seville, Ibn 'Abdun sharply objected to the employment of Muslims by *dhimmis* in menial occupations, to the purchase by Muslims of Jewishly slaughtered animals, and to ministrations of Jewish physicians to Muslim patients. A curious situation arose in 918–19, when a royal medical commission headed by Sinan was sent to Sura to combat a pestilence there. Although himself a Sabian, Sinan had previously been appointed head of all hospitals in a district which included Mecca and Medina. Now he was ordered by the scholarly but rather illiberal vizier, 'Ali ibn 'Isa, to extend medical treatment, first to the Muslims, then to the Jews, and finally to the animals of Sura—a city, which had a Jewish majority at that time. According to Abu Ḥanifa, a Muslim expressing condolence to a bereaved *dhimmi* had to use a formula reminding the mourner that only a believer returns to Allah: "Be patient with whatever happens to you. May Allah not diminish your numbers!" Sometimes it was the Muslim populace itself which tried to humiliate its Jewish neighbors. In Jerusalem (or some other community in the Faṭimid or Seljuk Empire) the Muslims refused Jews access to the local well, claiming that they could not be expected to share their water with infidels. They secured the support of the district governor, who did not yield even when the Jews obtained a favorable ruling from Cairo. The governor changed his mind, however, after receiving a handsome *douceur*. This story, incidentally, illustrates well the general instability of Jewish life, and also the double-edged sword of bribery. The governor here, and many like him, actually seems to have held out even against the express orders from Cairo, for no other reason than to extort from the Jewish community a substantial payment. More significantly, the very term "Jew" (or "Christian") was considered so obnoxious that Muslim jurists reiteratedly prohibited the use of that epithet in name-calling among Muslims. Such prohibitions did not, however, prevent Muslim sectarians from following the Christian example and calling one another "Jews" in their religious controversies.[31]

One must not imagine, however, that there was little friendly intercourse between members of the various denominations. Business and cultural interests brought them far more closely together than is indicated in our predominantly normative sources. Certainly the influential Jewish court bankers and counselors must have been in constant touch with Muslim officials. Scholars, too, frequently associated with their colleagues of other faiths, professionally as well as socially. Only thus was it possible for the famous Jewish physician, Isaac Israeli, to receive instruction from a distinguished Muslim doctor, and in turn impart his knowledge to Muslim as well as Jewish pupils, some of whom achieved fame in their own right. And master-pupil relationships at that time approximated close family ties! The impression made by Maimonides' great personality on some Muslim physicians is attested by a number of their extant comments. Sa'id ibn Sina al-Mulk, a medical man of considerable reputation, even composed an admiring poem in his honor, filled with the then usual hyperboles.

Galen's art heals only the body,
But Abu-Imran's [Moses'] the body and the soul.
His knowledge made him the physician of the century.
He could cure with his wisdom the disease of ignorance.
If the moon would submit to his art,
He would free her from her spots at the time of full moon,
Would relieve her of her monthly ailments
And at the time of her conjunction, save her from waning.

Ordinary Jews, too, often attended non-Jewish festivities and family celebrations, and entertained Muslim friends in their homes. While the poet Ibn Qutaiba (died about 889) mentioned a popular saying imputing to Jews a special odor, the early modern historian Al-Maqqari recorded medieval Spanish-Arabic sources extolling Andalusia as the country where "children and Jews have the instinctive qualities of politeness and poise." From the early days of Islam, when conversion of churches and synagogues had been a daily practice to accommodate the growing masses of worshipers, had come the rule permitting Muslims to pray in Christian and Jewish houses of worship. Even intolerant Mutawakkil insisted that spacious churches, however old, assign a special section for a mosque. Unbelievers were not supposed to attend services at mosques, but as a rule no one inquired about the faith of those present.[32]

Mohammed, to be sure, forbade his followers to take Jews or Christians as friends. The "Covenant of 'Umar" also enjoined the latter, as we recall, not to use Arabic *kunyas* for their family names. In fact, however, one of the difficulties in identifying a Jew in documents hailing from Muslim lands is the regular use by Jews, too, of the "Abu" and "Ibn" designations combined with purely Arabic names. How could one tell at first glance that the famous Spanish-Hebrew grammarian, Abu'l Walid Merwan ibn Janaḥ had derived the last name (the equivalent of "the winged one") from his Hebrew name Jonah? Nor must we ever lose sight of the deep cleavages created in Muslim society itself by religious and class distinctions. In Kufa there existed a separate mosque for the *ma-*

wali (clients, or fairly recent converts). Though generally open-minded and quite cosmopolitan, Mas'udi recorded a popular saying, "He that seeks shame, ignominy, and opprobrium, will find all combined amongst the *mawali*." On the other hand, an irate utterance attributed to the 'Abbasid courtier, Al-Fadl ibn Yaḥya, illustrates the disdain of the ruling clique for the masses of their coreligionists. Apart from the four classes of rulers, viziers, the wealthy, and the men of culture, Al-Fadl exclaimed, "the remainder are filthy refuse, a torrent of scum, base cattle, none of whom thinks of anything but his food and sleep." Certainly, no courtier could be more contemptuous toward unbelievers. Increasing feudalization of the Near East at the end of the Middle Ages ultimately introduced even distinguishing colors in the attire of various classes of Muslims, and the prohibition for most of them to ride on horseback.[33]

Nevertheless the basically egalitarian structure of Islam made it possible even for a most lowly Muslim to rise, through personal effort or chance, to higher ranks in society. A *dhimmi* could not completely emancipate himself from his status, however ill-defined. In the poisoned atmosphere of cultivated contempt, the Jew now more poignantly than ever before felt himself disparaged as an "infidel." This term, perhaps first applied to the Jews by Manethon (Josephus, *Against Apion,* 1.26.248), had come into more frequent use during their protracted civil and religious controversies with the Alexandrian Greeks. It was picked up by Christian assailants of Judaism, and even penetrated the legal verbiage of the Christian Empire. Not until the Caliphate, however, did it become the universal, willfully contemptuous designation of all those who differed from the established religion and used in a matter-of-fact, non-polemical context. Since humiliation, rather than vengeance, became the keynote of Muslim-Jewish relations, foundations were laid for the ghetto, the badge, and, as we shall see, also for the oath *more judaico*. Although in the oriental mode of life, as well as in the popular view, these signs of segregation never possessed that hateful character which they assumed in Christian Europe in the later Middle Ages (in which context they will be treated more fully), they symbolized even there the state of legal and social inferiority into which had sunk all those who refused to recognize Mohammed as the seal of prophecy.

OFFICIALS AND COURTIERS

The wide discrepancy between law and life became clearest with the appointment of Christians, Zoroastrians, and Jews to public office. Although prohibitions of such appointments were frequently renewed, an "unbelieving" Persian, Syrian, Berber, or Jew often occupied the most prominent place in the administration of the country. This was the case not only during the first century after Mohammed, when there evidently were not enough trained Muslims to man the vast bureaucratic machinery of the far-flung empire, but also in most periods thereafter.

Conditions under early Islam are well illustrated by the treatment of Christian prisoners of war attributed by tradition to 'Umar I himself. After the conquest of Tripolis the caliph allegedly gave some captives away as slaves, whereas others were made "clerks" and employed in forced labor for the government. At first the Jews played but a minor role. Having long been kept out of administrative posts in both Byzantium and Persia, they had far less to offer to the new conquerors than either Christians or Zoroastrians. For a while, as in Egypt immediately after the Muslim occupation, the administration was left largely in the hands of previous officials. In time, however, caliphs and governors increasingly began enlisting the services of Jewish advisers. Especially when it became clear that one of the main burdens of the new bureaucracy was to raise the state's revenue, which to so large an extent was derived from the taxation of non-Muslim subjects, the expert advice of some Jews began to be increasingly sought. Already 'Abd al-Malik made use of the Jew Sumer for the minting of his new coinage, and possibly for the general planning of his great fiscal reform. The Jewish share gradually increased thereafter, because more and more Persians embraced the Shi'ite version of Islam and, with the resurgence of the Byzantine peril in the ninth century, the Christians appeared less trustworthy. Only the Nestorian enemies of the Orthodox Byzantine emperors continued to find significant employment in the higher reaches of bureaucracy in the eastern provinces. The scribes of Deir Qunna, especially, often appear in the records as government clerks in ninth-century Baghdad.[34]

Such records are necessarily sporadic, and fail to present an adequate picture of the Jewish share in the Caliphate's public service. Apart from the general problem of preservation and accurate transmission of our texts, we learn far less about the numerous Jews employed in the lower echelons of officialdom than about their more powerful and exalted brethren. Arab political historiography was chiefly concerned with events at the headquarters of powerful monarchs and generals, the unceasing court intrigues, and the constant rise and fall of caliphs or their favorites. It preserved occasional data on *dhimmis* in high office as well, but rarely referred to lower clerks of any faith. Jewish letters, too, on the whole mentioned only some prominent leaders, whose elevation or downfall affected the entire community. The poems composed in honor of patrons of the arts were also more likely to be addressed to high-ranking officials than to some lowly state employees.

Many Muslims, moreover, mentioned such employment of "infidels" mainly in order to voice grievances over their purported maladministration and their preferential treatment of coreligionists. They also complained of the general violation of the established law which, ever since the "Covenant of 'Umar," had barred unbelievers from public office. Such complaints were repeated, for example, by Niẓam al-Mulk, an eminent vizier of the late eleventh century, who wrote "Today all distinctions have disappeared. If a Jew administers the affairs of the Turks and performs the expected services, they find him convenient. The same is true of Magians, Christians, or Qarmatians. Complete indifference reigns in this respect. They have no zeal for Islam, they are careless in the collection of taxes, and have no pity for the subjects" (*Siyasat namah,* ed. by C. Schefer, p. 139; French trans., II, 205). By that time, to be sure, such generalizations carried the less conviction, as the public had long learned to expect little altruism from officials of any faith. Nevertheless, echoing deep-rooted prejudices, they rarely failed to evoke some response even from less fanatical Muslims.

Not surprisingly, it was the pious 'Umar II who first reacted sharply, discharging all *dhimmi* officials. "I do not know," he wrote in a circular letter to the governors, "a secretary or official in any part of your administration who was not a Muslim but I dismissed him and appointed a Muslim in his stead." Of course, after nearly a century of mass conversions to Islam, the caliph had at his disposal a sufficient number of Muslim candidates for the vacant offices. However, it soon became apparent that the legal theory therewith embedded in the "Covenant" could rarely be fully upheld. Ibn an-Naqqash, to whom we owe the preservation of 'Umar's order, also mentions that the same procedure had to be employed again and again by that caliph's successors, Al-Manṣur, Al-Mahdi, Harun ar-Rashid, Al-Ma'mun, Al-Mutawakkil, and Al-Muqtadir. Sometimes, as in 1107–8, a vizier (Majd ad-Din) was reappointed to his high office under the express condition that he would employ neither Christians nor Jews. However, Al-Manṣur himself, within a few years after issuing his decree of 849, employed the Jew Masha'allah and the Zoroastrian An-Naubakht to plan for him the new capital. He also had in his employ the Jew Musa, whom he appointed one of the two chief collectors of revenue. Al-Muqtadir, who had ordered the employment of non-Muslims in menial occupations as a mark of their inferiority, on a par with his simultaneous prohibition of their riding on ordinary saddles (they had to use packsaddles), from the beginning exempted two categories of officials from his outlawry. Jews and Christians still could perform the important functions of court physicians and tax collectors. Their services in these two branches had by that time become quite indispensable, and the caliph wisely refrained from cutting off his nose to spite his face.[35]

Curiously, it was under Al-Muqtadir's regime that the Caliphate witnessed the rise of a Jewish family to the zenith of its power. This rise had been slow but persistent, and its duration was to be totally unprecedented in the Empire's annals. According to Aṭ-Ṭanukhi, two Baghdad bankers, Joseph ben Phineas and Aaron ben Amram, were employed already by Vizier Al-Khaqani (before 877) on certain financial errands. The nature of these semifiscal and semicommercial transactions will become clearer in the context of Jewish economic history of the period. But, if we are to believe a family chronicle paraphrased soon thereafter, it was early in Al-Mu'tadhid's reign (about 892) that Neṭira (Joseph's son-in-law) was able to perform a signal service to the Treasury by detecting a high-ranking embezzler. Such services seemed, indeed, to justify the affirmation of Mu'tadhid's vizier, "Not because of any sympathy on my part for Judaism or Christianity did I take the unbelievers into civil service, but because I found them to be more faithfully attached to thy dynasty than Muslims." Neṭira apparently behaved on that occasion with such personal magnanimity toward both the Caliph and his chief advisers that, even discounting the miracle tale of Elijah's appearance to Al-Mu'tadhid in his sleep in order to prevent a threatening anti-Jewish decree, we may believe that the monarch proved grateful to his loyal and disinterested servant.

> And Israel lived in peace and without disturbance [the chronicle continues] during the remaining nine and a half years of Al-Mu'tadhid's reign. They wore black clothes like the 'Abbasid family, the Gentiles lived in good relations with them, and enjoyed no superior status above them. Only some of the Sufi mystics behaved haughtily toward them and maltreated them [but were severely punished by the authorities]. After his [Al-Mu'tadhid's] death, his son Al-Muqtadir [the chronicler skipped here Al-Muqtafi's reign, 902–8] ascended the throne. Neṭira remained with the caliph in the same post for more than eight years until his death, may God have mercy on him. He was succeeded by his sons, Sahl and Isaac [Ibrahim?], since he had had no other children, male or female.

Despite many obvious errors, the chronicler's account, undoubtedly written originally in Arabic and subsequently suffering from the usual errors in translation and transmission, contains a solid kernel of historic truth, borne out by much outside testimony.[36]

The services of the "children of Neṭira" and the "children of Aaron" continued unabated throughout Al-Muqtadir's regime, despite the constant changes in administration. The caliph himself was rather unfriendly to "unbelievers." But being a man of "good sense and sound judgment," as he was characterized by the Arab historian Suyuti, and at the same time "addicted to sensuality and drinking, and profuse in his expenditure," he could not dispense with the services of the Jewish financiers. Even the prejudiced Vizier 'Ali ibn 'Isa made use of their financial expertness. But their heyday was during the three vizierates of the brilliant but unscrupulous Ibn al-Furat (908–12, 918, 924), for whom Ibrahim and Sahl, Neṭira's sons, performed all sorts of services, not always honorable according to our standards, but fully accepted by contemporary public opinion. Their power was so great even under the vizierate of Ibn Muqlah that the academic leaders utilized their political connections for the benefit of the academies, as well as of Jews living in more distant communities. In his letter of solicitation in behalf of the academy of Sura, addressed to an Egyptian community in 928, Saadiah extended to his correspondents the bait of favorable intervention in their behalf with the Baghdad authorities on the part of the children of Neṭira and Aaron. Only in the subsequent period of total chaos, which in the 930's and 940's brought the Caliphate to the brink of ruin, did these Jewish banking families, too, suffer irreparable losses. They never succeeded in regaining their influence at court. But the fact that for more than sixty years the "house of Neṭira" held sway despite constant political vicissitudes and many personal prejudices of viziers and caliphs, reveals how far economic power lent itself to being translated into political control, without the occupancy of a formal appointive office.[37]

More directly political and military was the influence of the Jewish counselors of the rising Faṭimid empire. Ever since the discovery of the Chronicle of Aḥimaaz more than half a century ago, the identity of the southern Italian Jewish leader, Palṭiel ben Shefaṭiah, with the Faṭimid general Jauhar, or vizier Ya'qub ibn Killis, has been one of the moot problems of contemporary historiography. But there is no question that a converted Jew could reach the acme of political influence in short order. After his conversion Ibn Killis, a native of Baghdad, indeed contributed greatly to the consolidation of the new Caliphate. At the court of the first caliph Al-Mu'izz (969–75), allegedly nothing could be achieved without the help of some Jew or other. His successor, Al-'Aziz, employed a Christian vizier, 'Isa ben Nestorius, who together with his Jewish associate, Manasseh ben Ibrahim al-Qzaz, governor of Syria, created bitter resentments among the Caliph's Muslim subjects. Each was said to have greatly favored his coreligionists over the Muslims. No wonder that sometimes an Arab poet felt like writing a bitter satire such as,

Today the Jews have reached the summit of their hopes and have become aristocrats. Power and riches have they and from among them are councilors and princes chosen. Egyptians, I advise you, become Jews, for the very sky has become Jewish.[38]

Clearly such Jewish officials were even more perilously exposed to changes in the momentary power constellations than were their Muslim counterparts. We possess an interesting autobiographical record of a Jewish officeholder in Egypt. It describes how, because of a court cabal, the author was suddenly deprived of his post and, to save his life, had to give away all his property. But the very calmness of his description and his continued gratitude to the authorities for allowing him to escape with his life and even giving him a minor office clearly show that these sudden changes in fortunes were generally taken for granted. Even after Ḥakim's intemperate outburst many Jews were employed in the Egyptian administration. One of them actually was saved from prison by his public profession of Judaism. Serving as supervisor of the Damietta district, Solomon Abu'l Munajja ibn Sha'ya constructed a canal in the Nile, which was long named after him. He was arrested soon after its formal opening in 1112, because of its allegedly excessive costs. Thereupon he circulated a copy of the Qur'an with the colophon reading, "Written by Abu'l Munajja, the Jew." Since theoretically Jews were not even allowed to study the Qur'an, such a sensational copy attracted public attention to his case and secured his early release.[39]

Spain, too, witnessed the early rise to affluence and power of many Jewish individuals. Here the occasional suspicion of Mozarab officials because of their proximity to hostile Christian powers was intensified by sharp Arab-Berber rivalries among the Muslims themselves, especially under the rule of the "petty princes" of the eleventh and early twelfth centuries. Jewish statesmen were often considered more loyal and trustworthy.

Already at the height of Spanish-Muslim power, 'Abd ar-Raḥman III made extensive use of the diplomatic and linguistic abilities of the distinguished Jewish physician and patron of learning, Ḥisdai ibn Shapruṭ. In 944 Ḥisdai received the ambassadors of Emperor Constantine VII Porphyrogenitus of Byzantium. Twelve years later he acted in a similar capacity on the arrival of an embassy from Emperor Otto I of Germany. On the other hand, the caliph sent him as an envoy to such Christian neighbors as Ordoño III of Leon and the old Queen Tota of Navarre. On that occasion the Queen availed herself of Ḥisdai's medical advice to reduce the obesity of her grandson, Sancho, the deposed king of Leon. Ḥisdai not only offered Sancho the required treatment, but also concluded with Tota an alliance which resulted in Sancho's return to his throne and the removal of Ordoño (960). The Jewish statesman was not guilty of gross exaggeration when, in his famous letter to the Jewish king of Khazaria, he boasted that the various embassies (which he enumerated) were not only received by him, but "their message arrives through my hands, and through me is determined the result." With equal grandiloquence, characteristic of the contemporary Arabic epistolary style, he also explained to the Khazar king his great influence on Spain's flourishing international trade. After describing the vast extent of the Spanish imports and exports yielding some 100,000 gold dinars annually from custom duties imposed upon foreign merchants alone, Ḥisdai declared, "And everything pertaining to them and their merchandise is determined exclusively by me, and on my say-so." Understandably, therefore, even Jews of Christian countries sometimes turned to him for intercession with their Christian rulers. Two such letters, apparently addressed by the Cordovan statesman to Empress Helena and her husband Constantine VII, have come to light in a Genizah fragment. Here Ḥisdai pleaded the cause of religious liberty in Byzantium not only on general grounds but also by referring to his own benevolent attitude toward the Christians living under the 'Umayyad caliph of Cordova.[40]

In many ways the career of Samuel ben Joseph ibn Nagrela, the Nagid of Granada, was even more startling. A refugee from Cordova after the sack of that imperial capital by the Berbers in 1013, this extraordinarily talented poet, grammarian, talmudist, and linguist (among his poems is one written in seven languages), seems to have gradually worked his way up from a humble shopkeeper and tax collector among his own coreligionists to the chief vizierate of the small but important principality of Granada. The story of his rise to power through his ability to write letters, which had first impressed a slave girl of the royal court, has been cherished by anecdotal historiography ever since Ibn Daud's chronicle. This tale need not be wholly unhistorical, however. The ability to compose state papers with many hidden allusions in the difficult rhymed prose of the period was considered a major prerequisite for all high chancery officials. The Berber dynasty, then reigning in Granada, must have indeed encountered considerable difficulty in finding elegant scribes among fellow Berbers, while it could not readily entrust to a suspect Arab any truly "sensitive" military or diplomatic position. Combining great statesmanship with personal courage and, wherever needed, absolute ruthlessness, Samuel served in an influential capacity under Ḥabbus. He became chief minister of state under the latter's son and successor, the profligate Badis, from 1038 to his own death in 1056. More remarkably, though hardly trained for warfare, Samuel frequently served as commanding general in the field. In fact, to judge from his immortal poems, many of which preserve vivid records of his campaigns, he enjoyed only two years of relative peace in the eighteen years he was in charge of Granada's political and military affairs. So great was the impact of his personality even upon the Arabs that a local poet, Muntafil, evidently on the Nagid's payroll, composed a poem extolling his greatness, which deeply aggrieved its later Arab copyists.

> Thou who hast united in thy person [Muntafil wrote] all the fine qualities of which others possess only a part each, and who hast rendered liberty to captive generosity, thou art superior to the most openhanded persons of East and West, just as gold is superior to copper. If only men could distinguish truth from error, they would apply their lips only to your fingers. Instead of trying to please the Lord by kissing the black stone at Mecca, they would kiss thy hands, for they alone dispense happiness. Thanks to thee I have secured what I wanted here below, and I hope that, thanks to thee, I shall also obtain what I desire on high. When I find myself near thee and thy people, I overtly profess the faith which prescribes observance of the Sabbath. When I stay with my own people, I profess it secretly.[41]

Of course, but few Arabs felt that way. The majority undoubtedly hated the Jewish master with the inveterate hatred of ages, made doubly poignant by envy of his successes. Samuel had to weather many a conspiracy at court, and he had implacable enemies even among the Arabs of neighboring principalities. He earned little thanks from those Arab grandees whose lives he had allegedly saved by warning them in advance of Badis' planned massacre. He himself still managed adroitly to escape the various snares laid for him by courtiers, and held off any violent moves on the part of the populace. But when he died, he was succeeded in his high office by his less gifted son, Joseph, on whose training he had spent many years of lavish care. Displaying more arrogance than finesse, Joseph, though celebrated later by Moses ibn Ezra as a successful general, brought down upon himself and the whole Jewish community of Granada the bloody vengeance of the aroused masses (1066). The immediate incentive to this massacre was given by a propagandistic poem of the pseudo-ascetic Abu-Isḥaq of Elvira, whose careerist advances had been brusquely repudiated by Joseph.[42]

During the frequent periods of political instability, both rise and fall of Jewish courtiers were meteoric. Even the apparently invincible "sons of Neṭira," we recall, who had made themselves indispensable enough to the imperial treasury to survive the execution of their patron, Ibn al-Furat, lost much of their influence under Ibn al-Furat's rival, 'Ali ibn 'Isa, and went into total oblivion in the anarchical 940's. Another prominent banking family, the sons of Sahl of Tustar (Abraham-Ibrahim Abu Sa'ad and Ḥesed-Abu Naṣr) achieved the acme of their power in the Faṭimid caliphate under Mustanṣir (1029–94), owing to the sheer accident that Ibrahim ben Sahl had sold a Negro slave girl to the caliph's father. Now regent, during her son Mustanṣir's childhood and adolescence, she was a loyal supporter of her former master (1036–47). Ibrahim was assassinated, however, in 1048, at the instigation of his own creature, the vizier Al-Fellaḥi, a converted Jew. The latter paid for his treachery with his life in turn. Ibrahim's son achieved power only after turning Muslim. In fact, power and wealth often created an easy bridge to conversion. We are told about the prominent Baghdad physician and philosopher, Ḥibat Allah (the Arabic equivalent of Nathan) Abu'l Barakat, who, disturbed by a satirical attack on his professional reputation inspired by anti-Jewish feelings, decided to turn Muslim. He made sure, however, that his grown daughters, who had refused to follow his example, would not lose their rights of inheritance. Abu'l Fadhl ibn Ḥisdai, on the other hand, influential adviser of Al-Muqtadir and Al-Mu'tamin in twelfth-century Saragossa, is said to have converted himself to Islam because of his love for a Muslim girl. His insatiable ambition and haughtiness, however, would probably have sufficed to make him overcome his scruples.[43]

For this ascendancy of some leaders the Jewish people paid a price—a higher price, perhaps, than its gains warranted. The flattery of external splendor may have played a part. In the case of the powerful viceroy R. 'Uzziel of Syrian Ḥamat, Yehudah al-Ḥarizi observed that all Jews were honored by the good deeds of their leader, "whose fame extends through all provinces." But Al-Ḥarizi and other poets were accustomed to shower upon Jewish grandees the inordinate praise characteristic of that age. Occasionally a Jewish leader may have sincerely believed that, by accepting high office, he was going to help other Jews, and possibly the entire community. At least one unnamed Jewish official (whose father had already served for fifteen years as supervisor of the Alexandrian harbor) tried to enlist the help of influential coreligionists by expostulating, "I have not engaged in royal service except in order not to depend on people and require assistance from Jews. I have done it only to earn a living, and to bestow upon Israel some of the bounty given me by the Lord." The people must have realized, however, that on balance it stood to lose much more through the downfall of these leaders than it could possibly gain from their rise to power. According to a widespread interpretation of two Qur'an verses (2:58, 3:108), many Muslims believed that it was preordained for Jews to be poor. Hence the sight of wealthy, luxury-loving Jewish bankers and courtiers must have irked orthodox Muslims as flaunting God's will. Since all political careers, moreover, were intertwined with factional strife, rapidly shifting power politics, and even personal whims of rulers, each debacle exposed the whole community to the vengeance of the opposing party. When the Baghdad Jewish banker, Abu 'Ali ibn Fadhlan, refused a loan to the emir in 998, the latter imprisoned many communal leaders. The successful Arab uprising against Joseph, son of Samuel ha-Nagid in Granada, led to a regular massacre, in which some 3,000 Jews lost their lives, and from which the community never fully recovered.[44]

The greatest weakness of the "protected" minorities was their extreme mutual animosity, which the Muslim rulers often utilized to impose their own will upon all. Originally, yellow was the required color of the badges of all unbelievers, but, probably under the prompting of Christians and Samaritans, the government often assigned to the latter such other hues as blue or red. The threat of being paraded through the streets of Cairo in Jewish clothes was considered by the Christian patriarch, Isaac, a supreme insult. This, of course, did not prevent other Christians in emergencies from securing safety by pretending to be Jews. When in 1265 certain Jews of Cairo were threatened with burning alongside Christians accused of arson, the Jewish banker, Ibn al-Kaziruni, allegedly pleaded against condemnation together with "these cursed dogs, your enemies and ours" (Tritton, *Caliphs*, pp. 116, 132). Even in modern Turkey Jews often suffered greater indignities from their Christian than from their Muslim compatriots. The self-assertion of the Arabs, on the other hand, artificially stimulated by the constantly inculcated feeling of superiority, largely prevented them from becoming normal citizens fully aware of their obligations toward their respective countries.

In this unnatural state of affairs, it was frequently under Muslim instigation that Jews and Christians held acrimonious public disputations, such as the two recorded between Jewish physicians and Christian priests in Cairo during the Faṭimid age. In the north, Jews were forced by Al-Manṣur to purchase those Armenian churches and their treasures which had been despoiled by the caliph in 757. This may, however, have been but a strategic move designed to strengthen the pro-Muslim elements in that exposed province. According to the Spanish Christian apologist, Samson, the Muslim administration of Cordova, following Visigothic precedents, tried to make use of the Christian church synods for its own purposes. Once such a synod was boycotted by the clergy of the diocese of Cordova. Forewarned, the administration allegedly sent in Jewish and Muslim substitutes. The enmity between the two groups on the Iberian Peninsula at times reached ridiculous extremes. In Portugal before the Reconquest, Theotonio, one of the founders of the monastery of Santa Cruz in Coimbra, refused to exchange greetings with Jews, as well as with heretics and "pagans" (Muslims), according to his admiring biographer. To be sure, the hatred among the Christian sects themselves, inherited from the Byzantine age, frequently exceeded even that between Jews and Christians. The Mandean opponents of orthodox Christianity libeled the Persian Christians by asserting that "they kill a Jewish child, take of his blood, bake it in bread, and offer it as food." At the same time they also taught that "he who consumes Jewish food shall not see the light; he who shows amity to Jews, shall die a second death." In the ninth century the Muslim governor of Antioch had to appoint a special guard, paid by Christians, to prevent the Christian sects from massacring one another during worship. Such excessess were to occur frequently even in modern times at the holy places in Palestine. Reciprocally, Jews allegedly took an active part in the serious anti-Christian disturbances in Jerusalem in 966 occasioned by the Patriarch's refusal to pay the governor's arbitrary impost. Maimonides, under the impact of Muslim hostility, counted the Christians among polytheists in view of their Trinitarian doctrine. Some such sectarians as 'Anan, the founder of Karaism, positively forbade a Jew to live among non-Jews.[45]

The masses did not always listen to such advice. We even hear of occasional collaboration between the three communities as such. During the last illness of the Egyptian ruler Aḥmad ibn Tulun, prayers for his recovery were recited by all three denominations. When the Black Death struck Damascus in 1348, Ibn Baṭṭuṭa tells us, Jews and Christians were allowed to join the Muslims in prayers at the neighboring Mosque of the Footprints (Al-Aqdam). Local pride had long asserted that this mosque had been erected on the original grave of Moses, whose alleged footprints were still visible on a rock. The three faiths may have considered it particularly appropriate during the great emergency to offer prayers at the tomb of the great lawgiver revered by them all. There must have been many more instances of such good will which, simply because they were less dramatic, escaped the attention of travelers and chroniclers.[46]

TAXATION

Thoroughgoing economic transformations accompanied these developments. Invoking Mohammed's injunction to "fight those . . . who do not practice the religion of truth from amongst those to whom the Book has been brought, until they pay the tribute by their hands, and they be reduced low" (Qur'an 9:29), the new rulers encouraged the *dhimmis* to pursue economic activities to their own and the state's advantage. From the outset the principle was well established: the Muslims should be the ruling, and consequently the military and administrative, portion of the population, while the non-Muslims should devote themselves to the economic upkeep of the country. They should also, through a general land and poll tax, help provide for the central and provincial administrations, for expenditures connected with the numerous wars, and for the large personal budgets of the caliphs and their officials.

At no time did the Caliphate succeed in establishing a single, uniform system of taxation and fiscal administration. From its inception it faced the sharp distinction between cities and provinces which had speedily surrendered to the invaders and concluded with them "irrevocable" treaties, and those which had been conquered by force and thus subjected to the conquerors' will. The Arabs found, moreover, especially in the formerly Byzantine provinces, a bewildering array of taxes, with enormous local variations from place to place, which had grown up in the course of centuries. While trying to simplify that fiscal structure whose complexities they were unable to master, they had enough respect for tradition to maintain many remnants of the older system, even though these might be inconsistent with their new arrangements or with one another. On the whole, the new caliphal administration preferred to follow the simplified patterns prevailing in Persia since Khosroe I's fiscal reform, and in time it imposed some Persian methods on the western provinces as well. But this was a slow, fitful process. Ultimately it led to fairly harmonious operations under the strong and prosperous regimes of the first century of 'Abbasid rule, but readily broke down in the subsequent, more anarchical periods.

Hence came that almost chaotic variety of traditions and legal interpretations which characterizes the pertinent discussions among Arab historians and jurists. Contradictions abound even in the works of individual writers, like the leading fiscal authority, Abu Yusuf, who had been ordered to prepare a treatise on the *Kharaj* (land tax) for the guidance of Harun ar-Rashid's groping officials. Nor are the Jewish sources particularly helpful. They occasionally voice loud grievances over fiscal exactions and the terrorization of recalcitrant or impecunious taxpayers. But they rarely furnish detailed data, which might supplement the information gleaned from the more or less official, and for the most part purely normative and theoretical, Arab sources by the record of practices affecting the minority taxpayers.[47]

Mohammed's treaties with the Christians and Jews of Najran, Khaibar, and other Arabian communities were often invoked as precedents by legislators, and they were keenly scrutinized by jurists. However, many new and unprecedented situations called for specific answers, which in turn established new precedents. For example, after their first raids into the Persian territories the Arabs made a treaty with Lakhmid Ḥira and generally laid foundations for the later taxation system in the important province of Sawad. These early decisions were permanently to affect the life of the conquered peoples in many eastern provinces. To cite Yaḥya ben Adam:

> The Sawad was at one time in the hands of the *Nabaṭ* [Nabateans], who were then brought under subjugation by the people of Persia, and they had to pay their new masters the *kharaj* [tax in the general sense]. When the country was conquered by the Arabs, the latter left the *Nabaṭ,* the *dahaqin* [Persian landlords], and all the Sawad in the same condition in which they found it. The Arabs put the *jizya* on the heads of men, and measured the lands of each, which was in their hands, on which they put the *kharaj* [here in its more specific meaning of land tax]. In addition they took possession of all the land not belonging to anyone [including that of the Crown and refugee landlords], and this land became the *ṣawafi* [domain] of the Imam.

It was this new land measurement which so impressed the apocalyptic author of the *Pirqe de-R. Eliezer* that he placed it at the head of the fifteen innovations introduced by the conquerors. He had in mind both the new assessments for a land tax and the expropriation of many estates which were given away as fiefs to members of the ruling class. Mu'awiya, particularly, even before his accession to the throne, sought to concentrate extensive landholdings in Syria and Palestine in his and his family's hands, so as to make the imperial center of Damascus less dependent on the rather unstable revenue from more distant and unruly provinces. This process led to the conversion of many Palestinian farmers, Jews among them, into sharecroppers, with the incidental features of personal subservience characteristic of the Byzantine colonate. Even the free peasants were now subjected to the new land tax on an individual, rather than a communal, basis under arbitrary rates and methods of collection.[48]

Since for a long time Muslims were exempt from that as well as from the capitation tax, such discrimination served as a powerful incentive to conversion, or else to flight from the land. We recall the probably numerous Jewish conversions during the early period of Muslim rule, while some Jewish farmers seem to have left their lands and escaped to the fiscally freer cities. In time, however, the state could not get along without imposing the land tax, that mainstay of most ancient and medieval fiscal systems, also on the new majority of Muslim landlords and farmers.

On the whole, the new system represented for the Jews a much milder degree of fiscal oppression than that which had existed during the declining Roman Empire. A tradition reported by Ibn Hisham claimed that, since the Jews had paid taxes to the former rulers, they were legally the clients of the Christians. For this reason they were included in the treaties with their protectors. According to Abu Yusuf's authoritative report, the vast majority of *dhimmis,* including even those exercising such fairly prosperous trades as dyeing, tailoring, and shoemaking, were to pay a poll tax (*jizya*) of only 12 silver dirhams or 1 gold dinar annually. This was the equivalent of some 4 dollars in present gold value, but at least three times that much in purchasing power. The middle class paid double that amount, while the few wealthy persons (Abu Yusuf enumerates specifically money changers, cloth dealers, landowners, merchants, and physicians) were taxed 48 dirhams or 4 dinars per capita. Theory had it that this tax was essentially the ransom paid by the "people of the book" in lieu of extermination. Hence only men after the age of pubescence were taxed; women, old men, and children were exempted, since combatting them in war was repugnant to Muslim ethics. Crippled and blind men were likewise exempted, unless they owned property, as were beggars and unemployed persons. Christian monks were tax-exempt unless their monasteries were wealthy enough to pay for them, but secular clergy were subject to the tax. Similarly rabbis and Jewish judges were liable, at least for a time, unless the community took over their share in its lump payments. In orderly times, therefore, only about one fourth of the Jewish population appears to have been subject to the poll tax.[49]

Jews probably resented the methods of collection even more than the taxes themselves. Although the treaty of surrender of Damascus in 635, which had served as a model for many other treaties, specifically promised the unbelievers that "so long as they pay the poll tax nothing but good shall befall them," there were too many powerful and greedy officials who tried to enrich themselves quickly at the expense of taxpayers. Only occasionally did the superior authorities intervene, as in the case of the Egyptian governor Qurra ben Sharik, whose order is preserved in a papyrus. The governor instructed the district office to punish any collector of more than the government's due by a hundred strokes, a fine of 30 dinars, and the cutting of his hair and beard. At times it was superior authority itself which was guilty of extortions. We learn, for example, that no sooner did Al-Baridi assume the emirate in 933 than he maltreated the Jewish merchants of Tustar "by outdoing every known form of outrage" (Miskawaihi) and imposed upon them the payment of 100,000 dinars. Conditions became particularly unbearable wherever collections were entrusted to tax farmers. Frequently combining greed with lust for power, tax farmers here, as elsewhere, considered the extortion of all that the traffic could bear a legitimate business profit. Sometimes even the Muslim populace lost patience. On one occasion it staged a riot in Baghdad, destroyed bridges, prevented Friday services at the leading mosques, and opened the prison gates—all in protest against the vizier himself assuming the function of tax farmer (919).[50]

More usually, however, public opinion condoned such peccadilloes. Only rarely did the administration realize, as did Qurra ben Sharik in his aforementioned order, that "whenever the populace suffers oppression and harm from its own officials, its ruin ensues." In the relatively rare instances when superior authorities stepped in and forced a high official to disgorge such excess revenue, he lost little prestige among his friends. On the contrary, already in the ninth century, according to C. H. Becker, the custom developed "to consider it the friends' social obligation, akin to that of wedding gifts, to contribute something to the discharge of the required fine." True, on a few occasions Jewish advisers to caliphs or governors used their influence to mitigate the evil. But precisely these interventions readily lent themselves to accusation of Jewish "solidarity" and mutual favoritism. At times they were used by Muslim demagogues as telling arguments for the removal of all *dhimmi* counselors. Typical of such mass appeals is a speech of Naṣr ben Sayyar to the people of Merv, as summarized by Ṭabari:

> Bahramsis [a Persian] used to prefer the Magi and to favor them; he released their share of the tax quota and loaded it upon the Muslims. Ashdad ben Jrijur [Gregory] used to favor the Christians, and 'Aqiba the Jew used to favor the Jews in just the same manner. I, however, will favor the Muslims and lift from them their burden and load it upon the unbelievers. . . . If any of you, Muslims, had to pay the *jizya* levied upon his head, or if the *kharaj* weighed heavily upon him while the unbelievers were taxed too lightly, then he may bring it before Manṣur ben 'Umar [the fiscal supervisor] who will remove it from the Muslim and charge it to the unbelievers.

Conversely, an ambitious upstart could appeal for the support of the religious minorities by lowering their taxes. This was one of Tamim Abu Ḥarb's early measures as leader of the Palestinian peasant revolt under Al-Mu'tadhim (833–42). But, quickly disappointed by the lack of *dhimmi* support, Tamim turned sharply and implacably persecuted both Christians and Jews. Much too frequently, indeed, the various classes of taxpayers, rather than making common cause against their extortioners, merely tried to shift the incidence of the exorbitant tax upon other shoulders.[51]

Against the powerful pressures of self-interest and constant fiscal needs, the injunctions of Muslim jurists to proceed humanely in the collection of taxes proved of no avail. Abu Yusuf voiced the regnant legal opinion when he wrote that "one must not strike taxpayers, expose them to the sun . . . or inflict upon them repugnant physical punishments. One ought to proceed with sweetness, imprison them . . . and not to discharge them until they pay up all their arrears." In fact, brutal house searches and even torture of suspected delinquents were quite frequent. Failure to pay was placed under severe sanctions, which seriously impeded the transaction of ordinary business. Especially in state-controlled Egypt, an unbeliever had to produce a receipt for his capitation tax before he secured an *aman,* or passport, indispensable for travel. From the eighth century on a native *dhimmi* traveling without a passport was to pay a fine of ten dinars. A foreign Jew caught without such a document was apparently subject to even more severe penalties. We recollect the moving letter written by a Jewish pilgrim to Jerusalem who had suffered shipwreck and landed in Alexandria. Here he lived in hiding for two months in fear of being caught on the street as an illegal entrant. All these chicaneries, however, were not specifically aimed at Jews or *dhimmis,* but rather reflected the general methods of supervision by the often desperate, because far from efficient, police state which the Faṭimid empire had inherited from the Egyptian governmental system of pre-Islamic times.[52]

Not that the Jewish community sought to free itself from all state taxation. Its enlightened leaders fully realized that the *dhimmis'* fiscal contributions were their main raison d'être from the standpoint of the Muslim state and society. A story told about the banker, Neṭira, even if apocryphal, well reflects this awareness. When Caliph Al-Mu'tadhid wished to relieve Jews from all special taxes, the family chronicle reports, the banker consented only to a reduction of the tax to its original size, but he pleaded, "Through the tax the Jew insures his existence. By eliminating it, you would give free rein to the populace to shed Jewish blood." All Jews, however, doubtless wished to see the collection of taxes purified of its purposely humiliating features. Mindful of the Qur'anic injunction, many Muslim rulers insisted on the personal payment of the poll tax by the communal leaders and invested the ceremony with many obnoxious features designed to show that the payers had been "reduced low." According to an old regulation,

> the *dhimmi,* Christian or Jew, goes on a fixed day in person to the emir, appointed to receive the poll tax, who occupies a high throne-like seat. The *dhimmi* stands before him, offering the poll tax on his open palm. The emir takes it so that his hand is on top and the *dhimmi*'s underneath. Then the emir gives him a blow on the neck, and a guard, standing upright before the emir, drives him roughly away. The same procedure is followed with the second, third, and following taxpayers. The public is admitted to enjoy this show.

On one occasion (about 1228) the distinguished head of the Baghdad Jewish academy, Ibn ash-Shuwaikh, requested in vain that he be permitted to make payment at night. That these humiliating practices continued at least sporadically, and were aggravated at times by overzealous officials, is evident from Ibn an-Naqqash's oft-quoted *fatwa.* Not surprisingly, such shameful proceedings increased the usual resistance of taxpayers to a point that, as a popular Arab adage had it, "a Jew will never pay his taxes till he has his head smacked." [53]

Public participation was, indeed, essential for the purpose of demonstrating, according to the Shafi'ite school, the political superiority (*ḥukm*) of Islam. Equally vexatious was the tax receipt, which, in accordance with an old Babylonian custom, was sometimes stamped upon the neck of the "unbelieving" taxpayer. This ancient mark of slavery, long before abolished in Ptolemaic Egypt and expressly prohibited in the Talmud under the sanction of the slave's forcible emancipation, occasionally reappeared here as a degrading stamp of "infidelity." According to Abu 'Ubaid, upon the conquest of Iraq two delegates of 'Umar I assessed the taxes due in Sawad and publicly proclaimed that "the one who does not come to us, so that we can put a seal on his neck, from him the *dhimmah* [protection] has been abolished." Al-Manṣur, too, on his visit to Jerusalem in 758, seems to have insisted on placing such stamps on the hands of unbelievers, a measure which, according to Theophanes, caused many Christians to emigrate to Byzantium. A Baṣran poet of about 800 C.E. sang "Love for her is stamped on my neck, it is stamped where the seal is impressed on the protected subjects." A choice simile for a love poem, indeed! [54]

The land tax (*kharaj*), frequently as high as one fifth of the crop value, lay more heavily on the agricultural population, although the prevalence of orchards and vegetable gardens in the immediate vicinity of towns helped make it less irksome to the majority of Jews. Occasionally it was so very burdensome that, even in the prosperous days of Harun ar-Rashid (he is said to have left to his successor a treasury filled with some $300 million in cash), it brought about a mass desertion of land by the Palestinian and other peasants. According to Baladhuri, the government had to issue public appeals to former owners to return to their estates, pledging permanent tax reductions to those returning within a specified period. In Egypt, where traditions of state control still were very vivid, more drastic measures were taken to enforce the return of fugitive farmers to their former lands.[55]

In addition to these basic taxes there were a great many other imposts and tolls, as well as legal and extralegal "presents," which burdened the entire economy but were felt most acutely by the defenseless "unbelievers." Jews must have been particularly affected by various taxes imposed upon merchants, their shops and goods. Overt "presents" and surreptitious bribes were often considered by them welcome means to forestall more drastic acts by religiously prejudiced officials. But this evidently was a double-edged sword. At times the prospect of such revenue sufficed to induce many a powerful bureaucrat to threaten to do something prejudicial to Jewish individuals or the community at large. He desisted only after receiving, as in the aforementioned reopening of a well, a tangible mark of appreciation. According to Ash-Shafi'i, as we recall, a Muslim administrator could confiscate up to two thirds of a *dhimmi's* property as perfectly legal "tribute," without running afoul of the Qur'anic injunctions. In a Cairo document of 1241, we hear indeed of a Jewish estate "from which the Sultan took a third." Drastic tax collections are also well illustrated by the reminiscences of Obadiah, the Norman proselyte, about conditions in Baghdad in the early twelfth century. The poll tax ranged, we are told, from one and a half gold dinars for the ordinary man to two and a half dinars for members of the middle class, and to four and a half dinars for wealthy Jews.

> If a Jew dies [Obadiah added] without paying the tax, and there are larger or smaller arrears, the Gentiles do not allow him to be buried until these arrears are paid up. If the deceased person leaves no estate, the Gentiles insist that the other Jews should ransom his corpse by paying the arrears out of their own funds. Otherwise, the Gentiles seek to cremate his body.

In Spain under Hisham I (788–96), we are told by an old French chronicler, fiscal pressure became so great that, in 793, many Jews and Christians "sold their sons and daughters into slavery, and only a few remained living in great poverty." This account, though exaggerated, doubtless reflected the existing oppression. It wholly fits the picture of Hisham's "despotic, harsh, and vindictive" character, as it emerges at least from one Arabic chronicle of the Spanish conquest. Despite the pious mouthings in his ethical will enjoining his son and successor to watch over the interests of his "protected" subjects and to punish severely undue exactions by local officials, Hisham was dictatorial enough to glory in forcing his Christian subjects to use Arabic, rather than Latin, in speech and in writing. Even Lucena Jewry, whose wealth was still extolled by Idrisi (about 1150), became so exasperated with the fiscal burdens imposed on it by King ‘Abd Allah (before 1090) that it rose up in arms and achieved a negotiated settlement.[56]

DELIMITED FREEDOMS

Fiscal oppression often made Jewish life under early Islam extremely burdensome. Uncertainty about the size of long-established imposts, whose rates varied from place to place and from period to period, and the unlimited possibilities of enactment of new taxes entirely depending on the ingenuity and self-imposed moderation of the existing powers, greatly complicated the long-range planning of Jewish communities and individuals. In many areas they had to live from day to day, meeting each emergency as it arose. When life seemed to become altogether unbearable, they sought redress by appealing to higher authority or to the generosity of their more fortunate brethren. Many such appeals are preserved, especially from Palestine, which always had a peculiar claim on the assistance of coreligionists of other lands and which, in Faṭimid times, could often be helped by a well-timed intervention of some highly placed Jew at the Faṭimid court in Cairo.

Equally galling, at least to the more sensitive souls, were the humiliating procedures. Before long the term *jizya* carried with it the subsidiary connotation of subjection. The prestige-minded Near Eastern population liked to flatter its own pride by lowering the dignity of the "protected" minorities. The various discriminatory provisions affecting dress and the use of animals for transportation, the size of buildings or interfaith social contacts, many of them completely unprecedented, were introduced principally for the purpose of underscoring the superiority of the true believers. Contempt toward the "infidels" and efforts to keep them "in their place" were, indeed, the guiding principles of the entire system of legislation and administration.

Extent and intensity of such discrimination varied from period to period and from province to province, depending upon the temporary socioeconomic tensions, the degree of "usefulness" of the *dhimmis* to the particular regime, and the personal temperaments or whims, of rulers. A minor breach in court etiquette, which especially in Faṭimid Egypt assumed the rigidity of the Byzantine ceremonial, sufficed to involve the individuals concerned, and even their communities, in serious difficulties. The importance of proper manners, occasional gestures, and a well-turned phrase was enormous in all political negotiations at Near Eastern courts and even in lower offices. That is why the frequent reports by chroniclers about what a Jewish representative said, or failed to say, to a king or statesman are not altogether owing to their general predilection for the anecdotal interpretation of history. A proper sentence, said or written at the proper time could, indeed, alter the course of history and particularly affect the fate of a defenseless minority. The Jew, who on his part never conceded his inferiority, felt that humiliation by unfriendly Gentiles was part of that complex system of sufferings going under the name "Exile." In tenser periods he preferred to go about his business calmly and unostentatiously. We shall see that occasional departures from this rule by the rich, publicly displaying precious garments and other luxuries, added fuel to the popular resentment of Jewish wealth. The majority sought to attract as little attention as possible. An Arab poet rightly spoke of entering the door "with bent heads as if we were Jews." [57]

Nevertheless, compared with conditions in other countries, the status of Jews in Islamic lands was fairly satisfactory in both theory and practice. Viewing the transition from Byzantine oppression to the relative security under the Caliphate, some Jewish observers must have felt inclined to echo, with the necessary modifications, the exclamation of the Nestorian *catholicos* Ishoyabh (650–60): "The Arabs to whom God has given at this time the government of the world . . . do not persecute the Christian religion; on the contrary, they favor it, honor our priests and the saints of the Lord, and confer benefits on churches and monasteries." Despite the subsequent vicissitudes in Judeo-Muslim relations, S. D. Goitein's sweeping generalization that "at the end of the Middle Ages the law governing the position of non-Muslims under Islam no longer diverged greatly from the attitude of the

Catholic Church toward the Jews," is unjustified even with respect to the Mameluk regime. To begin with, the mere fact of not being the sole minority, as Jews often were in Christian Europe, mitigated some of that oppressive feeling of living alone in a hostile world, which was to characterize so much of medieval Jewish thinking in Christian Europe. Nor must we lose sight of the fundamental difference that, under Islam, the Jews were never treated as "aliens." True, if they did not meet the original conditions of surrender, if they did not pay their taxes or committed some heinous crime, they lost their *dhimma,* their protected status under the law, and could readily be expelled or treated as outcasts. But even in theory this penalty affected only individuals, not the Jewish people at large. Hence the absence of any large-scale expulsions of Jews from entire countries such as were time and again to interrupt the continuity of Jewish history in many European lands.[58]

Insecure as life generally was in the troubled periods of Islam's decline, there was none of that feeling of personal insecurity which dominated the medieval Jewish psyche in the West. The Near Eastern, Moroccan, or Spanish Jew may have legitimately feared some sudden invasion or civil war. But he knew that he would then suffer not as a Jew, but together with other inhabitants of his locality, as if it had been struck by one of the recurrent earthquakes or famines. In peaceful times he was protected by law against personal assault almost on a par with the Muslim, and his average life expectancy was probably at least as high as that of his "believing" neighbor. His economic opportunities, too, as we shall see, suffered only from relatively minor restrictions. Outside of Egypt he was generally free to move from place to place. Like his Muslim confreres, he could traverse the vast expanse of the Muslim world in search of economic or intellectual benefits. The majority of Jews undoubtedly viewed all these disabilities and even the irksome humiliations as but a minor price they had to pay for their freedom of conscience and their ability to live an untrammeled Jewish life within the confines of their own community.

XIX
EASTERN EUROPE

COMPARED with their large, affluent, and intellectually advanced population in the Muslim world, Jews under Western Christendom and in the regions of Khazaria, India, or China represented before the end of the twelfth century somewhat peripheral settlements. They were more important for the promise they held out for the future than because of their actual numerical, economic, or cultural strength. True, from the standpoint of both Jewish and world history, by the twelfth century the center of gravity had already begun shifting to western Europe. Perspicacious observers, like Maimonides in his letter to the sages of Lunel, could already foresee that Western Jewries would soon become the chief standard bearers of Torah. But that philosopher's pessimistic description of the neglect of Jewish learning in Eastern lands must have sounded exaggerated to Maimonides' contemporaries; it hardly squares with the facts known to us today. Within Christendom itself, moreover, indomitable Byzantine Jewry outnumbered, and socioeconomically overshadowed, the awakening communities of western Europe, whose cultural contributions had begun to make themselves more widely felt only from the tenth century on.

Apart from sharing in the general cultural backwardness of the contemporary western nations, western Jews suffered from the greater instability of their legal status, and its great local and chronological variations. Despite Al-Ḥakim and the Almohades, Jews under Islam could generally look ahead with considerable equanimity toward their legal and political future. Threatened as they were by changing constellations of power, and by the ever unpredictable demands and whims of rulers and officials, they were at least certain of a more or less uniform legal doctrine which served as an underpinning for their legal structure in all Muslim countries. Superficially, the Western world, too, had established a fairly permanent *modus vivendi* with its Jewish minority by the basically interrelated teachings of the Catholic Church and the legislation of the Christian Roman Empire. In fact, that heritage of ancient Rome, as well as Persia, had also helped to shape the legal concepts which controlled the destinies of *dhimmis* under Islam. But owing to the constant internal changes in western Europe's dynamic society, which accounted for the ever changing power relationships between the various estates and between state and church, that basically uniform heritage underwent constant modifications. In the case of Jews, the European legislations ranged all the way from total outlawry of Judaism in one or another country, or even in the same country at different times, to a high degree of toleration bordering on equality with other large groups in the population. This instability was further accentuated by the frequency of mob action, even large-scale massacres, as well as by the caprices of individual rulers. The extreme swings in law and public opinion, which we had occasion to observe in the last century immediately preceding the rise of Islam, repeated themselves on a larger scale in the following centuries.

Under these circumstances, European Jewry betrayed its extraordinary adaptability and intrinsic vitality by embracing more numerous, and on the whole more populous, Jewish communities in 1200 than it had in 630 or even 500. Unwillingly, during these seven centuries, it laid the foundations for the rise of its Ashkenazic, that is Franco-German and later East European segment, whose numerical and cultural growth was ultimately to overshadow all other branches of the people.

BYZANTINE ERUPTIONS

Curiously, not the least affected by such temperamental changes was Byzantine Jewry living in the midst of an outwardly stable society. Otherwise the Eastern Roman Empire was successfully weathering all storms of barbarian and Arab invasions, maintaining its fundamental continuity with ancient Rome for a thousand years after the destruction of the Western Empire. The example of complete legal suppression of Judaism, however, set by Heraclius in 634, was not lost on his successors in other periods of great crisis.

Of course, the later emperors might have learned from that experience that a mere formal outlawry would not lead to the complete elimination of Jews. Enough Jews remained in the very capital of Constantinople to participate significantly in the street riots which followed Heraclius' death in 641, and again in the attack on Patriarch Pyrrhos and the cathedral of Hagia Sophia in 661. Although the imperial decree was never formally revoked, the Jews dared publicly to debate the merits of their faith with such distinguished ecclesiastics as Anastasios the Sinaite: "For there have arisen," Anastasios wrote, "many and frequent controversies and disputes between us and that people." They also ventured in 655 to seek official permission to rebuild some of their synagogues, like that of Syracuse in Sicily, destroyed some two centuries before during the military assault on the city by the Vandals. They were considered a sufficient menace to the orthodoxy of their Christian neighbors for the leading churchmen, assembled at the great Trullan ecumenical Council (the so-called Quinisext of 692), to expand the ancient segregationist legislation by the inclusion of several novel provisions. Clergymen, as well as laymen, were now forbidden under the sanction of defrocking or excommunication to consume the unleavened bread of Jews, to associate with them on a familiar footing, to receive medical treatment from Jewish physicians, or even to bathe with Jews in public baths. While generally in keeping with the tenor of ancient canon law, these regulations were aimed at making the barrier between members of the two faiths even more impenetrable.[1]

Provisions of this type were little more than pinpricks, only superficially affecting Jewish life in the Byzantine Empire. They attested, on the contrary, the presence of a fairly large and influential Jewish community. The situation became far more serious with the accession to the throne of Leo III, the Isaurian (717–41). Like Heraclius, this emperor rose to power at a moment of highest peril for the survival of his realm. An Arab army had reached the coast of Asia Minor facing Constantinople, while the Arab navy blockaded the capital from the sea. Only with the greatest effort and the aid of Bulgarians on the one hand, and a severe pestilence ravaging the Arab camp on the other hand, Leo succeeded in averting the fall of Constantinople, which might have entailed a rapid disintegration of the whole Empire.

Having warded off the immediate danger, the emperor sought to remedy the Empire's basic weakness stemming from its great sectarian diversity and the ensuing sharp conflicts. Not realizing that most of these divisions were deeply rooted in ethnic and other social factors, he thought that he could decree them out of existence by imposing basic doctrinal conformity on the entire population (722–23). "He began," Agapius of Menbidj informs us, "by converting to Christianity the sectarian groups of his empire and those who opposed Christianity. He made the Jews and the [Montanists] embrace Christianity, and they were called New Christians." In the case of Jews, Leo may also have been shocked by the irrational profundities of a frenetic messianic movement of those years. Although, as we shall see, this movement was led by a charlatan but recently converted to Judaism, it caught the imagination of many thousands of western Asiatic Jews and carried over into the Jewish communities of Byzantium. Many imperial Jews undoubtedly shared the belief of their coreligionists in the Caliphate that the struggle of titans before the gates of Constantinople presaged the approaching end of days. If the events of 717–18 had stimulated Muslim fanaticism and greatly contributed to the tightening of the anti-*dhimmi* laws under 'Umar II, they had an even more crucial effect on the ruling circles in Constantinople. In their quest for religious uniformity, the emperors were soon to embark on that grandiose iconoclastic reformation which for two centuries was to overshadow all other imperial issues and ultimately lead to the definitive breach between Eastern and Western Christendom.[2]

Agapius' concluding remark revealed, however, the essential inefficacy of Leo's decree of enforced conversion. As in Visigothic Spain before, and under the Almohades thereafter, sudden mass conversions did not lead to speedy amalgamation, but rather to the creation of a new separatist group of "New Christians." Since their legal status could no longer be governed by the traditional restrictive anti-Jewish legislation, while on the other hand public opinion resented their treatment on the basis of full equality with the Old Christians, they found themselves living in an uncomfortable, because ill-defined, intermediate position. They could also readily be designated "New Citizens," a term applied to them by

Michael Syrus and Barhebraeus. The earliest chronicler to record these events, Theophanes, claimed that, while the Montanists suffered martyrdom for their faith, the Jews "without much thought underwent baptism, but then washed it off. They partook of the holy communion after having eaten and thus contaminated the faith." Evidently taught by their previous experience under Heraclius, most Jews seem to have felt that by outwardly accepting Christianity they could continue professing their ancestral faith without suffering for it death or exile. Of course, there were many others who shunned such compromises and escaped to some more hospitable regions, including Khazaria. Still others may indeed have voluntarily embraced Christianity, or at least submitted to what they considered inexorable fate. But no one could clearly distinguish between such genuine converts and the numerous secret Jews, whose very presence helped nurture the schismatic movements within the Christian fold.[3]

In time, the ecclesiastical leaders themselves found the enforced conversion of Jews unpalatable on theological grounds. Although this attitude, clearly defined by Gregory the Great, was to become more pronounced in the more independent western than in the strongly "statist" eastern churches, the clergy viewed the presence of a large Neo-Christian community with considerable misgivings. Leo himself seems to have realized the inadequacy of his attempt. When in 726, only three or four years after his formal outlawry of Judaism, he and his son issued their brief recodification of Byzantine law, the *Eklogé,* they provided for the death penalty for Manichees and Montanists, but were strangely silent about sanctions for the profession of Judaism. During the next two generations the complications occasioned by the persevering mass of New Christians became ever more obvious. With the cooperation of Empress Irene, who was generally bent on undoing the harm brought about by the Isaurian dynasty's iconoclasm, the churchmen assembled at the Second Council of Nicaea in 787, decreed:

Certain deceitful adherents of the religion of the Hebrews, thinking to mock Christ our Lord, pretend to be Christians while secretly denying Him and stealthily observing the Sabbath and other Jewish customs. We prescribe that they be admitted neither to communion nor to prayer, nor into the church, but that the Hebrews should live openly according to their own religion. They should neither baptize their children, nor purchase slaves, nor possess them. Should one of them voluntarily convert himself and wholeheartedly confess, scorning their customs and pursuits, and in addition refuting and reforming others, then accept and baptize such an individual as well as his children. Moreover, guard him from apostasizing to the usages of the Hebrews. Never accept one who is not of this type.

No sharper distinction could have been drawn between the voluntary individual conversion which could only accrue to the benefit of Christianity, and the enforced mass conversion, which perpetuated in the midst of Christian society a clandestine, though outwardly identifiable group, directly and indirectly stimulating sectarian divergences.[4]

Not that we ought to take literally the recurrent denunciations of alleged Jewish influences on the iconoclastic movement. According to an old Christian, as well as Muslim, custom, opponents readily attributed any unpopular or unorthodox doctrine to the influence of Jews or Judaism. The violent struggle against icons lent itself particularly well to such accusation, since it so closely corresponded to the ancient Jewish opposition to religious imagery. An unorthodox emperor like Michael II (820–29), a native of Amorion in Phrygia, could the more readily be accused of being influenced by his former Jewish environment, as that district had indeed long been the home of an important Judaizing sect of Athinganoi. Though adhering to many Christian beliefs and the ritual of baptism, these sectarians celebrated their Sabbath on Saturday, and observed many other Jewish rituals. If we are even partially to believe the tenth-century continuator of Theophanes, Michael not only "oppressed the heritage of Christ," but actually freed the Jews from the burden of taxation, "for he loved and esteemed them above all mortals." It stands to reason that at least some of the iconoclastic leaders evinced sympathy for the Jewish point of view.[5]

For that very reason the iconodulic party saw in the Jews a major factor in keeping the controversy alive. Before long it began believing its own polemical assertions of the essentially "Jewish" inspirations of the iconoclastic fervor. Simultaneous attempts to eliminate also the other Christian heresies, especially that of the powerful Paulicians, combined with changing fortunes in the wars with the Arabs, reinforced the intolerant trends in the upper reaches of bureaucracy and Church. Powerful despots like Basil I, founder of the Macedonian dynasty (867–86), and the usurper Romanos I Lekapenos (919–44) were tempted to cut the Gordian knot by putting a violent end to the Jewish communities of their Empire. It appears that about 873–74, and again about 930, decrees were issued similar in nature to those of Heraclius and Leo III, although the latter's name was anathema to the new regimes.

Regrettably, the evidence for both these acts, too, is far from conclusive. Not only have the texts of these enactments not been preserved, but the testimony of contemporaries and early successors is often sharply contradictory. Our main source is an apocalyptic Hebrew "Vision of Daniel," which had caught some of the spirit of enmity toward Basil's predecessor Michael III, "the Drunkard" (842–67), permeating some similar visionary Christian documents in both Greek and Slavonic. After briefly describing Basil's rise to power and his extensive conquests, the author contended, in the usual vein of the *vaticinia ex eventu,* that that king "will set his face against the people of saints of the One on high, and baptize them against their will, with much suffering and compulsion. Afterwards he will sell their men and women into slavery. But he will die in his bed in great pain." Evidently, slavery was to be inflicted only on Jews resisting conversion. Even so this penalty has no parallel in the Empire's legislative acts. By its very nature, moreover, an apocalyptic source can hardly be considered a reliable guide for historic events.[6]

Its sweeping assertions are, in fact, modified and even controverted by other contemporary and more factual records. According to the generally well-informed continuator of Theophanes (in the fifth section, reproducing Constantine VII's enthusiastic biography of his grandfather Basil), the emperor merely summoned Jews from various parts of the Empire to debate the merits of their religion before him. If defeated, they were to accept the Christian faith. Well aware of the one-sided nature of that disputation, Basil strengthened his appeal by various worldly inducements. "To those who would join Christ," reports Basil's grandson-biographer, "he made offers of appointment to office. He also promised to relieve them from the burden of their former taxes, and to make noble and honorable men of obscure ones" (*PG*, CIX, 357; Starr, No. 69).

The same general impression is conveyed by the long-winded anecdotal account of Aḥimaaz of Oria, except that the Hebrew chronicler reported also the exemption from this rule of his own community, then still under Byzantine domination. We need not take too seriously his contention that this exception had been obtained by Shefaṭiah ben Amittai of that city, apparently one of the Jewish participants in the disputation, because he had healed the emperor's daughter from her obsession by a demon. This is an old miracle theme which often recurs in the Aggadah and medieval folklore. More likely, the emperor, himself a general of no mean attainments, was swayed by southern Italy's vulnerability to Muslim attacks and his fear of forcing the small but influential Jewish minority into the enemy's arms. The exemption of Oria and four other Italian communities is evidenced also by an otherwise garbled later account. Combining the tradition attached to the name of Shefaṭiah with his own imaginative interpretation of a verse in a prayer of forgiveness wrongly attributed to that author, Yehudah bar David described the tragic suppression of a thousand communities and the sparing of five owing to Shefaṭiah's successful treatment of the emperor's daughter. "How did they force them?" Yehudah elaborated, "Anyone refusing to accept their [the Christians'] error was placed in an olive mill under a wooden press, and squeezed in the way olives are squeezed in the mill. It is to that procedure that he [Shefaṭiah] referred in his *seliḥah* by praying: 'Save the rest from being squeezed in the olive press.' " [7]

Aḥimaaz' chronology, too, is obviously faulty. He claimed that the persecution had lasted twenty-five years, the duration of Basil's reign, and that it had been revoked by Basil's successor, Leo VI the Wise (886–912). In fact, Basil ruled somewhat less than nineteen years, and his anti-Jewish measures were not taken until some seven or eight years after his accession to the throne. We have, moreover, the clear testimony of *Novella* 55, enacted by Leo VI some time before 893, that his father had persuaded many Jews to "denounce their ancient doctrines and abandon their religious ceremonies, such as circumcision, the observance of the Sabbath, and all their other rites." Yet he did not by explicit decree revoke the older laws which "permitted them to live in accordance with their ancient customs." The *Novella* was intended to remedy this omission by ordering Jews not to "dare to live in any other manner than in accordance with the rules established by the pure and salutary Christian faith." Rather inconsistently, however, Leo threatened only relapsing Jewish converts with the penalties provided for apostasy, but said nothing about the consequences of a Jewish refusal to accept baptism in the first place. In any case, the *Novella* remained a dead letter. Very likely the generally enlightened emperor himself did not wish to see it enforced. He thereby earned the gratitude of Jewish writers, all of whom attributed to him the discontinuation of his father's persecution. "He will," wrote a later apocalyptic author, as a *vaticinium ex eventu,* "give respite and freedom to the people of the Lord's martyrs, and the Lord of Lords will enhance his realm." The *Novella* is also controverted by the entire tenor of the great legal code, the *Basilika,* enacted by the same emperor about the same time. As we shall see, this compilation repeated many of the older tolerant, as well as restrictive, provisions of Roman law concerning Jews and Judaism, but it clearly presupposed the continued existence of a Jewish community in the country.[8]

Whatever anti-Jewish measures were taken by Basil and Leo, obviously they were more of administrative than legislative nature, and probably were but short-lived. Nor did these emperors enjoy therein the unanimous backing of the Church. Within a few years after Basil's attempt at enforced conversion, a monk, Gregorios Asbestas, published "A Treatise Maintaining that the Hebrews Ought Not to Be Baptized with Undue Haste and without Previous Careful Examination." Not at all friendly to Judaism, the monk argued that such violence ran counter to the precepts of the Gospel and the apostolic and patristic canons. He also contended that hasty conversions must in the long run accrue to the disadvantage of the Church, for some of these "shameless and undisciplined fellows, after having learned that which they do not understand, will be thereby armed against us." Gregory could hardly have circulated such a tract without the approval of the patriarch, probably the famous scholar Photius, whose second term of office had begun in October of 877.[9]

Undeterred by these failures, of which he must have been fully cognizant, Romanos I made another inconclusive effort forcibly to suppress Judaism. The particular circumstances and even the date of this enactment are obscure, but it seems to have been occasioned by the great economic crisis resulting from a poor harvest and severe pestilence in 927–28. Personally, Romanos was not a simple fanatic. Possibly in his effort to combat the increasing accumulation of landed property in the hands of great landowners, whom he sharply attacked in his *Novella* 5 of 935, he considered Jews allies or agents of the aristocracy. However, such an assumption, based upon later East-European parallels, has no supporting data in the available sources, which are particularly sparse and inarticulate with respect to the economic activities of Jews in Asia Minor where these conflicts were most pronounced. Perhaps the controversy evoked by Romanos' appointment, in October, 931, of his sixteen-year-old, worldly son, Theophylaktos, to the patriarchal see at Constantinople, or the mere anticipation of such opposition, induced the emperor to conceive some dramatic action which would demonstrate his attachment to the Orthodox faith before ecclesiastical opinion from Jerusalem to Rome. All these crosscurrents in the Byzantine court and society may help explain both the anti-Jewish decree and its evidently half-hearted execution.[10]

According to a letter read at the Council of Erfurt in 932, Romanos had learned from the Patriarch of Jerusalem about a mass conversion of Jews in the Holy City which had resulted from a religious controversy and ensuing miracle. The Jerusalem churchman had allegedly urged the Byzantine emperor and other Christian rulers to follow that example, and either to convert their Jews, "or to exclude them from all of Christendom." The emperor, asserted another letter addressed to Germany by the civil and ecclesiastical leaders of Venice, "did indeed order all Jews to be baptized, but when the Hebrews themselves heard of God's miracles, they voluntarily believed and were baptized." Whatever one thinks of the extent of Jewish conversions to Christianity in Jerusalem, some sort of enforced conversion in the Byzantine Empire is attested also by a brief allusion in Mas'udi's "Meadows of Gold" and by a Khazar letter, both relating another large-scale emigration of Byzantine Jews to Khazaria.[11]

On the other hand, the obscure apocalypse of the "Vision of Daniel," apparently describing the sufferings of imperial Jewry during those centuries, emphasized that Romanos had been bent on the expulsion, not extinction, of his Jewish subjects, and that his hostile decree had been "carried out mercifully." Other sources seem to confirm the fact that "numerous Hebrews," to quote one of Romanos' ecclesiastical admirers, along with such Christian sectarians as the Athinganoi and Paulicians, were converted to Christianity while some others suffered martyrdom. But a great many either escaped to Khazaria and other neighboring lands, or went into hiding until the storm blew over.[12]

The change seems to have come soon after Romanos' deposition by his sons in 944 and the speedy assumption of full imperial power by the original heir to the throne, Constantine VII Porphyrogenitus (912–59). Of a more scholarly than bellicose bent of mind, Constantine was interested more in promoting the study of sciences than in religious strife. Noting that his grandfather Basil I's missionary efforts had failed and that most Jewish converts had "returned to their vomit," he became convinced that converting Jews is like changing the pigmentation of Ethiopians. He readily listened therefore to his wife Helena, who, though Romanos' daughter, did not share her father's intolerance. The empress may indeed have been moved by the plausible arguments in favor of Jewish toleration advanced by Ḥisdai ibn Shapruṭ. Moreover, the returning Byzantine embassy to 'Abd ar-Raḥman III of Cordova must have described to her the Jewish statesman's extraordinary position at the caliphal court and the great power and intellectual glory of Cordova, flourishing under a system of mutual religious toleration. Constantine and Helena may also have been swayed by an adverse reaction to Romanos' anti-Jewish decree in Khazaria. The anonymous Khazar letter seems to refer to the Jewish king's retaliatory anti-Christian persecution, which may indeed have deterred the new rulers from persevering in their anti-Jewish course.[13]

In one way or another Byzantine Jews thus weathered four

major mass conversion crises in each of the four centuries from the seventh to the tenth. Enforced baptism, never officially sanctioned by the leading Church organs with respect to the wholesale conversion of Jewish communities, was doubly frowned upon when applied to individuals. True, occasionally fanatics like St. Nicon Metanoites still advocated the elimination of Jews. Asked by a delegation from Sparta to ward off a ravaging pestilence, Nicon refused until the city would rid itself of its Jews, so that it might no longer "be contaminated by their disgusting customs and by the pollution of their religion" (about 985). But this demand evidently led but to their temporary exclusion from that ancient city, to which their ancestors of the Maccabean age had claimed special kinship. More revealing is the formula of abjuration extant in a Greek manuscript of 1027, which clearly mirrors the Church's official attitude at that time. Here the convert from Judaism was made to swear that he did not accept conversion

> because of force, nor of compulsion, nor of a special levy, nor of fear, nor of poverty, nor of a criminal charge against me, nor for the sake of worldly honor, nor for any gain, nor for money, nor for things promised by someone, nor because of any kind of need or human glory whatsoever, nor for the purpose of avenging myself on the Christians, as a zealot for the Law, nor because of having been wronged by them, but because I love Christ and his faith with my whole soul and heart.

Writing in the second quarter of the eleventh century, the Nestorian Elisha bar Shinaya rightly asserted that the Byzantines "tolerate a large population of Jews in their realm. . . . They afford them protection, allow them openly to adhere to their religion, and to build their synagogues." During Al-Ḥakim's persecutions, many Jews from the Faṭimid Empire successfully sought refuge in Byzantium. The powerful emperor Basil II (976–1025) did not hesitate to invite a Jewish scholar, Moses, from Cyprus to Constantinople to testify in a calendar controversy among Christian divines. According to Matthew of Edessa's Armenian chronicle, Moses "delivered a discourse on the principles of the calendar, exposed the error of the Greeks and covered them with confusion, while he heaped praises on the Armenian scholar [Samuel] for his demonstration." Another distinguished emperor, Manuel Comnenus (1143–80), defied the old ecumenical canon of 692 and employed a Jewish court physician, Solomon the Egyptian. Through him, Benjamin of Tudela observed, "the Jews enjoy considerable alleviation of their oppression." [14]

Such Jewish perseverance in the face of recurrent outlawry is truly amazing. It may partially be explained by the empire's size and internal divisions, and the complexities of carrying through such an oppressive program. Here each person constituted a problem. Only the whole-hearted cooperation of the public with a really convinced ecclesiastical and civil bureaucracy might have secured full execution. True, the Byzantine Church was generally more pliable to imperial wishes than the western Papacy. Traditionally it also was less insistent on the need of permanent toleration of Jews as witnesses for the Christian faith. Nevertheless it was keenly aware of the possible damage to the orthodoxy of the Christian masses arising from the presence in their midst of large groups of insincere converts. Convinced of Jewish "stubbornness," it preferred slow gradual conversion of individuals to the sudden baptism of a large, unassimilable group. The civil officials, on the other hand, were readily accessible to bribery. The gradual rise of a powerful aristocracy, too, strengthened the feudal trends in general society. While inimical to the economic well-being of many Jewish individuals, feudalism militated against effective centralized controls. It facilitated local evasions of all laws, particularly of those which did not enjoy the full support of the aristocratic grandees.

LEGAL CONTINUITY

Most remarkably, these intolerant episodes had little bearing on the permanent status of the Jewish communities, since imperial legislation took little cognizance of such abrupt departures from the established order. The very emperors who tried drastically to suppress Judaism often restated the existing law, regulating Jewish life under its special status.

In his *Eklogé* of 726 Leo III had recodified the prevalent law as derived from both the Code of Justinian and the actual usages. This constant dichotomy between imperial laws and local customs further explains the ineffectiveness of many imperial enactments concerning Jews, whose affairs were governed much more by the provincial observances. We recall that the *Eklogé* provided only for the death penalty to Montanists and Manichees, but placed no sanction on continued adherence to Judaism. This was also clearly the understanding of the author of the appendix to that code, apparently written between 797 and 802, which contained a number of restrictions of Jewish rights but never once suggested that professing Judaism was in any way unlawful. Nor did the Macedonian dynasty, in its general effort to restore the old legislation of Justinian to its pristine purity, in any way impinge upon the basic toleration of Judaism. The Legal Handbook (*Procheiros Nomos*), published by Basil I in 870–78 shortly before or after his anti-Jewish enactments contained only the traditional provisions against Jewish slave ownership and Jewish attacks on Christianity. Another traditional prohibition of entrusting to Jews civil or military offices was renewed by that emperor in his other legal manual, bearing the name *Epanagogé* and unofficially issued in 884–86 in cooperation with Leo VI, the Wise. Leo himself, whose *Novella* 55 professedly sharpened Basil's outlawry of Judaism, in his major Code of Laws, the so-called *Basilika,* added but little to the long-established regulations concerning Jews. Clearly, legal enactments tell only part of the story. They reflect at best the legislators' wishes and programs; often they merely restate older and outworn norms superseded by new realities. Remarkably, in her judicious biography of her father, Emperor Alexis, Anna Comnena sharply attacked the Muslim doctrines and way of life, but had nothing adverse to say about Jewish tenets. As pointed out by G. Buckler, the princess hardly mentioned Jews at all. Even the two Aarons and one Solomon, described in the *Alexias* as conspirators, and one Elias, possibly a runaway slave, probably were neither Jews nor converts.[15]

Legal conservatism dominated also the nature of penalties provided for the religious "crimes" committed by Jews. Otherwise, the progressive medievalization of Byzantine law is well illustrated by the new corporal punishments introduced by the *Eklogé* and its successors. The prevailing tendency among scholars to blame these new sanctions on Arab prototypes is disproved by the frequency of mutilations recorded in the Byzantine court cabals of the seventh century. It is doubly remarkable, therefore, that none of these newer codes provides for physical mutilation as a penalty for a "Jewish" transgression. They merely place various acts injurious to the Christian Church under the sanctions of capital punishment, confiscation of property, or both, that is under the traditional penalties of the codes of Theodosius and Justinian.[16]

The major codes, and not the temperamental outbursts of individual monarchs, reflected the permanent policy of the Empire and in the long run shaped the destinies of imperial Jewry. For all practical purposes they displaced the *Corpus* of Justinian in the administration and the judiciary of the Byzantine Empire. More, by their early translation into Slavonic languages, the *Eklogé, Procheiron, Epanagogé,* and *Basilika* profoundly influenced all legal thinking and institutions, including those relating to Jews and Judaism, among the Slavs of the Balkans and Eastern Europe. In canon law, two collections, known under the names of *Nomocanon* and the *Synagogé* by Johannes Scholasticus, influenced the Slavonic world from the time Methodius himself introduced the former to his new converts in its Old Slavonic garb.[17]

In substance the *Basilika,* containing the fullest restatement of the laws governing Jewish life since the Code of Justinian, differed only in some details from that, or from the Theodosian Code. Most of its regulations can be traced back to the basic principles laid down at the beginning of the Christian Roman Empire. That is why its general outlook on Judeo-Christian relations differs but slightly from the gradually evolving legislation in western Europe which was likewise based on the Theodosian Code. We find major exceptions only in the numerous discriminatory economic laws, reflecting the more rigidly feudalistic order emerging in the West.

To put it in a nutshell: the guiding principles of the new, as of the old, legislation were limited toleration of the Jewish minority and its perpetuation on an inferior social plane. All codes agreed on the denial to Jews of honors and public offices, civil or military. If the *Eklogé* still repeated the archaic exception in favor of Jews occupying the burdensome and undesirable *decurionate,* this "favor" was eliminated in the subsequent summaries. Moreover, unlike Islam and many western European countries, the Byzantine Empire seems to have taken this provision quite seriously. No names of

Jewish officeholders are unequivocally recorded. Even in the eleventh and twelfth centuries, when the sale of public offices became for a time standard procedure and Emperor Isaac II (1185–95) allegedly sold civil posts "like vegetables on the market" (Nicetas Choniates), we hear of no Jewish officials. The only exception may have been a Hungarian Jew, Astafortis, who in a letter of 1166 is described as an extortionist tax collector from the Latins. But even if a Jew, and not a convert, he appears in the record more importantly as a semicommercial taxfarmer than as a public official. Nor should we be misled into believing that the constant repetition, in successive codes, of the prohibition for Jews to own Christian slaves reflected the need to stem a widespread practice. Repetition was so basic to all these codes that even totally obsolete laws often found their way into later compilations for purely literary reasons.[18]

Probably more frequently needed were the reiterated prohibitions of the erection of new synagogues, which the *Basilika* put under the double sanction of a fine of fifty gold pounds (some $18,000) and the confiscation of the new buildings for the benefit of local churches. Certainly Jews settling in new areas under Byzantine domination, and Jewish resettlers in older communities after their temporary elimination by an intolerant enactment, must have had recourse to new houses of worship. We actually learn now of fewer appropriations of synagogues by churches, or by church-inspired mobs, than in the first generations after Constantine. The *Basilika's* specific prohibition, too, of any violence directed against synagogues, Jewish homes or persons, and the exemption of Jewish houses of worship from the billeting of soldiers, doubtless contributed to the security of the Jewish population, at least in calmer periods. There is a grain of truth even in J. B. Bury's overstatement that the early Byzantine legislator "was perhaps more often concerned to protect them [the Jews], than to impinge upon their freedom." [19]

As a matter of fact, the silence of our historical and juridical sources about penalties exacted from Jewish communities daring to erect new synagogues is truly amazing. Since outside the imperial capital Jews seem not to have lived in quarters of their own, they must frequently have acquired houses of worship in new neighborhoods. The expansion and contraction of the imperial boundaries, especially on the Balkan Peninsula, must also have entailed the speedy rise and decline of Jewish settlements. In their period of affluence, these communities undoubtedly sought to have their own institutional structures. Similarly, the growth of the Karaite sect from the eleventh century on must have been accompanied by the erection of sacred buildings dedicated to its new forms of worship. Yet we learn nothing about negotiations before, or punitive action after, the opening of Karaite synagogues.

Understandably, the legislators were greatly concerned with the protection of the Christian religion and churches. Jews were forbidden to acquire church property. Conversion of adult Christians was severely punishable, while circumcision of Christian children or slaves was declared a capital crime. Intermarriage was equated with adultery, and likewise subjected to the extreme penalty. "A Jew who throws stones at or in any other manner disturbs a convert to Christianity, will be burned." Leo VI even repeated Justinian's singular ordinance forcing Jews to read Scripture in synagogues in a Greek translation, preferably the Septuagint, and prohibiting the study of *deuterosis*. This may have been, however, but one of those academic repetitions, whose execution was entirely left to the zeal of local officials. At any rate, when soon thereafter the Jews of both the Balkans and the southern Italian communities underwent a cultural renaissance and brought forth a number of distinguished experts in Jewish lore, their intellectual pursuits were in no way handicapped by this statutory provision.[20]

Most remarkably, there were even occasional conversions to Judaism. According to a recently recovered portion of the autobiographical memoir by a twelfth-century Norman proselyte, an example had been set by Archbishop(?) Andreas of Bari (about 1094).

God put the love of the Law of Moses [the proselyte reported] into his [Andreas'] heart. He left his country, his priesthood and dignity, and went to the land of Constantinople, where he underwent circumcision. There he sustained great sufferings and he had to run away before the uncircumcised who had tried to kill him. . . . And strangers followed him. Seeing what he did, they imitated him and entered the covenant of the living God. And the man went to Egypt and lived there until his death. The name of the Egyptian ruler at that time was Al-Mustanṣir [1036–94]. . . . When the news about Archbishop Andreas spread all over Lombardy, and reached the sages of Greece and Rome, the center of the Edomite kingdom, the Greek and Edomite sages were ashamed.

Among those deeply impressed by Andreas' deed was the writer, a young southern Italian priest named Johannes, who upon his conversion adopted the Hebrew name Obadiah. However, even this story reveals the dangerous mode of living of converts arriving from other lands, and their usual quest for safety by escaping to a Muslim country.[21]

At the same time the lawgivers repeated many of the ancient protective laws intended to safeguard internal Jewish autonomy and religious observance. They insisted that in litigations with Christians, Jews had to repair to the general magistrates and not to "Jewish priests," and that, in some religious matters such as marriage (especially the outlawry of polygamy), Jews must be subject to state laws. But they also safeguarded full Jewish judicial autonomy in litigations among Jews. By stating that "Jews may not be required by law officers to desecrate their Sabbaths and holidays," the *Basilika* actually broadened the ancient prohibition of citing Jewish parties or witnesses before law courts on Sabbaths. Similarly outspoken was the provision that "no non-Jew may be an overseer over Jews," leaving the management of Jewish communal affairs entirely in the hands of Jewish elders. A sentence issued by a Jewish court in a civil litigation among Jews was "to be upheld by the civil official." In this formula the Empire strengthened the jurisdiction of Jewish tribunals, though still treating them formally as mere courts of arbitration according to the law of 398.[22]

SLIGHT FISCAL CONTRIBUTIONS

Such far-reaching protection of Jewish self-government seems to have been based upon tradition and the recognition that only Jews could supervise the proper religious and ethical conduct of their coreligionists, rather than upon the fiscal self-interest of the state. Elsewhere, the Jewish community had often been converted into an effective tax collecting agency of the state. Under ancient

Persia and medieval Islam, as well as in many western countries, the Jewish communal organs often had to assume the responsibility for the total revenue from Jewish taxpayers, or at least to assist the state's ordinary fiscal agents. For this purpose the state had to strengthen the hands of Jewish leaders so that they might the more effectively carry out their fiscal obligations. In Byzantium that motive played a minor role. Certainly, none of the extant sources mentions Jewish elders or rabbis taking an active part in the assessment or gathering of state taxes.

This silence need not be attributed merely to the general paucity of extant sources, but rather to the insignificance of Jewish taxation within the Empire's fiscal structure. Such leading experts on Byzantine public finance as F. Dölger and M. A. Andreades, after a prolonged debate, finally agreed that there existed something like a special Jewish capitation, or family, tax in Byzantium as well. But Starr, on reexamining the entire rather slight source material, denied the existence of such a tax, at least between the seventh and the twelfth centuries. The truth seems to be that, while special taxes were neither consistent nor universal, they were collected at various times in various parts of the Empire.

Going back to the ancient *fiscus judaicus,* introduced by Vespasian after the fall of Jerusalem, the original Jewish poll tax had gone into disuse even before its formal abolition by Julian the Apostate. But it was renewed under the guise of the *aurum coronarium* which, originally collected from all adult Jewish males for the benefit of the Palestinian patriarchate, was made compulsory and appropriated by the Treasury after the patriarchate's suppression about 425. The law transferring that tax to the government was reiterated in the Code of Justinian and again in the *Nomocanon* of the ninth century. Although by that time the term itself represented but an antiquarian reminiscence, it probably still reflected some contemporary practice. Writing about the same time (846 or 886), the well-informed postmaster of the Caliphate, Ibn Khurdadhbah, reported that the Empire collected from both Jews and the *Majus* (Zoroastrians, or, more likely, Normans) a gold dinar annually, probably per capita. Some two centuries later we hear again of a Jewish family tax, though called *kephaleiton* (capitation tax), in connection with an endowment established in 1049 by Constantine IX in favor of the monastery Nea Moné on the island of Chios. The emperor provided the monks with the permanent revenue from the island's serfs as well as from the fifteen Jewish families, "who are everywhere free and subordinate to no one." This was to be a hereditary tax, and for that purpose the island's Jewish population was not supposed to grow by further immigration. Nevertheless, a century later Benjamin found there 400 Jews, probably representing an increase of some 400 percent in the course of four generations. That this family tax, however, must have been much larger than a dinar, or whatever other amounts were collected from Jews elsewhere, is evidenced by the simultaneous exemption of the Chios Jews (and serfs) from all other imperial taxes. On the other hand, an obscure messianic epistle of 1096 related the general exemption of Salonican Jewry from the capitation tax (*gulgolet*) because of the government's alleged belief in the speedy advent of the Messiah. However little credence this report deserves, it does illustrate the occasional tax exemptions of individual Jews or entire communities. Arbitrary privileges were a characteristic feature of Byzantine autocracy.[23]

Such ambiguities were possible only because of the general insignificance of Byzantium's direct taxation. More consistently prosperous than its counterparts under both Islam and western Europe, the Byzantine Treasury placed its main reliance on revenue derived from state domains and industrial enterprises, and a vast array of indirect taxes paid both in money and in kind. To the latter belonged also certain *corvée* services, including the billeting of soldiers, from which, as we recall, the synagogues were specifically exempted. In his famous description of Constantinople, Benjamin of Tudela reported that the emperor's annual revenue "from the rents of shops and markets, and from the tribute of merchants who enter by sea and land" in the capital alone amounted to 20,000 gold pieces. These were evidently custom duties, taxes on consumption, and rents from state-owned bazaars. Their yield does not seem exaggerated. In view of the prevailing rate of 10 percent *ad valorem*, the custom duties alone collected in a great emporium of trade like Constantinople, which dazzled Benjamin and other visitors, must have been enormous. Although many emperors were lavish in rewarding partisans and churches by land grants, some of these losses were compensated by frequent confiscations. We recall that many religious offenses of Jews had been placed under that sanction, which must have been an incessant provocation to miscarriage of justice. Together with mines and quarries, the royal domains contributed a major share to the imperial budget, making the Treasury largely independent of direct taxation. As usual, however, the direct taxes, aggravated by more or less arbitrary methods of collection, were most directly felt and, hence, resented by the population.[24]

On the other hand, wherever the Byzantine armies found established methods of taxation in a conquered territory, they doubtless continued for a time to gather the customary taxes. This may indeed be the background of Ibn Khurdadhbah's contention about the annual dinar paid by each Jew and "Zoroastrian" or Norman. He may have had in mind not the entire Empire, but only some newly conquered provinces. Though less spectacular and of shorter duration than the campaigns conducted against the decaying Caliphate by Nikephoros II Phokas (963–69) and John I Tsimiskes (969–76), there were some minor conquests of this kind also in Ibn Khurdadhbah's lifetime, especially under Basil I.[25]

Perhaps because Jewish taxation played but a minor role in the fiscal system, the emperors could lightheartedly dispense with it altogether by repeatedly outlawing Judaism in their realm. Unlike many later western kings, they lacked the incentive of sudden expropriation of accumulated Jewish wealth. They resorted, therefore, to mass conversion, rather than expulsion, perhaps hoping to retain the bulk of the regular revenue from their former Jewish subjects. Basil I even tried to entice Jews to accept conversion by offers of honorable posts and special tax exemptions, thereby evoking the protest of Gregorios Asbestas. With some exaggeration the monk claimed that such an insincere Christian, as a result of his formal baptism, "would even lord it over the Christians, lead an idle and otiose existence abundantly supplied with necessities throughout his life, attaining honors he had never dreamed of, and perhaps marrying the well-born daughter of the local governor." On the other hand, in its accusation of Michael II's iconoclastic efforts, the iconodulic party spread rumors of the emperor's excessive friendliness to Jews, the alleged inspirers of imageless worship, and of his freeing them from all taxation. Even such total tax exemption did not, of course, exempt the taxpayer from the main, the indirect, taxes.[26]

In any case, the fiscal pressure, however great on the entire population, did not seriously interfere with Jewish economic endeavor. Unlike western Europe, the Byzantine Empire did not develop any elaborate system of economic discrimination again its Jewish subjects. Even Benjamin, who graphically described the governmental oppression and the popular hatred under which imperial Jewry lived, had to admit that Jews were found in numerous trades and that many had amassed considerable wealth. Precisely because they did not perform any peculiar economic functions, as they did in western Europe, their elimination must have appeared to rulers as a minor disturbance of the social equilibrium. At the same time, however, their fairly general economic integration doubtless diminished the competitive animosities of rivals and debtors. Perhaps for that very reason the public at large seems to have offered so slight cooperation in the execution of the intolerant decrees. Nor must we lose sight of the significant absence of large-scale massacres of Jews, such as were to blot the annals of Jewish history in the West. In Byzantium such outbreaks of popular frenzy were aimed at Christian heretics, or even oppressive Latin aliens, much more than at Jews.[27]

In short, the only significant contributions to anti-Jewish discrimination apparently made by the Byzantine Empire after Justinian were the aforementioned canons of the Trullan Council of 692, which forbade Christians to use the ministrations of Jewish physicians and publicly to bathe together with Jews. Convoked and presided over by emperors, such great church councils here, as in Visigothic Spain, represented state assemblies as well; their canons, when confirmed by an emperor, became part and parcel of imperial law. The resolutions of 692 are the first instances of these particular forms of segregation which, partly emulated also in neighboring Muslim lands, were to play a pernicious role in shaping Judeo-Christian relations in the West. Byzantine formulas of abjuration for new converts and of oaths *more judaico* likewise seem to have served as models for the Western lands. In fact, the aforementioned formula, first published by Beneshevich from a 1027 manuscript, probably represents the fullest text anywhere of an abjuration required from a Jewish convert. On the contrary, the oath included in a text dating from 963–68 and taken over in Manuel Comnenus' *Novella* 55 of 1148, was far less elaborate than some of the Western formulas. Our record reads briefly:

First, he [the Jewish litigant] must gird himself with bramble, and grasp the august [Torah] scroll in his hands. Then he shall say as follows: "In the name of the blessed Lord, the God of our fathers, who made the heaven and the earth and led us on dry land across the Red Sea, I do not lie. If I be found a perjurer, may the Lord God afflict me with the leprosy of Gehazi and Naaman, and with the punishment of Eli the priest; may the earth open up and swallow me alive, even as Dathan and Abiram."

However, the antecedents of both the oath and the abjuration reach back to the ancient Christian Empire and may have influenced both the West and the countries of Islam without the mediation of the subsequent Byzantine legislation.[28]

Most remarkably, despite these legal pressures and even occasional outlawry, and despite widespread anti-Jewish sentiments among the ruling classes and populace alike, the Jewish communities in Byzantium's Balkan, Asiatic, and Italian possessions maintained their economic, social, and intellectual vitality through the seven centuries here under review. In one of his responsa Hai Gaon mentioned scholars from Constantinople attending his academy in Baghdad. The Karaite Tobiah ben Moses and others traveled to Jerusalem in quest of higher education. Even Benjamin, coming from affluent and populous Spain, was profoundly impressed by the power and glory of Constantinople. He observed the presence of some 2,000 Rabbanite and 500 Karaite Jews in the capital's Jewish quarter in Pera, and emphasized that they "are rich and good men, charitable and religious; they cheerfully bear the burden of Exile [*galut*]." His successor, Petaḥiah, arriving from underpopulated central Europe, was even more deeply thrilled by the number and size of the Byzantine communities. Although commenting on their grievous *galut* and physical enslavement, he observed with amazement that "there are there so many congregations that the land of Israel could not contain them, were they settled therein." No better homage could have been paid

to any branch of the Jewish people. Resisting untold pressures, Byzantine Jewry succeeded in maintaining its historic continuity through a millennium of hostile Roman and Byzantine rule. It was to rise to new heights of achievement immediately upon the latter's displacement by the more friendly Ottoman regime.[29]

CONVERSION OF KHAZARS

Byzantine pressures were, however, in part responsible for Jewish migrations into the northern regions across the Black and Caspian Seas. As a result, the largest and last mass conversion to Judaism occurred in this period, when the royal house and large sections of the population of Khazaria adopted the Jewish creed. This conversion, which seems to have taken place by degrees during the eighth century, as well as the eventual disappearance of that notable Jewish Black Sea settlement (of mixed Khazarian and Jewish extractions), still needs elucidation in detail.

True, we have at our disposal a sizable number of primary sources, including fragments first published in 1912 and 1923. Most of them, however, were written by outsiders, often from mere hearsay. The paucity and general unreliability of the few Khazarian-Jewish sources and, particularly, of the crucial letter of King Joseph extant in both a shorter and a longer version, is the less astonishing as Jews of that period were generally inarticulate outside their main centers of learning. What would we know, for example, about the Jews of Spain from their own writings composed between 300 C.E., when the Council of Elvira warned Christians against too intimate association with them, and 900 C.E., when their Golden Age was being ushered in? Khazarian Jews were less fortunate, for they had few civilized Christians or Muslims in their midst, so that the extant non-Jewish sources, too, are distinguished by neither clarity nor reliability. Most of our data are supplied, therefore, by Muslim geographers and historians (with the significant exception of Ibn Fadhlan, who had at least visited the neighboring Volga Bulgarians) deriving all their information at second or third hand. Most of their knowledge, particularly of earlier periods, was based on rumors such as that known to Saint Jerome through some Jewish contemporaries, that "the Assyrians and

Chaldaeans had conducted the Jewish people into exile not only in Media and Persia, but also in the Bosporus and the extreme North." Assertions of this kind merely attested the feeling among Jews of those regions that they had lived there from time immemorial. The epigraphic evidence, on the other hand, some of which indeed reaches back to the Graeco-Roman Bosporus, has been obscured by Abraham Firkovitch's indubitable forgeries as well as by the Karaite-Rabbanite controversy which has colored all contemporary debates on the inscriptions published by him. Archaeological exploration of the vast area under Khazar control, which alone might supply new and decisive answers, is likewise still in its initial stages.[30]

It appears, nevertheless, that the ancient Jewish settlers on the northern shores of the Black Sea were reinforced by two streams of migrants coming from the south and east. The recurrent outbursts of Byzantine and Sassanian intolerance, and the ravages of international and civil wars often devastating Asia Minor, Armenia, and Iran, forced many Jewish refugees to look for shelter in the Caucasian mountains and beyond. According to a plausible recent theory, the region around Khiva, profoundly Judaized before the Muslim conquest, now yielded a great many migrants, including regular armed detachments, to countries west of the Caspian Sea. About 929, Saadiah Gaon mentioned without much ado a Jew who "went to Khazaria." As elsewhere, Jews engaged in various pioneering pursuits. They taught their fairly primitive neighbors belonging to a variety of racial and linguistic groups more advanced ways of cultivating the soil, and means of exchanging goods among themselves and with foreign nations. They may also have introduced various methods of irrigating the dry lands and cultivating rice. In any case, much rice was produced in the Volga region during the flowering of Khazaria, while it practically disappeared after the latter's downfall. Nor did Muqaddasi intend to be humorous when, describing Khazaria as a vast but arid land, he declared that "sheep, honey and Jews exist in large quantities in that land." Here, too, Jews seem to have taught their neighbors the art of writing, and another tenth-century Arab author (Ibn an-Nadim) stated tersely, "The Khazars use the Hebrew script."[31]

Religious influences were bound to follow. After the rise of

Islam, particularly, the sectarian strife which filled the entire Mediterranean world began to affect Khazaria too. Religious disputations between representatives of various faiths became very frequent; one between a Jew and a Christian in Khazaria is more or less reliably recorded. Another religious debate there may be alluded to by the author of *Tana de-be Eliyyahu,* if that passage dates from the ninth century. Hence the story told about the Khazarian king (*khagan*) Bulan (about 740) that, after listening to the presentation of the various religious systems, he decided to adopt Judaism, need not be altogether unhistorical.[32]

On the other hand, in their frequent diplomatic negotiations with the Khazars, who had already proved valuable allies to Heraclius in his campaign against Persia, Byzantine envoys doubtless indulged in occasional conversions. During his years of exile in Kherson (695–98), Justinian II married a Khazar princess, who became a Christian and assumed the name of Theodora, after the wife of Justinian I. Although no outright missionaries are recorded in Khazaria until the famous apostle to the Slavs, Constantine (Cyril) of Thessalonica, after the Russian attack on Constantinople in 860, the Christian mission had long been an effective instrument of imperial policy in that region as well. But these very political considerations also influenced the choice of the Khazarian rulers, who, like Dhu Nuwas before them, could preserve their total independence only by professing Judaism. As pagans they had been subjected to vigorous religious propaganda emanating from Byzantium and the Caliphate, each of which had tried to draw them into the orbit of its policies. Their conversion to Judaism was the equivalent of a declaration of neutrality between the two rival powers. Understandably, therefore, the Byzantine administration was not anxious to facilitate direct contacts between the Khazars and the Jews of Cordova, although the 'Umayyad caliphs, as perennial enemies of the 'Abbasids, could be considered friends of Byzantium. Through constant delays the Constantinople authorities prevented Ḥisdai's first messenger, Isaac ben Nathan, from reaching Khazaria.

The world-shaking events of the first half of the eighth century clinched the issue. The Byzantine menace, culminating in the invasion of Crimea in 710 with an alleged force of 100,000 men, was averted when the Caliphate attacked Byzantium and laid Constantinople under siege in 717. It was probably in connection with that major campaign that the Khazars first invaded Adharbaijan in the same year. They later vanquished a Muslim expeditionary force, in 730. This victory was followed by a series of reversals, from 732 on, climaxed by the surrender of the Khagan and his alleged temporary adoption of Islam in 737. The Khazars recovered speedily, however, and thenceforth stemmed Islam's advances in eastern Europe, just as Charles Martel's victory in 732 simultaneously checked its progress in the West. "But for the existence of the Khazars in the region north of the Caucasus," rightly observes D. M. Dunlop, "Byzantium, the bulwark of European civilization in the east, would have found itself outflanked by the Arabs, and the history of Christendom and Islam might well have been very different." [33]

Byzantine persecutions of Jews proved a serious handicap for the imperial statesmen in this strategically important area. Otherwise Khazar contacts with the Empire were far more direct than those with the Caliphate, whose principal centers were separated from the Khazar territories by the mountain ranges of the Caucasus and the inhospitable regions around the Caspian Sea. There also probably were in the Khazar realm as many Christians, those natural carriers of Christian ideals, as Muslims. Ibn Fadhlan's description confirms the impression that the two groups were about equal in size. Even in his day this well-informed Arab traveler observed that "the Jews constitute the smallest number, even though the king belongs to them." It stands to reason that before the conversion of the ruling classes the Jewish population was smaller still. Without the reinforcements constantly pouring in from the Empire, as a result of persecutions, they doubtless would have remained but a tiny minority, with negligible influence on Khazar affairs. As emphasized by the anonymous author of the Cambridge fragment, only the arrivals from other lands made it possible for the king of Khazaria, even before his conversion, to be circumcised. His wife, Seraḥ, her father, and a valiant Jewish warrior, all of whom took a hand in that conversion, evidently were either immigrants themselves or under the influence of new arrivals.[34]

Political considerations of this kind may also help to explain both the absence of missionary zeal on the part of the Khazar rulers and their apparent adoption of a watered-down version of Judaism. Unlike their Muslim and Byzantine neighbors, they did not view their faith as an instrument of imperial expansion and, hence, evidently treated their Judaism as a defensive rather than offensive weapon. Jewish influence made itself felt among such neighboring tribes as the Alans, described in the Cambridge fragment as "the most powerful and overbearing among the peoples in our parts," but there is no evidence of any governmental pressure behind it. There was perfect liberty of conscience in the whole Khazar empire. Visitors from the Caliphate or Byzantium witnessed with amazement the presence of a Khazar supreme tribunal consisting of seven judges, including two Jews, two Christians, two Muslims and one pagan, the latter according to Mas'udi being in charge of Slavonic, Russian, and other pagan judicial affairs. Nor was it at all surprising that one of the lesser Caucasian rulers, to satisfy all his mighty neighbors, celebrated the Sabbath on Friday with the Muslims, on Saturday with Jews, and on Sunday with Christians.[35]

KHAZAR SYNCRETISM

Khazar religion, too, especially in its early stages, was decidedly unorthodox—in many respects, unconsciously heterodox. Separated by great distances from the centers of Jewish learning, Bosporan and Caucasian Jews even in antiquity had revealed those strong syncretistic leanings. We recall, for example, their adoption of the pagan-Hellenistic method of liberating slaves in sanctuaries. Certainly the Jew, Pothos, son of Straton of Gorgippia (Anapa in the western Caucasus), who in 41 C.E. had recorded his liberation of a slave in the synagogue (*proseuché*) in an inscription beginning with the invocation of the highest and omnipotent God (*hypsistos pantokrator*) and ending with one addressed to God, the Earth, and the Sun (Frey, *Corpus,* I, No. 690; cf. Nos. 682 ff.), transmitted to his descendants a syncretistic faith which was the more dangerous to orthodoxy for its unconsciousness. Subsequent Jewish arrivals must have brought with them a variety of local customs and traditions which, in the strange and novel environment, tended to be reduced to the lowest common denominator. The seething sectarian strife in the whole Jewish world from the seventh to the tenth centuries also unavoidably communicated itself through newcomers and messengers to these distant regions.

When Bulan, perhaps the first hereditary king of Khazaria, adopted the monotheistic faith, he apparently embraced it only in the form of a minimal "religion of Abraham," which he had heard invoked by spokesmen of Christianity and Islam as well as of Judaism. He may have been attracted by a legend, current in Arab and Jewish circles, that Turks and other Mongols were descendants of Abraham's sons by Keturah. According to Ibn Fadhlan, the Khazar kings customarily had twenty-five wives. "Each of them is the daughter of one of the kings who confront him [the vassal princes], taken freely or by force. He also has sixty slave-girls, concubines, all of superb beauty. Each of them, concubines as well as free-born ladies, lives in a castle of her own." The khagan may indeed have felt that such a harem was a legitimate imitation of King Solomon's polygamous establishment and of the wise king's use thereof as an instrument of imperial policy. Hebrew books must have been extremely scarce. Certainly talmudic tractates had then only begun to be circulated in the more civilized countries. Even copies of Scripture had to be brought out of a cave, according to the Cambridge fragment. Later, too, the donation of a scroll of law or a scriptural codex to a synagogue, or the sale of such a costly object by one individual to another, was considered worthy of recording in an inscription.[36]

Only at the end of the century did King Obadiah conform more fully with the accepted tenets and observances of official Judaism. Afterwards, King Joseph, in his letter to Ḥisdai ibn Shapruṭ to which we owe that assertion, admitted the irregularity of the Khazar calendar. When Petaḥiah arrived in that vicinity he was shocked to learn that

> in the land of Kedar there are no Jews, only heretics. And Rabbi Petaḥiah asked them: Why do you not believe in the words of the sages? They replied: Because our fathers did not teach them to us. On the eve of Sabbath they cut all the bread which they eat on the Sabbath. They eat in the dark, and sit the whole day on one spot. Their prayers

consist only of psalms. And when Rabbi Petaḥiah imparted to them our ritual and prayer after meals they were pleased. They also said: We have never heard what the Talmud is.

Ignorance of talmudic laws, rather than outright Karaite influences as erroneously assumed by Petaḥiah, induced them to fall back upon the biblical legislation. This may, indeed, be the meaning of the cryptic remark in the Cambridge fragment that "the sages of Israel explained them [the books of the Torah] in terms of their first statements," and that they thus put an end to an internal religious controversy. Only thus can we explain also the Khazar reversion to the offering of animal sacrifices at local shrines, which embarrassed the eleventh-century Spanish jurist, Yehudah bar Barzillai al-Barceloni. Priests officiating at such temples seem to have been buried in full official attire, if we may so interpret a remarkable find in a cave near Phanagoria (Sennaja; the body was clad in leather vestments so tailored as to correspond roughly to the biblical descriptions). At the same time, the Khazars were not obstinate in their sectarian views. In adopting a great many Hebrew names, while apparently retaining also their native Khazar designations, they impartially accepted derivatives from biblical and postbiblical holidays such as Pesaḥ (Passover) and Ḥanukkah. The former name later became quite common among East-European Jews. Petaḥiah himself witnessed the arrival in Baghdad, a few years later, of a delegation from Meshekh (Khazaria) which induced some disciples of the wise to come with them to Khazaria. Of course, such sporadic teachers sent from Babylonia or Egypt were unable to keep the widely scattered Khazarian communities within the straight and narrow path of orthodoxy.[37]

The similarity between some Khazar customs, such as sitting in the dark on the Sabbath, and Karaite observances, and the fact that Firkovitch, the Karaite, had tried to marshal all possible evidence, genuine and forged, to persuade the Russian authorities of the antiquity of Karaite settlements in southern Russia, have influenced modern scholars to look for Karaite origins of the Khazar brand of Judaism. But Bulan's original conversion, we must remember, took place before the crystallization of 'Anan's schism in its home country. Many heterodox features of the Khazar faith, moreover, may readily be explained through a combination of ancient syncretistic antecedents, the influx of Jews from various lands, and sheer ignorance of postbiblical Jewish sources while the Pentateuch was readily available. Whatever sectarian influences existed emanated not only from Karaites, but also from the more radical eastern sects, which, at times sharply persecuted by the authorities, must have furnished a relatively large contingent of emigrés from the Caliphate. King Joseph's contention that Obadiah had imported Jewish scholars who interpreted for him "Scripture, Mishnah, Talmud and the whole order of prayers," even if authentic (the reference to a regular literary "order of prayers" before 800 is particularly suspect), need not refer to more than a temporary educational effort of the royal reformer, limited to a small circle at court and quickly spent in the inhospitable clime of widespread Khazar illiteracy. We may, nevertheless, accept on good faith the assertion of some Jewish scholars of Khazar descent encountered by Abraham ibn Daud in Toledo (they had undoubtedly acquired their learning in Spain) that their ancestors ("their remnant") had been Rabbanites.[38]

The preeminently political orientation of the Khazar rulers also injected certain peculiar elements into the religion of their people. Although generally tolerant, they were prepared to institute sharp reprisals for anti-Jewish measures in neighboring lands. On one occasion, we are told, when the Muslim populace destroyed a synagogue in an otherwise unidentified town called Dar al-Babunnaj, the Khazar regime reciprocated by demolishing the tower of the Muslim mosque and executing its muezzins in Khozran (923–24). Similarly, Romanos' forced conversion of Byzantine Jews was answered by King Joseph with the persecution of Christians in his realm. He apparently also induced his allies, the Alans, to expel all Christian priests (after 932). Since the Byzantines now instigated the Russians to attack their Khazar overlords, the Khazar commander, Pesaḥ, destroyed three Byzantine cities in Crimea. According to the Cambridge document, he also forced the Russian prince (whom the writer called Helgo-Oleg instead of Igor) to attack Con stantinople.[39]

Despite their abandonment of the originally elective khaganate and acceptance, perhaps in emulation of biblical precedents, of a hereditary dynasty, the Khazars shared with other Jews the belief in the ultimate restoration of the whole people to Zion. But they envisaged it chiefly in terms of a successful military campaign. Out of Khazaria apparently came that great twelfth-century messianic movement which, led by David Alroy (or Menahem ben Solomon Al-Roḥi; either David, or more likely, Menahem was the assumed messianic name), rapidly spread to Kurdistan, Adharbaijan, and other parts of Persia. It aimed at the military conquest of the Holy Land—not a completely hopeless undertaking, considering the prevailing anarchy in the intervening Muslim countries. Although this northern counterpart of the contemporary Christian Crusades failed to attract the active support of the Jewish masses in the Near East and was publicly repudiated by their "accredited" leaders in Baghdad, it seems to have left behind more than a mere romantic memory appealing to such modern writers as Benjamin Disraeli. Ever since, it has been suggested, the six-cornered "shield of David," theretofore mainly a decorative motif or a magical emblem, began its career toward becoming the chief national-religious symbol of Judaism. Long used interchangeably with the pentagram or the "Seal of Solomon," it was attributed to David in mystic and ethical German writings from the thirteenth century on, and appeared on the Jewish flag in Prague in 1527. Thus were laid the foundations for its ultimate glorification in the nineteenth century.[40]

Much as they were displeased by Khazar heterodoxy and lack of culture, the Jews of other lands were flattered by the existence of an independent Jewish state. Popular imagination found here a particularly fertile field. Just as the biblically minded Slavonic epics speak of "Jews" rather than Khazars, so did western Jews long after spin romantic tales around those "red Jews," so styled perhaps because of the slight Mongolian pigmentation of many Khazars whose main stock was of Ugro-Finnic extraction. At the same time their immediate neighbors, the Russians, called them "white Ugrians," in contrast to the Magyars, or "black Ugrians." Ḥisdai was typical in his delight to learn that "there is a place where there is a remnant and government for the Jewish dispersion and where they are neither oppressed nor ruled over." So enthusiastic was this Spanish-Jewish scholar and statesman that he was ready, upon verification of these reports, to leave his family and his influential post in Cordova and travel across land and sea to the

Jewish kingdom. Perhaps even more important was this matter for Jews in Christian lands, because of their age-old controversy with the Church over the nexus between the crucifixion and the fall of Jerusalem. No longer could writers like Isidore of Seville accuse them of "lying about I do not know what king of the tribe of Judah holding sway over some distant regions in the East." In Isidore's lifetime the Dhu Nuwas reign had been a matter of the past, but now there seemed to be a more enduring Jewish monarchy in Europe itself. Even before 864, a Westphalian monk, Christian Druthmar of Aquitania, noted that among the Gog and Magog, that is Hunnish, tribes there existed one called "Gazari," which is "circumcised and observes all of Judaism." Apart from the prestige factor some tangible benefits must also have accrued to Jewish merchants traveling through eastern Europe.[41]

Romantic tales of this kind, built around a solid kernel of historic reality, also helped to satisfy the curiosity of Jewish masses in Arab countries, long inured to story-telling of the most fantastic sort. To the European Jews they served as welcome news of a wider world, so different from that of their confined daily experience, and as a buoy in years of despair. Anticipating the Christian legends of Prester John, which they helped to form, Jews constantly elaborated ancient legends bearing on the survival of their Lost Ten Tribes in distant lands. They believed that, even in their day, the sons of Moses continued to live behind the mythical river Sambation, so called because its stream of stones (not water) regularly stopped flowing during their weekly day of rest.[42]

More realistic news from the Khazar kingdom continued to reach western Jewish communities through travelers, like Petaḥiah, even after that state's gradual disintegration under the blows of the Viking-Russian raiders in the latter part of the tenth century. The ancient community of Panticapaeum, continued under the Khazar name of Samkartsh, survived Sviatoslav's occupation in 965 and the subsequent vicissitudes, which in 1016 led to the establishment of the Duchy of Tmutarakan. Samkartsh al-Yahud, as Ibn al-Faqih called it, continued to play a role in Jewish history long after the city's name was shortened to Kertsh. In general, the reduced Khazar kingdom persevered. It waged a more or less effective defense against all foes until the middle of the thirteenth century, when it fell victim to the great Mongol invasion set in motion by Jenghiz Khan. Even then it resisted stubbornly until after the surrender of all its neighbors. Its population was largely absorbed by the Golden Horde which had established the center of its empire in Khazar territory. But before and after the Mongol upheaval the Khazars sent many offshoots into the unsubdued Slavonic lands, helping ultimately to build up the great Jewish centers of eastern Europe. As in many other lands, the destruction or departure of industrious Jewish farmers, artisans, and merchants left behind a void, which in those regions has only recently begun to be filled. During the half millennium (740–1250) of its existence, however, and its aftermath in the East European communities, this noteworthy experiment in Jewish statecraft doubtless exerted a greater influence on Jewish history than we are as yet able to envisage.[43]

AMONG SOUTHERN SLAVS AND MAGYARS

From Khazaria Jews began drifting into the open steppes of eastern Europe, during both the period of their country's affluence and that of its decline. In the era of Khazar overlordship over vast stretches of what is now southern Russia and the Ukraine, many Jewish officials and merchants appear to have settled in these subject territories. After Sviatoslav's victories and the ensuing decline of the Khazar Empire, on the other hand, refugees from the devastated districts, including Jews, sought shelter in the very lands of their conquerors. Here they met other Jewish groups and individuals migrating from west and south. Together with these arrivals from Germany and the Balkans, they began laying the foundations for a Jewish community which, especially in sixteenth-century Poland, outstripped all other contemporary areas of Jewish settlement in population density as well as in economic and cultural power.

Not that Jews had previously been an unfamiliar sight among the early Slavs and the non-Slavonic Magyars and Rumanians. Characteristic tombstone inscriptions, beginning with the second century C.E., have been found in various parts of the Balkans, in Pannonia (Hungary), and on the northern shores of the Black Sea. They testify to the presence of Jews, even organized Jewish communities, in these regions long before the formation of the first Slavonic states. Jews resided in Stobi, Oescus (Gigen), and Gran, we recall, as well as in other communities along Rome's Danubian frontier, under the protection of Roman law, before the arrival of the first "Serbs," Bulgars or Magyars, and certainly before the transformation of the Bulgarians from a Mongolian to a predominantly Slavic people. By one of the usual ironies of Jewish history, these new arrivals, adopting the general Christian reinterpretation of history, began viewing the Jews as "aliens," living amidst their own, the "native," majority.

Of course, in view of the extreme paucity of extant sources, these chance epigraphic records do not vouchsafe the continuity of Jewish settlement in all these regions from Roman to medieval times. These tombstones themselves reveal an unusual degree of assimilation of Balkan Jewry, understandable enough in sparse and scattered settlements maintaining but few contacts with the major centers of Jewish learning in Palestine and Babylonia. Even the Tiberian Jew, who died at the age of forty and was buried in Dalmatian Salona, bore the purely Roman name of Aurelius Dionysius. He who inscribed the tombstone of an eighteen-year old girl in Soklos, Pannonia, called her Septimia Maria Judea, and yet did not hesitate to introduce that inscription with the customary pagan siglum, D.M. (*Diis Manibus,* or to the Divine Shades of the Dead). The recently reconstructed inscription of a Jewish customs official and communal elder in another Pannonian city reads:

> In honor of the eternal God, for the salute of our lord, the pious and happy Emperor Severus Alexander and the Empress Julia Mamea, mother of the Emperor, Cosmius, head of the custom station of Spondill[a] and archisynagogus of the Jews, is glad to fulfill his vow.

Another archisynagogus, head of the community of Sofia, though himself bearing the Hebrew name Ioses, had a father named Maximinus, and a wife named Qyria, and followed the pagan custom of erecting a tombstone for himself and his wife while both were alive.[44]

Like their non-Jewish neighbors, these frail communities sustained grievous losses during the upheavals of the barbarian migrations. Yet their basic tenacity carried them through these recurrent crises, enabling them to maintain a measure of historic continuity until the emergence of new and more vigorous settlements from the tenth century on. The absence of positive records is not at all surprising. Diaspora Jewry outside Babylonia was long totally inarticulate, while the new barbarian settlers had to struggle for a long time before they learned the art of writing. Only after their adoption of Christianity did the Croats, Czechs, and Poles, as well as the Magyars, take over the Latin script together with the Catholic faith; the eastern Slavs found in the adaptation of the Greek script in the "Cyrillic" alphabet a more adequate phonetic instrument. We shall see presently that, with the aid of their Hebrew script, Jews may have been instrumental in helping the apostles to the Slavs, Cyril (Constantine) and Methodius, to perform this significant pioneering task.

With the conversion of many Khazars, Judaism gained strength not only in the far-flung possessions of the Jewish khagans, but also in all neighboring lands. If we are to believe the communication addressed by King Joseph to Ḥisdai, on one occasion the Alans inhabiting the Caucasian mountains came to the assistance of the Khazars, attacked by a vast and heterogeneous coalition brought together by the Byzantines, because "many of the Alans" had been converted to Judaism. As in Khazaria proper, these converts mixed with some native Jews who had settled in these mountains in ancient times, and they became the ancestors of the so-called Mountain Jews of the Caucasus, whose racial and cultural peculiarities were to attract considerable attention in modern times. It is to them as well as to the Khazars that Eldad ha-Dani referred in his description of the remnants of the tribes of Issaschar, Simon, and half of Menasseh who "receive tribute from twenty-five kingdoms including some Muslims." [45]

Far more significant for the subsequent destinies of the Jewish people and the western world as a whole was the impact of Khazarian Jews on the neighboring Slavonic countries. Our information concerning both the northern and the Balkan Slavs of the eighth and ninth centuries is extremely limited. But it seems that, on a lesser scale than in the early centuries of Christianity, the presence there of Jewish communities helped pave the way for the spread of the daughter religion as well. Even in neighboring Bulgaria the Byzantine mission had made but slow advances until the ninth century. Here the older Jewish settlements had received considerable reinforcements through Byzantine Jewish captives carried away by Bulgarian raiders, for example Czar Krum in 811. In their noteworthy correspondence with Pope Nicholas I of 866, the Bulgarian leaders still evinced considerable hesitation in choosing between the Eastern and Western forms of Christianity, and they expressed their theological bewilderment about the difference between either form and Judaism. They were uncertain, for example, whether they ought to emphasize faith or good works, celebrate their weekly day of rest on Saturdays or Sundays, and treat the meat of all animals as permissible for consumption. They even asked whether persons converted to Christianity by a Jew were to be considered Christians or Jews. Nicholas I, simply assuming that these persons had been baptized and quoting Augustine, declared that the deficiencies of a person administering baptism did not invalidate the act itself. This twilight situation between Judaism and Christianity explains also some aspects of Bulgarian sectarianism. The most important and enduring of the Balkan sects, the Bogomils, first appearing in the ninth century, betrayed principally Manichaean influences. Heirs of Marcionite gnosticism, they also repudiated the continued divine authority of the Old Testament. But in their persistent denial of the divine birth of Christ and their spiritual rather than literal interpretation of the Gospel miracles, they may well have been influenced by Jewish teachers.[46]

If we are to accept claims of some Bulgarian nationalists, Methodius and his younger brother Cyril (originally Tvardina, renamed for Christian reasons Constantine), though natives of Thessalonica, were Bulgarian Slavs. Cyril, especially, was able to acquire some knowledge of Hebrew on his missionary journey to the great commercial city of Kherson, where he is said to have studied under a Samaritan teacher. He put that knowledge to good use in developing both the Glagolitic and Cyrillic alphabets, the former used in Croatia to the seventeenth century. Its indebtedness to the Hebrew alphabet in at least eleven characters, representing in part the Slavonic sounds, has long been recognized. Cyril also utilized his knowledge of Jewish letters in seeking to persuade Jews of the superiority of Christianity. Although Cyril's controversial tract against Judaism, allegedly translated into Slavonic by his brother Methodius, is not preserved, we may reconstruct some of his arguments from three chapters in his biography. For all these efforts he received a commendatory letter from Patriarch Photius, himself probably of Khazar descent. Though never large, the Jewish settlement in the Bulgarian czardom included in the twelfth century such Jewish scholars as Tobiah ben Eliezer, author of the Midrash *Leqaḥ ṭob,* and his pupil, Moses of Castoria. A converted Jew, Leo Mung, became patriarch of Ochrida and Bulgaria's ecclesiastical head. Bulgarian Jewry, constantly reinforced by emigrés from Byzantium, who early formed a Greek congregation in Sardica (Sofia), thus succeeded in weathering the successive calamities which befell their kingdom until its subjection by the Ottoman Turks.[47]

No less obscure is the story of the Jewish communities in present-day Yugoslavia. Here too, the Jews look back to a fairly uninterrupted evolution from the days of the Roman Empire. Especially on the Dalmatian coast, where the Greek and Latin traditions intermingled with the new Slavonic civilization and where, as late as 1381 a trilingual inscription underscored the fusion of these three cultural strains, Jews seem to have persisted under the new conditions. They continued to live both in the areas which were permanently to come under the sway of Rome (Croatia and Slovenia), and in those where ultimately the Eastern Church was to prevail (Serbia, Montenegro, and Albania). According to one theory, the king of "Gebalim," who figured prominently in the Khazar correspondence, was none other than Krešimir II (958–90) of Croatia. Whoever this king may have been, his delegation to Cordova included two Jews, Saul and Joseph, who undertook to forward Ḥisdai's letter to the king of Khazaria. These Jewish envoys expected their monarch, evidently in recognition of Ḥisdai's good offices, to exert himself to send the letter through Hungary and Russia (the Ukraine) to the Volga Bulgars, from where it would reach its destination. Curiously, despite this roundabout journey required for the dispatch of a simple letter, the envoys recalled that, some six years before their departure, a blind Jewish scholar, Amram, claiming to have served at the court of the Khazarian khagan, had reached their country.[48]

Once converted, the Slavonic countries entered the stream of biblical tradition. They soon began making contributions of their own to Christian literature, first in the form of translations and later through their independent liturgy and works of scholarship in the Old Slavonic dialect. Since they often had access to eastern sources no longer extant today, they unwittingly enriched Jewish learning as well. In dealing with ancient times we have had several occasions to refer to data preserved only by the Slavonic Josephus. Students of Jewish Apocrypha and Pseudepigrapha have likewise been indebted to variant readings, even entire passages, preserved only in Slavonic translations. Most of these versions were reproduced from Greek texts circulating in the Byzantine Empire, in themselves often but renditions from lost Hebrew or Aramaic originals. We know too little about the time and circumstances which brought forth each particular translation; for instance, that of the important apocryphal book of Enoch. We cannot tell, therefore, whether Jews were consulted by the translators, or were otherwise instrumental in preserving and distributing some of these ancient texts. In any case, by helping to bridge the gap between the two Testaments, these translations brought the medieval Slav intelligentsia closer to an understanding of its Jewish neighbors and their religion.[49]

Frontiers then and long after being extremely fluid, the early history of the Jewish communities among the southern Slavs is in part also the history of Hungarian Jewry. Before and after the country's occupation by the Magyars in 895, Jews lived in many sections of the formerly Roman provinces of Pannonia and Dacia. Their continued existence in the tenth century is borne out by Ḥisdai's brief reference to Hungarian Jews who would help transmit his message to Khazaria, and by some such uncertain records as a document of 1526 in which the Jewish community of Sopron (Ödenburg) claimed that some of its tombstones were six hundred years old. There also was a close connection between the Magyars and the Khazars which went back some three centuries before the elevation of Arpad upon a shield in a Khazar manner, according to Constantine Porphyrogenitus. The twelfth-century Byzantine historian John Cinnamus mentioned a group of *Khalisioi* observing Mosaic laws among the Hungarian allies of Dalmatia in the war of 1154. Whether or not this obscure name has anything to do with the Hebrew term *ḥaluṣ* (pioneer), Cinnamus' statement attests the presence of a recognizable group of Jews, or at least of a Judaizing sect whose existence would in turn presuppose some direct Jewish influence. If we are to accept Tolstov's theory, these *Khalisioi* (to be identified with the *Khwalisi* of the Primary Russian chronicle), as well as the *Khabaroi* mentioned by Constantine Porphyrogenitus, were originally Jewish groups from Khwarizm-Khiva who reached the Hungarian plain in the ninth and tenth centuries.[50]

It was that Judaizing influence which induced the Council of Szabolcs in 1092 to forbid Jews to marry Christians, to own Christian slaves, and to work on Sundays and Christian holidays (canons 10, 26). While all these regulations had long been standardized in both Eastern and Western Canon law, their formal adoption by a Hungarian synod doubtless reflected a newly felt local need. The Council of Gran (about 1114) prohibited altogether the employment of Christian servants by Jews (canon 61). Clearly, even the Church did not agitate for the curtailment of Jewish rights beyond what it considered long-accepted practice. The government as such issued no formal laws concerning Jews, but let them enjoy practically all the rights of other subjects. This is indeed a contributory cause to the absence of reliable sources concerning Jewish life in that early period of the Hungarian kingdom. The situation changed after the passage of the anti-Jewish crusaders in 1097, against whom King Coloman (1095–1116) tried to protect not only the older Jewish inhabitants, but also many new arrivals from Bohemia and Austria. In 1098, we are told, even some of the remaining Jews of Bohemia had surreptitiously sent their accumulated treasures to Hungary and Poland. This sudden influx of Jewish refugees seems to have created sufficient resentments in the country for the king to issue a decree restricting Jewish settlement to the major episcopal cities. This restriction was in sharp contrast with the dispersal of Muslims through the countryside, combined with the general outlawry of Islam and the prohibition for its former adherents to marry within their own group. The king evidently merely wished to hold Jews under the bishops' closer surveillance. He thus hoped to promote Jewish commerce, and at the same time to remove Jews from rural areas and their resultant direct influence on the peasant masses. To obviate controversies, he also decreed that loan contracts between Jewish creditors and Christian borrowers, or vice versa, should be entered into only in the presence of witnesses of both faiths. On the other hand, he specifically guaranteed the Jews' freedom in signing contracts and their ability to testify in court, a prerogative often denied them in other Christian countries. From the novel prohibition of the Golden Bull of 1222 forbidding Jews to hold the posts of mintmasters, taxgatherers, and supervisors of the royal salt monopoly, we may judge that a sufficiently large number of Jews had previously occupied these positions to arouse the ire of the Hungarian gentry, under whose pressure recalcitrant Andrew II (1205–35) enacted that bull.[51]

IN RUSSIA AND POLAND

We know even less about the beginnings of Jewish settlement in the vast stretches of land located north of the Carpathian Mountains and the Black Sea. Since those territories lay outside the confines of the Roman Empire, we do not even possess that meager epigraphic material which sheds some light on the early Jewish settlements in the Danubian basin. The general history of that area is likewise shrouded in almost impenetrable darkness, with but few rays of light emerging from the nondescript references by ancient geographers like Pliny. Only in recent years have archaeological investigations conducted by Soviet scholars disclosed the existence, from the seventh century on, of a fairly affluent civilization in Kievan Russia. Excavations in Rostov on the Don, for example, have shown that this locality had at that time been the site of a fortified city, inhabited by many skilled craftsmen. We need not accept the archaeologists' overconfident conclusions from these admittedly spotty data and subscribe to their theory that these areas had an uninterrupted civilized life reaching back to 3000

B.C.E. And yet we must revise the formerly regnant view that civilization in these regions began only with the advent of Gothic and Scandinavian invaders.[52]

Such archaeological discoveries devoid of epigraphic materials do not enable us to distinguish between Jewish and non-Jewish inhabitants. Not only are clear-cut Jewish sources totally absent, but, unlike the western nations, the ancestors of the Slavonic peoples now inhabiting the vast stretches of the Soviet Union and its western neighbors remained almost completely inarticulate until the beginning of the second millennium. All one can now assert, therefore, is that Jews may have lived in these regions for several centuries before their first appearance in more or less reliable records.

Curiously, the few casual statements found in such Jewish sources as the Khazar correspondence and the travelogue of Ibrahim ibn Ya'qub belong to the oldest literary references of any kind to the Slavs of East Central Europe. Even the term "Canaan," often applied in later Hebrew literature to the Slavonic countries, reflected in many ways the consciousness of medieval Jewry of its immemorial ties with these lands, including the formerly Slavonic parts of eastern Germany. This designation, to be sure, was later rationalized as a derivative from the old identification of Slavs with slaves, of whom they were then indeed a major source of supply. The emphatic biblical prediction, "Cursed be Canaan; a servant of servants [*'ebed 'abadim,* or rather a slave of slaves] shall he be unto his brethren," led to the easy linkage of the Slavonic peoples with the descendants of Canaan. Benjamin of Tudela's characteristic comment evidently echoed a Jewish opinion widely held in the twelfth century. Referring to Bohemia and its capital, Prague, the traveler added: "This is the commencement of the land of Slavonia [Esclavonia] and the Jews who dwell there call it Canaan, because the men of that land (the Slavs) sell their sons and their daughters to the other nations." This identification seems, however, to have followed an older myth concerning the emigration from Palestine to Slavonic Europe of some ancient Canaanites after their displacement by the Israelites under Joshua —a myth undoubtedly reflecting memories of Semitic settlers there many centuries before their first appearance in historical records. Its origin would thus be akin to that which had led North Africans, too, to consider themselves descendants of Canaanite emigrés, because of the vivid memories of the Phoenician colonization of Carthage. Be this as it may, the very name "Canaan" must have evoked in the minds of medieval Jews associations of both kinship and hostility with their Slavonic neighbors.[53]

Living among these pagan peoples, Jews, especially those arriving from neighboring Khazaria where they had had a taste of political power, tried to propagandize for their faith. This is at least the bearing of the famous story of Vladimir of Kiev's (980–1015) conversion to Christianity. As told by the Russian Primary Chronicle, the story is largely a replica of that reported in connection with the previous conversion of the Khazar king to Judaism. Here, however, the debate of the representatives of the various faiths before the king ended with the defeat of the Jewish spokesmen, allegedly because the Jews' loss of national independence and their general political powerlessness did not seem inviting to the ambitious Rus grand-duke. Nevertheless the Jews seemed unwilling to concede defeat, and for years to come leading churchmen felt it incumbent upon themselves to persuade the Russian public of the superiority of the Christian faith. The first native Russian metropolitan, Hilarion—all his predecessors and many successors had to be recruited from Byzantium—wrote a special treatise contrasting "The Mosaic Law and the Grace and Truth of Jesus Christ" (after 1051). He doubtless borrowed some of his arguments from Constantine-Cyril, whose controversial tract may still have been at his disposal. The famous Petcherskii (Cave) Monastery in Kiev, founded by Hilarion after his deposition in 1053 under Byzantine pressure (he was apparently renamed Nikon), remained a center of anti-Jewish propaganda. Nestor's biography of another famous monk, Theodosius, abbot of that monastery (*ca.* 1062–74), reports with elation his clandestine meetings with Jews. The abbot hoped, we are told, that his missionary efforts would arouse his Jewish interlocutors sufficiently for them to murder him, and thus assure him the death of a martyr. Another member of that distinguished monastery, Nikita, is said on the other hand to have succumbed to Jewish arguments and tried to spread some Jewish doctrines among the other recluses, but ultimately to have repented.[54]

Nor did the Kievan Jews abandon their political ambitions. Upon the death of Swiatopolk II in 1113, and the election of reluctant Vladimir II Monomakh (1113–25), the latter's partisans attacked some Kievan grandees "and subsequently threw themselves upon the Jews and plundered them." This assault probably was but a popular reaction to some Jews siding with the sons of the deceased grand-duke, the community suffering here, as often elsewhere, for misplaced political ambitions of individual members. According to Vernadsky, "there was no general Jewish pogrom. Wealthy Jewish merchants suffered because of their association with Sviatopolk's speculations, especially his hated monopoly on salt." In any case, upon accepting the throne Vladimir restored order and apparently took no retaliatory measures against the Jews. More divided was Jewish opinion sixty years later, when a court cabal led to the assassination of Bogoljubov (1154–74). While two prominent court Jews, Ephrem Moisevich and Anbal Yassin, took a leading part in the conspiracy, other Jews seem to have remained loyal to the reigning monarch. We know even less about Jewish religious activities and their continued conversionist efforts, direct or indirect. Significantly, some of the important sectarian movements so characteristic of the later history of the Russian Church were known under the names of *Judaizanti* (Judaizers) and *Subotniki* (Seventh Day Observers), and possibly had their deeper roots in the earlier periods of Russian Jewish contacts. In view of the extreme paucity of documents concerning the more overt Judeo-Russian relations before and long after Vladimir's conversion, the much-debated problems of the rise of these sects and the direct Jewish influences on their beliefs and rituals are not likely to be satisfactorily solved for many years to come.[55]

In any case, these political and religious adventures did not interfere with the gradual growth of the Jewish community, which was steadily reinforced by arrivals from Khazaria, now increasingly under Russian control, as well as from Byzantium and the West. According to an unconfirmed report of a Czech chronicler, Hajek, some western Jews, arriving in Prague in 1064, were not allowed to stay there, and moved on to Greek (that is Greek Orthodox) lands. Kiev's Jewish quarter, located near the so-called "Jewish Gate," one of the three foremost entrances to the city, suffered from a devastating fire in 1124 and from frequent civil wars, such as that between two pretenders in 1146. It nevertheless embraced a community quite substantial in numbers and wealth, which began to show signs of intellectual awakening in the twelfth century. A local scholar R. Moses of Kiev, belonged to the distinguished band of disciples gathered around Jacob Tam in Rameru, France. He also corresponded on matters of law with the Baghdad gaon, Samuel ben 'Ali. Nor did the Jews encounter serious difficulties in pursuing their various occupations. If under Vladimir II a council of nobles, meeting in Wydobycz, enacted certain restrictions on the rate of interest charged by Jewish creditors, this regulation did not seriously handicap Jewish moneylenders. It certainly infringed on none of the other mercantile or industrial activities of Jewry in the Ukrainian metropolis which a western admirer, Adam of Bremen, called "the rival of Constantinople and the most shining gem of the Greek Church." [56]

In neighboring Poland, too, the beginnings of Jewish settlement are enveloped in the mist of the general historic evolution of several western Slavonic tribes, ultimately united by the strongest among them, named Polans. Remarkably, Jews appear in the earliest myths connected with the formation of the Polish state. An old legend reported that when the various tribes decided to choose a king, their choice fell on a Jew, Abraham Prochownik, who resigned, however, in favor of a native peasant named Piast, the alleged founder of the famed Piast dynasty. However anachronistic the reference to "powder" at that time may appear (if indeed the name Prochownik is derived from it), the presence of Jews at the birth of the first Polish dynasty is far from improbable.

Remarkably, the first outsider to mention the kingdom of Mieszko, the first historic king of Poland (963–92), was the Jew Ibrahim ibn Ya'qub, possibly Ḥisdai ibn Shaprut's envoy to Emperor Otto. In the brief excerpt from his travelogue quoted by Al-Bakri, Ibrahim left behind an interesting description of customs prevailing in the Slavonic countries, including Mieszko's realm, which he called the Kingdom of the North and "the most extended of Slav lands." Ibrahim's account confirms the general trade relations among the western Slavonic peoples and their Prussian and Hungarian neighbors, converging on Prague and other western cities. Although Jews are mentioned specifically only together with the Muslim and Turkish (Hungarian) merchants arriving from Hungary, there is little doubt that they came to Prague also from Khazaria and the West, and possibly from Karako (Cracow). There is, therefore, an element of truth also in another legend, which describes the arrival in Poland of a large delegation of German Jews, all of them curiously bearing Spanish Jewish names. It was in Poland, particularly, that this western Jewish wave encountered the equally large influx of Jews from the east, especially Khazaria, both leaving behind many place names like Żydowo (mentioned in the districts of Gniezno and Kalisz in 1203 and 1211 respectively), Kozari, and Kozarzów. Apparently entire villages were founded by Jews and Khazars as far west as Greater Poland.[57]

Whatever their origin, Jews seem from the outset to have played a certain role in the Polish state and economy. Among the most remarkable vestiges of Jewish life are the fairly numerous coins bearing Hebrew inscriptions. Apparently Jewish mintmasters, unfamiliar with the Glagolitic or the western Slavonic alphabets then still in the early stages of their evolution, used Hebrew characters to place on these bracteates (thin plates inscribed only on one side) such identifications as "Mieszko, king of Poland," "From the House of Abraham ben Joseph the Prince" (probably the minter himself) or else some such simple benedictions as "Blessing" or "Luck." These coins are extant in too numerous specimens to be dismissed as simple freaks. Of course, the name could also refer to Mieszko II (1025–34) or Mieszko III (1173–77, 1201–2). Mintmasters of that period, as M. Gumowski rightly observed, were "persons designated not only to coin ducal money, but also to distribute it in the provinces and to exchange older for newer coins. The latter privilege made them also bankers and money-changers. Such exchange, always resulting in a profit for the Treasury and a loss for the population, invariably turned the minters into unwelcome guests." But these unpleasant by-products of minting doubtless characterized later attempts at conversions with depreciated currency, more than the original coinage.[58]

We know very little about Jewish life during that early period, but Jews evidently enjoyed full freedom of action and were subjected to few, if any, legal restrictions. Bishop Adalbert (Wojtech) of Prague, the missionary among the then heathen Prussians (997), and Queen Judith, wife of the weak monarch Ladislas Herrmann (1079–1102), were praised by chroniclers for their charitable work in ransoming Christian slaves from Jewish traders. But both Adalbert and Judith came from Bohemia, where German concepts and institutions had already begun to take deeper roots. Obviously, the native Polish state and church had not yet attempted to outlaw Jewish ownership of Christian slaves, elsewhere one of the prime postulates of Christian legislation. It was only in the thirteenth century, as we shall see in a later context, that the Polish Church ventured to adopt resolutions aimed at segregating Jews from their Christian neighbors. Even then, however, it did not dare to propose the suppression of Jewish landholdings such as were recorded especially in the vicinity of Breslau before 1203.[59]

In the eleventh and twelfth centuries Polish and other Slavonic Jews make their first appearance in the growing Hebrew literature in France and Germany. Brutzkus has successfully identified R. Yehudah ha-Kohen, whose responsum was later reproduced verbatim in Isaac bar Moses of Vienna's *Sefer Or Zaru'a,* with the rabbi of Mayence by that name living in 1028–70. Mentioning the capture of Jews by Russians from the city of Przemyśl located on the frontier between Poland and Red Russia, this responsum attests the existence of a Jewish community there as early as 1031. A distinguished twelfth-century western rabbi, Eliezer bar Nathan, actually visited one of the Slavonic countries ("the land of Canaan") and from time to time referred to East-European Jewish customs.[60]

Through that mist of ages which engulfs eastern Europe before 1200, we thus note the emergence of Jewish communities amidst young and vigorous Slavonic tribes, then first to enter the scene of world history. The importance of these communities for the general history of the Jewish people still lay in the future. But the contours of the new evolution had already begun to take shape in that period.

NEW HORIZONS

Emergence of these new communities was connected with the perennial struggle for supremacy over the Mediterranean world between Byzantium and the Muslim states, during which Jews often sustained severe losses. Victimized along with other inhabitants in the war-torn lands, they also suffered as Jews from the changing power constellations. At least twice, under Heraclius and again under Leo the Isaurian, a great imperial crisis resulted in total intolerance and the formal suppression of Judaism throughout the empire. Two later decrees of expulsion and forced conversion likewise were but reflections of overwhelming international as well as domestic tensions.

At the same time, the constant wars and war preparations absorbed so many Byzantine energies that many imperial decrees were nullified from the outset by the lack of determined execution on the part of an unwilling, if not venal, bureaucracy. The deep internal divisions among the Christian majority and the great heterogeneity of local usages likewise hindered any concerted imperial action. In the case of Jewish mass conversions, the empire altogether lacked effective law enforcement agencies which, like the later Inquisitorial courts, might try to distinguish between sincere and insincere converts. After the passage of a few years, many secret Jews publicly reverted to their former faith. Some others returned from foreign countries where they had sought shelter during the periods of violent persecution. Under the more tolerant regimes—and we must not lose sight of the rather exceptional and temporary nature of the four attempts made totally to outlaw Judaism—there was even a modicum of new Jewish immigration from other lands. Prompted by the quest for economic betterment, that eternal mainspring of human migrations, some Jews left the politically and legally more hospitable Muslim lands and settled in the Byzantine Empire. Arrivals like these brought along with them the sectarian divisions which had emerged in the eastern lands. Only thus can we account for the rise of the influential Karaite community in Constantinople during the tenth and eleventh centuries.

Byzantine pressures, economic as well as political, on the other hand, forced many Jews to seek new opportunities in the underdeveloped areas across the Black Sea and the Danube. Here the dust of barbarian migrations began to settle only toward the end of the first millennium with the emergence of new and more or less stable nations. While closer to the Adriatic and Aegean Seas the permanent boundary lines between Greeks, Latins, and Slavs began to be drawn as early as the sixth century, Hungary, Rumania, and southern Russia were subject to many changes in their ethnic composition for several more centuries. These recurrent upheavals were not altogether inviting to a pacific population like the Jewish. Nevertheless, yielding to the strong external pressures, Jews expanded northwards and eastwards from the ancient Roman frontiers.

Forced conversions of Jews proved a boomerang for Byzantine policies in so far as the conversion of the ruling classes of Khazaria to Judaism, undoubtedly accomplished in part by Byzantine refugees, helped to withdraw this powerful empire from the control of Constantinople. Unwittingly, however, these Jewish refugees even in exile served Byzantium's imperial interests. They not only spread some rudiments of Graeco-Byzantine culture, but, as in antiquity, they also prepared the ground for the Christian mission by teaching their pagan neighbors the fundamentals of their historical and ethical monotheism, and by acquainting them with their biblical tradition. The conversion of Russians to Greek orthodoxy, an event of prime magnitude in the history of mankind, was symbolically accomplished by the Thessalonican missionary Cyril with the aid of the Hebrew alphabet and a new translation of Scripture. It demonstrated on another plane the historic function of the *praeparatio evangelica* performed by Jews beyond their own ken or will, and in a fashion entirely different from that usually defined by this patristic term.

At the same time, these Jews built also for their own future in a way transcending their wildest expectations. Saadiah may have known of Jews going to Khazaria, as he knew of those who went to India. But even in the years of his greatest despondency he hardly dreamed of the regions west of the Caspian Sea ever becoming major centers of Judaism. Two centuries later, Maimonides set his hopes for the perpetuation of Jewish learning on the youthful and struggling communities of western Europe. But even if he had heard from his rival Samuel ben 'Ali of an inquiry by a Jewish scholar stemming from remote Kiev, he would hardly have suggested that in these regions, inhabited by barbarian Slavs known in the Near East principally as the major sources of supply of white slaves, would before long arise populous, affluent, and learned Jewish communities, which within three or four centuries would assume the leadership of the Jewish people. Little informed as we are about that early period of gestation, and beset though we may feel with chronological and other uncertainties, we secure at least some glimpses of the new forces emerging on these sidelines of world history. Once again penetrating the periphery of human civilization, Jews performed a major pioneering service in helping to open up vast and promising lands for more advanced forms of human coexistence. Before long they also helped to integrate these young countries into the Western world then entering upon an era of its greatest expansion.

NOTES

ABBREVIATIONS

AASOR	Annual of the American Schools of Oriental Research
AHDE	Anuario de historia del derecho español
AJA	American Journal of Archaeology
AJSL	American Journal of Semitic Languages and Literatures
Annuaire	Brussels, Université Libre, Institut de philologie et d'histoire orientales et slaves, Annuaire
ATR	Anglican Theological Review
BASOR	Bulletin of the American Schools of Oriental Research
BJPES	Bulletin (*Yediot*) of the Jewish Palestine (later Israel) Exploration Society
BSOAS	Bulletin of the School of Oriental and African Studies (University of London)
BZ	Byzantinische Zeitschrift
CHE	Cuadernos de historia de España
CHR	Catholic Historical Review
CJ	Corpus Juris Civilis
CRAI	Comptes rendus de l'Académie des Inscriptions et des belles lettres
C.Th.	Theodosian Code
EI	Encyclopaedia of Islam
EJ	Encyclopaedia Judaica
HJ	Historia Judaica
HUCA	Hebrew Union College Annual
IC	Islamic Culture
JA	Journal asiatique
JAOS	Journal of the American Oriental Society
JNES	Journal of Near Eastern Studies (continuation of *AJSL*)
JPOS	Journal of the Palestine Oriental Society
JQR	Jewish Quarterly Review (new series, unless otherwise stated)
JRAS	Journal of the Royal Asiatic Society
JSS	Jewish Social Studies
Kohut Mem. Vol.	Jewish Studies in Memory of George A. Kohut. New York, 1935.
KS	Kirjath Sepher, Quarterly Bibliographical Review
Löw Mem. Vol.	Semitic Studies in Memory of Immanuel Löw. Budapest, 1947.
Marx Jub. Vol.	Alexander Marx Jubilee Volume. 2 vols. New York, 1950. A volume each of English and Hebrew essays.

MGH	Monumenta Germaniae Historica
MGWJ	Monatsschrift für Geschichte und Wissenschaft des Judentums
MIOG	Mitteilungen des Instituts für österreichische Geschichtsforschung, Vienna
MJC	Mediaeval Jewish Chronicles, ed. by A. Neubauer.
M.Q.	Mo'ed Qaṭan (talmudic tractate)
M.T.	Moses ben Maimon's Mishneh Torah (Code)
MW	Moslem World
OLZ	Orientalistische Literaturzeitung
PAAJR	Proceedings of the American Academy for Jewish Research
PEQ	Palestine Exploration Quarterly *or* Palestine Exploration Fund Quarterly Statement
PG	Patrologiae Cursus Completus, series Graeca, ed. by J. P. Migne
PL	Patrologiae Cursus Completus, series Latina, ed. by J. P. Migne
PO	Patrologia Orientalis
Poznanski Mem. Vol.	Livre d'hommage à la mémoire du Samuel Poznanski. Warsaw, 1927.
QDAP	Quarterly of the Department of Antiquities in Palestine
r.	Midrash Rabbah (Gen. r. = Bereshit rabbah; Lam. r. = Ekhah rabbati, etc.)
RB	Revue biblique (includes wartime *Vivre et Penser*)
REJ	Revue des études juives
Resp.	Responsa (*Teshubot* or *She'elot u-teshubot*
RH	Revue historique
RHPR	Revue d'histoire et de philosophie religieuses
RHR	Revue d'histoire des religions
RIDA	Revue internationale des droits de l'antiquité (II–V = Mélanges Fernand de Visscher, I–IV)
RSO	Rivista di studi orientali
Saadia Anniv. Vol.	American Academy for Jewish Research. Texts and Studies, Vol. II. Saadia Anniversary Volume. New York, 1943.
SB	Sitzungsberichte der Akademie der Wissenschaften (identified by city: e.g. *SB* Berlin, Heidelberg, Vienna)
Shorter EI	Shorter Encyclopaedia of Islam, ed. by H. A. R. Gibb and J. H. Kramers. Leiden, 1953.
Starr Mem. Vol.	The Joshua Starr Memorial Volume: Studies in History and Philology. New York, 1953. Jewish Social Studies, Vol. V
Vienna Mem. Vol.	Sefer ha-Zikkaron le-bet ha-midrash le-rabbanim. Jerusalem, 1946.
VSW	Vierteljahrsschrift für Sozial- und Wirtschaftsgeschichte

Weil Jub. Vol.	Gotthold E. Weil Jubilee Volume. Jerusalem, 1952.
YB	Yivo Bleter
Yellin Jub. Vol.	Minḥah le-David: Jubilee Volume in Honor of David Yellin. Jerusalem, 1935.
ZDMG	Zeitschrift der Deutschen Morgenländischen Gesellschaft
ZDPV	Zeitschrift des Deutschen Palästina Vereins. Vols. LXVIII (1948) ff. are entitled Beiträge zur biblischen Landes- und Altertumskunde.
Zlotnik Jub. Vol.	Minḥah li-Yehudah. Jubilee Volume in Honor of Judah Leb Zlotnik. Jerusalem, 1950.
ZNW	Zeitschrift für die neutestamentliche Wissenschaft und die Kunde der älteren Kirche

NOTES

CHAPTER XVI: THE PREISLAMIC WORLD

1. J. D. Mansi, *Sacrorum conciliorum . . . collectio,* IV, 1287 ff. (Ephesus), VI, 690 ff., VII, 102 ff. (Chalcedon; these and other early conciliar decisions are available also in English translations or summaries by W. R. Clark in C. J. Hefele, *A History of the Councils of the Church from the Original Documents,* III, 61 ff., 310 ff., 344 f.); Pseudo-Zachariah (Rhetor) of Mitylene, *Historia ecclesiastica,* VIII.1.6 (a near contemporary), in the Latin translation by E. W. Brooks, II, 42, 57, and in the English translation by F. J. Hamilton and E. W. Brooks, entitled *The Syriac Chronicle Known as That of Zachariah of Mitylene,* pp. 190–212; Michael Syrus, *Chronique,* VIII.12, ed. and trans. by J. B. Chabot, II, 218 (Syriac), 91 (French); repeated by John of Ephesus and a Coptic writer, cited by J. Juster in *Empire romain,* I, 229, n. 2, and by J. Parkes in *The Conflict of the Church and the Synagogue,* p. 303, where further instances of the use of "Jew" for mere name-calling are assembled. Juster has also pointed out (I, 80 n. 6) that the canons of both these councils, and hence also their anti-Jewish references, received formal approval by the respective emperors, Theodosius II and Marcian. Nor did Theodosius II or Justinian hesitate directly to equate Nestorians with Jews. Cf. *CJ,* Codex, 1.5.6 (ed. by Krüger, II, 51), *Novella* 109 of 541 (ed. by R. Schoell and W. Kroll, III, 517: "Nestorii Iudaicam sequuntur insaniam"), and *supra,* Vol. II, pp. 188, 191. In his collection of testimonies attacking the Council of Chalcedon, John Rufus, bishop of Mayuma, even reported that a revered old man once saw the vision of Jesus complaining that he had again been crucified by a mass of bishops. "And he was right," John added, "for the Nestorians suffer of the Jewish malady." Cf. his *Plerophories, c'est à dire témoignages et révélations,* ed. by F. Nau, p. 30. Cf. also other data cited by E. Honigmann in his *Evêques et évêchés monophysites d'Asie antérieure au VIe siècle,* esp. pp. 21 ff.

2. John Malalas, *Chronographia,* XV–XVI, ed. by L. A. Dindorf, pp. 389 f., 396 (the Zeno episode is reproduced more fully in the Slavonic version, in whose underlying codex of 1262 the editor, V. M. Istrin, detected generally an "unusual interest in Hebrew and Jewish materials"; cf. M. Spinka's translation from the Church Slavonic of the *Chronicle of John Malalas, Books VIII–XVIII,* pp. 6, 111 f.); Michael Syrus, *Chronique,* IX.6, ed. by Chabot, II, 254 (Syriac), 149 (French); Simeon Metaphrastes, *Vita S. Simeonis Stylitae,* XII.50, in *PG,* CXIV, 381 ff.; Zachariah of Mytilene, *Historia ecclesiastica,* VII.8, English trans. p. 171. Cf. S. Krauss's *Studien zur byzantinisch-jüdischen Geschichte,* pp. 3 ff.; M. Chaine's *La Vie et les miracles de s. Simon Stylite l'ancien;* and *supra,* Vol. II, p. 189. The report in Gregory Abu'l Faraj Barhebraeus' *Historia dynastiarum* (Chronography), ed. and trans. by E. A. W. Budge, pp. 74 (Syriac), 70 (English), that the Antiochians had burned the synagogue "and many of the Jews therewith," evidently is but a garbled restatement of the

older sources. It is clearly controverted by Zeno's irate exclamation. Our information concerning the Jewish role during the Persian conquest is extremely limited. But evidently Jews, too, suffered severely from the city's destruction, evidenced by archaeological excavations. Cf. J. Sauvaget's brief summary in his *Alep. Essai sur le développement d'une grande ville syrienne des origines au milieu du XIXe siècle,* pp. 57 f. n. 140. Cf. also G. Downey's critical reexamination of Procopius' account, "The Persian Campaign in Syria in A.D. 540," *Speculum,* XXVIII, 340–48.

3. Justinian's *Novella* 37 of 535, addressed to Solomon, governor of Africa, in *CJ,* ed. by Schoell and Kroll, III, 245; Procopius' *De Aedificiis,* VI.2.21–23; his *De Bello Gothico,* I [V].10.25, in his *Works,* ed. by H. B. Dewing, III, 98 f., and VII, 368 ff.; and *Acta Sanctorum,* ed. by Joannes Bollandus, January, I, 569b. On the latter's date, cf. P. Monceaux's *Histoire littéraire de l'Afrique chrétienne,* III, 108 ff., 156 ff.; and, more generally, H. Caplan's *Materials for the History of the Jews in the Roman Province of Africa* (typescript; a microfilm was graciously placed at my disposal by the author and Cornell University Library). Cf. also the list of twenty-three tombstone inscriptions dating from the first to the ninth centuries in the cemetery of Ifran, in the Anti-Atlas Mountains, compiled by V. Monteil in "Les Juifs d'Ifran," *Hespéris,* XXXV, 151–60; and the mixture of legend and history reported by J. Chaumeil in "Le Mellah de Tahala au pays des Ammelu," *ibid.,* XL, 228 ff. The emperor evidently acted in response to a petition of an otherwise undocumented Church "Council of all of Africa," which in turn harked back to demands often voiced before the Vandal conquest of 429. Cf. E. J. Jonkers, "Einige Bemerkungen über das Verhältnis der christlichen Kirche zum Judentum vom vierten bis auf das siebente Jahrhundert," *Mnemosyne,* 3d ser., XI, 309 f. Cf. also *supra,* Vol. II, pp. 179, 393 n. 45, 398 n. 10. Clearly the extreme measure of Belisarius (whose name remained a byword for a grandee in the Ladino speech of Balkan Jewry to the twentieth century; cf. A. Galanté's testimony in *Les Juifs de Constantinople sous Byzance,* p. 13 n. 2), forcing all the Jews of Borion to be baptized, was but a retribution for their unexpectedly stubborn resistance, although Belisarius' severity is considerably toned down in Procopius' account. In fact, a year after the receipt of the aforementioned *Novella,* Solomon had to repel a strong attack by the Berber tribesmen, on whose pro-Jewish leanings see *infra,* Chap. XVII, nn. 23–24. These Berber assaults were repeated in 544, 563, 569, and after. Cf. C. Diehl's data in *L'Afrique byzantine,* pp. 51 ff., and R. Devreesse's study of "L'Eglise d'Afrique durant l'occupation byzantine" in *Mélanges d'archéologie et d'histoire* of the Ecole française de Rome, LVII, 143–66. Borion's dejudaization, moreover, also fit the general scheme of the strategic, ecclesiastical, and urban reconstruction of the new administration. Cf. Ruinartius' Commentary on Victor Vitensis, *Historia persecutionis Vandalicae,* XII, in *PL,* LVIII, 430 ff.

4. Justinian's *Novella* 131, XIV.1 in *CJ,* III, 663. Cf. Arcadius' statement quoted by H. Grégoire in his chapter on "The Byzantine Church," in N. H. Baynes and H. St. L. B. Moss, *Byzantium: an Introduction to East Roman Civilization,* p. 131; Juster's *Empire romain,* I, 251 n. 1. Justinian's combination of the prohibition of new synagogues with that of the acquisition of Church property by Jews in that *Novella* of 545 was not merely coincidental. In at least one case, we are told, a fanatical Christian monk, Sergius of Mesopotamian Amida, was long thwarted by the local clergy in his efforts to destroy the synagogue and to eliminate the Jewish

community. The Jews were "settled in the territory of the Church of Amida," John of Ephesus reports, "and used to pay many contributions to the members of the Church; out of the desire for the abundance of their gold all the members of the Church became their supporters, threatening the blessed Sergius and saying, 'This man wishes to destroy the property of the Church.'" Cf. his *Lives of the Eastern Saints,* v, ed. and trans. by E. W. Brooks, I, 70 ff. According to John, Sergius' will ultimately prevailed, although the Jews retaliated by surreptitiously burning the saint's huts. John is, of course, not an impartial witness. As a leading missionary of that age, he prided himself on having converted 80,000 pagans during the thirty years of his missionary journeys in Asia, Caria, Phrygia, and Lydia. During that time he claims to have founded 98 churches and 12 monasteries, and transformed into churches an additional 7 synagogues. Cf. *ibid.,* XLVII (I, 681). Somewhat different figures are cited in other largely derivative sources. Cf. Honigmann's *Evêques,* p. 208 n. 6. On the other hand, though in the emperor's employ, John as a confirmed Monophysite was generally sympathetic to the monks of Amida, whose sufferings at the hands of "the champions of the corrupt council of Chalcedon" he so eloquently described. *Lives,* XXXV (I, 607 ff.).

5. Severus ibn al-Muqaffa', *History of the Patriarchs of the Coptic Church of Alexandria* (Arabic with a French translation), ed. by B. Evetts in *PO,* I, 467. Cf. also S. Krauss's brief summary of "The Christian Legislation Concerning the Synagogues" (Hebrew), *Melilah,* III–IV, 77–92 (mainly a collection of notes on medieval and early modern sources); and *supra,* Vol. II, pp. 189 f., 398 n. 13, 402 n. 25.

6. The individual stages in the successive Samaritan revolts and their repression by Zeno, Anastasius, and Justinian, culminating in the laws of 527–29 soon included under the title *De haereticis et Manichaeis et Samaritis* in *CJ,* Codex, I.5.12.17–18 (ed. by Krüger, II, 53 ff.), will be more fully described in the context of the general Samaritan history of the period, *infra,* Chap. XXV. The undated edict, 1.5.17 (II, 56), especially, not only ordered all Samaritan synagogues destroyed, but also disqualified these sectarians from testimony in courts even in their own affairs, and removed from them all rights of testamentary disposition.

7. *CJ* I.7.1–2; 9.3.6 (ed. by Krüger, II, 60 f.); Council of Chalcedon, canon 14 in Mansi's *Sacrorum conciliorum collectio,* VII, 363 f., 377, 388, 418 f. (with minor variations); and Hefele, *History,* trans. by Clark, III, 400 f. On intermarriage see *supra,* Vol. II, pp. 401 n. 24, 411 n. 17. Such latitude toward the marriage of Jewish converts did not necessarily conflict with "La Noblesse de race à Byzance," as explained by R. Guilland in *Byzantinoslavica,* IX, 307–44. It was only another aspect of the great impact of Christianity on the *Corpus* of Justinian, which has long been recognized by modern scholars. Cf., for instance, C. Hohenlohe's comprehensive *Einfluss des Christentums auf das Corpus juris civilis;* and, more specifically, R. M. Honig's observations on "The Nicene Faith and the Legislation of the Early Byzantine Emperors," *ATR,* XXXV, 304–23. Less attention has been paid by modern students, however, to the influence of Jewish law on the great Roman codes and their underlying sources. A few illustrations have been discussed *supra,* Vol. II, esp. pp. 415 n. 32, and 431 n. 11. Cf. also *infra,* Chap. XXVII, n. 1; and, more generally, J. E. Seaver's *Persecution of the Jews in the Roman Empire (300–438)*; and G. Ferrari delle Spade's careful studies of "Privilegi degli ebrei nell' Impero

romano-cristiano" (1944), and "Giurisdizione speciale ebraica nell' Impero romano-cristiano" (1947), reprinted in his *Scritti giuridici,* III, 267–77, 279–304.

8. Malalas, *Chronographia,* XVIII, ed. by Dindorf, p. 443. We must bear in mind, however, that, owing to their flimsy construction, most synagogues of the period were greatly exposed to the ravages of earthquakes. Certainly few communities could afford to build monumental houses of worship of the kind erected for their Christian compatriots by imperial benefactors. The scores of churches built by Justinian were sturdy structures which could easily withstand minor tremors—not to speak of that world's marvel, the Hagia Sophia in Constantinople, which, according to a fourteenth-century student of Byzantine administration, cost the emperor 300,000 gold pounds (some $108 million), and which was later so greatly to impress even a Jewish traveler like Benjamin of Tudela. In contrast thereto the contemporary synagogues, as evidenced by Palestinian excavations, were as a rule small buildings set up by amateur architects with limited funds raised mainly through small donations from individual members. Cf. the *De structura templi Sanctae Sophiae,* attributed to Georgios Codinos, in *PG,* CLVII, 613–34; *infra,* Chap. XIX, n. 7; and, on the Palestinian synagogues, the data briefly analyzed by M. Avi-Yonah in his *Bi-yeme Roma u-Byzantion* (In the Days of Rome and Byzantium), pp. 174 f.

9. Theodosius II's *Novella* 3 in *C.Th.,* ed. by Mommsen and Meyer, II, 7 ff. Cf. *supra,* Vol. II, pp. 398 n. 12, 400 n. 21; and *infra,* nn. 43, 50. On Domninus, who was more distinguished as a mathematician than as a philosopher; Marinus, head of the Athens school of philosophy from 485 to 525, and their Jewish or Samaritan antecedents, cf. S. Krauss's somewhat questionable findings in his "Domninus, a Jewish Philosopher of Antiquity," *JQR* [o.s.], VII, 270–77; and "Marinus, a Jewish Philosopher of Antiquity," *ibid.,* IX, 518–19. If true, the suppression of the famous citadel of independent thought, with its Jewish members, may have given rise to the vague tradition of the exclusion of Jews from Athens since early Byzantine times, mentioned by F. Gregorovius in his *Geschichte der Stadt Athen im Mittelalter,* 3d ed., I, 201 f.

10. Procopius, *De Bello Vandalico,* IV.9.6–9, in his *Works,* II, 280 f. On the whereabouts of the Temple vessels after the fall of Jerusalem, cf. the literature cited *supra,* Vol. II, p. 375 n. 29; and Galanté's *Juifs de Constantinople sous Byzance,* p. 13 n. 3 (telling the story of a reputed Temple chalice in a monastery of Mt. Athos, for which Baron Edmond de Rothschild offered 100,000 gold francs, but was refused). It is often assumed that the Jews had been excluded from residence within the congested center of the new capital by Theodosius II. This "expulsion" was allegedly connected with the confiscation of their synagogue in the Copper Market, reported by Theophanes (in his *Chronographia,* ed. by De Boor, I, 102; not reproduced by Anastasius, *ibid.,* II, 107). Cf. J. Starr's "Byzantine Jewry on the Eve of the Arab Conquest (565–638)," *JPOS,* XV, 281 n. 4, placing these events in 434–35. However, to postulate a regular expulsion of Jews into a separate quarter on the basis of the mere confiscation of a newly constructed, clearly unauthorized synagogue, seems too far-fetched. We must also bear in mind that Theophanes, the main source for this and many other events of the period, is far from a reliable guide. Cf., especially, K. N. Uspenskii's detailed analysis of "Theophanes and His Chronicle" (Russian), *Vizantiiskii Vremennik,* n.s., IV, 211–62. As a matter of fact,

Jews later inhabited various quarters in Constantinople and its suburbs. Cf. the data supplied by Galanté, pp. 23 ff.

11. Cf. Justinian's *Constitutio tanta,* ed. by Pringsheim in *RIDA,* V, 383 ff.; and *supra,* Vol. II, p. 425 n. 1. We may perhaps take the meaning of Justinian's prohibition of the *aliae legum interpretationes* of his legal code in the more restricted sense and apply it only to differences of opinions among jurists or outright perversions, "lest their verbosity discredit the Emperor's legislation by causing confusion." Cf. A. Berger, "The Emperor Justinian's Ban upon Commentaries to the Digest," *Bulletino dell' Istituto di Diritto Romano "Vittorio Scialoja,"* LV–LVI, 124–69, esp. pp. 150 ff. Yet one can readily see that the extended talmudic debates and their relative "verbosity" as compared with the few concise laws of the Bible aroused Justinian's deep suspicion. More difficult is the problem of the extent to which Justinian's *Novella* was applied in the Byzantine provinces including Palestine. In his "Was beweisen die Papyri für die praktische Geltung des justinianischen Gesetzgebungswerkes?" *Aegyptus,* XXXII, 131–37, A. Steinwenter draws the line between the *Digest,* which he considers as a mere "textbook" for lawyers, and the *Codex* and *Novellae* which dealt primarily with laws in practical use. This distinction seems exaggerated even with respect to the Byzantine jurists of the period who, like their Syriac and Jewish counterparts, doubtless saw even in purely theoretical works valid sources of practical law. On the other hand, when applied to Jews, these laws and their ancient antecedents often were greatly modified by local customs and attitudes. That is why even the outlawry of the *deuterosis* may have differently affected the various Jewish communities.

Justinian's *Novella* 146 (in *CJ,* III, 714 ff.) has given rise to endless debates, particularly in connection with its data on the internal heresies among Jews and its bearing on the rise of the new liturgical poetry in Palestine, the so-called *piyyuṭ.* These aspects will be more fully discussed, also in connection with some related statements by Yehudah bar Barzillai and Samau'al ibn Yaḥya, *infra,* Chap. XXXI. Here we need but refer to the vast literature summarized by Juster, Krauss, and Parkes. The latter offers a complete English translation of the *Novella* (in his *Conflict,* pp. 392 f.), from which our quotations are taken. Although starting with the controversy in Constantinople, the *Novella,* from its inception, was clearly intended to serve as imperial law affecting all provinces. Whether by mentioning the *archipherekitai,* the emperor had specifically in mind the leaders of the Jewish academy in Tiberias distinguished by that title, as suggested by Avi-Yonah (in his *Bi-yeme Roma,* p. 182; cf. p. 173), appears questionable. We know practically nothing about the titles used by leaders of Jewish communities in the dispersion during that period. However, we hear from a visitor to Rome in 1007, Jacob bar Yequtiel, that he had found there officials bearing such distinguished eastern titles as *nasi, gaon,* and *resh kallah.* Cf. *infra,* Chap. XXIII, n. 72. There is no reason for assuming that other communities, including that of the Byzantine capital, should have refrained from such borrowings. On the specific use of *archipherekitai* in the Muslim period, see my *Jewish Community,* III, 32 n. 34.

12. *CJ,* 1.9.8–9 (ed. by Krüger, II, 61); and *supra,* Vol. II, p. 254. Comprehensive lists of laws relating to Jews in both the Theodosian Code and that of Justinian, are offered by Juster in his *Empire romain,* I, 168 ff.; and by Parkes in his *Conflict,* esp. pp. 379 ff., 386 ff., and, according to their subject matter, pp. 389 ff. Cf. also,

more generally, P. Browe's analysis of "Die Judengesetzgebung Justinians," *Analecta Gregoriana,* VIII, 109–46. Of course, failure on the part of Justinian to include a law by a predecessor is no conclusive proof of its absence. Doubtless many ordinances were issued in the interval, particularly in individual localities and provinces, and only the neglect of contemporary jurists or chroniclers to mention them has obliterated their memory. Nevertheless it is characteristic that Justinian's legal advisers found only one relatively minor decree from the period of 439–527 worthy of repetition in the new code. They restated Marcian's rescript of 452, forbidding clerics and others to dispute matters of faith with Jews. The latter might thus have an opportunity to deride Christianity in those public, often riotous, debates, which characterized the sectarian controversies of that period. Cf. *CJ,* Codex, I.1.4 (ed. by Krüger, II, 6).

13. *Chronicon Paschale,* ed. by L. Dindorf, I, 619 f.; *CJ,* Codex, I.3.54.8–11; 10.2 (ed. by Krüger, II, 38, 62). In summarizing this legislation, Parkes missed the particular incentive which the emperor wished to offer to the Arian slaves in North Africa, and hence assumed that this decree, though addressed "in the first instance to Africa," was intended for the entire empire. Cf. his *Conflict,* p. 247. It was, however, only the extraordinary situation in the newly liberated province, which explains the Draconian penalty and the emperor's acceptance of ecclesiastical supervision. Elsewhere the penalty evidently did not exceed the fine of thirty pounds, mentioned in the undated decree (I.10.2). That silver pounds were meant there is likely. Thirty gold pounds would have amounted to $11,000 in present gold value, and several times that amount in purchasing power. Needless to say that few Jews, even among the wealthiest slave owners or slave traders, could have paid such a fine, and that it did not represent any approximation of the slave's real value.

14. St. Jerome's *Epistolae,* 126, 2; 127, 12, in *PL,* XXII, 1086, 1094. In his *Commentary* on Daniel 7:8 (*PL,* XXV, 555), written in 407, this Church Father observed bluntly that "all the ecclesiastical writers have handed down to us that at the end of the world, when the kingdom of Rome will be destroyed, ten future kings will divide up the Roman Empire." Cf. E. Demougeot's "Saint Jérôme, les oracles sibyllins et Stilicon," *Revue des études anciennes,* LIV, 83–92, pointing out that, because of this nexus between the Sibylline poems' early predictions of the downfall of Rome (*Rome, Ryme,* "Rome will become a village," etc.) and the Teuton invasions, Stilicho, the Teuton ruler of Rome, had ordered the burning of those poems (408). To Jews the downfall of the "kingdom of evil" was an even more convincing realization of the ancient predictions of their seers. On the conflicting Jewish and Christian chronologies based on the era of Creation see *infra,* Chap. XXXV.

15. Barhebraeus' *Chronography,* trans. by Budge, I (English), 70, 73 ff.; II (Syriac), 74, 78 ff.; Procopius, *Anecdota,* XVIII.30, in his *Works,* VI, 220 f. Cf. in general, A. Vasiliev, "Medieval Ideas of the End of the World: West and East," *Byzantion,* XVI, 462–502; and, with special reference to the Constantinople panic of 398 and an Augustinian sermon, *De Urbis excidio* (On Rome's Fall; in *PL,* XL, 715–24), J. Hubaux's description of "La Crise de trois cent soixante cinquième année," *Antiquité classique,* XVII, 343–54. Cf. also Malalas' *Chronographia,* ed. by Dindorf, p. 485; and the graphic description of the horrors of an earthquake which, in the

days of Justinian, nearly wiped out Antioch, in Malalas' Slavonic version, trans. by Spinka, pp. 125 ff. In this connection the Slavonic paraphrast illustrated the dissolution of all social life in the vicinity of the Syrian metropolis by relating the story of the robberies committed on the dead, as well as on surviving refugees, by one Thomas surnamed Evreos, a *silentiarius* by rank. Even if that criminal's surname were derived from "Hebrew," his name Thomas and his official rank proves that he was no more a real Hebrew than was Paul the Jew, the patriarch of Antioch in 519. See *supra,* n. 1.

16. *Sefer Eliyahu* (Book of Elijah), in Jellinek's *Bet ha-Midrasch,* III, 65 ff.; and in Yehudah ibn Shemuel's (Kaufmann's) collection of *Midreshe ge'ulah* (Jewish Apocalyptic Writings), pp. 29 ff. (includes on pp. 49 ff. a second version entitled *Pereq Eliyahu* [Chapter of Elijah]). On the date of this apocalyptic midrash, see the literature cited by Ibn Shemuel. His own dating at 627, although somewhat too precise for the available evidence, is fairly approximate. According to Theophanes, the final destruction of the Colossus of Rhodes, which had theretofore weathered all storms for 1,360 years (more correctly 933 years), was ordered by Mu'awiya after his occupation of that island in the twelfth year of Constans II (653). The purchaser, a Jew from Edessa or Emesa, allegedly carted away ninety camel loads of bronze, not, as is often asserted on ninety camels, whose use in Rhodes is very problematical. Cf. his *Chronographia,* ed. by De Boor, I, 345 (Greek), II, 216 (Latin; the latter reads "Iudaeus quidam Emesinus").

17. *Seder Eliyahu r.,* XX, ed. by M. Friedmann, pp. 113 f.; Malalas, *Chronographia,* XVIII, ed. by Dindorf, pp. 449 f., 455; Pseudo-Zachariah of Mitylene, *Historia ecclesiastica,* IX.23, Latin version by Brooks, II, 107; and in Hamilton and Brooks, *Syriac Chronicle* (English trans.), p. 282; Theophanes' *Chronographia,* ed. by De Boor, p. 179 (this passage is not extant in the Latin translation). On the chronological confusion of the Samaritan offer, see *infra,* n. 71. The quotation here given from *Seder Eliyahu r.,* like most other aggadic sayings of this kind, can not be precisely dated. W. Jawitz and others, who ascribed the compilation of that midrash to the pre-Islamic period, have extensively used it to illustrate the Palestinian conditions of the sixth and early seventh centuries. See Jawitz, *Toledot Yisrael,* IX, 5–41. However, equally plausible arguments have been presented for its origin in third-century Palestine (M. Margulies) or ninth-century Babylonia (V. Aptowitzer). Cf. *supra,* Vol. II, p. 434 n. 26; and *infra,* Chap. XXVIII n. 7. In any case, the saying itself doubtless reflected an age-old rationale of Jewish political neutrality in a divided world. First conceived in the period of Rome's perennial struggles with Parthia and Persia, this idea could readily be transferred to the world's new division between Islam and Christendom. The Jewish view, on the other hand, was but a variant of the opinion expressed, for instance, in Khosroe II's famous letter to Emperor Maurice of 590, that God had given the world the two great empires, "like two eyes," to guide it and to preserve order among men. Cf. the text reproduced by Theophylactus Simocatta in his *Historiae,* IV.11, 2, ed. by Bekker, p. 169 (ed. by De Boor, p. 169).

18. John of Nikiu, *Chronique,* XCIX.2, Ethiopic text, ed. with a French translation by H. Zotenberg, p. 415; and in R. H. Charles's English translation, p. 162. Cf. also *infra,* n. 73. The dramatic events of 590–92 have been carefully analyzed on the

basis of the vast documentation by P. Goubert in his *Byzance avant l'Islam,* Vol. I. Cf. also M. J. Higgins, "International Relations at the Close of the Sixth Century," *CHR,* XXVII, 279–315; and *supra,* Vol. II, pp. 182 f., 399 n. 15. We have little reliable information on the role played by the Jews, and the imperial policies toward them in the days of Maurice. The few casual references by the tenth-century Christian chronicler, Agapius (Mahbub) of Menbidj, and the sixteenth-century Hebrew writer, Gedaliah ibn Yaḥya, are emotionally tinged. According to the former in his *K. al-'Unvan* (Histoire universelle, ed. with a French translation by A. Vasiliev, II, 439 f.), a Jew of Antioch at one time insulted the image of the Virgin, whereupon Maurice ordered the entire community's ignominious expulsion from the city. Gedaliah, on the other hand, tells of an earthquake which destroyed the temple built by Julian (probably confusing it with Constantine's basilica) in Jerusalem, and its rebuilding by a gang of Jewish corvée laborers from Constantinople sent there by Emperor Valentinian (Maurice) in 589. Cf. his *Shalshelet ha-Qabbalah,* III (Chain of Tradition; an historical miscellany, Venice, 1587, fol. 109b). This event is ascribed more definitely to Maurice but less precisely to some year after 584 by David Gans in his *Ṣemaḥ David* (Scion of David; on Jewish and world history, Prague, 1592), Vol. II, fol. 44b. Neither fact is historically impossible or even improbable, but absence of more reliable records makes both stories rather suspect.

19. *Sefer Eliyahu* or *Pereq Eliyahu, supra,* n. 16; Michael Syrus, *Chronique,* trans. by Chabot, II, 379; and, less definitely, Agapius, *K. al-'Unvan,* ed. by Vasiliev, p. 449. Cf. also R. Devreesse's data in *Le Patriarcat d'Antioche depuis la paix de l'église jusqu'à la conquête arabe,* pp. 99 f. Phokas' decree is mentioned only by Pseudo-Dionysius of Tell-Maḥre, in his Syriac chronicle, *Makhtebanutha,* ed. by J. B. Chabot, IV, 5 (Syriac), 4 (French). Cf. also Chabot's earlier comments in his "Trois épisodes concernant les Juifs," *REJ,* XXVIII, 290 ff.; and, on the rather dubious date, Krauss's *Studien,* p. 22, and C. Lébeau's *Histoire du Bas-Empire,* X, 445.

20. Eutychius ibn Batriq (the Alexandrian), *Annales,* in *PG,* CXI, 1084 f.; ed. in Arabic by L. Cheikho *et al.,* I, 216. Cf. Starr's pertinent observations in *JPOS,* XV, 283 ff. The report that the Jews of Cyprus were urged to participate may not be significant for the story of the campaign, but certainly testifies to the recuperative powers of the community there. Cf. Sir George Hill, *A History of Cyprus,* I, 243 n. 1; and *supra,* Vols. I, pp. 375 n. 13; II, pp. 96 f., 371 n. 11. Avi-Yonah dates the assault on Tyre in 617, and tries to connect it with the Persian siege of Constantinople, or rather the Persian occupation of Chalcedon in that year (*Bi-yeme Roma,* p. 197). However, this hypothesis runs counter to the clear statement by Eutychius. Ibn Khaldun doubtless had in mind the Persians' first occupation of Chalcedon in 610. The figure of 20,000 Jewish combatants in the siege of Tyre, or that of 26,000 participating in the conquest of Jerusalem, should be considerably reduced. While one can not compare an agglomeration of enraged and armed civilians with a standing army, or even with occasional levies of warriors by Byzantine generals, we must bear in mind the smallness of contingents then generally involved even in major battles. Belisar had commanded only a force of some 15,000 men when he embarked upon his ambitious undertaking of incorporating North Africa, Italy, and Spain into the Empire. "The grand total," writes

N. H. Baynes, "of the Byzantine military forces in the tenth century was at most 140,000 men." Cf. the introduction to his and Moss's *Byzantium,* p. xxiii.

21. The enforced conversion of 607 still essentially stands and falls with the dependability of Pseudo-Dionysius of Tell-Maḥre, a Syriac chronicler of the ninth century. Cf. his *Makhtebanutha* (Chronique), IV, ed. by J. B. Chabot, pp. 4 f. (Syriac), 4 (French). His narrative is full of evident inaccuracies, however, including the date of 616–17, long after Phokas' demise. We have no other evidence for Phokas' general outlawry of Judaism. In fact, on another occasion Phokas himself allegedly imposed a severe fine on Christian communities of Syria and Mesopotamia, because, feeling themselves threatened, they took anticipatory reprisals against their Jewish neighbors. Cf. Agapius' *K. al-'Unvan,* p. 449. A frenzied reaction to the Persian conquests in 616–17, and hence also a radical decree of this kind, would appear far more credible. But that author is generally unreliable in regard to dates and other details. It would seem more prudent, therefore, to suspend judgment about the historicity of this anti-Jewish decree until the discovery of further sources.

Any estimate of the Jewish population in early seventh-century Palestine naturally is extremely tenuous. Avi-Yonah's estimate of 150,000 to 200,000 (*Bi-yeme Roma,* pp. 175 f.) is mainly based upon the questionable figure for Jewish combatants (see *supra,* n. 20). On the other hand, the total number of 43 recorded Jewish settlements, or about one fifth of the localities known to have had Jews after the Bar-Kocheba revolt, may indeed be indicative of some such minority status of 10–15 percent. On the strategic location of most of these settlements, see Avi-Yonah's graph of the route taken by the Persian invaders in 614 (p. 193).

22. Jacob's *Doctrina* (or *Didaskalia*) enjoyed considerable vogue, and is extant in Greek, Arabic, Ethiopic, and Slavonic versions. The Greek text was published under the title *Doctrina Jacobi nuper baptizati* by N. Bonwetsch, and republished by F. Nau in *PO,* VIII, 711–80. Portions of the Ethiopic text (Part I) had previously appeared, with a French translation by S. Grébaut, under the title *Sargis d'Aberga* (*Controverse judéo-chrétienne*), *ibid.,* III, 547–643; XIII, 1–109, while only an abstract of the Arabic text is available in P. Sbath's summary in *Echos d'Orient,* XXII. Cf. also S. Krauss's analysis of some of its data relating to Jewish history in his Hebrew essay "A Religious Disputation in Palestine at the End of the Byzantine Rule," *Ṣiyyon,* II, 28–37; and A. Sharf's "Byzantine Jewry in the Seventh Century," *BZ,* XLVIII, 107. On the political and ecclesiastical situation in Palestine before the Persian invasions, see the recent studies by L. Casson, "The Administration of Byzantine and Early Arab Palestine," *Aegyptus,* XXXII, 54–60; E. Honigmann's "Juvenal of Jerusalem," *Dumbarton Oaks Papers,* V, 209–79; F. M. Abel's *Histoire de la Palestine depuis la conquête d'Alexandre jusqu'à l'invasion arabe,* II, 387 ff.; and the literature mentioned by these authors.

23. *Doctrina Jacobi,* v.6, ed. by Bonwetsch, p. 77; *Sefer Zerubbabel* in Jellinek's *Bet ha-Midrasch,* II, 54–57, xxi f. (in S. A. Wertheimer's *Bate midrashot,* 2d ed., II, 495–505, and Ibn Shemuel's *Midreshe ge'ulah,* pp. 55 ff.; both include additional fragments). Although the text of the latter apocalypse twice refers to the date of 990 years from the fall of the Second Temple as the date of the prospective redemption, this figure was evidently inserted later by a messianically minded copyist. See *infra,* Chap. XXV, n. 3. Its generally optimistic tenor, despite the Jews' defeat by

Heraclius, is easily explained by the author's renewed hope after the Muslim conquest.

24. Eutychius, *Annales,* in *PG,* CXI, 1083; ed. by Cheikho *et al.,* I, 216. Cf. also P. Peeters's ed. of the Arabic version of "La Prise de Jérusalem par les Perses," *Mélanges* of the Université Saint-Joseph in Beirut, IX, 1–42; Y. A. Manadian's review of "The Itinerary of Emperor Heraclius' Persian Campaigns" (Russian), *Vizantiiskii Vremennik,* n.s., III, 133–53 (chiefly on the northern battles); other data analyzed by K. Hillkowitz concerning "The Participation of Jews in the Conquest of Jerusalem by the Persians in 614" (Hebrew), *Zion,* IV, 307–16; and M. Avi-Yonah's detailed topographical analysis "On the Sassanian Conquest of Jerusalem" (Hebrew), *Jerusalem* (quarterly), II, 228–30. On the Persian treaty concerning the non-burial of the dead in Armenia, see Procopius, *De Bello Persico,* I.12.4 in *Works,* I, 96 f.; and A. Christensen's explanation in *L'Iran sous les Sassanides,* pp. 356 f.; as well as the general background sketched in C. Toumanoff's "Iberia on the Eve of Bagratid Rule," *Muséon,* LXV, 17–49; LXVI, 103–4. Cf. also the more moderate description of these events in Barhebraeus, *Chronicon ecclesiasticum,* ed. by J. A. Abbeloos and T. J. Lamy, I, 261 ff., and his *Chronography,* trans. by Budge, pp. 86 f. We know next to nothing about the personality and early career of Benjamin of Tiberias. But *Seder Eliyahu r.,* XIV (ed. by Friedmann, p. 66) may contain an allusion to him as a native of Babylonia, for whom the emperor had built castles in Palestine (see *supra,* n. 17). The latter author also alludes frequently to Christian converts, of whom there doubtless was a large number during the period of Jewish domination over the Holy Land. Of course, there were also confirmed Christians who readily suffered martyrdom. On Radegund, see Gregory of Tours, *Historia Francorum,* IX.40, in W. Arndt's ed. (*MGH,* Scriptores rerum Merov., Vol. I), pp. 396 f.; and in O. M. Dalton's English translation, II, 413. In "La Vrai Croix et les expéditions d'Héraclius en Perse," *Revue des études byzantines,* XI, 88–105, A. Frolow contends that the recapture of the True Cross as the *main* motivation of Heraclius' campaign was an invention of the overheated Crusading fantasy after 1096. Yet one must not unduly minimize the sense of grief caused by the removal of the Cross to an "unbelieving" country among contemporary Christians as well. These and other more crucial problems of the age of Heraclius, including the emperor's complex reactions to the Jewish uprising, may receive new answers from the forthcoming dissertation, *Heraclius et les Héraclides* by a pupil (Guillou) of P. Lemerle. Cf. the latter's brief communication, "Les Etudes d'histoire de Byzance et du moyen-âge oriental," *Annales,* X, 543–46.

The tremendous impression created by the fall of Jerusalem is also attested by the growth of innumerable legends, some of which found an echo almost a thousand years later in Ariosto's *Orlando Furioso.* Cf. especially the texts, ed. by C. Bonner, in "The Maiden's Stratagem," *Byzantion,* XVI, 142–61 (on a girl martyr who sought to preserve her innocence during the invasion); and E. Cerulli's study of "La 'Conquista persiana di Gerusalemme' ed altre fonti orientali cristiane di un episodio dell' 'Orlando Furioso,'" *Orientalia,* XV, 453 ff. (includes a fragment from a Greek version in a Vatican MS); supplemented by his "Nuovi testi sulla 'Conquista persiana di Gerusalemme' como fonte di un episodio dell' 'Orlando Furioso,'" *ibid.,* XVI, 377–90.

25. The events in Jerusalem at the time of the Jewish seizure of power and subsequent breach with the Persians are extremely obscure. If we may take a clue

from the visionary author of the Book of Zerubbabel, "Nehemiah" offered a sacrifice in Jerusalem. He doubtless wished thus to proclaim the restoration of a Jewish commonwealth. After a while, however, he was executed by Siroe, son of the king of Persia, "and a misfortune befell Israel, the like of which had never been before." Cf. *Sefer Zerubbabel* in Jellinek's *Bet ha-Midrasch,* II, 56 (less sharply in Wertheimer's *Bate midrashot,* II, 499); and Israel Lévi's detailed analysis of "L'Apocalypse de Zerobabel et le roi de Perse Siroés," *REJ,* LXVIII, 129–60; LXIX, 108–21; LXXI, 57–65. Cf. also Ibn Shemuel's text and commentary in *Midreshe ge'ulah,* pp. 55 ff. Lévi identifies the Persian king with Siroe, Khosroe II's son and successor in 628, and points out certain parallels between this apocalypse and a liturgical poem by Eliezer Qalir. As usual, the contemporary Christian chroniclers attributed the change in the Persian attitude to such personal factors as disappointment over the Jews' failure to deliver treasures supposedly hidden in Jerusalem by previous rulers, or the influence of Khosroe II's Christian wives. While there may well have been some such contributory causes (see *infra,* n. 74), the real weakness of the Jewish community, combined with its exaggerated expectations and demands, doubtless decided the issue. No exact date for the reversal of Persian policy can be given, though it may have been connected in some way with the failure of the Persian armies to occupy Constantinople in 617. The particular nexus with the lifting of the siege of Tyre, postulated by Avi-Yonah (p. 197) on the basis of an equivocal statement by Ibn Khaldun (see *supra,* n. 20), must be rejected on chronological grounds. One can nevertheless see that the religiously inspired heroic defense of Constantinople against the combined onslaughts of Persians and Avars must have persuaded the Persian commanders to seek some reconciliation with the newly conquered Christian peoples of Asia and Africa.

26. Agapius, *K. al-'Unvan,* ed. by Vasiliev, p. 466; Sebeos, *Histoire d'Héraclius,* in F. Macler's translation, pp. 94 f.; Eutychius, *Annales,* in *PG,* CXI, 1089 f. (ed. by Cheikho *et al.,* II, 5 f.); and Theophanes, *Chronographia,* ed. by De Boor, I, 328; II, 205. Sebeos reports, however, that many Edessene Jews fled to the Arabs, and he connects their arrival with the rise of Islam—evidently an argument of *post hoc, propter hoc.* Cf. also F. Dölger, *Regesten der Kaiserurkunden des oströmischen Reiches von 565–1453,* I, 22 f. Nos. 195–99. On the events in Edessa, see S. Krauss's brief note "On the History of the Jewish Revolt in the Days of Emperor Heraclius" (Hebrew), *Ṣiyyon,* III, 17–21 (arguing for the historicity of Sebeos' report). These events may be better understood in the light of the previous evacuation of many Monophysites from the city by Khosroe, their return in 628–29, and the imperial attempt to replace them by Orthodox Christians. Cf. Barhebraeus, *Chronicon ecclesiasticum,* ed. by Abbeloos and Lamy, I, 263 ff.; and R. Duval, *Histoire politique, religieuse et littéraire d'Edesse jusqu'à la première croisade,* pp. 223 ff. Heraclius' arrival in Jerusalem is dated in either 629 or 630 by Starr in his "Contribution," *JPOS,* XV, 287 n. 36. On his need to placate the Church, see A. Frolow's observation in "La Déviation de la 4e Croisade vers Constantinople," *RHR,* CXLVII, p. 53.

27. The Tumai conversion, narrated with the usual embellishments by an anonymous Christian chronicler and summarized by R. Griveau in "Histoire de la conversion des Juifs habitant la ville de Tomei, en Egypte," *Revue de l'Orient chrétien,* XIII, 298–313, is the more remarkable, as Egypt was not only the citadel of anti-Byzantine Monophysitism, but also a mainstay of the continued pagan

resistance to Christian missionary efforts. Cf. R. Rémodon's data on "L'Egypte et la suprême résistance au christianisme (Ve–VIIe siècles)," *Bulletin de l'Institut français d'archéologie orientale du Caire,* LI, 63–78.

28. The Jewish participation in the Constantinople riots, attested by the ninth-century chronicler Nicephoros in his *Istoria syntomos* (in De Boor's ed. of his *Opuscula historica,* pp. 30 f.), shows the inefficacy of Heraclius' edict even in the imperial capital. On its text and date, sometime between 632 and 634, cf. Dölger, *Regesten der Kaiserurkunden,* p. 24, No. 207; and the more recent discussions by R. Devreesse, "La Fin inédite d'une lettre de Saint Maxime: un baptème forcé des juifs et des Samaritains à Carthage en 632," *Revue de science religieuse,* XVII, 25–35; G. I. Bratianu, "La Fin du régime des partis à Byzance et la crise antisémitique du VIIe siècle," *Revue historique du sud-est européen,* XVIII, 48–67; J. Starr's "Note on the Crisis of the Early Seventh Century, C.E." *JQR,* XXXVIII, 97–99; and Sharf's comments in "Byzantine Jewry in the Seventh Century," *BZ,* XLVIII, 109. The nexus, however, between the prolonged negotiations, abetted by the use of force, to establish an effective union of the Chalcedonian and Monophysite churches and the simultaneous decree enforcing baptism for Jews seems to have escaped the attention of scholars. On these negotiations see L. Bréhier's succinct summary in his and R. Aigrain's *Grégoire le Grand, les états barbares et la conquête arabe (590–757),* in A. Fliche and V. Martin's *Histoire de l'Eglise,* V, 116 ff.

29. We possess no West European Jewish literature from that early period. Only Italy may perhaps boast of one or another aggadic collection, the historic-folkloristic work going under the name of Yosephon, and the medical-mystic work of Asaf Judaeus, all possibly written before the Carolingian period. The pertinent hypotheses of modern scholars will be discussed in their respective contexts, *infra,* Chaps. XXVIII, and XXXVI. In any case, however, these writings shed little light on the social and political status of the Jews in Western Rome's turbulent successor states. Fortunately, numerous non-Jewish sources, historical, legal, and theological, have survived; they vouchsafe a few glimpses into the trials and tribulations, if not into the ordinary life, of Western Jews during the sixth and seventh centuries. Cf. S. Calderone's recent study, "Per la storia dell' elemento giudaico nella Sicilia imperiale," *Rendiconti* of the Accademia nazionale dei Lincei, Classe di sc. morali, 8th ser., X, 489–502, mainly referring to ancient Jewry and particularly to a Comiso (Syracuse) inscription, probably dating from the third century.

30. *Edictum Theoderici,* CXLIII, ed. by F. Bluhme, in *MGH,* Leges, V, 166; and *supra,* Vol. II, pp. 266 f., 419 n. 43. As pointed out there, Theodosius himself seems to have lost faith in the efficacy of his enactment, which was nevertheless repeated in the Code of Justinian. On Theodoric's general policies concerning Jews, see G. Pfeilschifter's excursus in *Der Ostgotenkönig Theoderich der Grosse und die katholische Kirche,* pp. 219 ff.; and W. Ensslin's more recent *Theoderich der Grosse.* It has been suggested that the king often delegated the investigation of anti-Jewish riots and the punishment of culprits to the old imperial authorities, such as the Roman Senate, in order to divert the ensuing popular resentment from the Gothic administration. Cf. H.-E. Giesecke's suggestion in *Die Ostgermanen und der Arianismus,* p. 123. Ensslin has convincingly shown, however, that this procedure re-

flected mainly the king's genuine wish to respect the jurisdiction of established authorities (pp. 214 ff.). It is possible, however, that Theoderic's anti-Catholic attitude made him view the Jewish minority in a more friendly fashion. Cf. G. B. Picotti's recent "Osservazioni su alcuni punti della politica religiosa di Teoderico" in *Settimane di studio* of the Centro Italiano di Studi sull' Alto Medio Evo, III, 173–226.

31. Cassiodorus Senator's *Variae*, II.27 ("quia nemo cogitur, ut credat invitus"); V, 37, ed. by T. Mommsen, in *MGH*, Auctores ant., XII, 61 f., 163. On the king's great concern for the *civilitas*, see the numerous passages culled from the sources by Ensslin, pp. 221, 380 f. Less convincingly Ensslin (p. 98) also argued that the passage pertaining to the impossibility of enforcing belief stemmed from Theodoric himself, rather than Cassiodorus. "No Roman of his day would have dared to make such a statement." One must bear in mind, on the other hand, the king's utter ruthlessness, which came to the fore also in his pro-Jewish measures. On one occasion, for example, Theodoric intervened sharply in a local disturbance in his own residence of Ravenna (519). The general facts, as reported by the author of the *Origo Constantini imperatoris*, known as the *Anonymus Valesianus*, 2d part, XIV, ed. by T. Mommsen, in *MGH*, Auctores ant., IX, 326, are fairly clear. After the mob had destroyed the local synagogues (there apparently had been more than one in existence), the king ordered full restitution. Those Christians who were unable to pay were to be publicly flogged. The motive behind the mob attack supplied by the chronicler, however, has given rise to various explanations. See Parkes, *Conflict*, p. 207 n. 2. Parkes's own interpretation of the sentence, "Quare Judaei baptizatos nolentes dum ludunt frequenter oblatam in acquam fluminis iactaverunt" is equally unsatisfactory. It supposedly tells of some forced converts who had marched together to the river and thrown there the consecrated bread given them at baptism. But this explanation presupposes a textual emendation, a forced interpretation of the term *frequenter*, and neglect of the phrase *dum ludunt*. Nor does one quite see why the ridiculing of Christianity by Jewish converts should have induced the mob to destroy the synagogues of professing Jews, if any remained after their supposedly general conversion. While the chronicler's command of Latin was evidently poor and the sentence will necessarily remain obscure, the more likely rendering is that "Jews, hating the baptized, frequently while playing threw bread into the river's water." This may have been a symbolic act of casting off the sinners, similar to the casting off of sins through emptying crumbs into the river during the widespread *Tashlikh* ceremony on New Year's day. In fact, Ravenna Jews may indeed have combined such an excursion to the river banks with some graphic elimination of apostates from their midst. At least they may have conveyed some such notion to Christian onlookers who doubtless were greatly puzzled by the entire performance. Even if erroneous, such a notion was certainly liable to inflame the accumulated hatreds. On the origins, still rather obscure, and manifold forms of the *Tashlikh* ritual, see J. Z. Lauterbach's analysis in his *Rabbinic Essays*, pp. 297–433.

32. Letter from Gelasius to Bishop Quingesius, included in the "Canons Attributed to" him in *PL*, LIX, 146; *Anonymus Valesianus*, Part 2, XV, in *MGH*, IX, 328. Ensslin goes too far in discounting that story, partly because he takes too seriously the legal exclusion of Jews from public functions, including the semiprivate

legal profession (pp. 327, 390 n. 3). The very repetition of that prohibition in the imperial enactments (cf. Juster's *Empire romain,* II, 250, 263 f.) is a clear indication of its essential inefficacy. On the attitude of the ancient Churches to Jews and Judaism, see the extensive literature listed *supra,* Vol. II, especially Chaps. XII–XIII, to which may be added J. E. Seaver's aforementioned monograph on the *Persecution of Jews in the Roman Empire (300–438)*; and, more generally, P. Browe's essay, "Die religiöse Duldung der Juden im Mittelalter," *Archiv für katholisches Kirchenrecht,* CXVIII, 3–76; and G. Franz's Nazi-oriented summary, "Der Jude im katholischen Kirchenrecht," *Deutschc Rechtswissenschaft,* II, 157–66.

33. Cf. R. Aigrain's note in L. Bréhier and his *Grégoire le Grand,* p. 54 n. 4. Gregory's attitude toward the Jews has been treated frequently and with constant repetition. Cf. esp. F. Görres, "Papst Gregor I der Grosse (590–604) und das Judentum," *Zeitschrift für wissenschaftliche Theologie,* L, 489–505; S. Katz, "Pope Gregory the Great and the Jews," *JQR,* XXIV, 113–36; and, in connection with the pope's other activities, F. H. Dudden, *Gregory the Great: His Place in History and Thought,* esp. II, 151 ff. Most of these investigations have been limited, however, to the pope's epistles, best available in P. Ewald and L. M. Hartmann's edition (in *MGH,* Epistulae, Vols. I–II). To the 24 letters (I.34, 45, 66, 69; II.6, 38; III.37; IV.9, 21, 31; V.7; VI.29; VII.21, 41; VIII.23, 25; IX.38, 40, 104, 195, 213, 228; XIII.3, 15), listed by Juster in his *Empire romain,* I, 81 n. 2, Katz (p. 115 n. 12) added a letter of May, 591 (I.42). These letters extend over practically the entire reign of the pope, being dated between March, 591, and November, 602. None of the other voluminous writings (covering the bulk of Vols. LXXV, LXXVI, LXXVIII, and LXXIX of the *Patrologia Latina*) have been subjected to careful examination, although, as we shall see presently, there is an obvious dichotomy between the restatement of the largely anti-Jewish theological position of the Church in Gregory's exegetical and homiletical works and the more moderate, practical approach characteristic of the Epistles. Cf. the numerous references to Jews summarized in the indexes to Gregory's works in *PL,* Vols. LXXV–LXXIX, including the few illustrations cited here. Precisely because this dichotomy between theory and practice is characteristic of a large body of medieval Church literature and helps to explain many of the apparent inconsistencies in the ecclesiastical policies toward Jews, a detailed examination of all of Gregory's works from this angle would shed significant new light on the origins of this polarity in thought and action.

34. Gregory, *Epistolae,* I.45; II.6, 38; IV.31; V.7; XIII.15 (in *MGH,* I, 71 f., 105, 134, 267, 288; II, 383). The lengthy quotation from I.45 is given here in Dudden's English translation, *Gregory the Great,* pp. 153 f. It should be noted that, despite his zeal, the pope could not rid even the ecclesiastical domains from Manichaean and pagan farmers. In his letters to Januarius, bishop of Sardinia, and to Cyprian of Palermo (IV.26; V.7, in *MGH,* I, 260 f., 288 f.). Gregory suggested also the use of tax concessions for the conversion of heathens. However, he drew a line between Jews, who should be given tax reductions if converted but maintained in their older status if they refused, and pagans, whose refusal was to be penalized by a tax increase. Manichaeans should forcibly be restored to the Catholic faith. On changes in the missionary methods in later periods, see *infra,* Chap. XXIV n. 39; and P. Browe's comprehensive study of *Die Judenmission im Mittelalter und die Päpste.*

35. Gregory, *Epistolae,* IV.31; XIII.3 (in *MGH,* I, 267; IV, 367 f.); his *Homilies on Ezekiel,* I.6.2–3; II.9.5–6; and his *I Reg. Expositio,* II.2.16 (on I Sam. 1:22), III.2.8 (on I Sam. 4:6–7), in *PL,* LXXVI, 829 f., 1044 ff.; LXXIX, 97, 163 f. We must bear in mind, however, that some of Gregory's exegetical works are of dubious authenticity and have, in part, been disavowed by their author himself (602; *Epistolae,* XII.6, in *MGH,* II, 352). Cf. H. Schwank's dissertation, *Gregor der Grosse als Prediger,* pp. 22 n. 98, 26 ff. Schwank also emphasized Gregory's great indebtedness in his methods and outlook to both Ambrose and Augustine. Generally, Gregory followed closely the regnant views of the ancient Church. In a far-fetched homily on Job 1:21, for instance, he insisted that "Christ, who arose from among the Jews, will revert to them at the end of the world." Cf. his *Moralia,* II.36, in *PL,* LXXV, 584 f. Even his paradoxical comparison of the Jewish people with Esau did not differ greatly from St. Ignatius' exclamation that "Christianity did not believe in Judaism, but Judaism believed in Christianity." Cf. *supra,* Vol. II, pp. 136 ff., 168 f., 381 f., 394 f. Cf. also Taio, the seventh-century bishop of Saragossa, *Sententiae,* I.40; II.4, in *PL,* LXXX, 774 f., 778 f. (expatiating on Gregory's ideas; see *infra,* n. 50). Nor was Gregory entirely immune to the eastern equation of Nestorianism with the "Jewish perfidy." Cf. his *Epistolae,* XI.52 (in *MGH,* II, 325); and the fanciful etymology supplied already by Melito of Sardis for the equation of the Jews with Edom, *infra,* Chap. XXIV, n. 56.

36. *Epistolae,* I.34; II.6; IX.38 (in *MGH,* I, 47 f., 105; II, 67). Cf. *supra,* Vol. II, pp. 189, 401 n. 24. The difference between Gregory and Ambrose can readily be understood. Apart from his general responsibility for maintaining public order in his domains, the pope was not then involved in any fundamental struggle between Church and State. Hence he did not have to make an issue of the state's failure to condone mob action with respect to synagogues, as had the archbishop of Milan two centuries earlier.

37. *Epistolae,* IV.21; IX.104 (in *MGH,* I, 255 f.; II, 111 f.). In all these matters the pope adhered strictly to the existing laws. In Italy, Jewish ownership of even would-be Christian slaves was sharply outlawed as a result of the Eastern Empire's earlier prohibitions incorporated in the Code of Justinian. In the other western countries, however, the much milder provisions of the Western Empire taken over in the Theodosian Code still remained in force. On this distinction, see Juster, *Empire romain,* II, 72 ff. Gregory may have scolded the Frankish rulers for tolerating Jewish domination over Christian slaves (see n. 38), but he could not put the onus on Jews who had merely availed themselves of their legal rights. Probably for this reason he was lenient also toward the slave trader's "oversight" in importing from Gaul Christian, among other, slaves. That is also why in 597 he ordered Candidus, papal presbyter in Gaul, to redeem, with all the necessary "subtlety and solicitude," four Christian captives who had been ransomed by a Narbonne Jew (*Epistolae,* VII.21, in *MGH,* I, 464). He simply did not-arrogate to himself the authority to order them set free without indemnity, as he undoubtedly would have done in an Italian city. Similarly he was within the letter of the law when he exempted even Italian *coloni* from the prohibition affecting Jewish employment of Christian slaves. The date of that epistle to Luna (May, 594) may help explain the special papal solicitude. At that time the Papal States were just beginning to recover from a devastating invasion of the Langobards, which had ended in a prolonged siege of Rome during the pre-

ceding year. For the sake of reconstructing the country's agricultural economy, the pope was prepared to make concessions to Jewish landholders. Cf. also A. Segré's analysis of the preceding three centuries of historic evolution of "The Byzantine Colonate," *Traditio,* V, 103–33, showing among other matters, how much the Italian economy, in particular, had become dependent on these half-free sharecroppers. Later generations, however, paid little heed to this emergency background, and readily considered the papal epistle as a significant legal precedent of general validity, so long as they themselves had an economic interest in continued Jewish landholdings. Cf., however, *infra,* Chap. XXII n. 6.

38. Augustine's sermon on the prodigal son (Luke 15:11–32), ed. by G. Morin in *Miscellanea Agostiniana,* I, 256 ff.; Gregory, *Epistolae,* I.66; II.6; III.37; IX.38, 213, 215, 223; XIII.3 (in *MGH,* I, 87, 105, 195; II, 67, 199 f., 203, 223, 367 f.); his *I Reg. Expositio,* I.3.3 on I Sam. 2:1 (*PL,* LXXIX, 63); and Schwank, *Gregor der Grosse,* pp. 30 f. Gregory's familiarity with this particular sermon of the bishop of Hippo cannot be proved. But the fact that he had always been a great admirer of Augustinian homiletics and that, not long before him, Caesarius of Arles had known this particular sermon or one like it, enhances the likelihood of its availability to the pope too. Cf. B. Blumenkranz's remarks on "La Parabole de l'enfant prodigue chez Saint Augustin et Saint Césaire d'Arles," *Vigiliae christianae,* II, 102–5. The attraction exerted by the Elijah altar may readily be understood in the light of D. B. Botte's data on "Une Fête du prophète Elie en Gaule au VIe siècle," *Cahiers sioniens,* IV, 170–77. On the international aspects of Gregory's interventions, see *infra,* n. 44.

39. *Carmen de synodo Ticinensi,* ed. by K. Strecker, in *MGH,* Poetae latini aevi Carolini, IV, 728. Although by its very nature this poem is neither historically precise nor entirely reliable, the fact of such an attempted large-scale enforced conversion need not be doubted. But the execution of a complicated measure of this kind, which depended on the inner convictions of numerous individuals, doubtless transcended the powers of the crude Langobard administrative machinery.

40. Cf. J. J. Rabinowitz's comparative study of "Jewish and Lombard Law," *JSS,* XII, 299–328, also reproduced in his *Jewish Law: Its Influence on the Development of Legal Institutions,* pp. 182 ff. As in some of his other investigations, Rabinowitz may have somewhat overdrawn the picture of the Langobard indebtedness to Jewish prototypes, but many of his illustrations can indeed best be explained by the influence of legal practices (especially legal formularies) observed by the Langobard rulers among their Jewish subjects. Cf. also *infra,* Chap. XXVII, n. 1; and, on the influence of Byzantine corporal punishments, R. S. Lopez's brief analysis of "Byzantine law in the Seventh Century and its Reception by the Germans and the Arabs," *Byzantion,* XVI, 445–61.

41. J. Amador de los Rios's *Estudios históricos, politicos y literarios sobre los Judios,* p. 4 n. 3; in the French translation, p. 24 n. 3, both giving the text of the spurious Toledo letter in Spanish. The alleged inscription reading, "This is the grave of Adoniram, King Solomon's servant, who had come to collect the tax and died on the . . ." still existed in the sixteenth century, when Moses ben Shem Tob ibn Ḥabib saw it at Muviedro and deciphered a few introductory lines and the name Amaziah. Cf. his *Darkhe no'am* (Pleasant Paths; on Hebrew prosody; Rödelheim,

1806), fol. 6b. Ibn Ḥabib seems unaware of the fact that, if authentic, this inscription should have been written in the ancient Hebrew-Phoenician alphabet. To any historically informed person the picture of King Solomon sending out a tax gatherer to a distant colony which he had never acquired was clearly but a borrowing from the biblical description of Solomon's reign, buttressed by medieval fiscal realities. Cf. J. B. Frey's *Corpus inscriptionum judaicarum*, I, 447 No. 665; and S. Katz's comprehensive monograph on *The Jews in the Visigothic and Frankish Kingdoms of Spain and Gaul*, pp. 141 ff. Cf. also the more recent archaeological and other data discussed *supra*, Vols. I, pp. 170, 370 n. 6, 374 n. 13, and II, pp. 210, 406 n. 42.

42. Menahem ben Aaron ibn Zeraḥ's *Ṣedah la-derekh* (Provisions for the Road; on rituals), Introduction (Lwów, 1859), fol. 2a. Cf. also R. Thouvenot's "Chrétiens et Juifs à Grenade aux IVe siècle après J.-C.," *Hespéris*, XXX, 201–13 (with reference to the Council of Elvira and the writings of a monk Gregory, bishop of that city). Cf. also P. Lombardía's recent study of "Los Matrimonios mixtos en el Concilio de Elvira," *AHDE*, XXIV, 543–58; and other data cited in my "Yehudah Halevi: An Answer to an Historic Challenge," *JSS*, III, 246 f. There is no way, however, of ascertaining even remotely the number of Jews living in Visigothic Spain and the neighboring province of Septimania. G. Kittel's estimate that they amounted to 8 or 10 percent of the total population on the island of Minorca, and possibly in all of Spain, during the early fifth century (*supra*, Vol. I, p. 370 n. 6) is not supported by any reliable evidence. Yet there is no question that at least some of the major urban centers embraced a significant proportion of Jews, who seem to have increased in number during the barbarian invasions, when Spain suffered relatively less than most other provinces of the Western Empire. Even if we greatly discount the oratorical praise of Spain's climate and wealth by Isidore of Seville (cf. his *Etymologiae*, XIV.4.28 in *PL*, LXXXII, 509), we may readily assume that to the end of the sixth century living conditions were sufficiently favorable for the local communities not only to grow speedily by natural processes, but also to attract many Jews from other lands.

43. *Lex Romana Visigothorum*, II.1.10; 8.3; III.1.5; 7.2; IX.4.4; XVI.2.1; 3.1–2; 4.1–2, ed. by G. Haenel, pp. 34, 44, 74, 82, 178, 248, 250 ff., 256 ff.; Council of Agde, canon 34, in Mansi, *Sacrorum conciliorum collectio*, VIII, 330 (Hefele, *History*, trans. by Clark, IV, 82). The Jewish provisions of Alaric's code are briefly analyzed by J. Juster in *La Condition légale des Juifs sous les rois visigoths*, pp. 3 f., largely following M. Conrat's detailed commentary of the *Breviarium Alaricianum, Römisches Recht im fränkischen Reich in systematischer Darstellung*, pp. 156 ff. Juster is in turn closely followed by all subsequent students, including Parkes and Katz. The Council of Agde may have had an anti-Jewish bias; it was presided over by Caesarius of Arles, an outspoken Jew-baiter. Cf. *supra*, Vol. II, p. 398 n. 10. However, the canonical prerequisite of an eight months' catechumenate certainly aroused no objections among Jews. In fact, if closely adhered to, it would have seriously impeded most attempts at enforced conversion.

44. Reccared's law cited in the *Leges Visigothorum*, XII.2.12, ed. by K. Zeumer in *MGH*, Legum I, Part 1, p. 417; Third Council of Toledo, canon 14, in Mansi, *Collectio*, IX, 996 (with the royal confirmation *ibid.*, p. 1000; in Hefele, *History*, trans. by Clark, IV, 420 f.); Gregory's *Epistolae*, IX.228 (in *MGH*, II, 223). Reccared's anti-

Jewish laws were evidently issued several years after the conclusion of the Council of 589. This sequence explains both the progressive sharpening of the royal legislation, and the fact that Gregory I waited until 599 with praising the king for having enacted "a constitution against the Jewish unbelief [*perfidiam*]." The pope had said nothing on this subject in his letter to Leander of 591 (1.41; in *MGH*, I, 57) in which he had congratulated the Spanish bishop on Reccared's conversion. That this was not owing to the mere slowness of communications and the interference of the Byzantine navy is almost self-evident, although the relative paucity of papal letters to Spain, in contrast even with such a distant country as England, is sometimes ascribed to this factor. Cf. the debate in Z. García Villada's *Historia ecclesiastica de España*, II, 134 f. There is no way of telling what other provisions were included in that "constitution." Evidently, for a Recceswinth or Erwig, the later compilers of the *Leges Visigothorum*, even Reccared's subsequent regulations seemed outdated because of their mildness.

45. Except for details, H. Graetz's summary review of *Die westgothische Gesetzgebung in Betreff der Juden*, published in 1858, has not been greatly improved upon by Görres, Juster, Parkes, and Katz. The general evolution of Visigothic law and the history of its kings in their relations to the Church have found careful investigators in Felix Dahn, Pius B. Gams, Rafael de Ureña y Smenjaud, and others. Cf. the bibliography listed in Katz, *Spain and Gaul*, pp. 166 ff. Of more recent provenance are, e.g., P. Meréa's *Estudos de direito visigotico* (although without direct reference to Jews, this volume sheds light on such legal institutions as parental authority and puts into bolder relief the removal of Jewish children from the control of their parents), and F. S. Lear's analysis of "The Public Law of the Visigothic Code," *Speculum*, XXVI, 1–23. On the other hand, H. Eicke's *Geschichte der westgotischen Könige seit Alarichs Tod*, generally undocumented, is interesting mainly for its Nazi interpretation. Most grievous is, of course, the total absence of Hebrew sources, so that even the few narrative records or polemics, such as have come down to us from Isidore of Seville or Julian of Toledo, are all works of opponents. Later generations of European Jews would at least have left behind some dirges or litanies on their great sufferings. Jewry under the Visigoths apparently produced no literature of its own, although its general level of culture must have been sufficiently high to account for its apparent attraction to Christian converts. To judge from the frequent discussions at the councils, Jewish missionary successes, however moderate in scope, were a permanent thorn in the flesh of the Spanish churchmen.

46. Although no contemporary source mentions this nexus between the Perso-Byzantine war and Sisebut's sudden decision, it alone seems to offer a reasonable explanation. The king certainly required no direct prompting by Emperor Heraclius, with whom he was to conclude a formal treaty in 616. Cf. Katz's *Spain and Gaul*, p. 12. There is no question, moreover, that the impact of Byzantium had made itself felt in all walks of Visigothic life. Cf. especially P. Goubert, "Byzance et l'Espagne visigothique (554–711)," [*Revue des*] *Etudes byzantines*, II, 5–78; and "L'Administration de l'Espagne byzantine," *ibid.*, III, 127–42; IV, 71–134. The latter essay discusses, in particular, the religious and political influences emanating from the Byzantine Empire. The legal consequences were even more pronounced, since many passages in the *Leges Visigothorum* were merely paraphrased from the Code of Justinian. Cf.

A. K. Ziegler's dissertation, *Church and State in Visigothic Spain,* pp. 74 ff., and the sources cited there.

47. Isidore of Seville, *Historia Gothorum, Wandalorum, Sveborum,* LX, ed. by T. Mommsen, in *MGH,* Auctores ant., XI, 291; *Leges Visigothorum,* XII.2.13–14, ed. by Zeumer, pp. 418 ff.; IV Toledan Council, canons 57, 59, in Mansi, *Collectio,* X, 633 (summarized in Hefele, *History,* trans. by Clark, IV, 456). Cf. *infra,* n. 50; and the anonymous *Chronicon Moissiacense,* ed. by G. H. Pertz, in *MGH,* Scriptores, I, 286. Although writing some two centuries after the event (about 819), this chronicler doubtless derived his data from some older source or oral tradition. Isidore of Seville's condemnation of these proceedings in his *Historia Gothorum (loc. cit.)* is somewhat softened by his concluding reflection that "after all, as it is written, Christ must be annunciated, be it through some incidental method, or according to the truth."

This polarity in approach to enforced conversion characterized also Isidore's other writings, including his apologetic treatise, *De fide catholica ex veteri et novo Testamento, contra Judaeos* (in *PL,* LXXXIII, 449–538), characteristically written at the request of his sister, Florentina, "for the edification of thy study." Nor is there any record that he had ever dared to protest directly to Sisebut. On the contrary, he often greatly praised the king for his piety. His censure was written after Sisebut's death under the calmer regime of Swinthila (624). Cf. also the somewhat forced arguments offered by P. Séjourné in his biography of *Saint Isidore de Séville,* pp. 252 ff. In general, however, this influential Spanish theologian and philosopher of history was anything but a friend of Jews. Cf. the excerpts from his polemical tracts, readily available in an English translation in A. L. Williams's *Adversus Judaeos,* pp. 215 ff.; and Williams's earlier analytical essay, "The Jews: Christian Apologists in Early Spain," *Church Quarterly Review,* C, 267–87 (discussing also Prudentius, Hildefonsus, and Julian; on the latter see also *infra,* n. 55). Characteristically, Isidore's anti-Jewish works did not deter such later Spanish-Jewish authors as Abraham bar Ḥiyya from accepting some of his teachings and outlook on history. Cf. *infra,* Chap. XXVIII, n. 98. The general, extremely complex and ramified problem of enforced conversion, and the attitude of the Christian Churches to its appropriateness before, and validity after, baptism, will be more fully analyzed in the light of the fine nuances drawn by the advanced canon jurists of the later Middle Ages.

48. Cf. the characteristic passages from the *Leges Visigothorum* and conciliar canons cited by Juster in *La Condition légale,* p. 10 n. 2. Juster also pointed out that we ought not to be misled by this equivocal terminology into believing, as did Graetz, that Recceswinth was prepared to tolerate professing Jews. As is well known, the accusation that the presence of an organized Jewish community was largely responsible for the "obduracy" of the converts was to play a particularly tragic role in the Judeo-Spanish relations during the fifteenth century.

49. Joseph ben Joshua ha-Kohen, *'Emeq ha-bakhah* (Valley of Tears; on Jewish sufferings), ed. by M. Letteris, p. 7 (in M. Wiener's German translation, p. 5, giving 616 as the year of Sisebut's decree). Cf. also Samuel Usque, *Consolaçam as tribulaçoens de Israel,* ed. by M. dos Remedios, III, pp. i–ii. That these sixteenth-century authors should have had access to some written Jewish sources dating from the Visigothic period, as is often asserted, is extremely unlikely. They probably had to

rely on oral traditions which, as we shall see, had generally become far less reliable than in ancient times. Cf. *infra,* Chaps. XXVII, nn. 21, 23, and XXVIII, nn. 62, 65.

50. Braulio, *Epistolae,* XXI, in *PL,* LXXX, 667 ff.; Wamba's pathetic decree in *Leges Visigothorum,* IX.2, ed. by Zeumer, pp. 370 ff.; and other sources cited by Lear in *Speculum,* XXVI, 3 ff. The text of Braulio's letter, too, is available only in a unique ninth-century copy. Cf. Z. García Villada's *Catálogo de los códices y documentos de la Catedral de Léon,* p. 54. In his reply Braulio clearly intimated that the pope himself had condoned the relapse of baptized Jews. Braulio may have been influenced in this firm stand by his close associate, "Samuel" Taio, apparently of Jewish descent and possibly himself a convert, who was to succeed him in the bishopric of Saragossa. Cf. Fidel Fita's detailed analysis of that correspondence, which he was the first to locate, in "Il Papa Honorio I y San Braulio de Zaragoza," *La Ciudad de Dios,* Vols. IV–VI; C. H. Lynch's biography of *Saint Braulio, Bishop of Saragossa (631–651),* pp. 60, 131 ff., 145 ff.; and *supra,* n. 35. Little is known about Honorius' attitude to the Jews of Rome, but he generally sought to avoid controversial issues, as in his much-debated letter to Patriarch Sergius of Constantinople on the subject of monenergism (634). Cf. also the other data cited by R. Aigrain in Bréhier and his *Grégoire le Grand* (Fliche and Martin, *Histoire de l'Eglise,* Vol. V), pp. 397 ff. This general complacency doubly underscores the pope's sudden initiative in Spain four years later, evidently in reaction to the intervening events in the Near East. It may also be noted that in 641, Braulio advised a fellow-bishop that Easter must not fall on April 1, because it would then coincide with the Jewish Passover, contrary to the decision of the Council of Nicaea. He suggested, therefore, the date of April 8, "for it is appropriate that theirs precede ours, just as the Old Testament comes before the New Testament." Cf. his *Epistolae,* XXII, in *PL,* LXXX, 671; and Lynch's analysis, pp. 116 f. Unwittingly, the Saragossan bishop ran counter to the express purpose of Justinian's *Novella* of 543, offering another proof of the latter's total ineffectiveness. See *supra,* n. 9, and Vol. II, p. 400 n. 21.

51. IV Toledan Council, canons 57–66; VI Council, canon 3; and Recceswinth's opening address at the VIII Council, in Mansi, *Collectio,* X, 633 f., 663 f., 1209 (in Hefele, *History,* trans. by Clark, IV, 456 f., 461, 470). The crucial canon 60 of the Fourth Council, which was attended by sixty-nine ecclesiastical dignitaries from the whole realm, concerned the handing over of Jewish children to genuine Christians. Its text is uncertain and has given rise to extended discussions. But the reading of several manuscripts, "Judaeorum filios et filias baptizatos," seems most acceptable. Cf. Hefele, *History,* IV, 456 n. 1. However, the presence of numerous such children in 633 is very unlikely. The relapsed Jews, whom the Council accused of overtly practicing circumcision among Christian proselytes, had hardly performed any baptismal rites on their own children since Swinthilas' accession to the throne a dozen years before. Evidently the Council wished to remove from untrustworthy parental control all children born to relapsed Jews, whether or not they had gone through the baptismal ceremony. The distrust, on the other hand, of even the baptized second generation went so far that, "on command of the King," the council forbade their appointment to public office (canon 65).

52. The *placitum* under Chintila is alluded to in *Leges Visigothorum,* XII.2.17, ed. by Zeumer, pp. 425 f., but only that given to Recceswinth is cited there in full

(also in Mansi, *Collectio,* X, 1229 f.). It is reproduced in English translation in Parkes, *Conflict,* pp. 394 f. The term *placitum,* as defined by some jurists, in contrast to *pactum,* designated an agreement which, although involuntarily entered into, nevertheless had to be scrupulously observed. Cf. Isidore of Seville's *Etymologiae,* v.24.19, in *PL,* LXXXII, 205 (not Isidore's opinion: *alii dicunt*). These formulas of abjuration were in many respects an innovation in the Church's treatment of converted Jews. Previously there had been various ceremonies connected with the return of heretics. In Spain herself we find a summary formula suggested by Pope Hormisdas (514–23) for some heterodox Greeks. Cf. his letter to the Spanish bishops, appended to Isidore of Seville's *Works* in *PL,* LXXXIV, 823 f. However, Jews had been treated more informally. Cf. the impressive array of data assembled by Juster in his *Empire romain,* I, 110 ff.

53. *Leges Visigothorum,* xii.2.18; 3.1–28, ed. by Zeumer, pp. 426 ff., 475 f.; IX Toledan Council of 655, canon 17; XII Council of 681, Introduction and canon 9; XVI Council of 693, Introduction and canon 1, in Mansi, *Collectio,* XI, 1023 f., 1035 f.; XII, 59 ff., 68 f. (in Hefele, *History,* trans. by Clark, IV, 473 f.; V, 208, 210 f., 243 ff.); Montesquieu's judgment in *The Spirit of the Laws,* xxviii.1, in the English translation by Thomas Nugent, 3d ed., II, 236. Apart from their intrinsic weaknesses such royal and conciliar enactments were often defeated also by the overwhelming force of old and deep-rooted local customs. Cf. T. Melicher's data on *Der Kampf zwischen Gesetzes- und Gewohnheitsrecht im Westgotenreich.* This dichotomy explains, in particular, also the great divergences of the later Spanish popular *fueros* from the Visigothic theory. Cf. *ibid.,* pp. 199 ff., 210 f.; W. Reinhart's more general observations on "La Tradición visigoda en el nacimiento de Castilla," *Estudios dedicados a Menéndez Pidal,* I, 535–54, esp. pp. 543 ff.; and *infra,* Chap, XX, n. 30.

54. *Leges Visigothorum,* xii.3.24, ed. by Zeumer, pp. 452 f. The widespread corruption even among bishops had induced the Fourth and Eleventh Councils to legislate against simony in episcopal elections. Other councils often had occasion to condemn further malpractices of the higher and lower clergy. Cf. Ziegler's *Church and State,* pp. 45 f. On the other hand, one must not lose sight of the self-interest of many churchmen in Jewish conversions. Although several councils reiteratedly prohibited charging fees for the administration of the sacrament of baptism, this very reiteration indicated how difficult it was to eradicate that practice. Moreover, these synods allowed the clerics to receive gifts for their ministrations. Certainly, in the case of mass conversions, it must have been extremely difficult to distinguish a gift from a fee. Cf. P. Glaue, *Zur Geschichte der Taufe in Spanien,* II, 34 f.

55. XVI Toledan Council, canon 1; XVII Council, canon 8, in Mansi, *Collectio,* XII, 68 f., 93 f., 102 ff. (in Hefele, *History,* trans. by Clark, V, 243 ff.). Cf. *Leges Visigothorum,* xii.2.18, ed. by Zeumer, pp. 426 ff., 481 ff. On the economic status and taxation of Spanish Jewry, see *infra,* Chaps. XX and XXII. Julian's *Liber Responsionum* is no longer extant, but it is mentioned by his biographer, Felix, in his *Vita,* xii, in *PL,* XCVI, 448. This tract must have been written in the same vein as his *De Comprobatione aetatis sextae, ibid.,* cols. 535–86. Remarkably, at that late stage a primate of Spain, writing at the king's request, still found it necessary to argue for Jesus' messianic character on chronological grounds, against the accepted Jewish chronology. He insisted, of course, that one must follow the figures given in

the Septuagint, rather than those found in the Hebrew Scriptures (cols. 539 f.). See *supra,* n. 14; and *infra,* Chap. XXIV, n. 50. Julian's anti-Jewish sentiments, a characteristic not infrequent among persons trying to hide their Jewish origin (in the case of Julian this origin, sometimes doubted, is attested by Isidor Pacensis), did not prevent him from entertaining friendly relations with individual Jews. On one occasion he was tactfully reproved by Idalius, bishop of Barcelona, for having sent him a book (Julian's *Prognosticon*) through a "crude" Jew, Restitutus. Cf. Idalius' letter of 688, included in Julian's preface, in *PL,* XCVI, 458, 816. It is impossible to ascertain, however, what role, if any, Julian played in the preparation of Erwig's twenty-eight anti-Jewish laws. Cf. J. Rivera, *San Julian Arzbispo de Toledo,* pp. 181 ff.; and F. X. Murphy, "Julian of Toledo and the Fall of the Visigothic Kingdom of Spain," *Speculum,* XXVII, 13 f. The generally close collaboration between the "Byzantine" usurper, Erwig, and this "Jewish" archbishop, whose joint rule over the Spanish Goths so greatly distressed the Nazi historian, Eicke (*Geschichte der westgotischen Könige,* pp. 300 ff.), makes Julian's co-authorship very likely.

56. Julian's *Historia rebellionis Pauli adversus Wambam,* v, xxviii, ed. by W. Levison, in *MGH,* Scriptores Merov., V, 504 f., 524. On the exception stipulated by Egica in favor of Jews inhabiting the strategically important places in Visigothic Gaul, see the king's aforementioned opening address to the XVII Council, in Mansi, *Collectio,* XII, 93 f.; or in the *Leges Visigothorum,* ed. by Zeumer, p. 485. Cf. also Juster's comments in his *Condition légale,* p. 22 n. 3; and, on the subsequent destinies of the great Jewish center of Narbonne, *infra,* Chap. XX, n. 58.

57. The nexus between the intolerant decrees of Sisebut and Dagobert, to be sure, seems first to have been clearly articulated by Paulus Aemilius of Verona in his *Res gestae Francorum,* p. 44, cited in Graetz, *Geschichte der Juden,* 4th ed., V, 58 n. 1. The argument was here advanced that "it appeared unseeming to a Frank to retain any longer the indomitable enemies of our faith who had been expelled by the Visigoths and admitted to his lands. He would thus seem to lag behind the Visigoths in his faith." But some such connection is also implied in statements by contemporary chroniclers. Cf. J. Aronius *et al., Regesten zur Geschichte der Juden im Fränkischen und Deutschen Reiche bis zum Jahre 1273,* p. 21 No. 59. Otherwise, we hear next to nothing about the Jews of the Frankish kingdom during the two decades of 613–33. We possess only one royal decree of 614—one of the few Merovingian decrees extant—and decisions of two or three councils (Fifth Paris of 614; Clichy of 626; and possibly Reims 627–30; see *infra,* n. 63) dealing with the Jewish question more or less in the traditional vein. The interrelated enactments of 614 (see *infra* n. 64), evincing serious concern about Jewish military or administrative control over Christians, may actually have preceded the marked influx of Spanish refugees, which the French Christian chronicler recorded under the year 615.

58. Legends connected with the prayer, *Ve-hu raḥum* (And He, the Merciful), cited in L. Zunz's *Literaturgeschichte der synagogalen Poesie,* p. 17; Josephus, *Antt.,* xvii.13.2.344; xviii.7.2.252. The frequent polemical preoccupation with Jews of the influential bishop of Arles, St. Caesarius, his denunciation of their allegedly treasonable attitude, and, on the other hand, his setting of their strict Sabbath observance as an example to be followed by Christians—all show that they occupied an important position in that city. Cf. his *Sermones,* ed. by G. Morin, esp. No. lxxiv in Vol. I,

pp. 308 f.; *supra,* Vol. II, pp. 165, 210, 398 n. 10, 406 n. 42; and, on Arles' focal importance for the evolution of French Christianity, J. Gibert, *Arles gréco-romain, seuil des Gaules chrétiennes.*

59. Frey, *Corpus inscriptionum,* No. 670. Cf. also the other inscriptions reproduced and analyzed *ibid.,* Nos. 666 ff., and Katz, *Spain and Gaul,* pp. 6 ff., 148 ff. The interesting inscription found at Auch in the Department of Gers and dating from approximately 700 C.E. (Frey, No. 671; Katz, pp. 152 ff.) evidently referred to a donation made to a synagogue by one Jonah. Cf. the reconstruction and translation of the text in L. Robert's review of Frey's *Corpus* in *REJ,* CI, 80 f.

60. *C. Th.,* XVI.8.3–4, ed. by Mommsen and Meyer, I, 887. In his careful topographic studies pertaining to the location of Jewish settlements, R. Anchel pointed out how closely most of these, even in the later Middle Ages, had clung to the original Roman highways. Cf. "The Early History of the Jewish Quarters in Paris," *JSS,* II, 45–60 (repeated in French in *Les Juifs de France,* pp. 59 ff.); and *infra,* n. 61. On the sources and recent debates concerning the Jewish settlement in the Rhinelands in Roman times, cf. *supra,* Vol. II, pp. 210, 406 n. 42. M. Haller's more general review of "La Question juive pendant le premier millénaire chrétien," *RHPR,* XV, 293–334, possesses mainly the merits of popularization.

61. All these statements are made here with considerable diffidence because of the extreme paucity and limited range of the extant sources. As in Spain, we hear practically nothing from the Jews themselves, except through the mute testimony of several inscriptions and some distorted traditions recorded by writers removed from the scene by several centuries. Even the legalistic decrees of kings and councils are far fewer and less informative than those of the Visigothic realm. On the other hand, we secure a few deeper insights through the narrations of Gregory of Tours and other chroniclers which, carefully edited and examined by competent scholars for many generations, have been exploited from various angles. Efforts have also been made to utilize more fully the findings of archaeology and to draw therefrom a more integrated picture of the social conditions in late Roman and Merovingian France. Cf. especially E. Salin's comprehensive review of *La Civilisation mérovingienne d'après les sépultures, les textes et le laboratoire;* and, on the progressive archaeological discoveries and reinterpretations, the successive volumes of *Gallia, fouilles et monuments archéologiques en France métropolitaine,* published by the Ministry of Public Education. In *Les Juifs de France,* pp. 41 ff., R. Anchel made a valiant effort to assemble all data for a "toponymie juive," and listed an impressive array of localities throughout France whose names owed their origin to the presence of Jews in their early historical stages. But most of these names either stem from later periods, or are undatable. In general, our knowledge of Jewish history in the Merovingian era has thus far received but minor stimuli from these new approaches, and we have advanced here but little beyond the state of Jewish historiography in the last decades of the nineteenth century.

62. Cf. *Lex Romana Burgundionum,* in *Leges Burgundionum,* ed. by L. R. de Salis, in *MGH,* Legum sectio II, Vol. I, pp. 123 ff. (only mixed marriages are prohibited; XX.4, p. 143); in K. Fisher's English translation, *The Burgundian Code,* p. 86, Art. CII. Although Burgundy lost her independence in 534, and many Visigothic posses-

sions were also taken over by the Franks in the following years, the continued impact of the Roman system was reinforced by the growing reverence for custom. We must bear in mind, moreover, that the Frankish law itself, and particularly the *Lex Salica,* was also influenced by Jewish legal concepts. Cf. J. J. Rabinowitz's somewhat overdrawn picture of "The Influence of Jewish Law upon the Development of Frankish Law," *PAAJR,* XVI, 205–24; and his *Jewish Law,* pp. 220 ff.

63. Councils of Vannes of 465, canon 12; Epaon of 517, canon 15; II Orléans of 533, canon 19; III Orléans of 538, canons 13, 30; I Mâcon of 581, canons 14–15; Clichy of 626, canon 13 (Reims canon 11; see below), in Mansi, *Collectio,* VII, 954; VIII, 561, 838, 861; IX, 15 f., 19, 934 f.; X, 596 (in Hefele, *History,* trans. by Clark, IV, 17, 111, 187, 207, 209, 404, 446). Childebert's decree of unknown date is not included in A. Boretius's ed. of the *Capitularia regum francorum,* in *MGH,* Legum sectio II, Vol. I, but is correctly mentioned by Aronius (*Regesten,* pp. 12 f., No. 32), on the basis of later references. The likelihood that this decree was intended to confirm the decision of the Third Council of Orléans is enhanced by the presence of a letter by the same king (included in Boretius's collection, No. 2, pp. 2 f.), apparently confirming a canon adopted by the Second Council of Orléans five years previously against Christian emulation of pagan practices. Cf. C. de Clercq's remarks in *La Législation religieuse franque de Clovis à Charlemagne,* pp. 16 f. De Clercq has also convincingly argued that the Council of Reims (627–30) was at best but a regional assembly, which in essence repeated only the decisions of Clichy (pp. 65 f.). No reference is therefore made here to that Council. The dates of some of these assemblies are likewise in doubt. We have generally followed their traditional dating, still accepted by De Clercq, rather than those given in Anchel's *Juifs de France,* pp. 27 f.

The problem of intermarriage will be more fully discussed in its better known later medieval context. However, it may be worth mentioning that the preponderance of males over females, characteristic of all countries of immigration, doubtless plagued also most of the early medieval Jewish communities in western Europe. Even in Venosa, located in an area of older and better established Jewish settlements, the extant inscriptions indicate a preponderance of 45 male over 29 female names. While there, as well as in Rome, some of that surplus may perhaps be accounted for by a larger number of epitaphs devoted to deceased men—such a difference is yet to be proved from any reliable source—the general impression of the numerical superiority of Jewish men seems incontrovertible. Cf. H. J. Leon's recent reexamination of the epigraphic evidence relating to "The Jews of Venusia," *JQR,* XLIV, 279.

64. Councils of Clermont, canon 9; III Orléans, canon 13; IV Orléans, canons 30–31; I Mâcon, canons 13, 16; V Paris, canon 17 (15); Clichy, canon 13 (Reims canon 11); Châlons, canon 9, in Mansi, *Collectio,* VIII, 861; IX, 15 f., 118, 934 f.; X, 542, 596 (Reims; see n. 63), 1191 (in Hefele, *History,* IV, 191, 207, 213 f., 404 f., 440, 446, 464). The decision of the Council of Paris, convoked by Clothar II, received royal confirmation in an edict issued within a few days (Oct. 18, 614). This edict included the provision barring Jews from public office (cap. 10). Cf. Boretius's ed. No. 9, p. 22; and De Clercq's comments thereon in his *Législation,* pp. 57 ff. Cf. also *ibid.,* pp. 67 ff. concerning the date of the Council of Châlon, which evinced special concern that Christian slaves not be sold outside the confines of the Frankish possessions where they might fall into the hands of Jews. In fact, however, other western countries

were more stringent in their outlawry of Jewish ownership of Christian slaves, seemingly already resolved by the Theodosian Code. It was this relative forbearance of the Frankish kings which called forth repeated censures by Gregory the Great. Cf. his aforementioned *Epistolae,* IX.213, 215 (in *MGH,* II, 199 f., 201 f.); and *supra,* n. 37. In evaluating these conciliar decisions one must also bear in mind that not all of them were national assemblies. In periods of the divided monarchy, especially, they represented but limited sections in the country. Nevertheless, by constantly adding to the mass of available canon legislation, they, too, often influenced the Jewish status beyond the confines of their immediate authority.

65. IV Orléans, canon 15, in Mansi, *Collectio,* IX, 115 (unduly abbreviated in Hefele's *History,* IV, 212); Gregory of Tours, *Historia Francorum,* IV.12; VI.5, in W. Arndt's ed. in *MGH,* I, 149, 247 ff.; and in the English translation by O. M. Dalton, II, 125, 235; see Aronius, *Regesten,* p. 5, No. 9; and *supra,* Vol. II, p. 398 n. 10. Priscus may be identical with a Jewish mintmaster by that name, mentioned together with one Domnulus in a coin of Cabillonum (Châlons sur Saône) by G. Ponton d'Amécourt in his *Description générale des monnais mérovingiennes,* ed. by A. de Belfort, I, 323. Cf. *Regesten,* p. 16, No. 45; and *infra,* Chap. XXII, n. 79. Ironically, in 589 the Council of Narbonne was to prohibit Jews from loudly reciting psalms even in funeral cortèges of their own (canon 9, in Mansi, *Collectio,* IX, 1016; in Hefele, *History,* IV, 423).

66. Gregory of Tours, *Historia,* VI.5, 17, 46, ed. by Arndt in *MGH,* I, 247 ff., 259 f., 286 (in Dalton's translation, pp. 235 ff., 250 f., 278). Despite his obvious bias, Gregory's narrative, a main source of information for Frankish history till 591, also includes a few significant references to contemporary Jews, while his statements about the ancient Israelites are all second or third hand. His general veracity has stood up quite well under modern criticisms. Cf., e.g., J. M. Wallace-Hadrill's analysis of "The Work of Gregory of Tours in the Light of Modern Research," *Transactions* of the Royal Historical Society, 1951, pp. 25–45.

67. *Historia,* V.11; VIII.1, ed. by Arndt, in *MGH,* I, 199 ff., 326 (in Dalton's translation, II, 177 ff., 329); and *supra,* n. 60. The events in Clermont were immediately extolled in a poem by Venantius Fortunatus. Cf. his *Carmina,* V.5, ed. by F. Leo, in *MGH,* Auctores ant., IV, 107 ff. The figure of more than 500 converts reported by Gregory is obviously exaggerated, since there were few medieval communities which had as many as 500 Jewish inhabitants. See the data analyzed in my *Jewish Community,* III, 106 ff., n. 19; and, on the generally small size of the Frankish towns, F. Lot's *Recherches sur la population et la superficie des cités,* Vols. I–III (he believes, for instance, that Clermont in the days of Gregory of Tours could not possibly have had more than 2,000–3,000 inhabitants; II, 111). The forced conversion in Clermont was allegedly preceded by a similar action of the pious bishop Ferreolus in Uzès, in southern France (about 558). Cf. Aronius, *Regesten,* pp. 11 f., No. 30. The chronicler's report is greatly vitiated, however, by his reference to the royal suspicions of Ferreolus' loyalty, because "he ate and drank with Jews and Saracens, and gave them gifts," which in the middle of the sixth century was a stark anachronism. Perhaps our writer merely misread his source, which might have mentioned the bishop's intercourse with Syrians and other partisans of Visigothic rule. The city

had only been occupied by the Franks for a short time, and, before Reccared's conversion to Christianity, many Jews, as well as Syrians, for commercial reasons, may indeed have longed for the restoration of Visigothic rule.

68. The story of Heraclius' dream, or astrological prediction, is recorded in Fredegarius' chronicle, IV.65; and the *Gesta Dagoberti,* XXIV, both ed. by B. Krusch, in *MGH,* Scriptores Merov., II, 153, 409. It echoed similar reports current in the East. Cf. the sources listed by J. Starr in *JPOS,* XV, 288 n. 41; and F. Dölger's remarks in his *Regesten der Kaiserurkunden,* pp. 19, No. 168, and 24, No. 207. Although the date of Dagobert's decree still is uncertain, it seems to have stemmed from the embassy sent by Dagobert to Constantinople in 629, soon after the unification of all Frankish possessions under his scepter. By signing with the Franks a treaty of perpetual peace, the Byzantine emperor evidently sought to secure his rear in the face of the new menace. It probably was not until 632–34, however, when, as we recall, Heraclius himself enforced baptism in North Africa, that the emperor may have addressed some such urgent message to the western monarchs. Dagobert, on the other hand, not personally a fanatic, seems to have wished not only to accommodate Heraclius' plans for all Christendom, but also to appease domestic public opinion and the Church, scandalized by his amours. He doubtless expected to secure much good will by the display of religious piety in enforcing Jewish baptism, as well as by his generous contributions to pious foundations. In view of the paucity of sources, even R. Barroux's more recent literary biography of *Dagobert, roi des Francs* (p. 157), contributes a little to the understanding of the king's motives.

69. H. Graetz, *Geschichte der Juden,* 4th ed., IV, 372 f.; S. Assaf's edition of *Teshubot ha-geonim* (Responsa Geonica ex fragmentis Cantabrigensibus, 1942), pp. 147, 165; M. Seligsohn, "Quatre poésies judéo-persanes sur les persécutions des Juifs d'Ispahan," *REJ,* XLIV, 87–103, 244–59; W. J. Fischel, "Isfahān: The Story of a Jewish Community in Persia," in *Starr Mem. Vol.,* pp. 111–28; Mutaḥḥar al-Maqdisi (Muqaddasi), *K. al-Bad' wal-Tar'ikh* (Le Livre de la Création et de l'Histoire), ed. by C. Huart, IV, 30 f. (Arabic), 28 f. (French). Cf. *infra,* Chap. XVII n. 43.

None of Zaradusht's or Mazdak's own writings have come down to us, although two different Arabic translations of Mazdak's works were still known to the famous tenth-century Arab bibliographer, Ibn abi-Ya'qub an-Nadim. Cf. his *K. al-Fihrist* (The List), ed. by G. Flügel, I, 342; II, 179. We are therefore entirely dependent on the information supplied by hostile writers. The more sympathetic authors, such as the well-known twelfth-century student of comparative religion, Abu'l Fath Muḥammad ash-Shahrastani, are far removed in time from the scene of events. To be sure, this heresiologue still knew of the more or less clandestine existence of four Iranian sects in his day, which professed doctrines in direct filiation from the teachings of Mazdak. However, there is no way of telling how closely these offshoots resembled their spiritual progenitor. Byzantine contemporaries or near contemporaries, like Procopius or Agathias Scholasticus, even if not generally hostile to everything Persian, were dependent on the official documents, even propaganda, emanating from the Persian court and priests after the suppression of Mazdakism. Cf., e.g., J. Suolahti's *On the Persian Sources Used by the Byzantine Historian Agathias.* That is why the absence of Jewish sources, be it only in the form of stereotype complaints about persecutions, is doubly grievous. Jews seem to have taken no direct part in the controversy. Christian, but not Jewish, leaders are recorded among the debaters in the religious disputation staged by the king before his formal condemnation of Mazdakism. Precisely for this reason Jewish sources might have contributed significantly to the elucidation of this mysterious historic evolution. In any case, the old antagonistic appreciation of the entire movement has given way to a more judicious evaluation in A. Christensen's analysis of *Le Règne du roi Kavadh I et le communisme mazdakite* and *L'Iran sous les Sassanides*, pp. 316 ff.; and even, for obvious reasons, to enthusiastic approval in N. V. Pigulevskaya's Russian essay on "The Mazdakite Movement," *Izvestiya* (Bulletin) of the Academy of Science of the USSR, I (1944), Part 4, pp. 171–81. It is evident that modern Jewish historians have greatly exaggerated the impact of Mazdakism on Persian Jewry. Cf. also *supra*, Vol. II, pp. 182, 399 n. 15.

70. The general nature of Khosroe I's fiscal reform is often overlooked. Cf. C. Huart's brief summary in *L'Iran antique*, pp. 386 ff. On the figures pertaining to the treasury's revenues and reserves in 607–26, see Christensen's *Iran*, pp. 453 f. (based on Nöldeke's and Ernest Blochet's estimates); and, more generally, F. Altheim and R. Stiehl, "Staatshaushalt der Sasaniden," *Nouvelle Clio*, V, 267–321. If these estimates are correct, Khosroe II's reserve was nearly four times the amount of the 320,000 gold pounds accumulated by the Byzantine emperor, Anastasius. Cf. Procopius, *Anecdota*, XIX.7, in *Works*, VI, 228 f.; and A. M. Andreades, "Public Finances," in Baynes and Moss, *Byzantium*, p. 79 n. 1.

71. Cf. Theophanes, *Chronographia*, ed. by De Boor, I, 178 f.; and Malalas, *Chronographia*, ed. by Dindorf, p. 455. The report of these two chroniclers is evidently confused. The story in Malalas may indeed refer to an earlier instigation of Samaritan refugees in Persia and their advocacy of continued warfare. However, the figure of 50,000 such refugees seems not only unlikely, but probably an interpolation by a later copyist, who confused this story with the report in Theophanes' chronicle relating to Khosroe. The latter is likewise far from clear, and was omitted by Theophanes' Latin paraphrast, Anastasius, in De Boor's ed., p. 134. Cf. also S. Krauss, *Studien*, p. 17 (itself far from unequivocal); and *infra*, Chap. XXV, n. 31.

72. Hormizd's declaration was reported, in part doubtless from Christian sources, by Abu Jafar Muḥammad ibn Jarir aṭ-Ṭabari in his *K. Aḥbar ar-rusul w'al-muluk* (Annales), ed. by M. J. de Goeje, II, 991 (in Nöldeke's abridged translation, pp. 268 f., especially emphasizing the king's toleration of Christians); G. Hoffmann's *Auszüge aus syrischen Akten persischer Märtyrer*, p. 122; and P. Devos's "Sainte Sirin, martyre sous Khosrau Ier Anošarvan," *Analecta Bollandiana*, LXIV, 128 f.

73. Theophylactus, *Historiae*, V.7.1; 7.5–8, ed. by Bekker, pp. 217 ff.; ed. by De Boor, pp. 200 ff. The events of 589–91 are described in detail by P. Goubert in his *Byzance avant l'Islam*, I, 119 ff. On the proximity of New or Roman Antioch to Maḥoza within the complex structure of the Persian "city of cities," Ctesiphon, see Christensen's *Iran*, pp. 383 ff.; J. Obermeyer's more detailed data in *Die Landschaft Babylonien im Zeitalter des Talmuds und des Gaonats*, pp. 161 ff., 180; and *supra*, n. 18. The talmudic data are well summarized in M. D. Yudlevitz's Hebrew monograph *Maḥoza* (Maḥoza: From Jewish Life in Talmudic Times), also making a case for the residence there of Exilarch Samuel, Raba's contemporary (pp. 96 f.).

74. Michael Syrus, *Chronique,* ed. by Chabot, II, 410 (Syriac), 410 (French); Sebeos, *Histoire d'Héraclius,* xxx, in F. Macler's French translation, pp. 94 f. Burzoe's autobiography has long been known from Ibn al-Muqaffa's introduction to his Arabic translation of the famous romance, the *Kelila and Dimna* (on this romance and its influence on Hebrew literature, see *infra,* Chap. XXXII). It is available in T. Nöldeke's German translation, entitled *Burzōes Einleitung zu dem Buche Kalīla waDimna,* p. 24. On Khosroe's Christian wife, or wives, see Goubert, *Byzance avant l'Islam,* I, 176 ff.

75. J. B. Pritchard, *Ancient Near Eastern Texts,* pp. 278 f.; Jer. 23:24. A. Guillaume goes decidedly too far, however, in suggesting (as had in some respects P. Haupt and others before him) that "the sons of 'Eber peopled the whole of the Arabian Peninsula" and that "Ḥabiru, Hebrew and Arab are interrelated much more closely than might otherwise be supposed." Cf. "The Habiru, the Hebrew and the Arabs," *PEQ,* 1946, p. 85. Similarly exaggerated, from another angle, is J. A. Montgomery's conclusion "that not from the wisdom of the Egyptian, Babylonian or Greek civilizations came our Western religions, but out of Arabia." Cf. his otherwise meritorious study, *Arabia and the Bible,* p. 188. A judicious critique of this view, pointing out differences as well as similarities, is given by S. D. Goitein in "The 'Arab' Source of Israel and Its Religion" (Hebrew), *Zion,* II, 1–18. Cf. also the related briefer study of "Arabia in the New Testament" by E. F. F. Bishop in *MW,* XXXIV, 192–98.

76. 'Erubin 63a; Shabbat 19b. The era of Nabatean expansion, roughly coinciding with Rome's rule over the Near East, has been illumined by many recent archaeological discoveries. Cf. especially A. Kammerer's *Pétra et la Nabatène;* N. Glueck's "Explorations" in *AASOR,* Vols. XIV–XV, XVII–XIX, XXVI–XXVIII; his more popular summary in *The Other Side of the Jordan;* and J. Starckey's briefer historical sketch of "The Nabateans," *Biblical Archaeologist,* XVIII, 84–106 (chiefly devoted to the period before 70). Cf. also G. and A. Horsfield, "Sela-Petra, the Rock of Edom and Nabatene, I–IV," *QDAP,* VII–IX (was to be continued); C. Kraeling's *Gerasa,* pp. 36 ff.; R. Devreesse's data on "Le Christianisme dans la Province d'Arabie," *RB,* LI, 110–46; and, more generally, M. Rostovtzeff's *Caravan Cities.* Far less is known about the conditions in the areas further north, except Palmyra. Our information about the Ghassanids and Lakhmids still depends largely on external and later sources, distorted by both bias and errors in transmission. The available material has been carefully analyzed by H. Z. Hirschberg in his *Yisrael ba-'Arab* (Jews in Arabia: History of the Jews in Ḥimyara and Hejaz from the Destruction of the Second Temple to the Crusades), pp. 36 ff. Of considerable interest are also such related studies as *Le Christianisme des Arabes nomades sur les limes et le désert syro-mésopotamien* by H. Charles, and "Arabes-Perses et Arabes-Romains. Lakhmides et Ghassanides," by R. Devreesse, *RB,* LI, 263–307; and esp. R. Dussaud's comprehensive analysis of *La Pénétration des Arabes en Syrie avant l'Islam,* including sections on Nabateans, Palmyrenes, and South Arabians in Syria. Talmudic references have been conveniently assembled by S. Krauss in his "Talmudische Nachrichten über Arabien," *ZDMG,* LXX, 325–53; and supplemented by E. I. Szadzunski in his "Addenda to Krauss," *AJSL,* XLIX, 336–37.

77. D. D. Luckenbill, *Ancient Records of Assyria and Babylonia,* I, Nos. 287, 308; II Chr. 8:4 (probably a misreading of the original "Tamar" in I Kings 9:18);

Malalas, *Chronographia,* XVIII, ed. by Dindorf, pp. 425 f. Cf. also *supra,* Vol. II, pp. 210 f., 407 n. 43; and P. K. Hitti, *History of the Arabs,* pp. 74 ff.

78. Writing before the onset of the era of extreme criticism, R. Dozy reconstructed on the basis of Arab legends a somewhat fanciful story of *Die Israeliten zu Mekka von Davids Zeit bis ins fünfte Jahrhundert unsrer Zeitrechnung.* Even in his day the book evoked considerable dissent, e.g., from J. H. Schorr. Cf. the latter's review in *Hechaluz,* XI, 47–49 (its belated publication in 1880 is attributed by M. Steinschneider to A. Geiger's influence in *Jahresberichte der Geschichtswissenschaft,* III, Part 1, 65). Subsequently scholars were inclined to disregard the Muslim legends entirely, until R. P. Dougherty identified in 1929 the city of Teima in Amurru, to which, according to a Babylonian tablet, Nabonidus had gone in 552 B.C.E., with the oasis Teima. Cf. his *Nabonidus and Belshazzar,* pp. 138 ff.; and "A Babylonian City in Arabia," *AJA,* XXXIV, 296–312. On this basis C. C. Torrey suggested that the beginnings of Jewish settlement in the area also date back to that period. Cf. his *Jewish Foundation of Islam,* pp. 10 ff. Nothing really convincing has since been said to disprove either Dougherty's or Torrey's theories. In fact, the publication of a Michigan tablet and the more recent excavation of a temple of Sin in the Ḥadhramaut have removed almost all doubts from Dougherty's identification. Cf. the data furnished by G. Caton-Thompson in *Tombs and Moon Temple of Hureidha (Hadhramaut)*; S. Smith in "An Inscription from the Temple of Sin at Ḥuraiḏha in the Ḥaḏhramawt," *BSOAS,* XI, 451–64 (referring in particular to the Caton-Thompson inscription No. 4); and in his *Isaiah Chapters XL–LV,* pp. 36 f., 136 n. 78; and F. P. Albright in "The Excavation of the Temple of the Moon at Mârib (Yemen)," *BASOR,* 128, pp. 25–38. Nor have critics of Torrey's view (e.g., Hirschberg in his *Yisrael ba-'Arab,* pp. 118, 295 n. 65) offered a satisfactory explanation as to why groups of refugees from Roman, but not from Babylonian, wars should have drifted into northern Arabia. Direct positive evidence is unfortunately lacking for either period, however.

79. Josephus, *Antt.* xv.9.3.317 (confirmed by Strabo); A. J. Jaussen and R. Savignac, *Mission archéologique en Arabie,* I, 148 ff., No. 44 (the reading *Yehudaya* is clear); II, 231, No. 386; 641 ff.; Ibn 'Abd Allah Yaqut's *K. Mu'jam al-buldān* (Geographisches Wörterbuch), ed. by F. Wüstenfeld, II, 504 f. The problems affecting the Jews on the Arabian Peninsula in the pre-Islamic age and their influence upon Mohammed have intrigued many scholars since Abraham Geiger published, a century and a quarter ago, his famous thesis, *Was hat Mohammed aus dem Judenthume aufgenommen?* Among more recent discussions, cf. J. Horovitz's "Judaeo-Arabic Relations in Pre-Islamic Times," *IC,* III, 161–99; F. X. Kortleitner's *De antiquis Arabiae incolis eorumque cum religione Mosaica rationibus;* I. Ben-Zeeb (Wolfensohn), *Ha-Yehudim ba-'Arab* (Jews in Arabia); and particuarly Hirschberg's *Yisrael ba-'Arab.* Cf. also the latter's reexamination of "Arabic Sources for the History of Jews in Arabia" (Hebrew), *Zion,* X, 81–101; XI, 17–37 (his suggestion, however, X, 94 f., that some younger midrashim were but an answer to Arab legends concerning the exercise of the *jus primae noctis* by a Jewish autocrat in Yathrib as the cause for Malik's revolt, is hardly plausible; he himself quotes earlier talmudic legends, in part going back to tannaitic times, which could well have given rise to similar elaborations). See also I. Lichtenstadter, "Some References to Jews in Pre-Islamic Arabic Literature," *PAAJR,* X, 185–94; J. Braslavsky's study

of "The Jewish Community of Khaibar" (Hebrew), *Zion,* I, 148–84 (discussing a later Genizah document published by Hirschfeld; cf. *infra,* Chap. XVII nn. 8, 16); and such general reviews as De L. O'Leary's *Arabia before Muhammad;* H. St. J. Philby's "sketch" of *The Background of Islam;* and G. L. della Vida's "Pre-Islamic Arabia," and J. Obermann's "Islamic Origins," in N. A. Faris's collection, *The Arab Heritage,* pp. 25–57, 58–120. The quotation in the text is taken from W. Caskel's lecture on "The Bedouinization of Arabia," which together with a summary of the following discussion appeared in the *Studies in Islamic Cultural History,* ed. by G. E. von Grunebaum, pp. 36–46, esp. p. 43.

Some new vistas have opened up with the successful reinterpretation of many North Arabian inscriptions written in the South Arabic alphabet by Enno Littmann, F. V. Winnett, and others. Cf. Winnett's *Study of the Lihyanite and Thamudic Inscriptions;* and "A Monotheistic Ḥimyarite Inscription," *BASOR,* 83, pp. 22–25. Cf. also Enno Littmann's "Jesus in a Pre-Islamic Arabic Inscription," *MW,* XL, 16–18. Littmann reads the name "Jesus" in a Thamudic inscription which he considers "the oldest native document of Christianity in Northern Arabia known so far." Since, however, Christian Arabs used, as far as we know, only the form "Yasu‘," it is conceivable that this was really a Jewish name. Cf. also G. Ryckmans's judicious analysis of "La Mention de Jésus dans les inscriptions arabes préislamiques," *Analecta Bollandiana,* LXVII, 63–73; and the list of Arab tribes at least partially professing Christianity in G. Graf, *Geschichte der christlichen arabischen Literatur,* I, 25 ff. Early North and South relationships and their bearings on the spread of monotheism are also illustrated by the Beth She‘arim discoveries. Cf. *infra,* note 83.

80. Philostorgius, *Historia ecclesiastica,* III.4.5, in *PG,* LXV, 481 ff. Cf. R. Devreesse's partly hypothetical data in "Le Christianisme," *RB,* LI, 110–46; D. S. Attema's lecture on *Het Oudste Christendom in Zuid-Arabië* (The Oldest Christianity in Southern Arabia); the broader surveys of "La religione nell' Arabia preislamica," by M. Guidi in *Studi e materiali di storia delle religioni,* XXI, 1–11; and *Les Religions arabes préislamiques,* by G. Ryckmans. Cf. also E. Dhorme's critical review of "Les religions arabes préislamiques," *RHR,* CXXXIII, 34–48. Of considerable value are also the extensive historical, as well as geographic, data supplied by H. von Wissmann and M. Höffner in their *Beiträge zur historischen Geographie des vorislamischen Südarabien,* with a succinct bibliography; and the former's "Geographische Grundlagen und Frühzeit der Geschichte Südarabiens," *Saeculum,* IV, 61–114.

81. *Inscriptiones Ḥimyariticae,* in *Corpus inscriptionum semiticarum,* published by the Academie des Inscriptions, 4th section, Vol. II, Part 3, pp. 262 ff., Nos. 540, 543; A. Jamme's "Inscriptions sud-arabes de la collection Ettore Rossi," *RSO,* XXX, 110 f. and Plate p. 128. The former two inscriptions, discovered and published by Eduard Glaser more than half a century ago, have been the subject of extensive debates, but their Jewish provenance seems perfectly clear. There are other items of Jewish, as well as Christian, interest in the approximately 3,000 inscriptions accumulated by Glaser and his equally famous predecessor, Joseph Halévy. The latter's journeys have been illumined by S. D. Goitein's publication of a travelogue prepared at the time by Halévy's Yemenite Jewish interpreter, Ḥayyim Ḥabshush.

Cf. his *Ḥezyon Teiman* (Travels in Yemen). Unfortunately, even at this late date, several hundred of Glaser's inscriptions have remained unpublished. Cf. M. Höfner's detailed analysis of *Die Sammlung Eduard Glaser,* pp. 42 ff. Cf. also her more general review of "Der Stand und die Aufgaben der südarabischen Forschung" in R. Hartmann and H. Scheel, *Beiträge zur Arabistik,* pp. 42–66. On the other hand, ever new inscriptions are being discovered or rediscovered. Among more recent publications, see especially Enno Littmann's *Safaitic Inscriptions;* H. St. J. B. Philby's "Three New Inscriptions from Hadhramaut," *JRAS,* 1945, pp. 124–33; G. Ryckmans's most comprehensive series of "Inscriptions sud-arabes," *Muséon,* XL–LXIX (covering till now 539 numbers; one item is more fully explained from the historical standpoint by J. Pirenne in "L' Inscription 'Ryckmans 535' et la chronologie sud-arabe," *ibid.,* LXIX, 165–81); his edition of inscriptions found by Miss Caton-Thompson in *The Tombs and Moon Temple;* his "Inscriptions du Yemen relevées par M. Ahmed Fakhry," *Muséon,* LXI, 227–43 (following Fakhry's brief description of his visit to Sirwâḥ, Mârib, and al-Gôf, *ibid.,* pp. 215–26); and A. van den Branden's compilation of *Les Inscriptions thamoudéennes.* Cf. also Ryckmans's earlier analysis of "Les Inscriptions monothéistes sabéennes" in *Miscellanea historica in honorem Alberti de Meyer,* pp. 194–205 (with reference to the inscriptions in the *Corpus,* Vol. IV, Nos. 539, 542–43); and his review article on "L'Epigraphie arabe préislamique au cours de ces dix dernières années," *Muséon,* LXI, 197–213. These and other sources have been utilized by S. Smith for his recent restatement of "Events in Arabia in the Sixth Century A.D.," *BSOAS,* XVI, 425–68 (the findings are more lucidly summarized in the chronological table, pp. 464 f.); and by J. Ryckmans in his detailed study of *L'Institution monarchique en Arabie méridionale avant l'Islam (Ma'in et Saba*). A fresh analysis of "La Légende de la Reine de Saba" in the Bible and its subsequent career is given by A. Chastel in *RHR,* CXIX, 204–25; CXX, 27–44, 160–74.

82. Cosmas Indicopleustes, *Topographia christiana,* I.140 f., in *PG,* LXXXVIII, 101 f. (in E. O. Winsted's critical ed., p. 72, and his note thereon, p. 338); letter from Simeon of Beth-Arsham to Abbot Simeon of Gabula, published in 1881 by I. Guidi, and republished with the extensive introduction and notes in his *Raccolta di scritti,* I, 1–60. This letter is cited here from A. Jeffery's translation in his "Three Documents on the History of Christianity in South Arabia," *ATR,* XXVII, 199 (reprinted in *MW,* XXXVI, 209). Cosmas' testimony is doubly relevant since, even if not a monk, he was a pious Christian writing in Alexandria, the main link in the negotiations between Ethiopia and Byzantium. Cf. M. A. Anastos's plausible arguments for "The Alexandrian Origin of the Christian Topography of Cosmas Indicopleustes," *Dumbarton Oaks Papers,* III, 73–80; and, on the international aspects of the Ethiopian-Ḥimyarite war, A. A. Vasiliev, *Justin the First,* pp. 282 ff.; N. Pigulevskaya, "Ethiopia and Ḥimyar in Their Mutual Relations with the Eastern Roman Empire" (Russian), *Vestnik drevnei istorii,* I, No. 23, 87–97; S. Smith's remarks "Events in Arabia," *BSOAS,* XVI, 425 ff.; and those by J. Ryckmans in *L'Institution monarchique,* pp. 320 ff. Clearly, the long-simmering conflict between the Monophysite Abyssinians and Alexandrians on the one hand, and the Orthodox regime in Constantinople on the other hand, did not prevent their cooperation against the Jewish kingdom. The Nestorians, however, themselves a sharply persecuted minority in Byzantium, were far less deeply involved. Cf. J. H. Hirschberg's

careful examination of the "Nestorian Sources of North-Arabian Traditions on the Establishment and Persecution of Christianity in Yemen," *Rocznik Orientalistyczny,* XV, 321–38. It should also be noted that the relative paucity of monotheistic, compared with the frequency of pagan, inscriptions may indeed "suggest a local revolt against the Jewish dynasty, which led ultimately to its overthrow with the assistance of Christian Abyssinia." Cf. H. St. J. B. Philby's "Note on the Last Kings of Saba," *Muséon,* LXIII, 273 ff.

83. Letter of Simeon of Beth-Arsham, in Jeffery, "Three Documents," *ATR,* XXVII, 199, 203 f. On the Ḥimyarite elder buried in the Beth She'arim catacomb No. 7, see the inscription and monogram reproduced and analyzed by H. Z. Hirschberg in his "Ḥimyarite Tombs at Beth She'arim" (Hebrew), *BJPES,* XI, 25–34; and his *Yisrael ba-'Arab,* pp. 53 ff. (the missing last letter of the Hebrew name Menaḥem was located in the monogram by C. Bar-Adon, cf. his "Note," *BJPES,* XIII, 172). Hirschberg's hypothesis that we deal here not with a visitor from Ḥimyara itself, but rather with the elder of a Ḥimyarite Jewish colony somewhere in northern Arabia, still fails to explain the major difficulty concerning the use of Greek by an Arabian Jew. Although one cannot speak confidently about the cultural life of the Jews in pre-Islamic Ḥimyara, Medina, or Khaibar, so long as these areas remain inaccessible to archaeological excavators, it would seem surprising if one were to find among them any real familiarity with Greek. We may rather believe Bishop Simeon that some Jews regularly traveled between Ḥimyara and Tiberias in the fifth century and earlier. When any such visitor from the South died in Palestine, he was provided by his relatives or hosts with a funerary inscription in Hebrew and Greek, according to the local customs of Tiberias and Beth She'arim, rather than with a South Arabic epitaph of the kind used in his home country.

84. Although the Byzantine refusal is recorded only by the great fourteenth-century Arab historian Ibn Khaldun, it is supported by other evidence, cited in Hirschberg's *Yisrael ba-'Arab,* pp. 108 f. Cf. also Sir E. A. W. Budge's data in *A History of Ethiopia, Nubia and Abyssinia,* I, 261 ff. In view of the slow pace of change in the life of the Arabian Peninsula, much can be learned about earlier conditions from contemporary ethnological studies. Cf. esp. E. Brauer's comprehensive study, *Ethnologie der jemenitischen Juden;* the Yemenite folktales, collected by S. D. Goitein in his *From the Land of Sheba;* and, on the Bedouin tribes of the Arabian Peninsula, M. Oppenheim's comprehensive anthropological work, *Die Beduinen,* Vol. III. Of interest is also the report, first made known in 1945, of the existence of an isolated Jewish community of some 450 souls in Ḥaban, Ḥadhramaut. According to local traditions their settlement existed in unbroken continuity from ancient times. Cf. T. Ashkenazi, "Jews of Ḥadhramaut" (Hebrew), *Edoth,* II, 58–71.

85. Procopius, *De Bello Persico,* I.19.3–4, in *Works,* I, 178 f. Cf. the data analyzed by F. M. Abel in "L'Ile de Jotabè," *RB,* XLVII, 525 ff., 529 ff.; and by P. Goubert in *Byzance avant l'Islam,* I, 247 ff., 264 f.

86. Jewish farmers were so conspicuously successful in the eyes of their Arab neighbors, both pagan and Muslim, that the latter ascribed part of that success to the effectiveness of Jewish prayers for rain. Such Jewish prayers, recorded in the Talmud, were now often secured by Arab peasants through suasion, money or even

force, Cf. W. Lammens's observations in *L'Arabie occidentale avant l'hégire,* pp. 92 ff.; Brauer's *Ethnologie,* pp. 366 f.; and, particularly, the data assembled by H. Z. Hirschberg in "The Keys of Rains" (Hebrew), *BJPES,* XI, 46–54.

87. Mutaḥḥar al-Maqdisi (Muqaddasi), *K. al-Bad' wal-Tar'ikh,* ed. by Huart, IV, 31 (Arabic), 29 f. (French). One poem (a *qasida*) attributed to Samau'al, to be sure, speaks of the house of David and extols many biblical heroes, including Moses, Saul, and Solomon. But its author may have been another Jewish poet, Samau'al, of the ill-fated tribe of Quraiẓa. In any case, it shows that the writer was familiar with the Bible only through some garbled, probably oral tradition. Arabian Jewry's intellectual equipment seems to have been limited to some scrolls of law, Hebrew prayerbooks, and other paraphernalia of worship and study, while the availability at that time of more than fragmentary Arabic translations from Scripture is extremely dubious. On the much-debated problems of the pre-Islamic Arabic-Jewish poetry, see especially J. W. Hirschberg's ed. of *Der Dīwān des as-Samau'al ibn 'Ādijā'* (with notes by T. Kowalski, pp. 76 ff.). Hirschberg successfully defended here the essential authenticity of many of those poems, impugned for instance by his teacher, Kowalski, in "A Contribution to the Problem of the Authenticity of the Diwān of As-Samau'al," *Archiv Orientalni,* III, 156–61. Cf. also *infra,* Chap. XXIV, n. 4; Chap. XXXII.

CHAPTER XVII: MOHAMMED AND THE CALIPHATE

1. A. Jeremias, *Das Alte Testament im Lichte des alten Orients*, 4th ed., p. 456 n. 2; Al-Bukhari, *K. al-Jamia' al-Saḥiḥ* (Les Traditions islamiques), in the French translation by O. Houdas and W. Marçais, III, 66 (in the name of the none-too-reliable Abu Huraira); W. Muir's data in *The Life of Mohammed*, new ed., pp. 391 ff.; Ibn Isḥaq's *Sirāt rasūl Allāh* (Life of Muhammad), p. 1021 (in A. Guillaume's English trans., p. 689). Different versions of Mohammed's alleged will are cited by T. Nöldeke in his *Geschichte des Qorans*, 2d ed., I, 13; H. Lammens in *L'Arabie*, p. 307 n. 1; and H. Z. (J. W.) Hirschberg in *Yisrael ba-'Arab*, pp. 155 f. The latter suggests that the original injunction was aimed at the elimination of polytheists from the Peninsula, and that it was later reinterpreted to include Jews and Christians as well. But one need not search for an authentic substratum for this purported saying, any more than for Mohammed's alleged reservation of the right to revoke his treaty with the Jews of Khaibar (see *infra*). These and many other sayings incorporated in the *ḥadith* in the name of the Messenger and his companions clearly owed their origin to such later needs as the justification of 'Umar's high-handed revocation of that treaty and his expulsion of the Jews from Khaibar. 'Umar's obvious inconsistency in allowing Jews to remain in other parts of the Peninsula caused much embarrassment to later commentators. Even the limitation of the term "Peninsula" to Hejaz, suggested by Yaqut and Al-Bakri, in itself hardly acceptable, was controverted by the continued presence of Jews in that province many generations after 'Umar. About the Christians, see W. Heffening's remarks in *Das islamische Fremdenrecht*, p. 45 n. 4.

Unfortunately, our information is almost exclusively derived from Muslim sources, the few Jewish reminiscences being of a legendary character. Tales concerning ten, or rather eleven, Jewish scholars who advised "the dumb, wicked man" have been recorded, for instance, in a Hebrew document published by J. Leveen in "Mohammed and his Jewish Companions," *JQR*, XVI, 399–406 (see also his and S. Gandz's additional remarks, *ibid.*, XVII, 235–37, 485). Cf. also M. Schwabe's "Mohammed's Ten Jewish Companions" (Hebrew), *Tarbiz*, II, 74–89 (with D. Z. Baneth's remarks thereon, *ibid.*, III, 112–16); and B. Cohen's text relating to "Une Légende juive de Mohamet," *REJ*, LXXXVIII, 1–17. Parenthetically one may mention also the curious legend of Mohammed's assassination by a Jewess. Cf. F. Macler's publication, from a Paris manuscript, of "Un Document arménien sur l'assassinat de Mahomet par une juive," *Mélanges Hartwig Derenbourg*, pp. 287–95, probably an elaboration of the story of the Messenger's attempted poisoning by a Khaibar Jewess. Cf. L. Caëtani, *Annali dell'Islam*, II, 36 ff. Both legends served to make Mohammed a martyr for his faith. On the other hand, Ṣafiya's marriage to Mohammed had practical repercussions in Fez, Morocco, as late as 1698–99. At that time, we are told, some Jews refused to pay the capitation tax, producing a purported copy of a privilege given by Mohammed to Ṣafiya's brother Musa, which allowed him and his descendants to wear a turban and freed them all from the capitation tax. The local Muslim doctors, however, not only questioned the authenticity of a copy written in 1323, but also denied that Ṣafiya had a brother Musa, and pointed out that that letter could not have been written in the year 9 of the *hejira* (631 C.E.), since that era had not been established until some eight years later. Cf. Aḥmad ben Khalad an-Nasiri as-Slawi's *K. al-Istiqṣa* (Histoire du Maroc), in the French translation by A. Graulle *et al.*, I, 60. Although written in the nineteenth century, this history is based upon earlier Arabic sources.

2. Qur'an 26:197, 45:15, in E. H. Palmer's English translation. Although somewhat antiquated and from a scholarly standpoint often superseded by R. Bell's more recent rendition entitled *The Qur'an: Translated with a Critical Re-arrangement of the Surahs,* it has the advantage of following the more widely accepted sequence by the length of the surahs. Bell's arrangement is highly debatable, as may be seen from the chronological table in his recent *Introduction to the Qur'an,* pp. 110 ff. Similar disagreements will arise also in connection with R. Blachère's new French translation of *Le Coran;* while J. J. Rivlin's incomplete Hebrew translation, *Al-Qur'an,* follows the traditional arrangement. Cf. also S. Vahiduddin's somewhat over-critical analysis of "Richard Bell's Study of the Qur'an," *IC,* XXX, 263–72.

Little progress has been made in recent years in our knowledge of the Jewish community of Mecca before 622, and of its relations with the budding prophet. But more recent investigations by H. Lammens and others have added considerably to the knowledge of the general socioeconomic and cultural conditions in the city. Cf. W. M. Watt's analysis of the meager extant data in his *Muhammad at Mecca.* In his excursus on "Arabian Monotheism and Judaeo-Christian Influences" (pp. 158 ff.) Watt unduly minimizes the Judeo-Christian influence on Mohammed, but he cannot deny that such influence doubtless helped to shape those monotheistic concepts and trends which the Messenger found in contemporary, overwhelmingly pagan Arabia.

3. In "The Ummi Prophet and the Banu Israil of the Qur'an," *MW,* XXXIX, 276–81, H. G. Reissner has pointed out, on the basis of previous researches by Nöldeke, Lane, and Wensinck, that the term *ummi,* combining the ideas of "Gentile" and "Arab of pure stock," had many similarities with the Hebrew term, *'am ha-areṣ.* On the latter's evolution, see *supra,* Vols. I, pp. 278, 414 n. 36; II, pp. 272, 413 n. 24. Even if Mohammed's professed illiteracy was more pretended than real, there is no question that he must have appeared as a simple *'am ha-areṣ* to those rabbis (*aḥbar* or *rabbaniyun*) with whom he associated. Cf. Qur'an 5:48, 68, for example; and, on the various explanations suggested for these terms, A. Jeffery's review in *The Foreign Vocabulary of the Qur'an,* pp. 49 f., 137 f.

4. The revival of Jewish messianic hopes, mentioned by Ibn Hisham and other Arab writers, was rightly stressed as an added reason for the stout Jewish resistance by Lammens in *L'Arabie,* pp. 89, 99. These messianic trends, known from Jewish sources (see *infra,* Chap. XXV, n. 30), were further elucidated through the reconstruction of a passage in a later Arabic romance by B. Heller in his "Yoûscha' 'al-Akbar et les Juifs de Kheybar dans le roman d' 'Antar," *REJ,* LXXXIV, 113–37. He successfully defended this thesis in his subsequent debate with R. Paret, *ibid.,* LXXXV, 56–62. These trends are more fully analyzed in H. Z. Hirschberg's Hebrew essay on "Footsteps of the Messiah in Arabia during the Fifth and Sixth Centuries after the Destruction of the Temple" in *Vienna Mem. Vol.,* pp. 112–24.

5. Qur'an 5:85. The far-reaching implications of Mohammed's agreement with the Christian community are emphasized by A. Abel in "La Convention de Nedjran et le

développement du 'droit des gens' dans l'Islam classique," *Revue internationale des droits de l'antiquité,* II, Part 2, pp. 1–17.

6. Shuraiḥ's poem is quoted here from the arrangement and Hebrew translation by Hirschberg in his *Yisrael ba-'Arab,* p. 257. Mohammed's frequent references to perennial Jewish internal discord (e.g., Qur'an 5:69: "for we have cast amongst them enmity and hatred till the resurrection day") are analyzed by S. D. Goitein in his "Banu Israel and Their Controversies" (Hebrew), *Tarbiz,* III, 410–22.

7. S. Tchernichovsky's *Shirim* (Collected Poems), published by Schocken, pp. 52 ff. (written in 1896). The bad conscience of Mohammed and his immediate associates also contributed to the inconsistencies in the subsequent Arab traditions concerning this miscarriage of justice. Cf. W. M. Watt's somewhat forced interpretation of these traditions in "The Condemnation of the Jews of the Banu Qurayẓah," *MW,* XLII, 160–71. Even later, however, the justice of Mohammed's treatment of this valiant Jewish tribe was heatedly debated. An Arab poet, Adh-Dhaḥḥak, was held up on this score to public contumely and accused of loving "the Jews rather than the Messenger" by a typical disloyalty hunter, Ḥassan ibn Ṭabit. Cf. O. A. Farrukh's dissertation, *Das Bild des Frühislam in der arabischen Dichtkunst,* p. 129. It is no longer possible to estimate the number of Mohammed's Jewish victims. Medieval tradition itself was far from uniform, Maimonides alone mentioning such divergent figures as 24,000 and 52,000. Even the lesser number seems exaggerated. Cf. Maimonides, *Iggeret Shemad* (Epistle on Conversion) in the two versions cited by me in "The Historical Outlook of Maimonides," *PAAJR,* VI, 82 n. 163.

8. Al-Zuhri ibn Sa'd, *K. Tabaqat* (Biographien Muhammeds), ed. by E. Sachau, No. 44; Baladhuri, *K. Futûḥ al-buldân* (The Origins of the Islamic State), ed. by M. J. de Goeje, p. 60 (Hitti's English version, I, 93 f., offers a somewhat different translation); Ibn Isḥaq, *Sirāt,* p. 956 (in Guillaume's trans. p. 643). These treaties have been studied frequently. Cf. J. Sperber's detailed analysis of *Die Schreiben Muhammads an die Stämme Arabiens,* and Caëtani's *Annali dell'Islam,* II, 31 ff., 247 ff. Of course, in view of subsequent developments both sides often tried to alter the record. The Muslim tradition began ascribing to the Messenger such spurious actions as an alleged reservation in the treaty with Khaibar Jewry which would enable him or any of his successors to revoke the treaty. Cf. Sulaiman Abu-Daud at-Tayalisi, *K. as-Sunnan* (Collection of Traditions), II, 25 f., 39. According to another version, Mohammed left the aforementioned will enjoining the complete elimination of non-Muslims from the Peninsula, or at least from Hejaz. The Jews, on the other hand, produced some spurious agreements to support their own legal contentions, and particularly to stave off disasters. In the Cairo Genizah was found the copy of another treaty between Mohammed and the Jews of Khaibar which was almost exclusively concerned with the safeguarding of the latter's rights, rather than the imposition of duties. Cf. the text published by H. Hirschfeld in "The Arabic Portion of the Cairo Genizah at Cambridge," *JQR,* [o.s.] XV, 169 ff., 177 ff.; with some improved readings by I. Goldziher, *ibid.,* pp. 526 ff. J. Braslavsky has plausibly suggested that this document, a fabricated version of an older authentic letter, was used by Khaibar Jews living in Egypt to counteract the persecutions of the Faṭimid caliph Al-Ḥakim (996–1021). Cf. his data in "The Jewish Community of Khaibar," *Zion,* I, 148 ff. Cf. also the Yemenite text published and translated by S. D. F. Goitein in "A Deed of

Privileges in Favor of the Jews Attributed to Mohammed" (Hebrew), *KS,* IX, 507–21; amplified in J. J. Rivlin's "Mohammed's Will Addressed to 'Ali ibn Abi-Talab" (Hebrew), *Yellin Jub. Vol.,* pp. 139–56; *supra,* nn. 1, 3; Chap. XVI. n. 79; and *infra,* n. 16.

9. Qur'an 74:30–32, 87:19. Modern scholars, as well as tradition, agree that these surahs were written in Mecca, as were indeed some three fourths of all surahs, though not the longest ones (for instance, 2–5). Cf. R. Bell's *Introduction,* pp. 110 ff., 113. In these early messages Mohammed did not yet invoke the shades of the ancient Hebrew patriarch in a polemical vein. See *infra,* n. 15.

10. Qur'an 2:136 ff., 17:1 ff.; Bukhari, *K. Al-Jamia',* French trans. by O. Houdas and W. Marçais, III, 66 (in the name of Ibn 'Abbas). Cf. R. B. Serjeant, "Hūd and Other Pre-Islamic Prophets of Ḥaḍramawt," *Muséon,* LXVII, 121–79; and the passage from Muqaddasi, cited *supra,* Chap. XVI. n. 87.

11. Cf. A. Jeffery's observations on *The Qur'ān as Scripture,* p. 17; G. Graf's *Geschichte der christlichen arabischen Literatur,* I, 29, 34 ff.; and A. Guillaume's plausible reconstruction of "The Version of the Gospels Used in Medina *circa* 700 A.D.," *Al-Andalus,* XV, 289–96. A. Baumstark, especially, has made numerous, though not altogether successful attempts to reconstruct, from later records, some pre-Islamic biblical and liturgical texts, especially those taken from the book of Psalms. He emphasized, particularly, certain divergences in later recorded texts from the Septuagint version, and argued that, therefore, these texts must have existed before 600. Cf. "Der älteste erhaltene griechisch-arabische Text von Psalm 110 (109)," *Oriens christianus,* XXXI, 55–66; his "Minbar-Thron und älteste arabische Psalmentexte," *OLZ,* XLVI, 337–41; and the literature cited *infra,* Chaps. XXIV, n. 4, and XXIX, n. 39.

12. Numerous more or less direct references to Jewish ideas and personalities have already been demonstrated in A. Geiger's *Was hat Mohammed aus dem Judenthume aufgenommen?* published a century and a quarter ago. This work is also available in an English and a Hebrew version (by F. M. Young and I. L. Baruch, respectively) and a revised German edition. Among more recent monographs on this much-debated problem of Mohammed's familiarity with Bible and Aggadah, see especially R. Bell's "Muhammad's Knowledge of the Old Testament," in *Studia Semitica,* II (Presentation Volume to W. B. Stevenson), pp. 1–20; H. Speyer's analysis of *Die biblischen Erzählungen im Koran;* that by D. Sidersky of *Les Origines des légendes musulmannes dans le Coran et dans les vies des prophètes;* and, with special reference to eschatology and the Sinaitic revelation, D. Künstlinger's "Eschatologisches in Sura 111," *OLZ,* XLI, 407–10; and J. Obermann's "Koran and Agadah, the Events on Mount Sinai," *AJSL,* LVIII, 23–48. In his "Zur Herkunft der monotheistischen Bekenntnisformeln im Koran," *Oriens christianus,* XXXVII, 6–22, A. Baumstark has plausibly argued that two positive and one negative formulas found in the Qur'an were derived from the "Hear, O Israel" in Deut. 6:4, or the Jewish liturgy. The context of the whole Medinese surah 2:96 shows that Mohammed had learned about the two fallen angels Ḥarut and Marut in Babylonia from the Jews. Cf. *supra,* Vol. II, p. 436 n. 31. In general R. Paret is doubtless right in saying that Mohammed "derives from history, or rather reads into history, what appears to him at any

particular moment relevant and important from his own standpoint." See "Das Geschichtsbild Mohammeds," *Die Welt als Geschichte,* XI, 224. Cf. also B. Heller's stimulating bibliographical and methodological discussion of "La Légende biblique dans l'Islam," *REJ,* XCVIII, 1–18.

13. Qur'an 4:158–59, 62:5 (cf. Gen. r. xcvii, ed. by Theodor and Albeck, p. 1222, for example). The change from three to five daily prayers took place toward the end of Mohammed's life. The Qur'an seems to presuppose only three services (11:116, etc.), but it was probably Mohammed himself who later added two more services to outdo the Jews. The abrupt change in calendar, on the other hand, has injected considerable uncertainties into the chronology of events during Mohammed's last years. Cf. H. A. 'Ali's recent harmonistic attempt to explain "The First Decade in Islam: a Fresh Approach to the Calendrical Study of Early Islam," *MW,* XLIV, 126–38. Cf. also J. J. Rivlin's recent analysis of "The *Qiblah, 'Ashura,* and Service in the Temple as Described in the Qur'an" (Hebrew), *Tarbiz,* XXVI, 17–48; J. Henninger's "Fêtes arabes et fêtes israélites," *Revista de Museu Paulista,* IV, 410–21; G. E. von Grunebaum's *Muhammedan Festivals;* and *infra,* Chap. XXIV, nn. 6, 37; Chaps. XXVII, XXXV. On Islam's attitude toward the Sabbath, cf. I. Goldziher's observations on "Die Sabbathinstitution im Islam," *Gedenkbuch . . . David Kaufmann,* pp. 86–105; J. J. Rivlin's *Gesetz im Koran,* pp. 17 ff.; and S. D. Goitein's story of the Yemenite Jew who escaped imprisonment on a Friday as soon as he invoked the shades of the Messenger as protector of the Sabbath. See "A Deed of Privileges," *KS,* IX, 507; and, more generally, J. J. Rivlin, "Mohammed as a Legislator" (Hebrew), *Keneset,* VII, 294–310; R. Bell's *Introduction,* pp. 166 ff.; and A. Guillaume's survey of "The Biography of the Prophet in Recent Research," *Islamic Quarterly,* I, 5–11. Of interest are also the transformations in the European image of the founder of Islam, particularly in the last centuries, briefly analyzed in J. J. Saunders's "Mohammed in Europe: a Note on Western Interpretations of the Life of the Prophet," *History,* XXXIX, 14–25.

14. Qur'an 3:72, 4:48; Baladhuri's *K. Futûḥ al-buldân,* p. 474, in F. C. Murgotten's English trans., II, 274. Cf. also the related traditions cited by Murgotten, *ibid.;* and, more generally, R. Paret's brief but pertinent observations in *Die Welt als Geschichte,* XI, 214 ff. From that time on the problems of authenticity of the biblical text and of its correct interpretation remained focal issues in all Muslim-Jewish polemics. Cf. *infra,* Chaps. XXIV, n. 9; XXIX, n. 10.

15. Qur'an 2:118 ff.; 3:58, 60, 78–79; 37:100 ff. Mohammed's rather belated realization in Medina of the importance of Abraham in his religious reformulation and his stress on the pure Abrahamic religion as antecedent to both Judaism and Christianity, which reminds us of a similar paradoxical Christian claim that true Christianity preceded Judaism, have often attracted the attention of scholars. Cf. Y. Moubarac's "Abraham en Islam," *Cahiers sioniens,* V, 196–212; E. Beck's careful analysis of surah 2:118–35 in "Die Gestalt des Abraham am Wendepunkt der Entwicklung Muhammeds," *Muséon,* LXV, 73–94; *supra,* n. 9; and Chap. XVI, n. 78. Cf. also J. Macdonald's related analysis of "Joseph in the Qur'an and Muslim Commentary," *MW,* XLVI, 113–31, 207–24; and E. Hilscher, "Der biblische Joseph in orientalischen Literaturwerken," *Mitteilungen des Instituts für Orientforschung* of the Deutsche Akad-

emie der Wissenschaften, IV, 81–108. Modern Muslim thinkers have sometimes sought to connect the term "Islam" with the idea of peace. However, such an emphasis seems hardly apposite to a bellicose empire builder like Mohammed and to a warlike atmosphere such as prevailed during the first decades after the *hejira.* The Messenger and his early successors evidently thought chiefly of the idea of the believer's resignation and total surrender to the will of God. Cf. J. Robson's analysis of "'Islam' as a Term," *MW,* XLIV, 101–9; and *infra,* Chap. XXVII, end.

Some authors are inclined to overemphasize the Jewish influence upon Mohammed. Others, leaning to the opposite extreme, ascribe this influence exclusively to Christians, whose number on the Peninsula was also very substantial. On the latter view see especially the comprehensive studies by R. Bell, *The Origin of Islam in its Christian Environment,* and T. Andrae, *Der Ursprung des Islams und das Christentum,* following C. H. Becker and others. Cf. also J. Henninger's "Spuren christlicher Glaubenswahrheiten im Koran," *Neue Zeitschrift für Missions-Wissenschaft,* I, 135–40, 304–14; II, 109–22; III, 128–40, and other literature briefly reviewed in G. Jäschke's "Muhammed und das Christentum nach neueren Forschungen," *Missions- und Religionswissenschaft,* VI, 16–28. Principal indebtedness to Judaism, on the other hand, has been ably defended by many authors from Geiger to Torrey. Cf. *supra,* Chap. XVI, nn. 78–80; and the literature listed in F. (S. D.) Goitein's article "Koran" in *EJ,* X, 307–23. A more moderate position is taken by J. W. Hirschberg in his *Jüdische und christliche Lehren im vor- und frühislamischen Arabien;* S. D. Goitein in his "Who Were Muhammad's Chief Teachers?" (Hebrew), *Weil Jub. Vol.,* pp. 10–23; and the various biographers of Mohammed such as Muir, K. Ahrens (in his *Muhammed als Religionsstifter*), or C. A. Nallino (in his posthumously published two lectures of 1916 on *Vita di Maometto*). On the latter publication, see also J. M. Peñuela's pertinent observations in his "Mahoma y los Israelitas de Arabia," *Sefarad,* VII, 395–416; and G. Trovato's essentially juridical study of *Maometto e gli ebrei nella biografia di Ibn Hišam.* In view of the paucity of reliable sources and the existence of many intermediary Judeo-Christian trends among the sectarian groups in and around Arabia, it is next to impossible precisely to segregate the Jewish from the Christian elements in the formation of Islam. In any case, E. Mainz is right in saying that, familiar as Mohammed may have been with Christian teachings, "he preferred to turn to Judaism in most matters out of choice, rather than ignorance." Cf. his review of Torrey's work in *Der Islam,* XXIII, 299–301. Later Arab poets referred therefore, as a rule, to the struggles of Mohammed with the Jews and his repudiation of the Jewish *din* (religion). Only a little-known poet from Najran mentioned the similar rejection of the Christian *din.* Cf. O. A. Farrukh, *Das Bild des Frühislam,* pp. 76 f., 80, 88 ff., 92.

Nor can one ascertain the extent to which certain ancient oriental traditions have penetrated early Islam through pagan, Christian, or Jewish channels. In his "Islam and the Religions of the Ancient Orient," *JAOS,* LX, 283–301, W. F. Albright reached the sharply negative conclusion that "the gap which separates Graeco-Roman civilization from ancient Oriental is much greater than that which divides Islam from Hellenism. Religiously Islam is an integral part of the Judaeo-Christian tradition and owes very little directly to the religions of the Ancient Orient." Cf., however, the qualifications suggested *ibid.,* p. 301 n. 61; and more poignantly in G. L. della Vida's "Dominant Ideas in the Formation of Islamic Culture," *Crozer Quarterly,* XXI, 207–16. Cf. also W. Thomson's "Islam and the Early Semitic World," *MW,* XXXIX, 36–

63. The background of pagan Arabia, on the other hand, has been greatly elucidated by the publication some forty years ago of Hisham ibn al-Kalbi's *K. al-Aṣnām* (The Book of Idols), now available also in an English translation by N. A. Faris.

Of great interest are also many monographic studies, such as J. Horovitz's attempt to trace Jewish influences through a detailed investigation of "Jewish Proper Names and Derivatives in the Koran," *HUCA*, II, 145–227; and J. Finkel's search for vestiges of ancient Israelitic concepts in early Islam, in his "Old Israelitish Tradition in the Koran," *PAAJR*, II, 7–21; and "Jewish, Christian and Samaritan Influences on Arabia," [D. B.] *Macdonald Presentation Volume*, pp. 147–66. Cf. also B. Heller, "Elements, parallèles et origine de la légende de sept dormants," *REJ*, XLIX, 190–218, and LIII, 111–14 (referring to Qur'an 18:8–25 and later Muslim legends assembled by I. Guidi in 1884 and reproduced in his *Raccolta*, I, 61 ff.); M. Papo, "Die sexuelle Ethik im Qorān in ihrem Verhältnis zu seinen jüdischen Quellen," *Jahrbuch für jüdische Volkskunde*, II, 171–291; J. W. Hirschberg, "Der Sündenfall in der altarabischen Poesie," *Rocznik Orjentalistyczny*, IX, 22–36; J. Rivlin's analysis of the term "Furqan in the Qur'an," (Hebrew), *Weil Jub. Vol.*, pp. 24–33; T. O'Shaughnessy, *The Development of the Meaning of Spirit in the Koran* (analyzing the term *ruḥ* in twenty Qur'anic verses from both Meccan and Medinese surahs and showing its progressive modification under the impact of Jewish, Christian, and gnostic-sectarian teachings); and *The Koranic Concept of the Word of God* (a similar analysis of the term *kallimat* Allah). In his *Judaism and Islam*, A. I. Katsh has offered a detailed, verse-by-verse commentary, from rabbinic sources, on surahs 2–3. This undertaking, similar in nature to Strack and Billerbeck, *Kommentar zum Neuen Testament*, will become fully meaningful only when carried through the entire Qur'an.

16. Cf. I. Ben-Zvi's Hebrew essays on "The Jews of Khaibar and Their Fate" (includes interesting contemporary testimony); and "Jewish Tribes in the Arabian Desert," reprinted in his collection *Nidḥe Yisrael* (The Dispersed of Israel), pp. 143 ff., 171 ff. (also in a forthcoming English trans. by D. A. Abbady entitled *The Exiled and the Redeemed*). Certainly the southern Arabian Jews succeeded in weathering all storms into the twentieth century. With respect to the Jews of Najran, see *infra*, n. 21.

17. Cf. the various excerpts from Arab historians quoted in Arabic, with a Hebrew translation, in the *Sefer ha-Yishub* (Book of Jewish Settlements in Palestine), Vol. II, ed. by S. Assaf and L. A. Mayer, pp. 1 ff., 47. On Gaza, see the scanty evidence of later date, *ibid.*, pp. 48 f., the editors' remarks in their Introduction, pp. xii f.; and those by H. Vincent and F. M. Abel in their *Jérusalem*, II, 930 ff. The Arabs seem to have been welcomed particularly by the Monophysite minority. Although less numerous than in Syria or Egypt—the latter was a hotbed of nationalistic Monophysitism which even the most orthodox emperors did not dare to attack—this sectarian minority doubtless proved quite helpful to the new conquerors of the Holy Land. That many of the Christian influences on Mohammed's teachings had come from Monophysite, rather than Orthodox sources, has conclusively been shown by H. Grégoire in his "Mahomet et le monophysitisme," *Mélanges Charles Diehl*, I, 107–19. Cf. also W. Hotzelt's study of "Die kirchliche Organisation Palästinas im 7. Jahrhundert," *ZDPV*, LXVI, 72–84; and more generally G. Le Strange's older, but still very useful, study of *Palestine under the Moslems;* and N. A. Mednikov's comprehensive Russian work, *Palestina* (Palestine: From Its Conquest by the Arabs to the Crusades, according to

the Arabic Historians). A French translation of *Textes géographiques arabes sur la Palestine,* arranged in the alphabetical order of Arabic localities, was prepared by A. S. Marmardji.

18. Despite considerable variations in the traditions recorded by Baladhuri, Ṭabari, Ya'qubi, and several Christian chroniclers (see the sources reproduced in *Sefer ha-Yishub,* II, 15 ff.; Ya'qubi actually recorded a controversy as to whether the treaty was concluded with Christians or with Jews, but decided in favor of the former), 'Umar's compact, including the stipulation to exclude Jews from settlement in the city, or at least from the protection of the law for such as might dare to enter it, may be regarded as more or less authentic. Cf. M. J. de Goeje's plausible reasoning in his *Mémoire sur la conquête de Syrie,* 2d ed., pp. 152 ff. The arguments advanced anew by S. D. Goitein against the historicity of the treaty in his "Did Caliph 'Umar Forbid the Jews to Reside in Jerusalem" (Hebrew), *Melilah,* III–IV, 156–65, while quite weighty, are not sufficient to invalidate this well-attested tradition. The contradictory evidence can largely be harmonized with the aid of the Arabic-Jewish document, published by S. Assaf. See *infra,* n. 33.

On the other hand, the historical connection between this treaty of 'Umar and the so-called Covenant of Omar, regulating the legal status of Jews and Christians (see *infra,* n. 29), often postulated by both the medieval chroniclers and some modern scholars, appears extremely dubious. According to Muslim traditions, the Arabic name of Jerusalem, probably abbreviated from *Medinat bet ha-maqdis* (City of the Temple), was first given it by the Jewish convert K'ab al-Aḥbar, who thus replaced the Christian-Hadrianic designation, Aelia. Cf. S. D. Goitein, "On the Arabic Names of Jerusalem" (Hebrew), *Zlotnik Jub. Vol.,* pp. 62–66. This ready acceptance of the Jewish name, on the other hand, may have been dictated by the religio-political quest to counterbalance the Christian claims. This quest was also responsible for the very erection there, by 'Abd al-Malik, of the magnificent Mosque "of the Rock," an abrupt deviation from the theretofore very austere forms of Muslim worship. Cf. Goitein's brief communication on "The Historical Background of the Erection of the Dome of the Rock," *JAOS,* LXX, 104–8. Here and in his Hebrew essay on "The Sanctity of Palestine in Muslim Piety," *BJPES,* XII, 120–26, Goitein has also rightly pointed out Qur'anic (5:21) and other antecedents for the Muslim recognition of the holiness of both Palestine and Jerusalem, and controverted the assumption that 'Abd al-Malik had sought totally to replace the pilgrimages to Mecca by visits to Jerusalem. These arguments were further expanded in J. W. Hirschberg's lucid analysis of "The Sources of Moslem Traditions concerning Jerusalem," *Rocznik Orientalistyczny,* XVII, 317 ff. Nevertheless, I. Goldziher's original proposal that the latter's holiness was overemphasized by the 'Umayyads for propagandistic reasons still has much to commend itself. Cf. also A. S. Marmardji's French translation of numerous Arabic sources pertaining to the Mosque of the Rock in his *Textes géographiques arabes sur la Palestine,* pp. 210 ff.; A. N. Poliak's keen analysis of the importance attached to the "Foundation Stone" of the Temple in certain Muslim circles, especially those recruited from Jewish converts, in his pertinent Hebrew article in *Sefer Dinaburg,* pp. 165–77 (fails to include the promised Hebrew translation of a passage in Ibn Sa'd's *Tabaqat;* cf. p. 166); C. D. Matthews's *Palestine—Mohammedan Holy Land* (translating two Arabic treatises on the subject); J. W. Hirschberg's serious reservations, in his review thereof in the *Israel*

Exploration Journal, II, 197–200; Hirschberg's own "Jerusalem's Place in the Muslim World" (Hebrew), *Jerusalem* (quarterly), II, 55–60; and, on the other hand, M. Gaudefroy-Demombyne's data on *Le Pèlerinage à la Mekke;* and *infra,* nn. 33–34.

19. Baladhuri, *Futûḥ al-buldân,* I, 127, 141 (in Hitti's English translation, I, 194 f., 217 f.). Baladhuri's report that Caesarea, theretofore the Byzantine capital of Palestine, had at that time some 200,000 Jews and 30,000 Samaritans in addition to 700,000 Byzantine soldiers (Yaqut reduced the Jews and the soldiers to 100,000 each but raised the Samaritan figure to 80,000) is, of course, grossly exaggerated. Cf. *Sefer ha-Yishub,* II, 54 f. But these very exaggerations indicate the continued presence there of a large Jewish community which survived the restoration of Byzantine rule in 629.

20. The Bustanai story is known to us only from later reports overladen with partisan bias, especially on the part of those who wished to disqualify the then officiating exilarchs. The data recorded in the various extant versions have been subjected to close scrutiny by H. Tykocinski in his Hebrew essay on "Bustanai the Exilarch," *Debir,* I, 145–79 (with important notes by J. N. Epstein). While Bustanai's union with the Persian princess and the subsequent controversy over the legitimacy of her offspring are fairly certain, many important details are still obscure. We are not even sure whether the caliph involved was 'Umar or 'Ali, and whether the princess was a daughter of Khosroe II or of Yazdegerd III. Although the earlier and more reliable sources attribute the benefaction to 'Umar, the first conqueror of Persia, there is no evidence that the latter had ever met Bustanai. Nor did he marry another daughter of Khosroe. An encounter between the exilarch and Mohammed's son-in-law is far more likely. Whether or not Ḥusain married Yazdegerd's second daughter, 'Ali certainly was in a position to give away the children of the last refugee king of Persia, assassinated in 651. The princess's name, Dara, may indeed have been but a Hebrew-Aramaic simplification of the Persian name Adragh, borne, according to Mas'udi, by one of Yazdegerd's daughters. We hear of no similar-sounding name belonging to one of Khosroe II's daughters, or for that matter to a daughter of either of the short-lived kings, Khosroe III or Khosroe IV, who appear among the shadowy rulers of Persia in the four years following the death of Khosroe II in 628. Since Yazdegerd, moreover, was himself a grandson of the great Khosroe, his daughter might legitimately have been counted among the latter's "daughters" (in Hebrew and Aramaic often the equivalent of "descendants") by both popular tradition and unwary chroniclers. Most significantly, from purely chronological considerations derived from the records of the exilarchic succession, Tykocinski has rightly deduced that the three sons of Bustanai from the Persian princess were not born before 660, but probably several years later. This late date would decidedly seem to favor Yazdegerd as Bustanai's father-in-law, and 'Ali as his immediate benefactor. See also *infra,* Chaps. XXIII, n. 5, and XXV, n. 3. Whatever one thinks of the merits of the subsequent dynastic-legalistic controversy, there is no question about the caliph's overt intention to show his high appreciation to the Jewish dignitary by giving him the Persian princess.

21. Benjamin of Tudela, *Massa'ot* (Itinerary), ed. and trans. by M. N. Adler, pp. 45 (Hebrew), 45 (English); and J. Obermeyer, *Landschaft Babylonien,* pp. 329 ff. The eleventh-century Syriac chronicler Elias of Nisibis was evidently mistaken when he noted under the date of 20 A.H. that 'Umar ibn al-Khaṭṭab had in that year

transplanted the Jews of Najran to Kufa. His statement may have been foreshortened by a copyist from an original record that Jews from Khaibar and Christians from Najran had shared that fate. Cf. F. Baethgen, *Fragmente syrischer und arabischer Historiker,* p. 111. A brief sketch of "The History of the Jews in Basra" was published by D. S. Sassoon in *JQR,* XVII, 407–69. Cf. also C. Pellat's pertinent remarks on the non-Arab sections of Baṣra's population in *Le Milieu basrien et la formation de Ǧaḥiz,* pp. 21 ff.; and, on Baṣra's various quarters, L. Massignon, "Explication du plan de Basra (Irak)," in *Westöstliche Abhandlungen Rudolf Tschudi . . . überreicht,* ed. by F. Meier, pp. 154–74. Here (p. 166) Massignon also quotes from a Manchester MS of Khasibi's *Diwan* the poet's assertion that Kufa was "neither Jewish, nor Christian, a mother of heresies . . . having committed Abraham and Daniel to the flames."

22. Eutychius, *Annales,* in *PG,* CXI, 1107 (ed. by Cheikho, II, 26); John of Nikiu, *Chronique,* CXVIII, CXX, trans. by Zotenberg, pp. 449, 455 (in Charles's translation, pp. 189, 194). Cf. *supra,* Vol. II, pp. 189 f., 402 n. 25. Needless to say that a community of 40,000 Jewish taxpayers hardly existed in Alexandria even after the restoration of its glory two or three centuries later. But it may well have been part of the boastful message sent to 'Umar by the conquering general, 'Amr ibn al-'Aṣ, who also claimed to have found in the city 4,000 palaces, 4,000 baths, and other visible signs of wealth staggering the imagination of these newcomers from the desert. Cf. also G. Wiet's history of *L'Egypte arabe de la conquête arabe à la conquête ottomane (642–1517).*

23. 'Abd ar-Raḥman Ibn Khaldun, *K. al-'Ibar,* in W. M. de Slane's abridged French translation, entitled *Histoire des Berbères,* III, 192 ff.; also other sources cited by N. Slouschz in his *Etudes sur l'histoire des Juifs au Maroc,* pp. 2 ff. The Canaanite-Phoenician antecedents of some segments of the North African population and their impact on the spread of anti-Jewish feelings in the Roman province of Africa are emphasized by A. H. Krappe in "Les Chananéens dans l'ancienne Afrique du Nord et en Espagne," *AJSL,* LVII, 229–43. Conversely, these feelings of kinship doubtless also played into the hands of Jewish visitors and settlers and paved the way for a successful Jewish mission among the local tribes. On the ancient evolution, cf. *supra,* Vol. I, pp. 176, 374 n. 13. Cf. also *supra,* Chap. XVI, n. 3.

24. The story of *Dehiyya al-Kahina malkat Afriqah* (Dehiyya al-Kahina, Queen of Africa) is told, largely on the basis of Ibn Khaldun, in a lengthy literary biography in Hebrew by N. Slouschz, who, however, leans too heavily upon the often purely legendary features of the later medieval Arab sources. Nevertheless this account is essentially confirmed and amplified in many significant details in the more recently published chronicle of an older Arab writer, 'Ubaid Allah ibn Ṣaliḥ ibn 'Abd al-Ḥalim. Cf. E. Lévi-Provençal's summary in his "Arabica Occidentalia, I: Un Nouveau récit de la conquête de l'Afrique du Nord par les Arabes," *Arabica,* I, 17–43. On Kahina, cf. pp. 32 f.; and the excerpts in French translation, pp. 40 f. Cf. also R. Basset's briefer summary in his article, "Al-Kahina," *EI,* II, 626–27; and, more generally, A. Guillaume, *Prophecy and Divination among Hebrews and Other Semites;* N. Abbott, "Women and the State on the Eve of Islam," *AJSL,* LVIII, 260; and E. Doutté, *Magie et religion dans l'Afrique du Nord,* pp. 32 ff. In "Les Juifs d'Ifran (Anti-Atlas marocain). Situation actuelle—cimetières—ancêtres—tombe de

Youssef ben Mimoun," *Hespéris,* XXXV, 151–60, V. Monteil discusses Yusuf's inscription allegedly dating from 5 B.C.E., but more likely placed on the tombstone a millennium later (996), and lists 22 other inscriptions from 239 to 896. Of interest are also A. Audollent's data on "La Diffusion du christianisme en Afrique au sud du térritoire soumis à Rome, après le Ve siècle," *CRAI,* 1942, pp. 202–16. There is little question that Judaism left a considerable imprint upon some Berber tribes, and that it is still noticeable in modern times in Tripolitania, the Aures mountains, and the fringes of the Sahara desert. Cf. the historical and anthropological data cited in Slouschz's *Travels in North Africa,* or, preferably, in his expanded Hebrew *Sefer ha-Massa'ot* (Travelogue); his brief historical sketch *Nefuṣot Yisrael be-Afriqah ha-ṣefonit* (Jewish Dispersion in North Africa from Ancient Times to Our Days); J. J. Williams, *Hebrewisms of West Africa;* A. H. Godbey, *Lost Tribes,* pp. 204 ff., 212 ff., 222 ff.; G. Colin, "Des Juifs nomades retrouvés dans le Sahara marocain au XVIe siècle," *Mélanges d'études luso-marocains* dedicated to David Lopes and Pierre Cénival, pp. 53–66; and R. Mauny's more recent survey of "Le Judaïsme, les Juifs et l'Afrique occidentale," *Bulletin de l'Institut français d'Afrique noire,* XI, 354–78. The Greek and Arabic sources recording "La Conquête de l'Afrique du Nord par les Arabes," have been subjected to a brief scrutiny by A. Gateau in his communication to the Sixth International Congress of Byzantine Studies in Algiers, 1939, pp. 122–30. Cf. also M. Simon's data on "Le Judaïsme berbère dans l'Afrique ancienne," *RHPR,* XXVI, 129 ff., 140 ff.; A. Bel's review of the religion of the preislamic Berbers in *La Religion musulmane en Berbérie,* I, 71 ff.; and, more generally, E. F. Gautier's study of *L'Islamisation de l'Afrique du Nord; les siècles obscures du Maghreb;* R. Brunschvig's "Ibn 'Abdalh'akam et la conquête de l'Afrique du Nord par les Arabes," *Annales de l'Institut d'études orientales,* Algiers, VI, 108–55; as well as other literature listed in C. Courtois's bibliographical essay on "Histoire de l'Afrique du Nord des origines à la fin du moyen âge," *RH,* CXCVIII, 228–49; and in the recurrent bibliographies published in *Hespéris.*

25. Cf. the sources cited by R. Dozy in his *Recherches sur l'histoire et la littérature de l'Espagne pendant le moyen âge,* 3d ed., I, 1–83; his *Histoire des Musulmans d'Espagne (711–1110),* new ed. rev. by E. Lévi-Provençal, I, 270 ff. (or in the English translation by F. G. Stokes entitled *Spanish Islam,* pp. 230 ff.); and Joseph ha-Kohen's *'Emeq ha-bakhah,* ed. by Letteris, pp. 10 ff. (in M. Wiener's German translation, p. 7). Cf. also C. Sánchez-Albornoz's detailed "Itinerario de la conquista de España por los musulmanes," *CHE,* X, 21–74. Once again the total absence of contemporary Hebrew sources makes all this evidence concerning the Jewish part in the Moorish conquest of Spain decidedly one-sided.

26. According to tradition Ka'b al-Aḥbar maintained some Jewish loyalties even after his conversion. He was supposed, for example, to have advised 'Umar to choose a site for his Mosque north of the Rock in such a way that the worshipers would turn toward the original place of Solomon's Temple. Cf. Abu Jafar Ṭabari, *K. Aḥbar ar-rusul w'al-muluk,* I, 2408 f.; and the literature cited *infra,* n. 33. Cf. also I. Wolfensohn (Ben-Zeeb), *Ka'b al-Aḥbar und seine Stellung im Ḥadiṭ und in der islamischen Legendenliteratur;* M. Perlmann's texts and analyses of "A Legendary Story of Ka'b al-Aḥbar's Conversion to Islam," *Starr Mem. Vol.,* pp. 85–99; and of "Another Ka'b al-Aḥbar Story," *JQR,* XLV, 48–58. A selection from the numerous sources mentioning early Jewish converts to Islam and the alleged

"Jewish" origin of the Qarmatian movement and the Faṭimid dynasty is given by A. N. Poliak in "L'Arabisation de l'Orient sémitique," *Revue des études islamiques,* XII, 35 n. 1.

Most of the Arab oral traditions, to be sure, are supposed to go back to the Messenger himself, their authenticity being safeguarded by the chain of authorities (the so-called *isnad*), who had allegedly transmitted them during the following generations. But even the Muslim traditionalists have long conceded the unequal value of these chains, and they have often classified the individual traditions (*aḥadith*) according to their degree of reliability. Cf. C. A. Nallino's brief but illuminating summary of the "Classificazione del 'ḥadīth' dal punto di vista dei tradizionisti" in his *Raccolta di scritti editi e inediti,* II, 142 ff. A good analytical review of the vast mass of these traditions from the point of view of their content is offered by A. J. Wensinck in *A Handbook of Early Muhammedan Tradition* (based on the twelve main collections in Arabic).

No comprehensive study of the Jewish ingredients of the *ḥadith* is as yet available. But there exists a long array of monographic investigations which should greatly facilitate the task of such a synthesis. The following essays are particularly noteworthy: S. D. Goitein's "Isra'liyat" (Hebrew), *Tarbiz,* VI, 89–101, 510–22, which shows the great influence of the talmudic Aggadah on a distinguished Muslim writer, Malik ibn Dinar, and his circle about 700 C.E.; W. R. Taylor's similar comparison of "Al-Bukhari and the Aggada," *MW,* XXXIII, 191–202; E. Hahn's "Hadith cosmogonique et Aggadah," *REJ,* CI, 53–72; S. Rosenblatt's illustrations of "Rabbinic Legends in the Hadith," *MW,* XXXV, 237–52; and other essays in his popular collection *The People of the Book.* Once again such researches ought not to cling to the more obvious borrowings alone. For example, Arab traditions concerning Abraham's introduction of such customs as cutting finger-nails, removing hair from arm-pits, and clipping mustaches (Bukhari) need not have any exact counterpart in the Aggadah. And yet the fundamental approach of ascribing to the first patriarch some contemporary cherished mores doubtless was taken over, however unconsciously, from similar efforts of Jewish homilists and creators of folklore. Some additional material of this kind is now available also in the published parts (Vols. IVb and V) of Al-Baladhuri's *K. Ansab al-Ashraf,* going beyond its strictly "Jewish Subject Matter" analyzed in S. D. Goitein's Hebrew essay in *Zion,* I, 75–81. Cf. also J. Finkel's edition of "An Arabic Story of Abraham," *HUCA,* XII–XIII, 387–409 (going back to a Muslim source sometimes ascribed to the Jewish convert, Ka'b al-Aḥbar); R. Bell's brief summary of Muslim views on "The Sacrifice of Ishmael," *Transactions* of the Glasgow University Oriental Society, X, 29–31; the strange lucubrations of a modern orthodox Muslim on "Did Abraham Offer His Son Ishmael for Sacrifice or Isaac?" *Review of Religions,* XXXVII, 297–310; and B. Heller's "Récits et personnages bibliques dans la légende mahométane" in *REJ,* LXXXV, 113–36, with special reference to R. Basset's *Mille et une contes,* Vol. III. Cf. also, more generally, S. D. Goitein's stimulating review in *Jews and Arabs: Their Contacts through the Ages;* P. K. Hitti, *History;* B. Spuler and L. Forrer's more recent survey of *Der Vordere Orient in islamischer Zeit;* the summarizing essays in T. Arnold and A. Guillaume, *Legacy of Islam;* and, from the sociological angle, the materials assembled by Reuben Levy in *An Introduction to the Sociology of Islam;* and G. E. von Grunebaum's *Medieval Islam.* Other studies can readily be gleaned from J. Sauvaget's mainly bibliographical *Introduction à l'histoire de l'Orient musulman;* R. Ettinghausen's briefer compilation of *A Selected Bibliography of Books and Periodicals in Western Languages Dealing with the Near and Middle East;* and the various articles in the *Encyclopaedia Judaica* and the *Encyclopaedia of Islam.*

27. *Nistarot* (Mysteries) of R. Simon bar Yoḥai in Jellinek, *Bet ha-Midrasch,* III, 78 (reprinted in Eisenstein's *Ozar Midrashim,* p. 555); *Pirqe de-R. Eliezer,* XXIX, ed. by M. Higger in *Horeb,* X, 193; and in G. Friedlander's English translation, p. 221. The *Pirqe,* however, quoted another, slightly later, homily directed *against* the new regime. "Why was his [Abraham's son's] name called Ishmael?" the preacher asked. "Because the Blessed be He knew that He would some day hear the groaning of the people over what the children of Ishmael were going to do on earth, He called him Ishmael," that is, "God shall hear" (*ibid.,* XXXI, *Horeb,* X, 196; a different translation offered by Friedlander, p. 231). On the date of the *Pirqe,* see L. Zunz, *Gottesdienstliche Vorträge,* pp. 271 ff.; and, with additional data by C. Albeck in his translation of *Ha-Derashot be-Yisrael,* pp. 135, 140, 420 n. 25. Cf. also B. Heller's "Muhammedanisches und Antimuhammedanisches in den Pirke Rabbi Eliezer," *MGWJ,* LXIX, 47–54 (chiefly relating to folklore). The *Nistarot* is related in both spirit and content to several other midrashim of the same kind, and especially to the so-called *Tefillah* (Prayer) of R. Simon bar Yoḥai, the first part of which leans heavily on the "Mysteries." The "Prayer" first appeared in Jellinek's *Bet ha-Midrasch,* IV, 117–26 (with Jellinek's introduction *ibid.,* pp. viii f.); and was reprinted in Eisenstein's *Ozar,* pp. 551 ff. Both midrashim, together with several others of related content, have again been reproduced in vocalized texts, with extensive introductions and comments, by Y. Ibn Shemuel (Kaufmann) in his *Midreshe Ge'ulah,* pp. 161 ff. More recently, B. Lewis has translated the "Prayer" into English and subjected it to careful scrutiny in "An Apocalyptic Vision of Islamic History," *BSOAS,* XIII, 308–38. He has made a strong case for dividing the text into four sections. Only the first section, largely a reedition of the material in the "Mysteries," dates essentially from the seventh century. The second section, relating to Faṭimid, Qarmatian and Byzantine invasions of Egypt was composed approximately in 969–76. The third section alone introduced new material relating to the First Crusade by a more or less contemporary writer. The midrash concludes with a messianic vision, probably written by the latter author. This is a very plausible reconstruction, although opinions may vary as to details, especially since all these texts have often been tampered with by copyists and include a great many interpolations. Cf. also the earlier literature cited by both Ibn Shemuel and Lewis.

28. Abu Yusuf Ya'qub, *K. al-Kharaj,* (Livre de l'impôt foncier), pp. 13 f., 28 f.; in E. Fagnan's French translation, pp. 38 f., 77 f. Evidently the stipulation of revocability in Mohammed's treaty with the Jews of Khaibar, here quoted, was added by later historians as an afterthought to justify 'Umar's expulsion of the Jewish sharecroppers. See *supra,* nn. 8, 16. Abu Yusuf himself (pp. 20 f.; in Fagnan, pp. 56 ff.), and others quoted a number of divergent traditions concerning the new land tax introduced by 'Umar, for which there existed no clear Qur'anic precedents. Only the Messenger's treaties with the surrendering Jews and Christians, who had to obligate themselves to pay unspecified amounts for *zakat* (poor tax) for the support of the impoverished Muslims in Medina, could serve as a *post facto* rationalization. Although it underwent a number of modifications, the very term *kharaj* betrays its adaptation from the conquered lands, where the Pehlevi *kharaj*

itself apparently was but an Aramaic loan word. Cf. W. Henning's "Arabisch ḫarağ," *Orientalia,* IV, 291–93; M. A. Khan's "Jizyah and Kharaj (A Clarification of the Meaning of the Terms as They Were Used in the 1st Century H)," *Journal of the Pakistan Historical Society,* IV, 27–35; and *infra,* Chap. XVIII, nn. 48 ff.

29. Cf. A. S. Tritton's detailed analysis of the Covenant of 'Umar in *The Caliphs and Their Non-Muslim Subjects;* and other literature mentioned *infra,* Chap. XVIII, n. 12. The keen disappointment over the repulse at Constantinople is reflected in the legends analyzed by M. Canard in "Les Expéditions des Arabes contre Constantinople dans l'histoire et dans la légende," *JA,* CCVIII, 61–121. On the messianic expectations about 100 A.H., cf. Vasiliev's observations in *Byzantion,* XVI, 471 ff.; and *infra,* Chap. XXV, n. 58. Their nexus with the ascetic and anti-alien trends under 'Umar II would bear further examination. Needless to say that then, and later, the enforcement of such detailed provisions affecting millions of subjects scattered over the vast expanses of the Empire would have required the constant vigilance of a far more efficient bureaucracy than was at the caliphs' disposal. On the conditions during the first century, see S. A. Q. Husaini's *Arab Administration.* Husaini's data could be greatly elaborated by further utilization of the Arabic and Greek papyri, since Greek still was the main official language of the western provinces during most of the seventh century. However, H. I. Bell is undoubtedly right in pointing out the gradual erosion of Hellenism in the last generations before Islam. Cf. his *Egypt from Alexander the Great to the Arab Conquest;* A. Grohmann's *Arabic Papyri in the Egyptian Library;* his *From the World of Arabic Papyri;* his slightly antiquated review of the "Stand und Aufgaben der arabischen Papyrologie im Rahmen der Arabistik," *Muséon,* LII, 325–36; and his more recent analysis of "The Value of Arabic Papyri for the Study of Medieval Egypt," *Proceedings* of the Royal Society of History, Cairo, I, 41–56. Among the extant papyri of the early Muslim age there are also a few of considerable Jewish interest. Cf. V. Tcherikover's forthcoming *Corpus* of these papyri. Of considerable importance also are the numerous Arabic inscriptions of the Muslim period, for which the *Répertoire chronologique d'épigraphie arabe,* published by the Institut français d'archéologie orientale of Cairo, serves as a basic reference work. Its latest volume (XIV), published in 1954, lists 400 items (Nos. 5201–5600) covering the period of 706–31 A.H. Cf. also *supra,* Chap. XVI, n. 81.

30. The racialist debates in medieval Islam have been briefly analyzed by I. Goldziher in his *Muhammedanische Studien,* I, 143 ff., 147 ff.; and "Die Šu'ubijja unter den Mohammedanern in Spanien," *ZDMG,* LIII, 601–20. Cf. also I. Lichtenstadter's more recent survey, "From Particularism to Unity: Race, Nationality and Minorities in the Early Islamic Empire," *IC,* XXIII, 251–80; and B. Spuler's succinct observations on "Die Selbstbehauptung des iranischen Volkstums im frühen Islam," *Die Welt als Geschichte,* X, 187–91. A fuller and more up-to-date treatment of this ramified problem is clearly indicated, however. See e.g., J. Lecerf's analysis of "La Signification historique du racisme chez Mutanabbi" in *Al-Mutanabbi,* published on the poet's thousandth anniversary by the Institut français de Damas, pp. 31–43. On the stimulus which these debates doubtless gave to Halevi's and Maimonides' racial theories, see my "Yehudah Halevi: An Answer to an Historic Challenge," *JSS,* III, 266 ff.; my remarks in *PAAJR,* VI, 101 f.; and *infra,* Chap. XXXIV.

31. 'Ali ben Yusuf ibn al-Qifṭi's *K. Ta'riḥ al-ḥukama* (History of the Philosophers), ed. by J. Lippert, p. 194; the anonymous Syriac chronicle, ed. by I. Guidi in "Un nuovo testo siriaco sulla storia degli ultimi Sassanidi," included in the *Actes* of the VIIIth International Congress of Orientalists, Semitic Section B, pp. 7 ff. (in T. Nöldeke's German translation, in *SB* Vienna, CXXVIII, Part 9, p. 22); *Iggeret* (Epistle) of Sherira Gaon, ed. by B. M. Lewin, p. 101. On Mosul's designation as Ḥesna Ebraya, cf. also the letter written in 1288 by Exilarch David of Mosul and excerpted in J. Mann, *Texts and Studies,* I, 477 n. 4. The fact that all the Sherira manuscripts agree on the figure of 90,000 Jews greeting 'Ali, that it was not rounded up to 100,000 (a number frequently occurring, for instance, in Agapius' chronicle), and that Sherira was generally rather careful in regard to numbers, heightens the likelihood that here, too, the gaon quoted a rough contemporary estimate. The welcome extended to 'Ali was in line with the neutralist position apparently assumed by Babylonian Jewry during the earlier periods of the Arab invasions. At least Baladhuri creates the impression that, during the conquest of Mosul and its close neighbor Nineveh (hence the Jewish equation of Mosul with Ashshur), the large Jewish quarter (*maḥallat al-yahud*) quickly surrendered. Cf. his *K. Futûḥ al-buldân,* pp. 332 f. (in Murgotten's translation, pp. 31 ff.). Cf. also J. Obermeyer's *Landschaft Babylonien,* pp. 135 ff.

32. Ibn an-Naqqash, "Fetoua rélatif à la condition des Zimmis," ed. and trans. by M. Belin in *JA,* LIX, 444; Benjamin of Tudela, *Massa'ot* (Itinerary), ed. by M. N. Adler, p. 38 (Hebrew), p. 39 (English). Cf. J. C. Russell's *British Medieval Population,* cited *infra,* Chap. XX, n. 99. Cf. also Obermeyer, *Landschaft,* pp. 147 ff.; Reuben Levy's general data in *A Baghdad Chronicle,* pp. 11 ff.; and, on Masha'allah, *infra,* Chap. XXXV.

Evidence on the Jewish population in medieval Baghdad is far from satisfactory. We may merely assume that the number of both the general and Jewish inhabitants permanently declined, rather than increased, after the ravages of the half-century from 923 to 972. At one time the depopulation became so serious a problem that houseowners paid their tenants for keeping the houses in a state of repair. 17,000 lives were lost in the fire of 972 alone. Cf. A. Mez's comprehensive survey of *The Renaissance of Islam,* pp. 6 f. Unfortunately we have no information at all about the size of the Jewish population there before Benjamin. It is also still subject to debate which of the two figures, 1,000 or 40,000 Jews (or Jewish taxpayers) in Baghdad, mentioned in the different manuscripts of Benjamin's *Massa'ot,* ed. by M. N. Adler, p. 38 n. 25 (Hebrew), p. 39 n. 1 (English), is correct; 40,000 seems to be much nearer the truth. On the general trustworthiness of the information furnished by Benjamin, see *infra,* Chap. XXVIII. Mez (pp. 37 f.) deduced from the head tax recorded for the early ninth and tenth centuries that there were altogether some 15,000 *dhimmi* taxpayers in the city, and therefore he believed that there were no more than 1,000 Jews in Baghdad as against 40,000 or 50,000 Christians. But such a disproportion in itself bears the mark of improbability; it is further disproved by Benjamin's reference to the 28 large synagogues, and the large Jewish settlements recorded by him in the neighboring cities of Harbal (15,000), Hilla (10,000), Kufa, and Mosul (7,000 each). On the Arab testimony (first published in 1908) concerning the 36,000 Jewish taxpayers in 1258, contrasted with a total Christian population of 43,000 worshiping in 56 churches, see Y. R. A. Ghanima, *Nuzhat al-Mushtak fi Ta'rikh Yahud al-Iraq* (History of the Jews in Iraq), p. 156;

quoted in J. Finkel's review thereof in *JQR,* XXVI, 239. Such relative strength of the two denominations is not unlikely, in view of the prolonged decline of Christianity in its Babylonian center after the tenth century. Neither is the resulting total of less than 200,000 *dhimmis* in a city, whose population probably still exceeded 1,000,000, altogether impossible. In any case, the great influence exercised, from the tenth century on, by Baghdad Jewry would be entirely inexplicable without a populous and thriving community. Cf. also D. S. Sassoon's more popular summary of *A History of the Jews in Baghdad;* his *Massa' Babel* (Babylonian Journey: With Matters Pertaining to the History of the Jewish Community in Baghdad), Hebrew trans. with Introduction and Notes by M. Benayahu; his aforementioned "History of the Jews in Basra," *JQR,* XVII, 407–69 (all three more valuable for modern than medieval times); W. J. Fischel's "Arabische Quellen zur Geschichte der babylonischen Judenheit im 13. Jahrhundert," *MGWJ,* LXXIX, 302–22; and *supra,* n. 21.

33. Cf. the data supplied by J. Mann in *The Jews in Egypt and in Palestine under the Faṭimid Caliphs,* I, 43 ff., and II, 189 ff. (dating the Jerusalem letter in 1057); B. Z. Dinaburg in "A Jewish 'Synagogue and Academy' on the Temple Mountain in the Arab Period" (Hebrew), *Ṣiyyon,* III, 82 f. (arguing in favor of an earlier date of 973, or rather 977, and correspondingly emending the text); and S. Assaf in "The Beginnings of Jewish Settlement in Jerusalem after the Arab Conquest" (Hebrew), reprinted in his *Meqorot u-meḥqarim* (Texts and Studies in Jewish History), pp. 17–23, with the discussions thereon by S. Yeivin, I. Press, Z. Baneth, and J. W. Hirschberg in *BJPES,* VII, 85–89; IX, 79–80; XII, 141–53; XIII, 156–64. We have no reason to doubt the Jews' claim to having first shown the Arabs the location of their ancient Temple, although it conflicted with similar Christian claims and was obviously colored by the desire to explain their presence in the city. The Christians must originally have resented the idea of seeing another sanctuary arising from the ruins, an issue so long and ardently debated among Jewish and Christian controversialists. Cf. *supra,* Chap. XVI, nn. 24–25, and Vol. II, pp. 107 f., 374 n. 23. The story of the three-cornered negotiations is probably apocryphal, since 'Umar spent only a short time in Jerusalem. Nor did Patriarch Sophronius long survive the occupation; he died in March 638 or 639, at most one year after his surrender. No successor was appointed until 706. Of course, it is barely possible that 'Umar, contemplating the willful neglect to which the Christians, for dogmatic reasons, had exposed the entire area of the former Temple of Solomon, changed his mind speedily and forced the Christian leaders to modify the anti-Jewish clause in their treaty of surrender. Cf. also T. Salomon's somewhat uncritical "Who Revealed the Place of the 'Foundation Stone' to the Arabs?" (Hebrew), *Luaḥ Yerushalayyim* for 5710, pp. 148–57; and *supra,* nn. 17–18.

34. Salmon ben Yeruḥim's Commentary on Ps. 30:10, in J. Mann, *Texts and Studies,* II, 18 f.; Mohammed ben Aḥmad ben Abu-Bakr al-Muqaddasi, *K. Aḥsan al-taqâsîm* (Best of Divisions for the Knowledge of Climates, or *Descriptio imperii islamici,* 985–86), ed. by M. J. de Goeje, p. 167 (in G. Le Strange's English translation), both reproduced with a Hebrew translation in *Sefer ha-Yishub,* II, 20 No. 20, 23 No. 36. Cf. also the editors' interesting summary in their introduction, *ibid.,* pp. xvi ff.; other Arab sources cited in French translation in Marmardji's *Textes géographiques,* pp. 26 ff.; S. D. Goitein's cursory Hebrew review of "Jerusalem in

the Arab Period (638–1099)," *Jerusalem* (quarterly), IV, 82–103; and J. Prawer's detailed examination of "The Vicissitudes of the Jewish and Karaite Quarters in Jerusalem during the Arab Period (640–1099)" (Hebrew), *Zion*, XII, 136–48. Goitein's explanation that otherwise prohibited services at a mosque were tolerated here because of the messianic tension is questionable even with respect to the inception of that arrangement. It could hardly have continued to operate several centuries thereafter. The intensive interest of modern scholars in the return of Jews to Jerusalem after 638, and their assistance in the recovery of the Temple site, is not altogether academic; it was heightened by the recurrent conflicts in modern times between Arabs and Jews over the latter's free access to the Wailing Wall. Among the vast literature on that remnant of the ancient sanctuary, see especially C. Adler's *Memorandum on the Western Wall;* and I. Y. Yahuda's "Western Wall" (Hebrew), *Ṣiyyon*, III, 95–163. Cf. also, from another angle, A. Guillaume's renewed query, "Where Was al-Masjid al-Aqṣà?" *Al-Andalus*, XVIII, 323–36; *supra*, n. 17; *infra*, Chap. XXI, n. 26; and, more generally, the aforementioned older but still valuable works by G. Le Strange, Mednikov, and Vincent and Abel; Z. Vilnai, *Toledot ha-'Arabim veha-Muslamim be-Ereṣ Yisrael* (A History of the Arabs and Muslims in Palestine); M. Assaf, *Toledot ha-shilṭon ha-'arabi be-Ereṣ Yisrael* (History of Arab Domination over Palestine); and S. Klein, *Toledot ha-yishub ha-yehudi be-Ereṣ Yisrael* (History of the Jewish Settlement in Palestine).

35. Cf. the extensive documentation given under the respective cities in *Sefer ha-Yishub*, Vol. II; with some additional data in J. Braslavsky's review of this work in *KS*, XXI, 144–50. The biblical and linguistic studies in Tiberias will be discussed *infra*, Chaps. XXIX–XXX. Cf. also H. Z. Hirschberg's more recent study of "Ramleh as an Intermediary Station before Jerusalem" (Hebrew), *Jerusalem* (quarterly), IV, 123–28 (chiefly offering data from later periods); and F. M. Abel's general review of the story of "Jaffa au moyen âge," *JPOS*, XX, 6–28. On the other hand, the ancient community of Hebron was now primarily but a center of attraction to Jewish pilgrims. Early under the Muslim regime the Jews secured permission, previously denied to them by the Byzantine authorities, to erect a synagogue at the entrance to the Cave of Machpelah, the burial place of the ancient patriarchs. The neighboring communities also frequently sent their dead for burial in the vicinity of that sacred ground. At times even more distant coreligionists dispatched there caskets containing bones of relatives. When Benjamin of Tudela visited Hebron, after the bloodletting of the First Crusade, he apparently found there no permanent Jewish settlers; their former synagogue had been converted into a Church of St. Abraham. Cf. his *Massa'ot*, ed. by M. N. Adler, pp. 26 f. (Hebrew), 25 f. (English); and other sources, cited in *Sefer ha-Yishub*, II, 6 ff. Of some interest are also the "Documents sur certain waqfs des Lieux saints de l'Islam, principalement . . . à Hebron et . . . à Jérusalem" published by L. Massignon in the *Revue des études islamiques*, 1951 (1952), pp. 73–120; and I. Ben-Zvi's brief sketch of "The Jewish Settlement in Ramleh" (Hebrew), *Sura*, I, 9–16.

36. Theophanes, *Chronographia*, ed. by De Boor, I, 342, 430 (to year 6249); II, 214 f., 282; Yaḥya of Antioch's report, cited with a French translation in Vincent and Abel, *Jérusalem*, II, 245; and M. Schwabe's "Khirbet Mafjar. Greek Inscribed Fragments," *QDAP*, XII, 20–30, esp. pp. 29 f. Cf. also I. Ben-Zvi's interrelated Hebrew essays on the Mustarabs or "Pseudo-Arabs" in Palestine in *Sinai*, III, Nos.

30–31, pp. 379–86, and IV, Nos. 39–40, pp. 38–41; and "On the Jewish Origin of the *Fellaheen* in Our Country" in the Annual of *Davar,* entitled *Tu shin yod dalet* (5714 = 1953–54), pp. 283–94. However, one must not forget the bitterness permeating the internecine struggles at the Church of the Holy Sepulcher among the Christian denominations themselves, although G. Every may be right in saying that their vehemence increased only after the twelfth century. Cf. his "Syrian Christians in Palestine in the Early Middle Ages," *Eastern Churches Quarterly,* VI, 363–72; his "Syrian Christians in Jerusalem, 1183–1283," *ibid.,* VII, 46–54; and L. Bréhier's older study of "La Situation des chrétiens de Palestine à la fin du VIIIe siècle," *Moyen Age,* XXX, 67–75. On the alleged Frankish protectorate, see *infra,* Chap. XX n. 57. Unfortunately, only few papyri which might throw light on such daily relationships have survived Palestine's inclement soil conditions. Cf. in particular the story related by N. Abbott in "An Arabic Papyrus in the Oriental Institute," *JNES,* V, 169 n. 3; N. Lewis's "New Light on the Negev in Ancient Times," *PEQ,* 1948–49, pp. 102–17 (on the period of 400–700; what the author says about the effects of the Arab domination on the Christians of southern Palestine largely applies also to Jews); and Tcherikover's forthcoming *Corpus.* The impact of the Crusades on the Near Eastern Jewries will be described *infra,* Chap. XXI.

37. Baladhuri's *K. Futûḥ al-buldân,* p. 127 (in Hitti's English trans., pp. 194 f.); Benjamin, *Massa'ot,* ed. by M. N. Adler, pp. 20 f., 31 f. (Hebrew), 18 f., 31 (English); Petaḥiah of Ratisbon, *Sibbub* (Travels), ed. with an English trans. by A. Benisch, pp. 52 f.; and in the critical ed. by L. Grünhut, pp. 28 (Hebrew), 38 f. (German); more readily available in J. D. Eisenstein's Hebrew anthology of travelogues, *Ozar Massa'ot,* pp. 46 ff., 54; and in E. N. Adler's corresponding collection in English, entitled *Jewish Travellers,* pp. 64 ff., 85 f.; Jacob's report on the graves of the patriarchs, in Eisenstein, *Ozar,* pp. 65 ff., 70 (Adler, *Jewish Travellers,* pp. 115 ff., 126 f.); *Sefer ha-Yishub,* II, pp. 51 ff.; Mann, *Jews in Egypt,* I, 107 f., 161 f.; II, 118 f., 182 f., 359 n. 4. Cf. also S. Assaf, "From the Old Records of the Damascus Community" (Hebrew) in his *Meqorot u-meḥqarim,* pp. 64–69 (includes four documents of 933 C.E. which, it may be noted, were still dated by both the eras of Creation and of Sabbatical cycles). On Petaḥiah's work and its value to historians and geographers, see *infra,* Chap. XXVIII. In "The Jews in the Latin Kingdom of Jerusalem," *Zion,* XI, 77 ff., J. Prawer argues in favor of dating Jacob's journey some time between 1153 and 1187. On Palmyra, see also the literature listed *supra,* Vol. II, p. 407 n. 43, in part pertaining to our period as well.

38. Petaḥiah, *Sibbub, supra,* n. 37; M. Sobernheim and E. Mittwoch, "Hebräische Inschriften in der Synagoge von Aleppo," *Festschrift . . . Jakob Guttmann,* p. 279; E. N. Adler, "Aleppo," *Gedenkbuch . . . David Kaufmann,* pp. 128–37; J. Sauvaget, *Alep,* pp. 60 f.; and, more generally, P. K. Hitti, *History of Syria, including Lebanon and Palestine.* On the reasons for giving earlier dates to synagogue inscriptions in Aleppo and elsewhere, see *infra,* Chap. XVIII, n. 18.

39. Mann, *Jews in Egypt, passim; Texts and Studies,* I, 359 ff.; Benjamin, *Massa'ot,* pp. 62 ff., 69 (Hebrew), 69 ff., 77 (English); S. Assaf's Hebrew sketch of "The Ancient Synagogue at Damwah (Egypt)" in his *Meqorot u-meḥqarim,* pp. 155–62. Among other more recent publications see, e.g., M. Fargeon's brief historical sketch of

Les Juifs en Egypte; L. Blau's "Fusṭāṭ, la residenza di Maimonide," *Annuario di studi ebraici,* II, 65–85 (also in Hungarian in the Blau Memorial Volume, *Zikhron Yehudah,* pp. 321–39); S. Assaf's "Relations between the Jews of Egypt and Aden in the XIIth Century" (Hebrew), *BJPES,* XII, 116–19; and, more generally, G. Wiet's survey of *L'Egypte arabe.* Some Christians claimed later that the synagogue of Damwah had originally been a Christian monastery. They seem to have confused, however, that synagogue with some other Jewish houses of worship which had, indeed, been converted from churches and monasteries for reasons to be explained *infra,* Chap. XVIII, n. 18. On the other hand, one need not take seriously the synagogue's alleged association with Moses. It was in line with the four mosques "of Musa," which existed in Egypt, including one built by Ibn Tulun on the spot where Moses "had talked with the Lord." Cf. Maqrizi's *Khiṭaṭ,* IV, 36; and J. Pedersen's article "Masdjid" in the *Shorter EI,* ed. by H. A. R. Gibb and J. H. Kramers, p. 333. Of course, the Jewish tradition may have had pre-Islamic roots and served as a model for the Muslims. Cf. *supra,* Vol. II, p. 20. On the Fusṭaṭ Genizah and its contents, see esp. P. E. Kahle's *Cairo Geniza* (mainly concerned with its contribution to biblical and linguistic studies); and A. Marx's broader, though succinct, discussion of "The Importance of the Geniza for Jewish History," *PAAJR,* XVI, 183–204. Cf. also D. Gonzalo Maeso's observations on "La Gueniza de El Cairo y sus exploraciones," *Boletin de la Universidad de Granada,* XXIII, 145–67; and particularly S. D. Goitein's searching inquiries into "What Would Jewish and General History Benefit by a Systematic Publication of the Documentary Geniza Papers?" *PAAJR,* XXIII, 29–40; and "The Cairo Geniza as a Source for the History of Muslim Civilization," *Studia Islamica,* III, 75–91.

40. N. Slouschz, *Etudes sur l'histoire des Juifs au Maroc,* Vol. II; Al-Bajan, cited by I. Goldziher in his *Muhammedanische Studien,* I, 205 n. 2; S. Poznanski's mainly literary data in his *Anshe Kairuwan* (Men of Kairuwan), *passim,* supplemented by B. M. Lewin's more recent data in "The Community of Kairuwan during the Geonic Period" (Hebrew), *Sinai,* VI, Nos. 71–72, pp. 337–42. The complex problems of Jewish participation in early Faṭimid campaigns will be discussed *infra,* Chap. XVIII n. 38. On the date of Mar 'Uqba's arrival in Kairuwan and its historic significance for interterritorial Jewish relations, see my "Saadia's Communal Activities," *Saadia Anniv. Vol.,* pp. 25 ff., 33 f.; and *infra,* Chap. XXIII, n. 46. The erection of the Kairuwan mosque on formerly Jewish land is reported by a fourteenth-century Arab chronicler (Ibn abi Zer of Fez, or Ibn 'Abd al-Halim of Granada), doubtless on the basis of older local sources. Cf. his *Annales regum Mauritaniae a condito Idrisadarum imperio ad annum fugae 726,* ed. with a Latin trans. by J. C. Tornberg, p. 47. Cf. also H. Z. Hirschberg's historical introduction to his new Hebrew translation of Nissim bar Jacob's *Ḥibbur yafeh me-ha-yeshu'ah* (Worthy Book of Comfort), on which see *infra,* Chap. XXVIII, n. 38. While the literary history of Kairuwan Jewry has found several competent investigators, its sociopolitical evolution would also merit a comprehensive monographic study.

41. Aḥmed as-Slawi's *K. al-Istiqṣa* (Histoire de Maroc), in the French translation by A. Graulle *et al.,* II, 102; and other data assembled by Slouschz in his *Etudes;* M. L. Ortega in *Los Hebreos en Marruecos,* 4th ed.; and J. M. Toledano in his *Ner ma'arabi* (Western Light; a History of the Jews in Morocco). To be sure, an official Arab chronicler, cited by Toledano (p. 12 n. 3) highly extolled Idris I for his victories

over the unbelievers and claimed that he had converted most of them to Islam by force. However, one may the more readily discount such pious assertions, as the author followed an obviously stereotype formula and included the Magi (Zoroastrians) among that mass of converts. Cf. also Ortega, pp. 43 f. In writing a moving elegy on the communities suffering from the Almohade persecutions, Abraham ibn Ezra singled out next to Fez also the Moroccan communities of Ceuta, Mequinez, Dra'a, and Segelmessa. Cf. *infra,* Chaps. XVIII, n. 6 and XXI, n. 54. It should also be noted that the aforementioned official chronicler reported a protracted conflict between a Christian and a Jewish tribe in the district of Dra'a adjoining the northern Sahara desert as late as the tenth century. Allegedly the Jews came out victorious. Cf. the text reproduced by Toledano, pp. 22 ff., and the literature cited *supra,* nn. 23–24. Cf. also, more generally, H. Terrasse's *Histoire de Maroc;* and E. Lévi-Provençal's more succinct review of *Islam d'Occident; études d'histoire médiévale.*

42. Cf. E. Lévi-Provençal's ed. of *La Péninsule Ibérique au moyen âge d'après le Kitab ar-Rawd al-mi'ṭar fi ḥabar al-akṭār d'Ibn 'Abd al-Mun'im al-Ḥimyari,* XIX, XLII, pp. 23, 42 f. (Arabic), 29 ff., 53 ff. (French); Idrisi, (Edrisi) *Description de l'Afrique et de l'Espagne,* Arabic text, ed. with a French trans. and notes by R. Dozy and M. J. de Goeje, pp. 191 (Arabic), 231 (French); Naṭronai's resp. in B. M. Lewin's *Otzar ha-gaonim* (Thesaurus of Gaonic Responsa and Commentaries), III, Part 1, pp. 24 f., No. 64; and Menaḥem ibn Zeraḥ's statement, cited *supra,* Chap. XVI, n. 42. According to Al-Ḥimyari, the population of Barcelona, too, was equally divided between Jews and Christians. However, located in the Christian part of the country, the present Catalan metropolis could not compare in size with the larger contemporary Muslim cities. Hence Benjamin was not altogether unjustified in speaking of it as a "small city." Cf. his *Massa'ot,* pp. 2 (Hebrew), 2 (English). Nor is it surprising that a scroll seen by an informant of Ibn Daud, which had allegedly been addressed by Saadiah Gaon to the communities of Spain, was directed only to cities in the Muslim parts of Spain, headed by their celebrated capital Cordova. Cf. Ibn Daud's *Sefer ha-Qabbalah* (Book of Tradition) in *MJC,* I, 74; and *infra,* Chap. XXIII, n. 13. On the demographic conditions in the latter, see my remarks in *JSS,* III, 246 n. 10; and R. Ramirez de Arellano's *Historia de Cordoba desde sa fondacion hasta la muerta de Isabel la Católica.* Cf. also P. David's *Études historiques sur la Galicie et le Portugal du VIe au XIIe siècle* (chiefly concerned with Church history); and, more generally, E. E. Lévi-Provençal's study of the Muslim social life and institutions in *L'Espagne musulmane au Xème siècle;* and esp. his comprehensive *Histoire de l'Espagne musulmane.* On the literature dealing chiefly with Christian Spain, but incidentally shedding also much light on Jewish life in the Muslim regions, see *infra,* Chap. XX.

We know very little, on the other hand, about the Jews of Sicily and southern Italy (for the most part centered around the fortified city of Bari) during the two centuries of Muslim domination. Often we must resort to mere reconstruction from conditions existing under the preceding Byzantine and the following Norman regimes. Cf. *infra,* Chap. XX, n. 20. Only a few details may be gleaned from such general works as the long renowned *Storia dei Musulmani di Sicilia* by M. Amari (now available in a rev. ed. by C. A. Nallino). Cf. also F. Gabrieli's suggestive comparison of "Arabi di Sicilia e Arabi di Spagna," *Al-Andalus,* XV, 27–45 (including excerpts from contemporary Arabic poems), and his recent bibliographical survey, "Un Secolo di studi arabo-siculi," *Studia islamica,* II, 89–102 (covering the publications since the appearance of Amari's first volume in 1854). However, further detailed scrutiny of the Arabic and other non-Jewish sources, together with the data yielded by the Chronicle of Aḥimaaz, some Genizah fragments, and references in later Hebrew letters, would surely produce new insights and facts which, in turn, would justify monographic treatment.

43. Moses ibn Ezra, *K. al-Muhadhara,* in B. Z. Halper's Hebrew trans., *Sefer Shirat Yisrael,* p. 59 (the author himself expresses doubts about the veracity of his informant; on this *ars poetica,* see *infra,* Chap. XXXII); Benjamin, *Massa'ot,* pp. 54 (Hebrew), 59 (English); Muqaddasi, *K. Aḥsan al-taqâsîm,* ed. by De Goeje, pp. 323, 388, 394, 414, 439. Cf. also A. J. Wensinck and B. Carra de Vaux, "Al-Dadjdjal," *Shorter EI,* p. 67; other data assembled by W. J. Fischel, especially in his "Yahudiya: On the Beginnings of Jewish Settlement in Persia" (Hebrew), *Tarbiz,* VI, 523–26; and in *Starr Mem. Vol.,* pp. 111–28; *supra,* Chap. XVI, n. 69; and, more generally, B. Spuler's comprehensive work, *Iran in früh-islamischer Zeit.*

44. As C. Toumanoff has pointed out, the legend of the Bagratid family's Hebrew origin mentioned by Moses of Khorene (cf. *supra,* Vols. I, p. 169, and II, pp. 204, 404 n. 36) was elaborated in the tenth century to include its alleged Davidic descent. Indicated already by Constantine Porphyrogenitus, this genealogy was fully developed in Sumbat ben David's eleventh-century Armenian history of that family. Cf. Toumanoff's study of "The Early Bagratids: Remarks in Connexion with Some Recent Publications," *Muséon,* LXII, 21–54. Cf. also the numerous local sources, many decidedly legendary, cited in A. H. Godbey's *Lost Tribes,* pp. 289 f., 314. The history of the Jews in Armenia would likewise merit greater attention than has hitherto been given to it by specialists. The country's vital geographic position has rightly been emphasized by J. Laurent in *L'Arménie entre Byzance et l'Islam* (citing also various sources on the debate concerning the Jewish origins of Armenia's animal sacrifices, p. 137 n. 1), and by R. Grousset in *Histoire de l'Arménie des origines à 1071.* The Jews in the neighboring districts of the Caucasus will be treated, in connection with the story of the Khazars, *infra,* Chap. XIX.

Much less is known about the early Jewish communities in the mountain recesses of Afghanistan. Cf. the few data marshaled from Hebrew sources by N. Slousch (Slouschz) in "Les Juifs en Afghanistan," *Revue du monde musulman,* IV, 502–11. It was gratifying therefore, when A. Dupont-Sommer published "Une Inscription hébraïque d'Afghanistan," *CRAI,* 1946, pp. 252–57. This inscription offers considerable difficulties. For example, instead of the date suggested by Dupont-Sommer, namely 749 C.E., W. J. Fischel has plausibly argued in favor of an improved reading which gives the date of 1198. Cf. his note in *JA,* CCXXXVII, 299–300. The conclusion of the inscription seems also to read better: *he-ḥasid ha-yare ha-yashish* (the old and God-fearing pious man). Cf. also I. Ben-Zvi's chapter on "The Tribes of Afghanistan and the Tradition of Their Descent from the Ten Tribes" in his *Nidḥe Yisrael,* pp. 183 ff. (also in the forthcoming English translation, *The Exiled and the Redeemed*); A. Brauer's more contemporary review of "The Jews of Afghanistan," *JSS,* IV, 121–38; and some of the general studies listed in M. Akram's *Bibliographie analytique de l'Afghanistan.*

Our knowledge of the history of Jews in other Middle Eastern countries must also often be reconstructed from such later sources as were assembled by Mann in his *Texts and Studies,* I, 477 ff., and analyzed by S. Assaf in a chapter "On the History of Jews in Kurdistan and Vicinity" in his *Be-Ohole Ya'aqob,* pp. 116–44; such comprehensive modern anthropological studies as Brauer's *Yehude Kurdistan* (Jews of Kurdistan); or some stray literary references as have been assembled by W. J. Fischel in "The Jews in Central Asia (Khorasan) in Medieval Hebrew and Islamic Literature," *HJ,* VII, 29–50; amplified in the debate thereon between him and L. Rabinowitz, *ibid.,* VIII, 61–67. Cf. also Fischel's other regional studies, including "Azarbaijan in Jewish History," *PAAJR,* XXII, 1–21; and "The Region of the Persian Gulf and Its Jewish Settlements in Islamic Times," in *Marx Jub. Vol.,* pp. 203–30; such useful general handbooks as the *Atlas of Islamic History* by H. W. Hazard; *A History of the Islamic Peoples* by C. Brockelmann; and *Geschichte der islamischen Länder,* Vol. I: *Die Chalifenzeit,* by B. Spuler.

45. R. Gottheil and W. H. Worrell, *Fragments from the Cairo Genizah in the Freer Collection,* No. 13, p. 68 line 35. The Qur'anic passages pertaining to apostasy from Islam, and the ramified legislation based thereon in later sources, are analyzed, with considerable anti-Muslim bias, by M. Zwemer in *The Law of Apostasy in Islam.*

46. Cf. the fragments of the *Sefer ha-Ma'asim,* ed. by B. M. Lewin and J. Mann respectively in *Tarbiz,* I, Part 1, p. 97, and Part 3, p. 12 (on the date and significance of this rabbinic compilation, cf. *infra,* Chap. XXVII, n. 71); Sherira Gaon, *Iggeret* (Epistle), ed. by Lewin, p. 101, and the sources listed in Lewin's notes thereon; Maimonides, *Teshubot* (Responsa), ed. by A. H. Freimann, pp. 151 f. No. 154, 198 No. 202. Cf. also *Pirqe de-R. Eliezer,* xxxii (ed. by Higger in *Horeb,* X, 198 ff., in Friedlander's trans., pp. 231 ff.), which chapter has long been interpreted as a mirror of the disintegration of the established modes of Jewish life in Palestine during the first century after the Arab occupation. Cf. *supra,* n. 27. The loose morals prevailing in the entire Near East during the early Muslim period are well illustrated by the sources cited in Obermeyer's *Landschaft Babylonien,* p. 121 n. 1. Hence arose those numerous precautions for the safeguarding of feminine chastity such as veils and segregated harems. Some Jews went so far as to complain to rabbis when one of their members, an innkeeper, accommodated Gentiles and merchants, because "these men look at their [the Jews'] women." Cf. *Teshubot ha-geonim mi-tokh ha-genizah* (Gaonic Responsa from Geniza MSS), ed. by S. Assaf, 1928, p. 116 No. 203. Cf. also *infra,* Chap. XVIII, nn. 25–26; and, on slavery, *infra,* Chap. XXII.

47. Mann, *Jews in Egypt,* I, 32 ff.; Samau'al ibn Yaḥya, *K. Ifḥam al-Yahud* (Silencing of the Jews), cited by M. Schreiner in his "Samau'al b. Yaḥya al-Maġribi und seine Schrift Ifḥâm al-Jahûd," *MGWJ,* XLII, 260. On this important controversial tract, a critical edition of which is being prepared by M. Perlmann, see *infra,* Chap. XXIV, n. 4. The extent and impact of Al-Ḥakim's and the Almohade persecutions will be discussed more fully in the next chapter.

48. All these estimates are submitted here with considerable diffidence. The data for the twelfth century are even less satisfactory than those relating to the first century, analyzed briefly *supra,* Vol. I, pp. 370 ff. n. 7. At that time reference could at least be made to some global figures of the Jewish population in the Roman Empire, supplied by Bar-Hebraeus, whatever one thinks of its scholarly worth. Modern research, too, has evinced considerable interest in these facets of social life, and minutely examined the few extant data, in a way allowing for some tentative,

but quite plausible conclusions. In contrast thereto, no one has seriously tried to come to grips with the basic population problems for the entire world of medieval Islam. The Jewish data, too, are both sparse and scattered, and no sustained scholarly effort has yet been made to subject them to careful and comprehensive scrutiny. Even our main source of information, Benjamin's travelogue, has suffered greatly from errors in transmission. As is well known, figures belong to textual elements least well reproduced by ancient or medieval copyists, because any alteration in them has as a rule little bearing upon the general context. In Hebrew, particularly, a change from *shalosh* (three) to *shesh* (six) is obtained by the deletion of a single letter. More significantly, to save space many copyists used alphabetical letters for figures. The result is that one could debate whether Benjamin found 200 (R) or only four (D) Jews in Jerusalem, since both letters look very much alike. See *infra,* Chap. XXI, n. 32. Similarly the omission of the letter M in his account of the visit to Baghdad could give rise to the obviously erroneous assumption that he had found only 1,000, rather than 40,000, Jews in the Muslim metropolis. Cf. *supra,* n. 32. Even where the figures are more or less certain, there still remains the problem, mentioned in the text, whether our traveler had in mind a city's total Jewish population, or only its taxpaying members. In many cases the latter is more likely. On the other hand, the simple shrugging off of the entire question and the equally simple admission of total ignorance are too facile an escape. The size, density, distribution, and especially growth or decline of population are factors too fundamental in all historical evolution for the conscientious historian to be satisfied with such a noncommittal *ignoramus et ignorabimus.* The present writer hopes some day to be able to submit more careful investigations of Jewish population trends through the ages. For the time being, these few very general remarks must suffice here.

49. Saadiah's *Beliefs and Opinions,* Intro., VI, ed. by S. Landauer, p. 21; in the Hebrew translation by Yehudah ibn Tibbon, ed. by Slucki, p. 48; and in the English translation by S. Rosenblatt, p. 26; D. G. Mandelbaum's eyewitness report on "The Jewish Way of Life in Cochin," *JSS,* I, 423–60; and J. Braslavsky's ed. of the Indian letter dated Tishre 8, 1461 (Sept. 12, 1149) in his "Jewish Trade between the Mediterranean and India in the Twelfth Century," (Hebrew), *Zion,* VII, 135–39. Fuller information on this significant segment of medieval international trade is to be expected from the forthcoming publication of a number of pertinent Genizah documents by S. D. Goitein. See his "From the Mediterranean to India: Documents on the Trade to India, South Arabia, and East Africa from the Eleventh and Twelfth Centuries," *Speculum,* XXIX, 181–97; and other data given *infra,* Chap. XXII. The part played by Jews in communicating to the Western world the methods and findings of Indian mathematicians and other scientists will be mentioned *infra,* Chap. XXXV. It is to be regretted that Benjamin of Tudela apparently never reached India —the very use of this term in his travelogue is equivocal, as it is in most contemporary writings. He apparently did not visit even those areas which had already been won over to Islam and are now largely included in Pakistan. Cf. *infra,* Chap. XXVIII.

50. An anonymous fragment from the Cairo Genizah, translated into German by E. N. Adler in his *Von Ghetto zu Ghetto,* pp. 197 ff. (not in its English original, *Jews in Many Lands*), and reproduced in English translation in his *Jewish Travellers,* pp. 101 f.; A. C. Burnell, "The Original Settlement-Deed of the Jewish Colony at

Cochin," *Indian Antiquary,* III, 333–34 (with facsimile); D. G. Mandelbaum, "Jewish . . . Life in Cochin," *JSS,* I, 425. The stray early sources, mainly Jewish, on Jews in India are briefly analyzed by N. Slouschz in "Les Juifs et le Judaïsme aux Indes," *Revue du monde musulman,* IV, 728–69; and by L. Sternbach in his "India as described by Mediaeval European Travellers, I: Jewish Dwelling Places," *Bharutiye Vidya,* VII, 10–28. Another interesting Arabic letter in the usual Hebrew script, dated 1153 and describing "A Journey to India" in a ship owned by the Fusṭaṭ *nagid* Ḥalfon which ended in shipwreck at Aden, is published by E. Strauss in his Hebrew essay in *Zion,* IV, 217–31. Cf. also two other letters of 1134 and 1148 respectively, published by Strauss, *ibid.,* VII, 145 ff. A noteworthy document in mixed Pehlevi and Arabic, but with an attestation in Hebrew square script, reporting alleged concessions granted the Christians was published by A. C. Burnell in his "On Some Pahlavi Inscriptions in South India," *Indian Antiquary,* III, 308–16. Cf. also the "Grant to the Early Christian Church in India," bearing among others four Hebrew signatures and published in *JRAS,* 1843, pp. 343–44 (with six lithographs). An interesting inquiry later addressed to David ibn Abi Zimra (died about 1573) states that Cochin embraced at that time 900 Jewish families, of whom only 100 were of pure Jewish extraction. Although less well off economically, the latter refused to intermarry with the majority, whom they called "[offspring of] slaves." Cf. the text published by A. Marx in his "Contribution à l'histoire des Juifs de Cochin," *REJ,* LXXXIX, 297; and his introduction thereto, in English, in his *Studies in Jewish History and Booklore,* pp. 174 ff. These stray bits of information, often of later date, shed some light, if used with the necessary caution, also on conditions before 1200. For this reason we may refer here also to some data assembled by W. J. Fischel in his "Jews and Judaism at the Court of the Moghul Emperors in Medieval India," *PAAJR,* XVIII, 137–77; and, more generally, by H. S. Kehimkar in *The History of the Bene Israel of India;* also the shorter studies by S. Lévi, "Quelques documents nouveaux sur les Juifs du sud de l'Inde," *REJ,* LXXXIX, 26–32 (include a funerary inscription of one Sarah bat Israel of 1269); S. S. Koder, "The Jews of Malabar," *India and Israel,* III, (Special Independence Issue of May 10, 1951), pp. 31–35; H. G. Reissner, "Jews in Medieval Ceylon," *Eastern World,* V, Part 5, pp. 14–16 (citing comments by Abu Zaid al-Hasan of Siraf of 911, Idrisi of 1154, and others); and his "Benjamin of Tudela on Ceylon," *Zeitschrift für Religions- und Geistesgeschichte,* VI, 151–55 (reproduces Asher's translation I, 141 ff., with an introduction and comments).

51. There is a considerable, though largely repetitious, literature on the intriguing problems of Chinese Jewry. Cf. R. Löwenthal's annotated bibliography on "The Jews of China" in *Chinese Social and Political Science Review,* XXIV, 113–234. More recently W. C. White has compiled the extant historical, epigraphic, and genealogical sources concerning the *Chinese Jews,* and thereby has greatly facilitated all future research, but he has himself refrained from drawing definite conclusions. Cf. also J. Tobar's older but still useful *Inscriptions juives de K'ai-fong-fou;* A. von Rohr-Sauer's reexamination and new German translation of *Des Abû Dulaf Bericht über seine Reise nach Turkestân, China und Indien,* pp. 20, 25, 49, 56 f. (the text had been edited with a Latin translation by K. von Schlözer in 1845, with new materials published in 1923); L. I. Rabinowitz's *Jewish Merchant Adventurers: a Study of the Radanites* which, though including some necessarily questionable hypotheses, is truly

suggestive. Of some interest is also G. Lambert's query, "Le Livre d'Isaïe parle-t'il des Chinois?" *Nouvelle Revue théologique,* LXXV, 965–72 (pointing out that the reading of the Dead Sea Isaiah scroll, 49:12, definitely proves that the prophet referred to the *Sevaniyyim,* or people of Assuan, Upper Egypt, and not to the *Sinim,* or Chinese). Cf. also J. Sauvaget's new ed. of the text, with a French translation, of *Aḫbar aṣ-Ṣin w'al-Hind* (Relation de la Chine et de l'Inde redigée en 851), which he attributes to an anonymous author, rather than, as was previously done, to Ḥasan ibn Yazid as-Sirafi; T. Lewicki's review of "Les Premiers commerçants arabes en Chine," *Rocznik orientalistyczny,* XI, 172–86; S. M. Ziauddin Alavi's "Arab Explorations during the 9th and 10th Centuries A.D.," *IC,* XXII, 265–79; and other writings discussed *infra,* Chap. XXII, n. 42. It may be noted that, at least according to Ibn Baṭṭuṭa's observations of 1346, the Chinese city of Al-Khansa (Hangchow) included a "Jews' Gate" and even seems to have had separate quarters for Muslims, Christians, Jews, and "Turkish" sun worshipers. Cf. his *K. Tuḥfat an-Nuẓẓar* (Voyages), ed. with a French trans. by C. Defrémery and B. R. Sanguinetti, IV, 283 ff.; and the English excerpts therefrom in H. A. R. Gibb's *Ibn Batuta, Travels in Asia and Africa 1325–1354,* pp. 293 f.

52. Eldad's narratives, ed. by A. Epstein in his *Eldad ha-Dani, passim; supra,* Vol. I, p. 321 n. 3. Cf. R. Hennig's *Terrae incognitae: Eine Zusammenstellung und kritische Bewertung der wichtigsten vorcolumbinischen Entdeckungsreisen,* 2d ed., II, 474 ff.; and A. M. Godbey's somewhat questionable data on ancient Israelitic vestiges among the tribes of the district of Usambara (inland from Mombasa) and Madagascar in *The Lost Tribes,* pp. 201 ff., 550 f. Cf. also A. Audollent's related study in *CRAI,* 1942, pp. 202–16. Some further data may also be culled from the fairly extensive literature relating to the Abyssinian Falashas, listed *supra,* Vol. II, p. 407 n. 44, to which is to be added A. Z. Aešcoly's *Recueil des textes falashas: introduction, textes éthiopiens,* published in 1951; and M. Wurmbrand's recent analysis of "Fragments d'anciens écrits juifs dans la littérature falacha," *JA,* CCXLII, 83–100 (mainly of liturgical content).

53. Cf. Epstein's introd. to his *Eldad ha-Dani;* the additional data supplied by A. M. Habermann in his edition of Epstein's *Kitbe* (Collected writings), I, 1–188, 357–90 (includes a list of printed editions of Eldad's work); and *infra,* Chap. XXVIII, n. 85. Modern scholars have, for the most part, completely discounted Eldad's stories as sheer inventions. Little scholarly progress has been made, therefore, in the investigation of some historically valuable ingredients in these narratives since the critical publication of the extant fragments by A. Epstein; D. H. Müller in *Die Recensionen und Versionen des Eldad ha-Dani;* and M. Schloessinger in his ed. of *The Ritual of Eldad ha-Dani.* F. (E.) Kupfer and S. Strelcyn's recent Polish communication, "Un Nouveau manuscrit concernant 'Eldād Haddāni," *Rocznik orientalistyczny,* XIX, 125–41 (with an additional description by K. Kwiatkowski on the tentative results of an ultraviolet-ray examination of the MS *ibid.,* pp. 142–43; the article itself appeared also in Yiddish in *Bleter far Geshichte,* VII, 131–50). The authors claim that the one page recovered from Nazi loot and now at the Warsaw Jewish Historical Institute dates from about 900. However, the palaeographical evidence appears questionable. At any rate, the 34 lines here transcribed differ but little from the text published by Epstein pp. 84 f. Cf. also S. Krauss, "New Light on Some Geographic Data in the Works of Eldad ha-Dani and Benjamin of Tudela" (Hebrew), *Tarbiz,*

VIII, 208–32; and L. Rabinowitz, "Eldad Ha-Dani and China," *JQR,* XXXVI, 231–38, pointing out in particular the similarity of several biblical names found in both Eldad's report and a Kaifeng Codex (in W. C. White, *Chinese Jews,* III, 35 ff.). Here and in his *Jewish Merchant Adventures,* pp. 71 f., Rabinowitz has also marshaled various arguments to prove that, before going west, Eldad had reached China. But the evidence is inconclusive.

CHAPTER XVIII: PROTECTED MINORITY

1. Cf. G. Wiet's brief summary of the long-regnant scholarly opinion concerning "L'Empire néo-byzantin des Omeyyades et l'empire néo-sassanide des Abbasides" in *Journal of World History,* I, 63–71. Regrettably, there is very little information on the political and legal developments affecting Jews, or the role they played in shaping their own status and that of the other *dhimmis* during the crucial first two or three centuries of Muslim rule. Even the somewhat more articulate Christian writers of the period have left behind but stray data from which we can reconstruct only a very incomplete picture of the legal and political situation of the Christian communities. Cf. the mutually complementary observations by J. E. Janot in "Les Chrétiens devant l'Islam au premier siècle de l'Hégira," *En Terre d'Islam* (1945), pp. 149–58; L. Massignon in "La Politique islamo-chrétienne des scribes nestoriens de Deir Qunna à la cour de Bagdad au IXe siècle de notre ère," *RB,* LI, 7–14; and the literature listed *supra,* Chap. XVII, n. 28, and *infra,* n. 9. In the case of Jews we must for the most part deduce from later conditions the happenings of the earlier formative, and hence more vital, stages of their political interrelations with the Muslim world. It stands to reason, however, that just as in the various scientific disciplines the Jewish contribution was greatest, though not necessarily qualitatively superior, in the first two or three centuries of Islam (see *infra,* Chap. XXXV), the impact of the Jews on political life, too, was felt most strongly in those early periods when the new rulers were feeling their way through the maze of unfamiliar political and economic institutions. Particularly in the treatment of religious minorities Jewish experiences must often have served as guideposts for the new regime.

2. Agapius, *K. al-'Unvan,* II, 267; Sherira Gaon's resp. in *Sha'are Ṣedeq,* IV.1.20, fol. 32ab; and *supra,* Chap. XVII, n. 41. Cf. the sources cited in my "Saadia's Communal Activities," *Saadia Anniv. Vol.,* pp. 14 f. It should be noted that, compared with the prevailing personal insecurity of many caliphs and other Muslim dignitaries, the life expectancy of Jewish leaders was quite high. We hear of the violent deaths of only two exilarchs, and of none of the heads of the academies. A legendary Arabic source mentions Caliph Marwan II's displeasure over what he saw in a miraculous mirror given him by the exilarch as the reason for the latter's execution (744–50). Cf. Ṭabari, *Annales,* III, 165 f.; and I. Goldziher's "Renseignements de source musulmane sur la dignité de resch-galuta," *REJ,* VIII, 124. But it seems likely that, if the story is at all true, the exilarch was condemned because of some involvement, real or alleged, in the plots which soon thereafter led to the overthrow of the 'Umayyad regime. A second exilarch, or rather candidate for the exilarchic office, is said to have lost his life on account of some blasphemous utterances against Islam. Cf. *infra,* n. 15. Such behavior is likewise understandable only during the period of anarchy prevailing in the mid-tenth century, and it may well have been connected with some sort of political partisanship. The case of the last universally recognized exilarch, Hezekiah (died in 1058), was different. According to Ibn Daud's chronicle (*MJC,* I, 67) he was imprisoned and tortured because of a denunciation

by some Jewish adversaries, probably the result of an internal Jewish conflict whose resolution was left to the imperial administration. Cf. *infra,* Chap. XXIII, n. 8.

3. Cf. the texts published by Mann in his *Jews in Egypt,* II, 30 ff.; his comments thereon, *ibid.,* I, 30 ff.; and A. Mez's statement in *The Renaissance of Islam,* English trans., p. 215. Unfortunately, the beginnings of the two versions of the Scroll are missing. The anonymous letter, published by Mann (II, 26), in which the accusation leveled at the Jews of Fusṭaṭ during the funeral of R. Shemariah is mentioned, could not be read by the editor in the crucial line 13. But the whole affair evidently resulted from some rumors spread against the Jewish communities of the whole land—hence the fear that the riots might spread to the environs of Fusṭaṭ and even to Alexandria. One could understand neither the excitement of the mob, nor the initial unawareness of the royal authorities, if the matter were "connected with taxes" (Mann, I, 31). Certainly the king and his advisers would have known more about such fiscal deficiencies than did the ordinary citizens, and the search for witnesses would not have been limited to some four chance bystanders. It appears, however, that not one Jew lost his life, or suffered permanent injury. The great fears of the Jewish community, recorded in a permanent liturgical memorial, can only be explained by the tense feelings prevailing in Egypt at that time. It is rather a testimonial to the general atmosphere of calm and security in the preceding generations for Egyptian Jewry now to have magnified such a relatively minor disturbance into a world-shaking event.

4. Joseph Sambari's chronicle, *Dibre Yosef,* excerpt published from a Paris MS by R. J. H. Gottheil in "Dhimmi's and Moslems in Egypt," in *Old Testament and Semitic Studies in Memory of William Rainey Harper,* II, 365 n. 2; Mann's *Egypt,* I, 32 ff. The caliph's frequent changes of mind, and the sadism characterizing his anti-Jewish and anti-Christian decrees, doubtless reflected his diseased mentality, which is otherwise attested. Cf. B. Bouthoul's literary biography, *Le Calife Hakim. Dieu de l'an mille,* esp. pp. 105 ff.; and, on the international as well as domestic conflicts explaining his extreme measures, P. J. Vartikiotis, "Al-Hakim Bi-Amrillah: The God-King Idea Realized," *IC,* XXIX, 1–8. But Ḥakim seems not to have been unaware of the tensions among the various groups in the population. Nor is Sambari's tradition quite so fantastic as it appears. The Passover Haggadah seems, indeed, to have aroused considerable ill-feeling already under the Hellenistic successors of the ancient Pharaohs (see *supra,* Vol. I, pp. 189, 381 n. 30). The longer the Faṭimid regime lasted in Egypt, the more did the memory of ancient Egyptian greatness loom large in the Arab minds as well. On the time lag between the persecution of Christians and of Jews, and on the repercussions of these hostile acts in Judeo-Christian relations in Western Europe, cf. *infra,* Chap. XX, nn. 17, 74.

5. 'Abd al-Halim of Granada's Arabic history of Fez, cited from MS by J. A. Condé in his *Historia de la dominación de los Arabes en España,* p. 408; R. Dozy, *Histoire des Musulmans d'Espagne,* III, 158 f. In evaluating this episode one must also bear in mind that, like the rest of the Almoravids, Yusuf was not only a puritan who by his religious rigidity antagonized even most Spanish Muslims, but also an obedient follower of the expounders of Muslim law. That is why he was swayed with equal ease by the first *faqih,* who claimed to have discovered an unknown legal tradition, and by the *qadhi,* who produced juristic arguments to the

contrary. See also, in general, E. Lévi-Provençal, "Reflexions sur l'empire almoravide au debut du XIIe siècle," in *Cinquantenaire de la Faculté des Lettres d'Alger (1881–1931)*, published by the Société historique algérienne, pp. 307–20; E. Fagnan's older summary of a contemporary Arab geographic work, *K. al Istibṣar*, in *L'Afrique septentrionale au XIIe siècle de notre ère;* and A. Huici Miranda's more recent documentation in his Spanish translation of the anonymous *K. al-Hulal al-mawshiyya* (written in 1381) in his *Collección de Crónicas árabes de la Reconquista,* I, supplementing his earlier edition of *Crónicas latinas de la Reconquista;* and *infra,* Chap. XX.

6. Excerpt from Shams ad-Din Muḥammad ibn Aḥmad adh-Dhahabi's "Life of Ya'qub al-Manṣur" reproduced from MS with a French translation by S. Munk in his "Notice sur Joseph ben Iehouda," in *JA,* 3d ser., XIV, 42 ff.; *Chronicon Adefonsi Imperatoris,* No. 101, ed. by H. Florez in his *España sagrada,* XXI, 398 f. The Jewish sources are generally vague and nondescript; for instance, Abraham ibn Ezra's poem, *Ahah yarad 'al Sefarad* (Woe, upon Spain) on the fall of Lucena and other cities in his *Diwan,* ed. by J. Egers, pp. 68 f. No. 169 and frequently elsewhere (cf. I. Davidson's *Oṣar ha-shirah,* I, 61 f. No. 1301) and commented upon by D. Cazès in his "Antiquités judaïques en Tripolitaine," *REJ,* XX, 84 ff.; and by F. Cantera in his "Elegía de Abraham ben Ezra a la toma de Lucena por los Almohades," *Sefarad,* XIII, 112–14. See also the variants discussed by S. Bernstein in his recent *'Al neharot Sefarad* (Spanish Litanies on the Fall of Jerusalem and Persecutions to 1391), pp. 114 f. No. 52, 243 ff.; *supra,* Chap. XVII, n. 41; and *infra,* n. 7; and Chap. XXI, n. 54. Only Joseph ibn 'Aqnin (on his personality and the question whether there were two scholars by that name, cf. *infra,* Chap. XXXIV) offers, in the sixth chapter of his *K. Ṭubb an-nufus* (Recreation of Souls: a Mental Hygiene), a few striking illustrations of the conditions prevailing in Spain and Morocco at the end of the twelfth century. Cf. A. S. Halkin's summary of these data from a Bodleian MS in his "On the History of the Forced Conversion under the Almohades" (Hebrew), *Starr Mem. Vol.,* pp. 101–10, supplemented by his "Ibn 'Aḳnīn's Commentary on the Song of Songs," *Marx Jub. Vol.,* pp. 389–424. Nor were the Christian writers of the time much more articulate. We must therefore lean heavily on the few accounts of such nearly contemporary Arab writers as 'Abd al-Waḥid, who composed his chronicle in 1224 (see *infra,* n. 8), or some chance letters surviving from both the Almoravid and Almohade periods, such as the *Trente-sept lettres officielles almohades,* ed. by E. Lévi-Provençal in 1941, and provided by him with a careful analysis in "Un Recueil de lettres officielles almohades" in *Hespéris,* XXVIII, 1–80 (the Colin codex includes also 21 letters dated 1106–23). Cf. also *infra,* Chap. XX, n. 43; A. Huici Miranda's Spanish translation of Ibn 'Idhari al-Marrakushi's *K. al-Bayān al-Maghrib,* in his *Collección de crónicas árabes de la Reconquista,* II–III; his earlier data on "La Leyenda y la historia en los origenes del imperio almohade," *Al-Andalus,* XIV, 339–76; F. J. Simonet's *Historia de los Mozárabes de España,* pp. 759 ff.; and the pertinent chapters of such more general works as A. Ballesteros y Beretta's voluminous *Historia de España,* II, 408 ff., or J. Calmette's more recent *Histoire de l'Espagne,* pp. 78 ff., summarizing especially the Moorish struggles with the resurgent Christian kingdoms of the eleventh and twelfth centuries.

7. Maimonides, *Ma'mar Qiddush ha-Shem* (Treatise on the Sanctification of the Name of the Lord, or on Martyrdom; also known under the title of *Iggeret ha-*

Shemad, or Epistle on Conversion) in his *Qobeṣ teshubot ha-Rambam* (Collection of Responsa and Epistles), ed. by A. L. Lichtenberg, II, fols. 12–15, esp. fol. 14d. While rather vague about the details of the Almohade enactments, and even about what happened to him and his family, the great jurist-philosopher only pointed out the unprecedented nature of that persecution. He advised his co-religionists, when confronted by such acts of intolerance, to escape as quickly as possible to another country. Otherwise he found it incumbent upon himself to instill hope in the ultimate survival of the Jewish people despite all sufferings. This optimistic affirmation is the keynote of his famous "Epistle to Yemen," as well as of the "Letter on Consolation" written by his father, Maimun ben Joseph. Their theoretical views on the meaning of this catastrophe will be treated more fully in the context of their ethical teachings (*infra,* Chap. XXXIV).

Because of this vagueness on the part of the main protagonists themselves, the behavior of Maimun's family during the years of their sojourn in Spain and their migrations through North Africa has become one of the moot questions in Maimonidean research. Particularly their settlement for many years in Fez, the very citadel of the Almohade regime, appeared puzzling. The usual explanation, offered by scholars bent on seeking purely intellectual connections, that Maimonides went to Fez to study under Yehudah ibn Sosan, gratuitously assumes that there were no scholars of equal standing in Cordova. Moreover, it fails to explain why Maimun's whole family moved there. Much more likely is the explanation here offered that the supervision of the conformity of former *dhimmis* was less rigid in the Moroccan capital, which was out of reach of Christian crusaders. Cf. Simonet, *Historia de los Mozárabes,* p. 770; A. Berliner's overtly apologetical essay, "Zur Ehrenrettung des Maimonides" in *Moses ben Maimon,* ed. by Jakob Guttmann *et al.,* II, 104–30; and my remarks in "The Historical Outlook of Maimonides," *PAAJR,* VI, 83. Maimonides' most distinguished pupil, Ibn 'Aqnin, was far more specific. Admitting his own guilt in temporarily yielding to Almohade pressure, he spoke bitterly of such compromises and demanded immediate emigration. At the same time he fully realized that such a step could not be taken lightly, and that for many individuals it meant total uprooting and permanent maladjustment. He actually considered exile from one's country the severest of all penalties short of execution. Cf. Halkin's summary in *Starr Mem. Vol.,* pp. 103 ff. Nor was emigration quite simple from the standpoint of public administration. Some Muslim jurists argued that protection for the *dhimmis'* life and property ceased upon their planned departure to "enemy territory," under which term were included also lands dominated by another Muslim sect. Hence such emigrés were supposed to leave all their property behind. Cf. S. D. Goitein's *Jews and Arabs,* pp. 76 f. It is small wonder then that many people believed that "one should rather die than leave one's home." This saying was actually attributed to the ancient sages by some poverty-stricken patients at the warm springs of Tiberias who considered their temporary expatriation in search of healing a sufficient tragedy to arouse the compassion of would-be charitable supporters. Cf. their letter published in Mann, *Jews in Egypt,* I, 167, and II, 193. Cf. also *infra,* n. 26.

This sharp discrepancy in the attitudes of master and pupil may perhaps to some extent be accounted for by the progressive deterioration of the status of the secret Jews during the last decades of the twelfth century. In the first years the Almohade rulers, and especially their local organs, were overwhelmed by the staggering task of suddenly converting millions of unwilling subjects. They had to be satisfied with some such verbal declarations as intimated by Maimonides. In time, however, they realized the inefficacy of such "conversions." They now began insisting on true allegiance to Islam, and severely persecuted the resisters, some of whom had undoubtedly been born under Almohade rule and hence should have grown up as orthodox Muslims. Writing in the 1190's, or about half a century after the Almohade conquest, Ibn 'Aqnin undoubtedly faced a much more despondent generation. Hence came also his own much more despairing mood. It may also be noted that, despite his understandable hostility to everything the Almohades stood for, Maimonides himself could not help being impressed by Ibn Tumart's uncompromising insistence on the absolute unity of God. Cf. I. Heinemann's pertinent observations on "Maimuni und die arabischen Einheitslehrer," *MGWJ,* LXXIX, 102–48; and *infra,* Chap. XXXIV. Nor is it at all surprising that a Christian cleric should have produced Latin translations of Ibn Tumart's works. Cf. M. T. d'Alverny and G. Vajda, "Marc de Tolède, traducteur d'Ibn Tumart," *Al-Andalus,* XVI, 99–140, 259–307, and XVII, 1–56.

8. Ibn 'Aqnin, summarized by Halkin in *Starr Mem. Vol.,* pp. 103 ff.; and Alfonso VI's decree reproduced by A. González Palencia in *Los Mozárabes de Toledo en los siglos XII y XIII,* Prelim. Vol., pp. 118 f. On the generally widespread application of the Visigothic *Liber Judicum* among the Spanish Mozarabs, cf. also *supra,* Chap. XVI, n. 53; and *infra,* Chap. XX, n. 30. The enactment of the sharp discriminatory provisions concerning the attire of the new converts is attributed by 'Abd al-Waḥid al-Marrakushi to Al-Manṣur during the last years of his reign (d. 1198). Cf. his *K. Al-Mujib* (The History of the Almohades), ed. by R. Dozy, 2d ed., p. 223; in E. Fagnan's French translation, *Histoire des Almohades,* pp. 264 f. (this excerpt was already cited by Munk in his "Notice," *JA,* 3d ser., XIV, 40 ff.). This sharpening of long-existing regulations by a personally less intolerant monarch was but the sign of growing despair over the failure of the Almohade experiment in religious unification. Cf. also *infra,* n. 22.

9. A fairly good review of the pertinent Arabic sources, including some heretofore unpublished, is offered by A. Mez's all-embracing survey of conditions prevailing in the Great Caliphate during the tenth century in *The Renaissance of Islam.* Cf. in particular, pp. 32 ff. Interesting additional data may be gleaned from A. S. Tritton's aforementioned study of *The Caliphs and Their Non-Muslim Subjects,* as well as from his supplementary essay, "Islam and the Protected Religions," *JRAS,* 1931, pp. 311–38; and his brief selection of legal maxims on "Non-Muslim Subjects in the Muslim State," *ibid.,* 1942, pp. 36–40. Cf. also Ibn al-Wasiti's "Answer to the Dhimmis" in *JAOS,* XLI, 383–457, where the history of the treatment of the "infidels" until the author's time (about 1300 C.E.) is given in the then prevalent anecdotal form; the similar, but more technically juristic, "Fetoua relatif à la condition de Zimmis, et particulièrement des chrétiens, en pays musulmans," by Ibn an-Naqqash, ed. with a French trans. by M. Belin in *JA,* LIX, 417–516; LX, 97–140 (to the mid-fourteenth century); and E. Fagnan's collection of excerpts of "Arabo-Judaica" in *Mélanges Hartwig Derenbourg,* pp. 103–20. On Ibn 'Ubayya, cf. *infra,* n. 17. A succinct review of "The Actual and Legal Position of the Jews under Arab Islam" is offered by Goitein in his *Jews and Arabs,* pp. 62 ff. Although not documented, this review is based in part on the author's personal observations of the "medieval" conditions of Yemenite Jewry in the twentieth century. Because of its brevity, however, it cannot do justice to the great differences in the treatment

of *dhimmis* in the different countries and periods. Interesting data on the "Ex-Territorial Capitulations in Favour of Muslims in Classical Times" are assembled in M. Hamidullah's pertinent essay in *Islamic Research Association Miscellany,* I, 47–60.

Neither has the material pertaining specifically to the political and legal status of the Jews in the respective countries or provinces found adequate treatment. Only in regard to Faṭimid Egypt does J. Mann's circumspect monograph, *Jews in Egypt,* serve as a reliable guide. But even in his first volume the author tried to elucidate more fully the new sources published by him in Volume II, rather than to present a balanced picture of Jewish life in Egypt during the crucial tenth to twelfth centuries. Cf. also B. Halper's extensive review of this work in *Hatekufah,* XVIII, 175–212. Other pertinent material is scattered in various periodicals or publications of sources. Of significance in this respect is J. Mann's more recent collection of *Texts and Studies in Jewish History and Literature.* B. Dinaburg's compilation and Hebrew translation of selected source material in his *Yisrael ba-Golah* (Israel in Exile) is likewise very useful. Of considerable value are also such comparable Christian materials as "A Charter of Protection Granted to the Nestorian Church in A.D. 1138 by Muktafi II, Caliph of Baghdad," ed. from a John Ryland MS and translated into English by A. Mingana in *BJRL,* X, 127–33. Cf. also the literature listed *supra,* Chap. XVII, n. 28.

10. 'Umar's letter is cited here in Tritton's English translation, *Caliphs,* pp. 5 f. Tritton himself quotes three other texts, finally reaching the conclusion that "it would seem that it was an exercise in the schools of law to draw up pattern treaties" (p. 12). This conclusion goes too far in minimizing what seems to have been the authentic core of the original treaties, later doubtless expanded to include provisions borrowed from actual practice. The authentic texts of these treaties seem to have disappeared quite early. Even As-Suyuti could find no earlier record than that written down by Ibn Zabr of Damascus in 780–81. Cf. E. Amar's French translation of the text concerning "La Soumission des Chrétiens en Syrie," *Revue du monde musulman,* II, 358–61; and R. Gottheil's remarks in *Studies . . . Harper,* p. 357. More authentic, but for that very reason less detailed, is the treaty of surrender signed by the Visigothic king Theodemir. It is carefully analyzed by M. Gaspar Remiro in his *Historia de Murcia musulmana,* pp. 11 ff. Most of the extant early texts, moreover, stem from Syria and Palestine rather than Egypt or Persia. This is doubly regrettable, as the arrangements with the Zoroastrians may have been considerably at variance with those included in the Christian treaties of surrender. One may look forward, therefore, to R. N. Frye's forthcoming publication of an Arabic *waqf* document from Biyabanak in central Iran, which may shed some new light on the terms imposed on the local population by the conquerors of the Sassanian Empire. Cf. Frye's review of F. Rosenthal's *History of Muslim Historiography, Speculum,* XXIX, 314. Of course, most of the *waqfs* were established by Muslims, first to help finance the holy wars, then for the building of mosques and for other pious causes. Cf. J. Schacht's analysis of the "Early Doctrines of Waqf," *Fuad Köprülü Armağani* (Mélanges), pp. 443–52.

Jews, not representing a political or military entity, undoubtedly signed no such treaties of surrender. Their status was, therefore, largely regulated by the treaties concluded with their "protected" neighbors. The Babylonian heartland of the Jewish people was, therefore, more deeply affected by such arrangements between the invaders and the Persian administrators than by what happened simultaneously in Jerusalem or Damascus. However, in time there evidently evolved a certain synthesis between these various treaties and the administrative practices in the various provinces, leading to a more uniform legal theory, if not genuine uniformity in practical application. Cf. also, from another angle, A. Steinwenter's juridical analysis, "Zu den koptischen Schutzbriefen," *Zeitschrift der Savigny-Stiftung, Rom. Abteilung,* LX, 237–41 (with reference to texts published by W. Till and discussions by A. Schiller and H. Liebesny).

11. Cf. A. Jeffery's brief summary in "The Political Importance of Islam," *JNES,* I, 387 f. (largely oriented toward contemporary conditions). One could, of course, also forfeit the status of a protected subject. This was especially the legal sanction for high treason, or even for simple refusal to pay tribute. If a *dhimmi* went over to the enemy and was captured by the Muslims, he was considered booty and thus devoid of any legal protection. Cf. Tritton's citation in *JRAS,* 1942, p. 38.

It seems that all Jews indiscriminately enjoyed the same legal status, regardless of their country of origin. True, Islam knew of a special category of "foreigners" (*must'amin*), who enjoyed fewer rights than the *dhimmis.* Cf. W. Heffening's careful analysis of their status in *Das islamische Fremdenrecht,* pp. 37 ff. Nevertheless, so great was the power of the Jewish community and so strong appeared its inner cohesiveness to Muslim administrators and jurists, that Jews from Christian countries, ransomed, for instance, by their Egyptian coreligionists, seem sooner or later to have joined the membership of the local communities on the basis of perfect equality. True, shipwrecked and penniless arrivals seem to have had a very hard time in Egypt. We learn from a pathetic letter written by an unfortunate would-be pilgrim to Jerusalem that when he had entered Alexandria "the Gentiles wished to punish me, but I was saved by a Jew who brought me here [Fusṭaṭ]. For two months I am now hiding here, for I fear to go out of doors, lest the tax official find me and put me in prison. I should die there because I have nothing to give [him] to save my soul." Cf. S. Assaf's ed. of the letter in his "On the History of Jewish Settlement in Palestine" (Hebrew), in *Meqorot u-meḥqarim,* pp. 59 f. Yet others seem to have found means of settling permanently there without serious difficulty.

12. 'Umar's statements cited by Gottheil in *Studies . . . Harper,* p. 358, and by Tritton in *JRAS,* 1931, p. 311. These utterances clearly reflect 'Umar I's desire to restrain his conquering hosts. Tritton's general conclusions (*Caliphs,* pp. 5 ff.), therefore, that the "Covenant" could not possibly have been enacted by 'Umar I and that its main provisions were, in fact, entirely unknown during the seventh century, has rightly become the regnant opinion. Most scholars are prepared to substitute 'Umar II for his famous predecessor as the author of this compilation. R. Levy's argument (*A Baghdad Chronicle,* pp. 65 f.) for Harun ar-Rashid as the real compiler, has been effectively controverted in J. Finkel's review in *JQR,* XXIII, 271. On 'Umar II, see C. H. Becker's older but still valuable "Studien zur Omajjadengeschichte," *Zeitschrift für Assyriologie,* XV, 1–36; and *supra,* Chap. XVII, n. 33. Cf. also *infra,* n. 21.

13. Baladhuri, *K. Futûḥ al-buldân,* p. 162 (in Hitti's English trans., p. 251); Ghazzali, *K. al-Munqidh min adh-Dhalal* (Deliverance from Error), ed. by J. Saliba

and K. Ayyad, pp. 69 f. (in W. M. Watt's English translation, *The Faith and Practice of Al-Ghazālī,* p. 21); his *Iḥya 'ulum ad-din* (Revival of Religious Sciences), I, 90; Mez, *Renaissance,* p. 33 (with a note by the editor of *IC*). It goes without saying that, like Pope Gregory the Great, the Muslim jurists saw nothing wrong in persuading infidels to join their faith by offering them such worldly advantages as tax reduction. In fact, we shall see that mass conversions on this score created quite a serious problem for the fiscal administration of the Caliphate. Cf. D. C. Dennett Jr., *Conversion and the Poll Tax in Early Islam,* and *infra,* n. 48. The existing prohibition explains the relative paucity of conversions from one minority faith to another, although it could not totally eliminate them. Particularly during the religiously turbulent ninth and early tenth centuries, no less a figure than the philosopher David al-Muqammiṣ seems to have encountered no insuperable obstacles in first adopting Christianity and then reverting to Judaism. Cf. *infra,* Chap. XXXIV.

14. Bukhari, *Saḥiḥ,* IV, 19 f.; in Houdas's French translation, IV, 421. Cf. E. Sachau, *Muhammedanisches Recht nach schafiitischer Lehre,* pp. 786 f. Perhaps because of the remoteness of his Meccan residence from Iran, Shafi'i taught that the *wergeld* of a Zoroastrian was only one fifteenth that of a Muslim, indicating his low estimate of the Zoroastrian creed as compared with the monotheism of Jews and Christians. Certainly in his day the number of Parsees still was far from negligible. Cf. B. Spuler, *Iran in früh-islamischer Zeit,* pp. 190 ff.; and *infra,* Chap. XXIV, nn. 31--32.

15. Abu Yusuf, *Kitab al-Kharaj* (Le Livre de l'impôt foncier), pp. 110 ff. (Arabic), 278 ff. (French); Mann, *Jews in Egypt,* I, 32 ff., 72 f. See also, more fully, Tritton, *Caliphs,* pp. 178 ff.; and Zwemer, *Law of Apostasy, passim.* A lurid story of the seizure of a Jew accused of cursing the king, despite the efforts of all other members of a Jewish caravan to conceal his identity, his subsequent execution, and the attempts of his relatives to wreak vengeance on the forced informer, is told in a remarkable inquiry addressed to Shalom Gaon of Jerusalem and published from a New York MS by A. I. Agus in "A Responsum of a Palestinian Gaon" (Hebrew), *Sura,* I, 17–25. One wonders whether the copyist of that MS of *Mordecai,* did not misread the name Shalom for Shelomo, namely the well-known Palestinian Gaon, Solomon ben Yehudah, whose period of activity (1027–51) was sufficiently disturbed to offer a proper background for that narrative. According to Nathan the Babylonian's well-known report, the only qualified candidate for the exilarchic office after Saadiah's death in 942 was executed because he allegedly cursed Mohammed during a public quarrel with a Muslim. Cf. *MJC,* II, 82 f. Although Nathan's account is somewhat confused here and cannot be verified by the fragment of the Arabic original, ed. by I. Friedlaender (in *JQR,* [o.s.] XVII, 747–61), the fact of the execution itself is probably historical. At least it documents the possibility of the invocation of the existing laws of "blasphemy," whenever somebody in authority wished to get rid of an unwelcome Jewish subject. On Nathan's general reliability and the confused background of that execution, cf. my "Saadia's Communal Activities," *Saadia Anniv. Vol.,* pp. 25 ff. The fairly accepted Muslim notion that the toleration of *dhimmis* was in so far only temporary, as upon the arrival of the redeemer all would have to be converted, is stressed by C. Snouck Hurgronje in "Der Mahdi" (1885), reprinted in his *Verspreide Geschriften,* I, 152 f. On religious controversies, cf. *infra,* Chap. XXIV.

16. Cf. Gottheil's extensive data in *Studies . . . Harper*, II, 351 ff.; Maqrizi's *K. Taqi ad-din: al-mawa'iz w'al-i'tibar fi dhikr al-khiṭaṭ w'al-aṭar* (Report on Countries and Monuments), II, 472; A. Galanté's *Documents officiels turcs concernant les Juifs de Turquie*, pp. 52 ff.; and many other sources cited in Tritton's *Caliphs*, pp. 37 ff., and in my *Jewish Community*, I, 162 ff., and III, 35 f. It should be noted, however, that Maqrizi himself recorded, in another connection, various traditions relating to Jewish places of worship in Egypt before the Exodus. He did not mind repeating the anachronism of Moses' and his followers turning in their prayers toward the Meccan *Ka'abah*. Cf. his *K. al-Khiṭaṭ*, I, VIII; in U. Bouriant's French translation, *Description topographique et historique de l'Egypte*, I, 62. Of the polemical literature generated by these controversies one need cite here only "Ibn 'Ubayya's Book concerning the Destruction of the Synagogue of Jerusalem in 1474," which includes numerous excerpts from older *fatwas* and law books, particularly from the Shafi'ite school. Cf. S. D. Goitein's Hebrew analysis thereof, on the basis of a Jerusalem manuscript, in *Zion*, XIII–XIV, 18–32. Cf. also S. Krauss's survey of "Ancient Synagogues in Palestine and the Near East" (Hebrew), in *Yerushalayim* (in Memory of A. M. Luncz), pp. 221–49; J. M. Toledano's "Ancient Synagogues in Alexandria and Its Environs" (Hebrew), *HUCA*, XII–XIII, 701–14; and J. Pinkerfeld's more recent monograph on the architecture of the *Bate ha-kenesiot be-Ereṣ Yisrael* (Synagogues in Palestine from the End of the Geonic Age to the Immigration of Ḥasidim) which occasionally refers also to some legal aspects.

17. Goitein's summary of Ibn 'Ubayya's arguments in *Zion*, XIII–XIV, 24 ff.; Tritton's *Caliphs*, pp. 48, 56. As in the Eastern Roman Empire, the conversion of a synagogue into a house of worship of the dominant faith could not easily be undone. Muslim law, to be sure, was much less outspoken in this respect than Canon law, which considered a church, however unlawfully consecrated, a sacred structure never to be defiled by restoration to its former owners for ritualistic or private use. In fact, in the nineteenth century, a Transjordanian Jew quoted an evidently spurious liberal decision by 'Umar I. On the appeal of an injured Jewish houseowner, the caliph, then in Medina, supposedly sent an order written on the jawbone of an ass, "Pull down the mosque, and rebuild the Jew's house." This was an etiological legend woven around a house in Busrah, bearing from time immemorial the curious name, "the house of the Jew." Cf. the story told by the British visitor J. L. Porter, in 1854, in his *Five Years in Damascus*, 2d ed., p. 235. As a rule, Jews had to be satisfied, as were those of Tripolis (about 1030) when their request for permission to build a synagogue elsewhere was granted. Cf. Mann, *Egypt*, I, 72 f., and II, 73.

Incidentally, it may be worth mentioning that the Mosque not only owed its entire organization and system of worship to the synagogue (its very name is a variant of the term *misgeda*, already found in the Elephantine papyri; cf. Cowley's ed. of these *Aramaic Papyri*, No. 44 line 3), but that it at first seems to have emulated even certain architectural patterns developed earlier by Jews in Dura-Europos and elsewhere. Of course, some of that imitation may have been indirect and based upon the emulation of the architecture of certain Christian churches indebted to Jewish prototypes. Cf. E. Lambert's pertinent observations on "La Synagogue de Doura-Europos et les origines de la mosque," *Semitica*, III, 67–72; and J. Sauvaget's more general archaeological data on *La Mosquée omeyyade de Médine. Etude sur les origines architecturales de la mosquée et de la basilique; supra*, Vol. II, p. 331 n. 9; and *infra*, Chap. XXVII, nn. 12 ff.

18. Bukhari's *Sahih,* in the French translation by Houdas and Marçais, I, 160 (the tradition is cited in the name of Abu Huraira); *Churches and Monasteries in Egypt,* attributed to Abu Salih, the Armenian, ed. and trans. by B. T. A. Evetts in *Anecdota Oxoniensia,* Semitic Series, VII, 136 (English; cf. also A. J. Butler's note 3 thereon), fols. 43b f. (Arabic); Mann's *Egypt,* I, 14. On the antiquity of the synagogues mentioned in the text, alleged or real, cf. *supra,* Chap. XVII, nn. 38–39. However, the story told by Abu Salih does reflect the prevailing attitude of mutual hostility among the minorities rather than of pulling together in the face of common danger. Curiously, the appropriation of synagogues, churches, and even private houses for use as mosques could also have adverse effects. According to Ibn al-Hajj, Christians and Jews planted, in places accessible to powerful men, old-looking documents purportedly showing that some ancient treasure was immured in one or another mosque. Such a lead was sufficient to induce the finder to destroy that mosque in search of the lost treasure. "That Christian or Jewish buildings are seldom destroyed by these means is proof that they are authors of this evil." Cited by Tritton in *JRAS,* 1942, p. 40. On the importance of treasure troves in the Islamic civilization, see *infra,* Chap. XXII, n. 80.

19. Al-Mas'udi, *K. Muruj adh-dhahab* (Les Prairies d'or), ed. and trans. by C. A. Barbier de Meynard and A. Pavet de Courteille, II, 388 ff.; Mann, *Egypt,* I, 14; Zwemer, *Law of Apostasy,* p. 92 (quoting a correspondence in *The Near East,* Nov. 24, 1921); *infra,* n. 22. Cf. also M. Z. Hasan's dissertation, *Les Tulunides.* These Muslim restrictions were less serious, however, than the earlier Zoroastrian disturbances occasioned by Jews and Christians "defiling" the earth through burial of corpses, rather than exposing them to birds of prey. See *supra,* Vol. II, p. 290. In any case, we hear few Jewish complaints on this score. Nor were the Jews prevented from adhering to their age-old funereal customs, which often differed from country to country. Such differences between Palestine and Babylonia called forth a responsum from Natronai Gaon, offering a noteworthy naturalistic explanation. Cf. the text of that reply cited by Isaac ibn Gayyat in his *Sha'are Simhah* (Chapters of Joy; a halakhic treatise), ed. by I. D. Bamberger, II, 44; *Sefer ha-Yishub,* II, 122 n. 27; and S. Assaf's comments thereon in his "Palestine in the Responsa of the Babylonian Geonim" (Hebrew), *Siyyon,* I, 23 f.

20. Cf. *Pirqe de-R. Eliezer,* XXIX, ed. by Higger in *Horeb,* X, 193 (in Friedlander's trans., XXX, p. 221); Hai's resp. cited in Ibn Gayyat's *Sha'are Simhah,* II, 72; and interpreted by Assaf in *Siyyon,* I, 29. Patriotic Jews, like the Karaite Salmon ben Yeruhim, deeply resented such outward marks of foreign domination as the presence of a Muslim cemetery in the immediate vicinity of the Temple mountain in Jerusalem. Cf. "The Prayer of Salmon ben Yeruhim the Karaite (?)" (Hebrew), ed. by S. Assaf in *Siyyon,* III, 88–94. Salmon's authorship is postulated here on the basis of certain similarities in the ideas expounded in his Commentary on Lamentations. Some illustrations of the extremes to which Muslim administrators were prepared to go in taxing Jewish funerals are given, largely from more recent records, by J. Ben-Hanania in his "Burial Taxes and Burial Difficulties in Jerusalem" (Hebrew), *Jerusalem* (quarterly), I, 43–46, with "Additional Notes" by M. Benayahu and J. Prawer, *ibid.,* pp. 47–49, and II, 100–101. This problem would merit closer examination.

21. Cf. 'Umar I's alleged letter, cited *supra,* n. 17; and Gottheil and Worrell, *Fragments,* No. xlvii, pp. 232 f. That it was a private house, rather than a synagogue

as suggested by the editors, is evident from both the term "house" and Nissim's explanation that as a result of its destruction "his wife [would be] alone among gentiles." Her situation was doubtless aggravated by the climate, "the greatest heat of the lowest *She'ol* [nether world]."

22. Mutawakkil's later decrees are likewise cited in R. Levy, *Baghdad Chronicle,* pp. 104 f.; that of Abu Shuja is in "A New Fragment of the 'Life of Obadiah, the Norman Proselyte'" (Hebrew), ed. by A. Scheiber, *KS,* XXX, 98 (somewhat differently translated by J. L. Teicher in the English version of this essay in *JJS,* V, 37); and that of Al-Manṣur is in 'Abd al-Waḥid Marrakushi's *History of the Almohades* as cited *supra,* n. 8. Obadiah's report probably reflected conditions still prevailing in Baghdad after his arrival there some time after his conversion in 1102. See *infra,* Chap. XIX, n. 21. On Al-Manṣur, see Terrasse, *Histoire de Maroc,* I, 333. Cf. also Ibn 'Aqnin's dramatic description cited by Halkin in his summary in the *Starr Mem. Vol.,* pp. 107 ff. Al-Manṣur's successor, An-Naṣir, however, was satisfied with a yellow cloak and turban.

The decree of 849–50, issued by the "God-trusting" caliph three years after his accession to the throne, offers the most elaborate formulation of the "Covenant of 'Umar." See *supra,* n. 12. It resulted from a combination of earlier practices and the caliph's personal intolerance, which found expression also in his sharp persecution of the Shi'ites and other dissenters. Curiously, despite its short duration, Ḥakim's extremist decree left a more permanent imprint on later historiography than did the more enduring enactments by Mutawakkil and other predecessors. It appears in a variety of formulations. Cf. the numerous sources excerpted in *Sefer ha-Yishub,* II, 75 ff. The eleventh-century Kairuwan scholar, Nissim bar Jacob, relating an ancient tale, felt impelled to emphasize that "one may deduce from these words that the Jews of those days were not accustomed to wear black shoes." Cf. his *Ḥibbur yafeh,* p. 2, and Hirschberg's introduction thereto, p. 75. A convenient summary of the more familiar regulations concerning "The Distinctive Dress of Non-Muslims in Islamic Countries" is found in I. Lichtenstädter's article in *HJ,* V, 35–52, which also lists and explains many technical Arabic terms in the Jewish wardrobe (p. 41 n. 22). The author fails to mention, however, the Almohade legislation, which, as we shall see in another context, was far more responsible for the introduction of the European "badge" than any eastern decree. Cf. also E. Fagnan's older study of "Le Signe distinctif des Juifs au Maghreb [Morocco]," *REJ,* XXVIII, 294–98; Habib Zayat's Arabic essay on "Distinguishing Marks of Christians and Jews under Islam," *Al-Machriq,* XLIII, 161–252; and more broadly, E. Strauss's data, largely culled from later Muslim juridical sources, on "The Social Isolation of Ahl adh-dhimma," *Pál (Gershon) Hirschler Memorial Book,* pp. 73–94.

23. Cf. the texts published by B. Chapira in his "Documents provenant de la Gueniza du Caire," *REJ,* LVI, 237 f. (Arabic), 240 ff. (French); and by J. Starr in his "Contribution to the Life of Naharai ben Nissim of Fusṭaṭ" (Hebrew), *Zion,* I, 443. In his famous letter to Samuel ibn Tibbon describing his extremely busy days, Maimonides spoke of his daily return home from court in the nondescript term, "I dismount from the animal [*ha-behemah*]." Cf. his *Qobeṣ teshubot,* II, fol. 28c. His apparent daily routine of riding on horseback the distance between Fusṭaṭ and Cairo and back seems not to have aroused too much antagonism. On the other hand we learn from Ibn abi-'Usaibia that another distinguished Jewish physician, Al-

Muwaffaq ibn Shawa, court surgeon and occulist of Saladin, was attacked by a visiting eastern Sufi because he was riding on horseback. The stone thrown by the fanatic permanently blinded one of the doctor's eyes. Cf. M. Meyerhof's summary in his "Jewish Physicians under the Reign of the Fatimid Caliphs in Egypt," *Medical Leaves,* II, 138.

24. Council of 692 (Quinisextum or Trullanum), canon 11, in Mansi, *Collectio,* XI, 933 f., 945 f.; and in Hefele, *History,* trans. by Clark, V, 225 (cf. Starr's note in *The Jews in the Byzantine Empire,* pp. 89 f.); Abu 'Umar al-Kindi's *K. al-'Umara'* (The Governors and Judges of Egypt), ed. by R. Guest, p. 69; Fagnan, "Arabo-Judaica," in *Mélanges Derenbourg,* p. 114; Ghazzali's *Iḥya 'ulum,* II, 235; Fagnan's trans. of Ibn Idhari's *Histoire de l'Afrique et de l'Espagne intitulée Al-Bayano'l-Mogrib,* I, 305 f. (citing Al-Bakri); Terrasse, *Maroc,* I, 125. Cf. M. Gonzalez Simanca's data on *Las Sinagogas de Toledo y el baño liturgico judio;* and M. Gomez Moreno's "Baño de la juderia en Beza," *Al-Andalus,* XII, 151–55 (with plates). Located in the province of Granada, with its dense Jewish population, the Beza bath, covering only an area of some 56 by 40 feet, is a good illustration of what Jewish bath-houses looked like in a Muslim environment. But catering chiefly to Jewish ritualistic requirements, they rarely took the place of public baths, especially along seashores or rivers. On conditions in contemporary Byzantium, cf. *infra,* Chap. XIX, n. 28.

25. Cf. Abu Yusuf, *K. al-Kharaj,* pp. 99 (Arabic), 252 f. (French); Tritton's *Caliphs,* pp. 187 ff.; his remarks in *JRAS,* 1942, p. 38; and Solomon ibn Parḥon's *Maḥberet he-'Arukh* (Lexicon hebraicum), ed. by S. G. Stern, fol. 57bc. Ibn Parḥon may never have seen a veiled woman, since he describes the veil as covering the entire face with but an opening for *one* eye in the corner. This may have been with him but a literary reminiscence harking back to the talmudic passage (Shabbat 80a), from which a modern scholar, too, was to deduce that in antiquity Jewish women had worn veils. Cf. E. Marmorstein's somewhat forced arguments in "The Veil in Judaism and Islam," *JJS,* V, 1–11. In fact, three centuries earlier, Daniel al-Qumisi the Karaite had attacked the Rabbanites for allowing their women to expose their faces to Gentiles. Cf. his Commentary on Minor Prophets in Mann, *Texts and Studies,* II, 78. Mohammed's action, evidently based on a confused recollection of Phinehas' deed (Num. 25:8; see n. 26), seems to have been first recorded by the famous jurist Ash-Shafi'i in his *Kitab al-Amm* (Collected Writings and Lectures on Muslim Law), IV, 186. As a member of the Quraisha tribe and long-time resident of Mecca and Medina, Ash-Shafi'i (767–820) had access to numerous more or less authentic traditions about the prophet. Nevertheless his report may reflect postulates of his own day much more than an existing practice in the days of Mohammed. The Muslim attitude to intermarriage can be understood only against the background of the ramified Muslim laws of marriage and divorce, and the general debates in the four main schools of jurisprudence. Cf. the vast literature listed *infra,* Chap. XXVII, n. 4. The numerous recorded instances have neither been assembled nor critically examined from a sociological point of view. See, in general, O. A. Farrukh's Arabic work on *The Family in Moslem Jurisprudence.* That intermarriage might have had repercussions even for parents is evidenced by the recently published "Autograph Diary of an Eleventh-Century Historian of Baghdad [Abu 'Ali ibn al-Banna]," ed. by G. Makdisi in *BSOAS,* XIX, 25 (Arabic), 43 (English). Here we are told about disputes in the Christian community of Baghdad in 1069, over a man who had given away his daughter in marriage

to a member of another faith. The Catholicos had allegedly declared: "I have already excommunicated him, and his property has become licit for confiscation by the Sultan of the Muslims."

26. Al-Jaḥiẓ, *Risala,* trans. by Finkel in *JAOS,* XLVII, 326, 328; *infra,* Chap. XXIV, n. 25; Maimonides, *M.T.* Issure biah xii.4–5; Sanhedrin, xviii.6; Commentary on M. Sanhedrin, ix.6; Zedekiah ben Abraham 'Anav's *Shibbole ha-Leqet* (On Law and Rituals), cited from a Montefiore MS by H. Tykocinski in *Die gaonäischen Verordnungen,* pp. 174 ff. Maimonides himself set up so many qualifications on lynching as to make it totally unrealistic. It was permitted only during the sexual act performed in the presence of ten or more Jews. If the transgressor killed his assailant in self-defense he escaped punishment. Tykocinski correctly observed that the punishment of exile for sexual transgressions is recorded nowhere in the geonic literature, nor is there any evidence for its application in 'Anav's own thirteenth-century Rome. One wonders whether the authors of that ordinance did not have in mind the old rabbinic advice for a man whose lust gets the better of him to leave his residence, settle in a place where he is totally unknown, and wear only black clothing. Cf. Ḥagigah 16a; *M.Q.* 17a. R. Ḥananel, and more distinctly, Ibn 'Aqnin, himself a sufferer from the agonies of expatriation, explained that exile, because of the miseries it entails, may be considered the most effective antidote to overbearing desires. Cf. Ḥananel's Commentary on Ḥagigah and M.Q., *loc. cit.* (Rashi quotes here an analogous explanation by Hai Gaon); Ibn 'Aqnin's comment communicated by Halkin in *Starr Mem. Vol.,* p. 105; and *supra,* n. 7. It may also be noted that, to stem illicit relations between Jews and Gentiles at the transition from Byzantine to Muslim rule in the Holy Land and probably elsewhere, the author of *Sefer ha-Ma'asim* ordained that "a woman who puts on cosmetics and visits [houses of] idols shall be flogged and her hair shaved off." Cf. the fragment, ed. by J. Mann in *Tarbiz,* Vol. I, Part 3, p. 12. On the ironical choice of the Sabbath by a Spanish Muslim for meeting his Jewish mistress, see the poem cited by H. Z. Hirschberg in "The Image of Jews in Early Arabic Letters" (Hebrew), *Hatekufah,* XXXIV–XXXV, 693 f. This essay mentions also other interesting sidelights of Arab-Jewish social relations. In general, the impact of the environment could not be entirely denied; at least, according to two Karaite controversialists, Daniel al-Qumisi and Sahl ben Maṣliaḥ, some Rabbanite Jews, in imitation of their Gentile neighbors, even indulged in pederasty. Cf. Qumisi's Commentary on the Minor Prophets in Mann, *Texts and Studies,* II, 77; and Sahl's introduction to his "Book of Precepts," cited in *Sefer ha-Yishub,* II, 125, where some related passages are likewise quoted. However, these assertions were doubtless polemically exaggerated. Cf. *infra,* Chap. XXVI, n. 39.

27. Cf. the data assembled by M. Schreiner in his "Notes sur les Juifs dans l'Islam," *REJ,* XXIX, 208 f.; Tritton's *Caliphs,* pp. 97, 136; and the various handbooks of Muslim jurisprudence. On the communities' "eminent domain" over the members' property, and their inheritance rights in heirless estates, see *infra,* Chap. XXIII, n. 17. In his *Jews and Arabs,* pp. 78 f., Goitein has rightly stressed the financial interest of many Arabs in the conversion of Jewish girls to Islam. In a polygamous society good-looking and talented wives commanded a rather high purchase price. But fathers lost all their claims to their "converted" daughters' price, for conversion automatically canceled all former family relations, according to both Muslim and Jewish law. On the other hand, a typical folk tale reported that Muslim officials, finding an

abandoned Jewish orphan girl, placed her with Jewish foster parents. Cf. Nissim bar Jacob, *Ḥibbur yafeh,* pp. 102 f.

28. The geonic responsum was addressed to an unnamed correspondent, probably by Saadiah. It was published by A. E. Harkavy in his *Teshubot ha-geonim* (Responsen der Geonim), p. 266, No. 541. A similar decision had previously been rendered by Naṭronai Gaon in a responsum published in the collection *Sha'are Ṣedeq,* IV.3.25, fol. 48b; and in J. Musafiah's edition of *Teshubot ha-geonim* (published in Lyck), Nos. 23–24. On the Christian legislation, see *supra,* Vol. II, p. 253, and *infra,* Chap. XIX. Once again the import of the interfaith hereditary rights can be comprehended only against the background of the ramified inheritance laws in both Islam and Judaism. The latter grew so complex, both legally and mathematically, that already Saadiah found it necessary to devote to them a special halakhic monograph. See *infra,* Chaps. XXVII n. 75, and XXXV.

29. Cf. H. Terrasse's detailed study of the Andalusian mosque built in Fez in 859–60 (about the same time as the Kairuwanese mosque) in *La Mosquée des Andalous à Fez,* with the sources listed there; Idrisi (Edrisi), *Description de l'Afrique et de l'Espagne,* ed. by R. Dozy and M. J. de Goeje, pp. 79 f.; E. Lévi-Provençal's study of "La Fondation de Fès," reprinted in his *Islam d'Occident,* pp. 1–41; Mez, *Renaissance,* p. 43; and, more generally, F. Taeschner's "Kulturgemeinschaft und nationale Sonderheiten in mittelalterlichen Orient," *Zeitschrift für Missionswissenschaft,* XXXV, 128–41. On the Jewish quarter in Baghdad, which included also the so-called old section (*Al-'Atiqa*), where the exilarchs resided, see Obermeyer's *Landschaft Babylonien,* pp. 147 ff. Of course, here too much depended on arbitrary decisions of officials and popular whims. There was, for instance, a violent reaction in fifteenth-century Cairo when the Jews cut a new lane in their own quarter. Cf. Gottheil's observations in *Studies . . . Harper,* p. 368. On the other hand, G. E. von Grunebaum's assumption that Jewish quarters were frequently located in the vicinity of the main government buildings "for better protection" (cf. "The Structure of the Muslim Town" in his *Islam: Essays in the Nature and Growth of a Cultural Tradition,* p. 148), is hardly justified even for western Islam, where imitation of Christian patterns was more pronounced. We shall see that under Christendom, too, general historical, rather than security factors accounted for the location of most Jewish streets. Cf. *supra* Chap. XVI, n. 60; and *infra,* Chap. XX, n. 32.

30. Jaḥiẓ, cited by Tritton in *JRAS,* 1931, p. 329; the geonic responsum addressed by an unnamed gaon to Shabib bar Jacob of Kairuwan (who during the latter part of the ninth century exchanged many letters with the Babylonian sages), published in S. Assaf's *Teshubot ha-geonim,* 1928, pp. 1 ff., 35, and parallel decisions by other sages listed there; Maimonides, *Resp.,* No. 254. The Maimonidean responsa themselves, however, offer unmistakable testimony for the frequency with which these rules were broken. In another case, brought to the sage's attention, a Jew had rented his section of the house to Gentiles. When asked about the neighbors' claims for damages, Maimonides had to admit that such claims could not be legally upheld. He merely advised his questioner to put the transgressor under a ban, lest the latter continue leasing his part to non-Jews. *Ibid.,* No. 255. Other such cases are recorded *ibid.,* Nos. 296, 312, and elsewhere. On Maimonides' efforts slightly to liberalize the existing rabbinic laws relating to the disposal of property, see my remarks on "The

Economic Views of Maimonides" in *Essays on Maimonides,* pp. 157 ff. Cf. also, more generally, G. Tchernowitz's detailed analysis of *Ha-Yaḥas ben Yisrael la-goyim le-fi ha-Rambam* (The Relations between Israel and the Nations according to Maimonides).

31. Cf. the excerpts cited by Tritton, *JRAS,* 1942, pp. 36 f.; Muḥammad ibn Aḥmad ibn 'Abdun's treatise, ed. by E. Lévi-Provençal in "Un Document sur la vie urbaine et les corps de métiers à Séville au début de XIIe siècle: le traité d'Ibn 'Abdun," *JA,* CCXXIV, 177–299, secs. 153, 157, 169, 206; and in Lévi-Provençal's French translation, entitled *Séville musulmane au début du XIIe siècle,* pp. 108, 110, 114, 128; Ibn abi-'Usaibia and Ibn al-Qifṭi cited by me in *Saadia Anniv. Vol.,* p. 50 n. 89; Abu Yusuf, *K. al-Kharaj,* pp. 132 f. (Arabic), 333 f. (French); Mann, *Egypt,* I, 153 ff.; II, 175 ff.; Mez, *Renaissance,* p. 40; and *infra,* Chap. XXXV. The controversy over the well, reported by Mann, seems to have occurred during some change in the regime of the country. Since the beginning and the end of the document are missing, the first lines referring to the Arabs gaining the upper hand would better fit some Palestinian or Syrian locality after its reconquest by the Seljuks, rather than a Faṭimid city. This change in regime would also explain the sudden closing of a well, long in Jewish use, by arrogant Muslim neighbors. Conversely, Jews were accused by some Muslims of greeting Gentiles with *as-sam 'alaikum* (death, or disgust be with you) instead of the customary *as-salam 'alaikum* (peace be with you). Cf. the data cited by C. Vajda in *JA,* CCXXIX, 87 f. Curiously, by a sort of reciprocity, the Byzantine emperor Nicephoros I (802–11) forbade his subjects to call the Arabs Saracens. According to Mas'udi, he was prompted by a faulty etymology of that designation as the equivalent of "Sarah's slaves." Cf. *K. at-Tanbiḥ,* ed. by De Goeje (in his *Bibliotheca,* Vol. VIII), p. 168; with E. Honigmann's comments thereon in his "Notes sur trois passages d'Al-Mas'oudi," *Annuaire,* XII, 183 f.

32. Sa'id ibn Sina al-Mulk's poem, cited in English in H. Friedenwald's essays *The Jews and Medicine,* p. 215; Abu Muḥammad 'Abd Allah ben Muslim ibn Qutaiba, *K. Adab al-katib* (Education of the Scribe), ed. by M. Grünert, p. 26; Abu'l 'Abbas Aḥmad ben Muḥammad al-Maqqari, *K. Nafḥ aṭ-ṭib* (Smell of Perfumes), ed. by R. Dozy *et al.,* under the title *Analectes sur l'histoire et la littérature des Arabes d'Espagne,* II, 259 (although writing in the seventeenth century, the author preserved excellent records from the period of Arab domination in Spain); Za'id ibn 'Ali, *Corpus juris,* ed. by E. Griffini, No. 364; Barhebraeus, *Chronography,* I, 141 (English). On Israeli and his school, see A. B. Milad's study of *L'Ecole médicale de Kairouan (aux Xe et XIe siècles)*; and *infra,* Chap. XXXVI. The prohibition for infidels to visit Mecca was placed under the sanction of capital punishment, and even today Christians and Jews can only surreptitiously visit Arabia's holy cities. On the other hand, Jewish law, which was not totally averse to Gentile visitors in synagogues, strenuously objected to Jews attending non-Jewish houses of worship. The few medieval Jews who cared to disregard their own laws certainly were not seriously impeded by the Muslim unwillingness to admit them to mosques.

33. Qur'an, 5:56; R. Levy, *Sociology,* pp. 84 (citing Mas'udi), 96 (citing the geographer, Abu Bakr); A. N. Poliak's brief review, "The Jews of the Middle East at the End of the Middle Ages" (Hebrew), *Zion,* II, 263 ff. Al-Fadl's remarks related to free Muslims. The contempt in which slaves were held, even if in practice they were treated with considerable kindness, is evident from all discussion of slavery in

Muslim letters. Cf. also *infra,* Chap. XXII. The use of the Arabic *kunya* remained unimpaired even though some Spanish Jews preferred to pronounce their name Abn or Aben (for instance, Aben Ezra). On the correctness of the modern transliteration of these names, see the discussion between M. Gaster and D. Herzog in their notes on "Abn oder Ibn in hebräischen Namen?" *MGWJ,* LXXVII, 210–11 (Gaster, favoring Abn, as still frequently pronounced in Sephardic names), 386–87 (Herzog, preferring Ibn). Cf. also J. Ruska's "Zur Umschrift der syrischen und hebräischen Eigennamen," *Archeion,* XXI, 99–102. The Spanish Christians, too, frequently had Arabic names and *kunyas* alongside of their Romance names. See the examples cited by A. González Palencia in *Los Mozárabes de Toledo,* Prelim. Vol., pp. 123, 143 ff.; and, more generally, Habib Zayat's "Christian Names, Given Names, and Surnames of Christians and Jews under Islam" (Arabic), *Al-Machriq,* XLII, 1–21. On the general social divisions under Islam, see also Von Grunebaum's *Medieval Islam,* pp. 170 ff.; and E. Strauss's mostly later medieval illustrations of "The Social Isolation of the Ahl adh-dhimma"; see *supra,* n. 22.

34. Baladhuri, *K. Futûḥ al-buldân,* p. 142 (English trans., I, 218); L. Massignon's observations in *RB,* LI, 7 ff.; and, more generally, Tritton, *Caliphs,* pp. 18 ff. The attitude of the early caliphs, known from scattered references in literature, is confirmed by a number of Egyptian papyri, including "An Official Circular Letter of the Arab Period," republished by Sir I. H. Bell in the *Journal of Egyptian Archaeology,* XXXI, 75–84. It shows that shortly before 706 (according to its first editor, Medea Norsa, as late as 779) a high Christian official could issue instructions in Greek to district authorities threatening death in case of noncompliance. Persians of the Shi'ite persuasion were as suspect as the *dhimmis.* Nevertheless, former Zoroastrians played a preponderant role in both the central and the provincial administrations of the Caliphate. Massignon's explanation (*loc. cit.*), however, of the influence of Nestorian scribes in Baghdad as owing to the numerical preponderance of Christians over Jews in ninth-century Iraq, is not borne out by the available evidence. Cf. *supra,* Chap. XVII, nn. 31–32. He himself has insisted, moreover, that the appointment of some Jewish leaders to influential posts took place during that very century. Cf. *infra,* n. 36.

35. Ibn an-Naqqash in his "Fetoua" communicated by Belin in *JA,* LIX, 428 ff.; Reuben Levy, *Baghdad Chronicle,* pp. 202 f. (pointing out the connection between Majd ad-Din's conditional appointment and some popular resentment against the Sultan's Jewish agent, Abu Sa'd ibn Simḥah, in 1091); Tritton, *Caliphs,* p. 22 f.; Jalalu'ddin as-Suyuti, *History of the Caliphs,* trans. by H. S. Jarrett, p. 397; and *supra,* Chap. XVII n. 32. There were very good reasons why Al-Muqtadir's discriminatory decree "did not last long" (Ṭabari). A combination of great needs of the state, general maladministration under ever changing viziers, and the reckless spending of the court quickly dissipated the tremendous treasury accumulations of the previous reigns. Cf. Bowen, *'Ali Ibn 'Isa,* p. 100; and *infra,* Chap. XXII, n. 83.

36. Cf. the chronicle published by A. E. Harkavy in his "Neṭira and his Sons: a Prominent Jewish Family in Baghdad at the Beginning of the Tenth Century," *Festschrift Berliner,* Hebrew section, pp. 34–43. I. Friedlaender has plausibly identified the author of this chronicle as Nathan the Babylonian, from whose pen we have the famous description of the central agencies of the Babylonian Jewish communities.

Both narratives may well have been but fragments of a history of Babylonian Jewry. See *infra,* n. 53; and Chap. XXVIII, n. 76. The emphasis in this chronicle on the wearing of black clothes by these bankers throws into bold relief the arbitrariness of the entire color legislation. See *supra,* n. 22.

The dates of Neṭira's and his sons' activities are nowhere indicated in the chronicle and must be surmised from other data. W. J. Fischel has correctly identified Neṭira with Joseph ben Phineas' son-in-law. Cf. his *Jews in the Economic and Political Life of Mediaeval Islam,* pp. 42 ff. He was too reserved, however, in interpreting Aṭ-Ṭanukhi's statement concerning Joseph's and Aaron ben Amram's appointment. He placed it in the time of Vizier Mohammed ben 'Ubaid Allah al-Khaqani (912–13), rather than that of his father, 'Ubaid Allah ben Yaḥya, who had served under Mutawakkil and Mu'tamid from 850 to 877 (pp. 10 f.). Fischel thus ran counter not only to the express statement of Aṭ-Ṭanukhi, whom he had to emend, but also to the sequence indicated in the chronicle of the house of Neṭira relating to the year 892. Neṭira may, indeed, have been one of those loyal servants to whom Al-Mu'tadhid's vizier pointed in his apology for employing non-Muslims. To be sure, uninterrupted service of a family of Jewish bankers for three generations is in many ways exceptional. But this perseverance against tremendous odds is by itself insufficient to controvert clear statements in the sources, confirmed also by many other bits of evidence. Cf. L. Massignon's data in "L'Influence de l'Islam au moyen âge sur la fondation et l'essor des banques juives," *Bulletin d'études orientales de l'Institut français de Damas,* I, 3–12; his observations in *RB,* LI, 12 n. 6; and *infra,* Chap. XXII, nn. 65–66.

37. Suyuti, *History of the Caliphs,* trans. by Jarrett, pp. 402 f.; Saadiah's letter in L. Ginzberg's *Geonica,* II, 87 f.; or, in a somewhat improved version in B. M. Lewin's critical edition of Sherira Gaon's *Iggeret* (Epistle), p. xxv; Fischel's *Economic and Political Life,* pp. 34 ff.; and my remarks in *Saadia Anniv. Vol.,* pp. 32 ff., 51 f. The position of *jahbadh* held by some of these bankers and the question of the Jewish "monopoly" in the revenue of Aḥwaz, held by Sahl ben Neṭira, will become clearer from the general economic developments of that period discussed *infra,* Chap. XXII, nn. 65, 78.

38. Mann, *Jews in Egypt,* I, 19 ff.; II, 11 ff.; A. Neubauer, "Egyptian Fragments, II," *JQR,* [o.s.] IX, 35 f. On the name of the Arab satirist, see three versions cited in Fischel's *Economic and Political Life,* p. 88 n. 1. The story of Palṭiel is told, with obvious family pride, by his descendant, Aḥimaaz of Oria, in *Sefer Yuḥasin* (Chronicle), ed. and trans. by M. Salzman, pp. 16 ff. (Hebrew), 25 ff., 88 ff. (English), and B. Klar's improved edition, pp. 39 ff., 126. On his unlikely conversion and identity with either Jauhar or Ibn Killis, see Klar's note, pp. 169 f., and, in greater detail, A. Marx's *Studies in Jewish History and Booklore,* pp. 3 ff.; Fischel's remarks, *op. cit.,* pp. 64 ff., and *infra,* Chap. XXIII, n. 47. At the same time we must remember that Mu'izz was anything but a lukewarm Muslim. His real attitude came clearly to the fore in his correspondence with the Byzantine emperor and his oral exchange with the latter's ambassador (probably in 962–63, several years before his conquest of Egypt). Replying to a Byzantine offer of a treaty of perpetual peace between the two empires, the caliph is supposed to have bluntly stated that "religion and the canon law [*as-shari'a*] did not admit such a perpetual truce. . . . Allah has sent his prophet Mohammed and set up the Imams after him from among his descendants in order to call mankind to His religion and to make holy war [*jihad*] against the recalcitrant till they

embraced the religion or 'pay the tribute by their hands and be subdued' [Qur'an 9:29], accepting the sovereignty of the Imam of the Muslims and seeking his protection [*dhimma*]. Truce is admissible for a fixed time only." Quoted here in S. M. Stern's translation, "An Embassy of the Byzantine Emperor to the Fatimid Caliph Al-Mu'izz," *Byzantion,* XX, 245 f. The reference here to the *imams'* descent from Mohammed was, of course, part and parcel of the Faṭimid propaganda and its glorification of the dynasty's descent from the Messenger's beloved daughter, Faṭima. Cf. also M. Canard's emphasis on the domestic importance of that propaganda in "L'Impérialisme des Fatimides et leur propagande," *Annales de l'Institut d'Etudes Orientales,* VI, 156–93; and, more generally, the detailed analysis of the sources for the *Ismaili Tradition concerning the Rise of the Fatimids* by W. Ivanow. The latter, incidentally, cites four significant traditions, clearly borrowed from Jewish messianic teachings (pp. 120 ff.). Not surprisingly, therefore, opponents tried to impute to the Faṭimid dynasty descent from Jews. Cf. the three versions analyzed by B. Lewis in "The Legend of the Jewish Origin of the Faṭimid Caliphs" (Hebrew), *Melilah,* III–IV, 185–87; and, more generally, P. H. Mansour's *Polemics on the Origin of the Fatimid Caliphs,* esp. pp. 101 ff.

39. A. Neubauer, "Egyptian Fragments, II," *JQR,* [o.s.] IX, 35 f.; Mann, *Egypt,* I, 215 ff.; II, 264 ff. On the general Jewish ignorance of the Qur'an and, on the other hand, the occasional quotations therefrom even by orthodox leaders, cf. *infra,* Chap. XXIV, n. 4. The ease with which unbelievers could reach the highest ranks of officialdom in Egypt is well illustrated by the career of an Armenian Christian refugee, Baḥram, who for a decade (1131–40) served as the all-powerful vizier of the Faṭimid Empire. Cf. M. Canard's well-documented description, "Un Vizir chrétien à l'époque fâtimite: l'arménien Bahrâm," *Annales de l'Institut des Etudes Orientales,* Algiers, XII, 84–113 (another article was to follow).

40. Ḥisdai's letter to the king of Khazaria, published many times since the sixteenth century and much debated as to its authenticity (see *infra,* Chap. XIX, n. 30), is best available in P. K. Kokovtsov's critical edition, with a Russian translation, in his *Evreisko-khazarskaya perepiska,* pp. 7 ff. (Hebrew), 51 ff. (Russian). Unfortunately, neither Ḥisdai's authorship of the letters, published by Mann in his *Texts and Studies,* I, 21 ff., nor their address to the Empress and Emperor of Byzantium is absolutely certain. Cf. S. Krauss, "Zu Dr. Mann's neuen historischen Texten," *HUCA,* X, 265–96, 307–8; and Mann's effective "Rejoinder," *ibid.,* pp. 297–307. But nothing would have been more natural for the Jewish patriot Ḥisdai than to make use of his personal contacts with the Byzantine embassy for the amelioration of the status of his coreligionists in the Empire. In fact, Ḥisdai may have sent his message back through the very Byzantine envoys of 944, a year before Romanos' deposition and the sole assumption of power by Constantine. Perhaps for this reason the letter was addressed to the Empress, who could intercede with both her father, Romanos, and her husband, Constantine. Ḥisdai may also have remembered that a century earlier (839–40) Yaḥya al-Jazal, sent as an envoy from Cordova to Constantinople, owed much of his success to the favorable impression he had made on the empress. Cf. E. Lévi-Provençal's description of "Un Echange d'ambassades entre Cordoue et Byzance au IXe siècle," *Byzantion,* XII, 1–24. M. Landau's suggestion that the recipient of Ḥisdai's first letter was Princess Agatha, Constantine's learned daughter, rather than his wife Helena, has little to commend itself. Cf. his *Beiträge zum*

Chazarenproblem, pp. 22 f. On Ḥisdai's diplomatic activities, see the sources cited by E. Lévi-Provençal in *L'Espagne musulmane,* pp. 111 f., and Calmette's *Histoire de l'Espagne,* p. 74. Their background has been further elucidated by another contemporary Arabic chronicle, edited with a Spanish translation by E. Lévi-Provençal and E. García Gómez under the title *Una cronica anónima de 'Abd al-Raḥman III al-Naṣir.* It is even possible that Ḥisdai returned the courtesy of the Holy Roman emperor by sending to Germany a Spanish-Jewish envoy, Ibrahim ibn Ya'qub, author of the well-known travelogue. Cf. *infra,* Chap. XIX, n. 57. If this suggestion should be verified by further finds, it would increase the likelihood that the aforementioned letter was indeed addressed by the Jewish statesman to the Byzantine empress. Ibn Ḥauqal doubtless confused Ḥisdai with his envoy, Ibrahim, when in drawing a map of the Alps and Carpathians (in his *K. al-Masalik,* ed. by J. H. Kramers, pp. 193 f.), he invoked the testimony of Ḥisdai who had traveled there and met kings and other dignitaries. Understandably, many fundamentalist Muslims resented the employment of the Jewish diplomat. According to a story reported by Averroës, a Muslim official tried to arouse 'Abd ar-Raḥman by a poem, "The Prophet for whom alone thou art honored,/ Is designated a liar by this Jew." Cf. the quotation from Averroës' commentary on Aristotle's *Poetics* in S. M. Stern's "Two New Data about Ḥisdai ibn Shapruṭ" (Hebrew), *Zion,* XI, 141–46. Ḥisdai's diplomatic correspondence was considered sufficiently typical of the contemporary Arabic epistolary style for one of his letters to be cited in full in Maqqari's *K. Nafḥ aṭ-ṭib,* I, 351.

41. The fascinating story of Samuel ibn Nagrela can largely be reconstructed from his own poems and their informative headings, with the aid of a number of other contemporary sources, both Jewish and Muslim. Cf. especially, R. Dozy, *Histoire des Musulmans d'Espagne,* III, 18 ff.; J. Schirmann's brief bibliographical sketch of "Samuel Hannagid, the Man, the Soldier, the Politician," *JSS,* XIII, 99–126; his remarkable reconstruction of "The Wars of Samuel ha-Nagid" (Hebrew), *Zion,* I, 261–83, 357–76, and II, 185–87; and J. Lewin's more recent Hebrew essay on "R. Samuel ha-Nagid," *Orlogin,* IX, 132–51, and XI, 225–50. Muntafil's poem, as well as an equally flattering letter addressed by him to the Nagid, is now available in the poet's work published in Cairo in 1942. It is quoted in a Hebrew translation by S. M. Stern in his "Notes on the Life of R. Samuel ha-Nagid" (Hebrew), *Zion,* XV, 135–45. Here Stern also adduces an interesting parallel to Samuel's rise to power because of his ability to write beautiful Arabic letters, and publishes from Bodleian and British Museum MSS two Hebrew poems in the Nagid's honor. On the internal discords not only between Berbers and Arabs but also among the latter, in so far as they considered themselves of Yemenite, Medinese, or Syrian origin, see M. M. Hussain's dissertation, *Essai sur la chûte du califat umayyade de Cordou en 1009,* blaming the downfall mainly on these internal dissensions. The date of Samuel's first appointment is rather uncertain; that given in Ibn Daud's chronicle (in *MJC,* I, 71 ff.) is almost surely erroneous. Cf. the discussion on this score between Schirmann and Z. (H.) Lichtenstein, in *Zion,* I, 266 f., and II, 185 f. Nor is the origin or spelling of the name Nagrela (Nagdela or Nagrila) altogether certain. Among the many theories advanced on this score, including the more recent one equating it with Nagralla, an Arabic-Spanish diminutive of *naghra* (the crow; see G. S. Colin's suggestion in E. Lévi-Provençal's introduction to the latter's edition of "Les 'Mémoires' de 'Abd Allah, dernier roi ziride de Grenade," *Al-Andalus,* III, 244 n. 23) probably the most

acceptable is the name's long-recognized connection with Samuel's title, *nagid* (prince, or leader, of the Jews). But the preference for spelling it Ibn Nagrela may perhaps go back to Samuel himself, or his son Joseph, "r" and "d" being easily interchanged in Hebrew. Samuel will frequently be mentioned here as both scholar and poet. Cf. esp. *infra,* Chap. XXXII, which will furnish additional data on his political and military activities as well.

42. Ibn Daud, *Sefer ha-Qabbalah,* in *MJC,* I, 73; R. Dozy, *Recherches sur l'histoire et la littérature de l'Espagne pendant le moyen âge,* I, 292 ff., LV ff. No. xxiii; Dozy, *Histoire des Musulmans,* III, 61 f., 70 ff., (both quoting at length the vitriolic attack upon Joseph by the disgruntled Abu Isḥaq al-Ilbiri, or, of Elvira). The full Arabic text has been reedited by E. García Gómez in *Un Alfaqui español—Abu Isḥak de Elvira,* pp. 148 ff. No. xxv, and commented on in his introduction, pp. 38 ff. On the underlying religious controversies, including the sharp exchange between Samuel and Ibn Ḥazm, the distinguished student of comparative religion, see *infra,* Chap. XXIV, esp. n. 19. Lévi-Provençal's suggestion that Samuel's success may in part be explained by the presence in the royal harem of some of his relatives, is not borne out by any evidence. Certainly, the women Samuel used to warn the Arab grandees could have been mere acquaintances. Cf. also, in general, J. Schirmann's interesting essay on "Le Dīwān de Šemū'el Hannāgīd considéré comme source pour l'histoire espagnol," *Hespéris,* XXXV, 163–88 (quoting also, pp. 167 f., Moses ibn Ezra's poem relating to Joseph's military exploits, published in *Haaretz,* Sept. 29, 1939). More recently, F. P. Bargebuhr has shown that Joseph had also been a distinguished builder, largely responsible for the construction of the famous Alhambra of Granada. Cf. "The Alhambra Palace of the Eleventh Century," *Journal of the Warburg and Cortauld Institutes,* XIX.

43. Fischel, *Economic and Political Life,* pp. 1 ff., 68 ff.; Mann, *Egypt,* I, 76 ff., and II, 75 ff.; R. Levy, *Baghdad Chronicle,* p. 231 (quoting Ibn Al-Qifṭi and Barhebraeus); and the sources cited by H. Pérès in *La Poesie andalouse en arabe classique au XIe siècle,* pp. 266 ff. Abu'l Barakat's financial arrangements were evidently facilitated by the aforementioned theory of Muslim law that religious communities should not be deprived of their property through the conversion of members. See *supra,* n. 27. Ibrahim at-Tustari's Hebrew name, Abraham, is attested, for example, by a typical letter of solicitation addressed to him by a Caucasian or Khazarian Jew. See Gottheil and Worrell, *Fragments,* No. 31, pp. 142 ff. On Ḥesed-Abu Naṣr and his family, see also S. D. Goitein, "Petitions to Fatimid Caliphs from the Cairo Geniza," *JQR,* XLV, 36 f.

44. Yehudah ben Solomon al-Ḥarizi, *Sefer Taḥkemoni* (Macamae), XLVI, ed. by J. Toporowski, p. 357 (P. de Lagarde, ed., pp. 174 f.); Mann, *Egypt,* II, 274; Aḥmad ibn Miskawaihi's *K. Tajarib al-'Umam* (Experiences of Nations), the concluding section of which appeared under the title, *The Eclipse of the 'Abbasid Caliphate,* ed. and trans. by H. F. Amedroz and D. S. Margoliouth, III, 282 (Arabic), VI, 300 (English). Of course, the people had little to say about such appointments; it could only rejoice in or mourn them after the event. We shall see that at times it had enough difficulty in staving off infringements on its own autonomy by such grandees not of its choice. Cf. also Goitein, *Jews and Arabs,* p. 75.

45. *Ginza,* German trans. by M. Lidzbarski, pp. 225 ff.; Mas'udi, *Muruj,* II, 386 ff.; Yaḥya ibn Sa'id of Antioch, *Histoire,* ed. with a French trans. by J. Kratchkovsky and A. Vasiliev, in *PO,* XVIII, 802; Simonet, *Historia de los Mozárabes,* p. 360; *Vita Sancti Theotonii,* in *Portugaliae Monumenta historica, Scriptores,* Vol. I, fol. 87a; Maimonides, *Responsa,* No. 369; 'Anan, *Sefer Ha-Miṣvot* (Book of Precepts), ed. by Harkavy, in *Zikhron,* VIII, 6 f. On the frequent Muslim persecutions of Armenian Christians, which were so greatly at variance with the general policies of the Caliphate, see J. Laurent's illustrations in *L'Arménie entre Byzance et l'Islam,* p. 158 n. 1.

We do not possess actual transcripts of the religious disputations. But their general tenor probably did not differ very much from the debate which allegedly took place in Palestine about 634, according to the convert Jacob ibn Tanuma, except that now the Christians lacked the power to silence Jewish debaters by a slap in the face. Cf. F. Nau's edition of the Greek text of his *Doctrina Jacobi* (Didascalie de Jacob) in *PO,* VIII, 711–80; S. Krauss's comments thereon in *Ṣiyyon,* II, 28 ff.; Starr's notes in *JPOS,* XV, 288; and *supra,* Chap. XVI, n. 22. These religious controversies will be more fully analyzed *infra,* Chap. XXIV.

46. Ibn Baṭṭuṭa, *Travels,* trans. by H. A. R. Gibb, pp. 68 f.; G. Wiet, *Egypte arabe,* p. 101. Nor must one lose sight of the frequent good will and cooperation between Christian and Jewish officials, for example 'Isa ben Nestorius and Manasseh. See *supra,* n. 38. The fact that the Christian Copts tried, for religious and possibly economic reasons, to familiarize themselves with the Jewish calendar, likewise indicates closer relationships than is evident from the few extant sources. Cf. F. Hintze, "Ein koptischer Glossar jüdischer Monatsnamen," *Mitteilungen des Instituts für Orientforschung* of the Deutsche Akademie der Wissenschaften, III, 149–52 (from a Berlin ostracon). On the Damascus tradition concerning Moses' tomb some two miles from the city, see A. S. Yahuda's remarks in his *'Eber va-'Arab,* pp. 283 ff. (based on a fourteenth-century Arab manuscript). Yahuda also points out that in recent generations this tradition has been completely eclipsed by the one current among Palestinian Arabs, that Moses had been buried in a place near Jericho. Stimulated by political considerations, the pilgrimages to this tomb of Moses have assumed mass character, and the annual *Nebi Musa* celebrations during the Easter season are still among the greatest religious events of Muslim life in Palestine and its vicinity.

47. The confused and often outrightly contradictory statements in the sources themselves have caused much grief to modern investigators. In the hypercritical age of Julius Wellhausen and his disciples, including Carl H. Becker and Leone Caetani, one had the simple expedient of assuming that later writers substituted contemporary conditions for those at the inception of the Islamic empire. Apart from being the result of historic ignorance, the last generation was told, this substitution was often intended to serve as a historic justification of relationships whose origin had become obscure and unintelligible. Cf. esp. Wellhausen's still valuable work, *The Arab Kingdom and Its Fall.* A somewhat similar explanation had already been offered by the early Muslim jurist, Sha'arani, for those who were puzzled by the wide differences of opinion on the laws and traditions governing the various imposts found among the luminaries of the four main schools of jurisprudence. "These differences are owing," he wrote, "to the fact that the *imams* take into account the conditions prevailing in the countries in which they live." More recent scholarship, however, reflecting our generally more conservative temper toward higher criticism, has been less prone to

discount the historic validity of these traditions. The undeniable discrepancies among the sources may often be explained by genuine local variations developed during the successive stages of the first conquest. Each momentary situation doubtless called for some specific adjustment which, even if at variance with some previous decision, likewise obtained the force of precedent. Cf. especially the strong arguments advanced against the radical view by D. C. Dennett, Jr., in his *Conversion and the Poll Tax.* Cf. also R. N. Frye's review of that work in *Speculum,* XXVII, 214–15. Frye incidentally mentions a twelfth-century Persian MS showing that, on one occasion, the population of Nishapur had refused to pay the tax on the grounds that it had never been conquered, but had peacefully surrendered. We recall that Jews, too, often advanced claims, genuine or spurious, of some such treaty arrangements, the alleged immutability of which was to safeguard them against the imposition of new and arbitrary taxes. Cf. *supra,* Chap. XVII, n. 10. See, however, the debates on this score mentioned *supra,* n. 17; and *infra,* n. 49. These arguments were facilitated by the governmental practice, illustrated by early Coptic papyri, of levying all these taxes "in a lump sum, either on a village community, a church, a monastery, or some other corporate body." Cf. E. M. Husselman, "Some Coptic Documents Dealing with the Poll Tax," *Aegyptus,* XXXI, 336. Hewing somewhat more closely to the Wellhausenian line, but likewise very informative, is F. Løkkegaard's *Islamic Taxation in the Classic Period, with Special Reference to Circumstances in Iraq.* Of considerable interest are also such monographs as A. S. Ehrenkreutz's "Contributions to the Knowledge of the Fiscal Administration of Egypt in the Middle Ages," *BSOAS,* XVI, 502–14; and C. Cahen's careful analysis of "Fiscalité, propriété, antagonismes sociaux en Haute-Mésopotamie au temps des premiers 'Abbasides d'après Denys de Tell-Mahré," *Arabica,* I, 136–52. Although Jews as such were rarely mentioned in the sources, the subject of their taxation, legal and extralegal, is so vital for the understanding of their entire political and economic history under medieval Islam that a comprehensive monograph reviewing the widely scattered data relating to them seems imperative. Of course, any analyst will be baffled also by the uncertainties of the earlier Jewish taxation under both Persia and Byzantium. See *supra,* Vol. II, p. 399, n. 18, to which add F. Lot, *Nouvelles recherches sur l'impôt foncier et la capitation personnelle sous le Bas Empire.*

48. Yaḥya ben Adam, cited by Dennett in *Conversion,* p. 28; *Pirqe de-R. Eliezer, supra,* n. 20; cf. B. Z. Dinaburg's commentary thereon in his *Yisrael ba-golah,* I, 59. The concentration of land in the hands of Mu'awiya and his relatives and friends is reported with particular clarity by Ya'qubi in his *K. al-Buldan,* ed. by De Goeje (in his *Bibliotheca geographorum arabicorum,* Vol. VII), pp. 277 f. As most Jews in the formerly Byzantine, Persian, or Visigothic provinces seem to have welcomed the new conquerors, probably very few of their landowners fled before the onrushing Arab armies. It seems likely, therefore, that they suffered relatively little from such expropriation of ownerless property. On the later land flight of Palestinian and other farmers, see *infra,* Chap. XXII, n. 2.

49. Baladhuri, *K. Futûḥ al-buldân,* p. 124 (Arabic), I, 190 f. (English); Abu Yusuf, *K. al-Kharaj,* pp. 69 ff. (Arabic), pp. 187 ff. (French); and the analysis thereof in Mahmoud Moursi's thesis, *L'Impôt foncier d'après le livre d'Abu Youssef.* Not surprisingly, a special pleader like Ibn 'Ubayya failed to mention Baladhuri's report, which evidently reflected the historic realities far better. See *supra,* n. 17. The rates

enumerated by Abu Yusuf seem to be borne out by a few extant tax lists. For example, in an Egyptian list, evidently recording arrears of various Jews on their poll tax, we find among the fifty-five debtors only six owing 1 or 2 dinars. The majority owed only a fraction of a dinar, for the most part one quarter or less. Of course some of the latter (especially those listed under entries 18, 19, 29, 53 and 55) may also have been originally assessed at 2 to 4 dinars each. These arrears seem to indicate also a method of payment by instalments. Cf. Gottheil and Worrell, *Fragments,* No. 13, pp. 66 ff. Only gradually did the rationalization emerge that the "unbelievers" owed this tax to the state in substitution for the military service from which they were freed. But not until 1855 was this impost so formalized in modern Turkey. See, in general, Ahmed el Emary's rather sketchy observations on *La Conception de l'impôt chez les Musulmans.*

50. Baladhuri, *Futûḥ,* pp. 121 (Arabic), I, 187 (English); C. H. Becker's ed. of *Papyri Schott-Reinhardt,* Vol. I, No. III, pp. 72 f.; Amedroz and Margoliouth, eds., *The Eclipse of the Abbasid Caliphate* by Miskawaihi, I, 257 (Arabic), IV, 291 f. (English); Mez, *Renaissance* (German), pp. 124 f. (omitted in the English translation). On the other hand, once the system of tax farming was established under Al-Mu'tamid, Jews too had access to this semicommercial occupation. Sahl ben Neṭira, for example, seems to have taken over the collection of all taxes from the slow-paying province of Aḥwaz. We have no information about the behavior of such Jewish taxfarmers, but they probably ran true to form. The legal justification for the most severe extortions from infidels was not too far to seek since, at least according to the extreme teachings by the Shafi'ite school, the caliph was entitled to take away up to one half or even two thirds of a *dhimmi's* property as tribute. Cf. Tritton's citation in *JRAS,* 1942, p. 40; and *infra,* n. 56.

51. C. H. Becker's ed. of *Papyri Schott-Reinhardt,* I, 74 f.; his *Islamstudien,* I, 205; Ṭabari's *Annales,* II, 1688, in I. Lichtenstadter's English translation in *IC,* XXIII, 269 f. The latter text is used by Wellhausen to support his theory of the relatively late origin of the division between land and poll taxes. Cf. *The Arab Kingdom,* pp. 282 f., 498 ff.; and Løkkegaard's reservations in his *Islamic Taxation,* pp. 128 ff. Needless to say that not all influential Jews exercised their office to the advantage of their coreligionists. The twelfth-century *Megillat Abiatar* movingly describes the rise to power during the 1080's of a newcomer to Egypt, David son of Daniel Gaon, and his ruthless tax collections. "And he made their [the Jewish communities'] yoke extremely heavy, as it had never been before." Cf. the text in Schechter's *Saadyana,* pp. 89 f., with Mann's explanation of underlying conflict in *Jews in Egypt,* I, 187 ff.; and *infra,* Chap. XXIII n. 41. However, we must not only discount here the testimony of a biased witness in the midst of a raging controversy, but also the fact that David Gaon evidently collected only Jewish taxes owing to the central authorities of the Jewish community, even if he had subsequently to deliver part of it to the Faṭimid Treasury. On this important function of the Jewish community, see *infra,* Chap. XXIII, n. 17.

52. Abu Yusuf, *K. al-Kharaj,* pp. 70 (Arabic), 189 (French); J. Karabaček's summary and comments in *Papyrus Erzherzog Rainer, Führer durch die Ausstellung,* pp. 153 ff., Nos. 601–2, 631; and *supra,* n. 11. Some early Egyptian papyri show entries of as little as 2.5, 5, and 11.5 dirhem. Cf. C. Leyerer's careful "preliminary" analysis of

"Die Verrechnung von Steuern im islamischen Aegypten," *ZDMG,* CIII, 40–69. See also, more generally, L. Casson, "Tax Collection Problems in Early Arab Egypt," *Transactions of the American Philological Association,* LXIX, 274–91; R. Remondon, "Ordre de paiment d'époque arabe pour l'impôt de capitation," *Aegyptus,* XXXII, 257–64 (publishing a brief Greek text of about 700 with detailed comments); and A. S. Ehrenkreutz, "Contributions to the Knowledge of the Fiscal Administration of Egypt in the Middle Ages," *BSOAS,* XVI, 502–14.

53. Harkavy's edition of the text in *Festschrift Berliner,* Hebrew section, pp. 36 (Arabic), 39 (Hebrew); the regulation cited by J. Karabaček in "Das arabische Papier," *Mitteilungen aus der Sammlung der Papyrus Erzherzog Rainer,* II–III, 173; the popular adage, cited in Tritton's *Caliphs,* pp. 95, 227; Fischel, *Economic and Political Life,* p. 130 (quoting Ibn al-Fuwati); Ibn an-Naqqash's "Fetoua," ed. by Belin in *JA,* LX, 103 ff. Ibn al-Fuwati cited the text of a letter written about 1230 by Ibn Fadhlan, the then newly appointed official in charge of the Bureau *(Diwan)* for Protected Subjects. This letter, arguing in favor of unlimited taxation of *dhimmis* and describing in exaggerated terms their influence and prosperity, was translated into Hebrew and analyzed by A. Ben-Jacob in his "New Sources with respect to the History of the Jews in Babylonia in the 12th and 13th Centuries" (Hebrew), *Zion,* XV, 62 ff. Neṭira allegedly also argued against the sudden cancellation of the Jewish poll tax because he feared that, at some future date, another ruler might reverse Al-Mu'tadhid's decision and suddenly confront the Jewish community with a tax bill covering all the accumulations during the intervening years. Cf. S. Fraenkel's comments on Harkavy's text in *JQR,* [o.s.] XVII, 386 f. If Friedlaender's suggestion is correct and this family chronicle originally formed a part of Nathan the Babylonian's history of Baghdad Jewry (cf. his comments *ibid.,* pp. 747 ff.), it would share the latter's strengths and weaknesses. Cf. *infra,* Chap. XXVIII, nn. 76–77.

54. Abu 'Ubaid, cited by Løkkegaard in his *Islamic Taxation,* p. 139; Theophanes, *Chronographia,* I, 446, and II, 295 (this is evidently the meaning of this passage and not a wholly unprecedented order to tattoo the *dhimmis'* hands, as suggested by Goitein in *Jerusalem,* IV, 91); *K. al-Aghani,* III, 26, cited in Mez's *Renaissance,* p. 48. Cf. also C. Cahen's observation in *Arabica,* I, 147. One wonders whether this practice was not widespread enough to account for the strange Arabic designation of the capitation tax, as an impost resting on the taxpayers' "necks." It often runs concurrently with the phrase of its being imposed on their "heads." Remarkably, neither Jewish nor Christian authors seem to be concerned with these humiliating features of the tax, about which they otherwise are far from silent. They apparently acquiesced in such outward manifestations of the realistically undeniable political superiority of the Muslims.

55. Baladhuri, *Futûḥ,* p. 144 (Arabic), I, 221 (English); Bell's data in *Journal of Egyptian Archaeology,* XXXI, 77, 83. Even in fertile Babylonia the sharp decline of state revenue from the ninth to the tenth century—some districts in Al-Aḥwaz paid only about one thirtieth of what they had paid a century earlier (cf. H. Bowen, *'Ali Ibn 'Isa,* p. 123)—was doubtless owing in part to flight from the land.

56. Ash-Shafi'i and other jurists discussed by J. Schacht in his "Zur soziologischen Betrachtung des islamischen Rechts," *Der Islam,* XXII, 229; Gottheil and Worrell,

Fragments, No. 8, p. 40 line 11; *Chronicon Moissiacense* under the year 793, ed. by G. H. Pertz in *MGH,* Scriptores, I, 300; Obadiah's "Fragment," ed. by A. Scheiber in *KS,* XXX, 98 (in English in *JJS,* V, 37); *supra,* n. 22; and *infra,* Chap. XIX n. 21. J. A. Condé's *Historia de la dominación de los Arabes,* pp. 114 f.; E. Lévi-Provençal's ed. of "Les Mémoires' de 'Abd Allah," *Al-Andalus,* IV, 115 f.; and F. Cantera y Burgos's data on "La Juderia de Lucena," *Sefarad,* XIII, 345 f. The story of the parents' sale of children into slavery, although reported by an almost contemporary chronicler (the *Moissiacense* was composed about 819; see *supra,* Chap. XVI, n. 47), seems decidedly exaggerated. More likely was the seizure of such children by some ruthless tax collector. According to strict legal theory, *dhimmis* failing to pay their taxes forfeited their "protection," which meant that adult males could be massacred, while women and children might be sold into slavery. But this theory seems to have received rare, if any, practical application. On Hisham's character cf. E. García Gómez's "Novedades sobre la crónica anónima titulada 'Fatḥ al-Andalus'," *Annales de l'Institut d'Etudes Orientales,* Algiers, XII, 35, with reference to Joaquin de González ed. of that anonymous chronicle, esp. pp. 71 ff.

57. Cf. S. Mahmassani's remark in *Les Idées économiques d'Ibn Khaldoun,* p. 154; the sources cited by I. Lichtenstadter in *IC,* XXIII, 269; and *supra,* n. 44. On the court etiquette in Cairo and its great similarity, whether by coincidence or by conscious imitation, with that of Constantinople, see M. Canard's comparison of "Le Cérémonial fatimite et le cérémonial byzantin," *Byzantion,* XXI, 355–420.

58. 'Ishoyabh's statement cited by A. Mingana in *BJRL,* X, 128; Goitein's remark in *Zion,* XIII–XIV, 28; further elaborated in his *Jews and Arabs,* pp. 62 ff. Even Abu 'Ubayya's assertion that Jews, being "aliens" everywhere, should legally enjoy no rights whatsoever (cited in *Zion,* XIII–XIV, 26) apparently is so singular an exception in Arab jurisprudence, and so starkly contradicts all historic facts, that it must be ascribed entirely to the heat of argument during a litigation. It is quite possible, moreover, that Ibn 'Ubayya picked up that notion from one of the western pilgrims in the Holy City.

CHAPTER XIX: EASTERN EUROPE

1. Nicephoros, *Istoria syntomos,* ed. by C. de Boor, in the former's *Opuscula historica,* pp. 30 f.; Anastasios Sinaites, *Anagogicarum contemplationum in Hexaemeron libri* (Latin version), in *PG,* LXXXIX, 931 ff.; *De S. Zosimo episcopo Syracusano,* in *Acta Sanctorum,* under March 3, p. 839; Mansi, *Collectio,* XI, 945 (in Hefele, *Histoire,* III, Part 1, p. 564; not in the English translation). All these sources are quoted or summarized and fully commented upon in J. Starr, *Jews in the Byzantine Empire,* pp. 84 ff. Nos. 2, 4, 6, 8. Cf. also A. Galanté's survey of *Les Juifs de Constantinople sous Byzance;* and *supra,* Chap. XVI, n. 28. Anastasios Sinaites is to be distinguished from two of his predecessors by the same name, the second allegedly killed in a Jewish tumult in 609 during the Perso-Byzantine war. Cf. J. P. Migne's introduction to his edition in *PG,* LXXXIX, 11, contrasting with J. Gretser's statements *ibid.,* cols. 29 ff. Cf. also the literature listed by M. Jugie in his "Anastasio Sinaita, santo," *Enciclopedia cattolica,* I, 1157–58. A sample of his debates is offered by Anastasios himself in his *Adversus Judaeos disputatio* (in *PG,* LXXXIX, 1203–82), which seems at times to summarize statements of Jewish interlocutors; for instance, in the introductory explanation of the Hebrew etymology of the terms Hebrew, Israelite, and Jew. In this context Starr also quotes an oblique statement by Michael Syrus that about that time (*ca.* 660), "many Jews believed and became Christians" (No. 5). However, Starr's contention (p. 1), that had conversion been voluntary we might have expected the mention of the successful missionary, is far from cogent. If our twelfth-century chronicler correctly summarized his source, the latter might only have referred to some sporadic conversions in the crucial years after the conclusion of the treaty of 659 between Emperor Constans II (641–68) and Caliph Mu'awiya. Owing to the civil war between the latter and 'Ali, the Arabs suspended temporarily their attack on Byzantium and even acceded to a humiliating payment of tribute. Quite possibly some Asiatic Jews and non-Jews saw in this treaty a turning point in favor of the Christian Empire. Having been disappointed in their own messianic expectations concomitant with the rise of Islam, some individuals may indeed have embraced Christianity, just as others joined the Muslim ranks. On the canons of the Trullan Council, see *infra,* n. 28; and *supra,* Chap. XVIII, n. 24.

2. Agapius, *K. al-'Unvan,* p. 244 (*PO,* VIII, 504); reproduced by Starr, p. 91 No. 11. Cf. *supra,* Chap. XVII, n. 29; and, on the messiah Severus, *infra,* Chap. XXV, nn. 46, 58. The year of Leo's decree may be reconstructed from Theophanes (*Chronographia,* ed. by De Boor, I, 401; in the Latin version, II, 260), the earliest chronicler to record it. Theophanes claimed that it occurred in the year following the appearance of the false messiah. The chronological confusion, arising from that historian's two systems of dating, does not affect the years 714–26. Hence the fifth or sixth year of Leo III, whose accession to the throne on March 25, 717, is fairly certain, would lead us to the year 721–22 for the messianic movement, and 722–23 for the date of the suppression of Judaism. Cf. G. Ostrogorsky's *Geschichte des Byzantinischen Staates,* 2d ed., pp. 72 f. The obscurities in the reports of the various chroniclers and the absence of any reference to that decree in the more official legal records, however,

cast some doubts on the historicity of this radical outlawry of Judaism by the founder of the Isaurian dynasty. There is, moreover, no supporting evidence from Jewish sources. S. Krauss's attempt to connect the obscure passages in both the *Nistarot* (Mysteries) and the *Tefillah* (Prayer) of "R. Simon bar Yoḥai" (reprinted in Y. Ibn Shemuel's [Kaufman's] *Midreshe ge'ulah,* pp. 195 ff., 277 f.) is quite far-fetched. Cf. his *Studien zur byzantinisch-jüdischen Geschichte,* pp. 37 ff.; and the literature listed *supra,* Chap. XVII, n. 27. Evidently Leo's measures made no lasting impression on either the Byzantine jurists or Jewish writers.

3. Michael Syrus, *Chronique,* ed. by Chabot, II, 489 f. (French), 457 f. (Syriac); Theophanes, *Chronographia, supra* n. 2; Starr, *Jews in the Byzantine Empire,* p. 91 No. 11. On the confusion between Jews and Montanists, see *ibid.,* pp. 92 f. No. 12, and 180 No. 121 end.

4. Leo III and Constantine IV, *Eklogé,* XVII.52, ed. by J. Zépos and P. Zépos in *Jus graecoromanum,* II, 61; in E. H. Freshfield's English translation, entitled *A Manual of Roman Law, the Ecloga,* p. 113 (follows A. Monferratus' ed. of 1889); Second Council of Nicaea, canon 8, in Mansi's *Collectio,* XIII, 427 (Hefele's *Histoire,* Vol. III, Pt. 2, pp. 782 f.; abridged in the English translation, V, 381); Starr, pp. 94 ff. Nos. 15, 18. The much-debated date of the proclamation of the *Eklogé* is given here as of March, 726, in accordance with the authorities cited by Ostrogorsky in his *Geschichte,* p. 122 n. 5. Incidentally, the increasing moderation of Leo III's policies toward non-Christians is evidenced also by his permission to erect a mosque in Constantinople—an unprecedented liberality in the Byzantine-Muslim relations. These later developments further strengthen the doubts concerning the severity of Leo's original anti-Jewish enactments. One wonders whether the inscription in the Church of St. Sophia, prohibiting entry to the ungodly, had not been inspired by canon 8 of the Second Council of Nicaea. On the problem of its authenticity, see C. A. Mango's brief remarks in "The Byzantine Inscriptions of Constantinople: a Bibliographical Survey," *American Journal of Archaeology,* LV, 57 f. It is to be hoped that the projected *Recueil des inscriptions historiques de Byzance* under preparation by P. Lemerle and his associates (*Annales,* X, 544) will come to fruition, enabling students of Jewish history, too, to make better use of the epigraphic sources.

5. *Theophanes continuatus,* ed. by J. Genesius, in *PG,* CIX, 61; Starr, *Byzantine Empire,* p. 105, No. 28. On the growth of the legend concerning Michael's pro-Jewish sympathies until he was called "belonging to the Jews" by the twelfth-century chronicler Zonaras, and even supplied with a Jewish grandfather by Michael Syrus, see the data cited by Starr in "An Eastern Christian Sect: The Athinganoi," *HTR,* XXIX, 95 f. Cf. also *supra,* Chap. XVI, n. 1.

6. The Hebrew *Ḥazon Daniel* (Vision of Daniel) was first published by L. Ginzberg in his *Ginze Schechter,* I, 313–23, and republished, with additional comments by Y. Ibn Shemuel in his *Midreshe ge'ulah,* pp. 232 ff. The material was independently reviewed by S. Krauss in "Un Nouveau texte pour l'histoire judéo-byzantine," *REJ,* LXXXVII, 1–27 (also in German in *Byzantinisch-griechische Jahrbücher,* VII, 57–86). Cf. also the briefer comments by Starr, in his *Byzantine Empire,* pp. 6 f. Krauss's interpretation is effectively controverted by Ibn Shemuel. By largely following Ginzberg's explanations, and rather too freely blaming the copyist for the existing

confusion, Ibn Shemuel succeeded in introducing a semblance of order into the lucubrations of our apocalyptic author. But many vital questions still remain unanswered. Most remarkably, none of the modern authors made use of the significant comparative material available in the fairly extensive Christian apocalyptic literature concerning the reign of the much-hated Michael III and his successor. That literature includes also Greek and Slavonic versions of a Christian "Vision of Daniel," which had been known since 1898 in V. Istrin's Russian study of "The Revelation of Methodius of Patara and Apocryphal Visions of Daniel in Byzantine and Slavo-Russian Literatures," in *Chteniyya v obshchestvie istorii i drevnostei rossiiskikh* (1898), Part 1, pp. 133–210. A good corrective to these hostile presentations of Michael III and his reign, which obviously affected our Hebrew author, is offered by A. A. Vasiliev in "The Emperor Michael III in Apocryphal Literature," *Byzantina-Metabyzantina,* I, Part 1, pp. 237–48.

Much confusion has also arisen from the fact that the Hebrew apocalypse mentions as Basil's predecessor not Michael III, but rather one cryptically referred to by the number *ARB*. Various *gemaṭrias* have been suggested for that name—all extremely artificial. Cf. for instance, those mentioned by Ibn Shemuel, p. 249. Perhaps we need not take the word "number" too literally, and rather see in this symbol some allusion to Bardas, Michael's uncle and coregent, distinguished by the title of Caesar, who was the main administrator of the realm and restorer of icons—a restoration emphasized also in our "Vision." Even before Michael, Bardas was assassinated by the upstart, Basil. This conclusion, which the present writer first reached on purely logical grounds, is strongly confirmed by the way the Arab writers discuss the Byzantine raid on Egyptian Damietta. The contemporary Ya'qubi, followed by Ṭabari and Ibn al-Aṭir, uniformly reproduce the name of one of the three Byzantine commanders through the cryptic consonants *alif, m.r.d.n. q*. H. Grégoire and A. Vasiliev detected in this crytogram the three crucial letters, ARD, which the latter read WRD, a symbol for Bardas. Cf. Grégoire's "Etudes sur le neuvième siècle," *Byzantion,* VIII, 515 f.; and Vasiliev's *Byzance et les Arabes,* I, 214 n. 3, 276, 315, 354. It is possible that the Hebrew text, too, read ARD, rather than ARB, which would confirm Vasiliev's selection of these three consonants.

7. Aḥimaaz of Oria, *Sefer Yuḥasin* (Chronicle), ed. and trans. by M. Salzman, pp. 6 ff. (Hebrew), 69 ff. (English); ed. by B. Klar, pp. 20 ff., 57 ff., 71 ff., 125 ff., 162 ff., 174 ff. The alleged anachronism in the mention of the garden of Boukoleon, where Shefaṭiah's exorcism took place (Klar ed., pp. 163 f.), is eliminated by R. Guilland's plausible arguments that it had existed as early as the ninth century. Cf. his "Constantinople byzantin: Le Boucoléon, la Plage de Boucoléon," *Byzantinoslavica,* X, 16–27. On the debate concerning the relative costs of building the Temple of Solomon and the Church of St. Sophia, cf. *supra,* Chap. XVI, n. 8. Klar reprinted also an apocalyptic passage from the Vision of Daniel (cf. n. 6), the statement of Yehudah bar David, and a poem by Shefaṭiah, *Yisrael nosha'* (Israel Is Saved by God's Eternal Redemption) which, somewhat obliquely, refers to the redemption from Basil's persecution. The latter poem is still widely recited during Jewish services on the Day of Atonement. Our legend concerning the olive press was further elaborated by a miracle tale reported in connection with Solomon the Babylonian, the real author of that *seliḥah,* whose picturesque language seems to have stirred the imagination of story tellers. According to that legend, an unnamed elder was to suffer martyrdom through the oil press when the latter got out of hand and destroyed everything

around it. As a result the decree was revoked. Cf. the sources cited by Klar, p. 128. Cf. also other important data furnished in Starr, *Byzantine Empire,* pp. 127 ff. Nos. 61–72.

8. Leo VI's *Novella* 55, in P. Noailles and A. Dain, eds., *Les Novelles de Léon VI le Sage,* pp. 208 ff. (in S. P. Scott's English translation, *The Civil Law,* XVII, 255); the laws of the *Basilika,* ed. by G. E. Heimbach *et al.,* excerpted, with comments, in Starr, *Jews in the Byzantine Empire,* pp. 144 f. No. 83. Cf. also Leo's *Novellae* 65 and 66, and G. Ferrari delle Spade's comments thereon in his *Scritti giuridici,* I, 24. The contrast between the Jewish sources and the *Basilika* as opposed to the clear text of *Novella* 55 likewise awaits further elucidation.

9. Gregorios Asbestas' "Treatise" ed. with a Flemish trans. by E. de Stoop in his "Antisemitism in Byzantium under Basil the Macedonian" (Flemish), in *Verslagen en Mededeelingen* of the Flemish Academy, 1913, pp. 449–511; Starr, *Jews in the Byzantine Empire,* pp. 137 f., No. 74. The general Church attitude toward enforced conversion of Jews was discussed *supra,* Vol. II, pp. 180, 398 n. 12; and Chap. XVI, n. 28. It will be more fully analyzed in the context of the later medieval debates during the periods of highest tension.

10. Zépos and Zépos, *Jus graecoromanum,* I, 205 ff.; M. Landau, *Beiträge zum Chazarenproblem,* pp. 36 f. Cf. also S. Runciman's detailed study of *The Emperor Romanus Lecapenus and his Reign,* esp. pp. 76 f. (the emperor's anti-Jewish measures are nowhere mentioned, however); and, on the other hand, A. P. Kazhdan's pointed denial of Romanos and his successors' friendliness to the peasants in "The Peasant Situation in Tenth-Century Byzantium and the Agrarian Policy of the Emperors of the Macedonian Dynasty" (Russian), *Vizantiskii Vremennik,* n.s. V, 73–98.

11. The summary of the canons of Erfurt and the letter of Peter II Candianus *et al.* to Emperor Henry I and others, ed. by L. Weiland in *MGH,* Legum sectio IV, Vol. I, pp. 4 f., 7; Mas'udi, *K. Muruj adh-dhahab* (Prairies d'or), ed. by Barbier de Meynard *et al.,* II, 8 f.; anonymous letter from Khazaria, ed. by Schechter in *JQR,* III, 208 (Hebrew), 217 (English), and reedited by P. Kokovtsov with a Russian translation in his *Evreisko-khazarskaya perepiska v X veke* (Jewish-Khazar Correspondence in the Tenth Century), pp. 35 (Hebrew), 117 f. (Russian); all summarized in Starr, *Byzantine Empire,* pp. 151 f., Nos. 90–92. On the authenticity of that anonymous letter, see *infra,* nn. 30, 34. In his *Regesten zur Geschichte der Juden,* pp. 53 f., Nos. 123–24, J. Aronius has made a good case for considering the Doge's letter independent of the one read at the Council of Erfurt. True, Peter II assumed office at the beginning of 932 (his title is mentioned already on January 14 in a treaty reprinted by G. L. Fr. Tafel and G. M. Thomas in their *Urkunden zur älteren Handels- und Staatsgeschichte der Republik Venedig,* I, 5 ff., No. X), and the Council of Erfurt listened to the reading of the letter some five months later. The tenor of that epistle, however, indicates that it was the copy of a transcript of the original letter sent out directly from Jerusalem to Constantinople which had reached Rome. Despite the strong similarity of this international action to suppress Judaism in all Christian lands with the move initiated by Heraclius almost exactly three centuries earlier, we need not doubt its essential historicity.

The astonishing fact that the Christian minority in Jerusalem should have enjoyed so much power is borne out by Muqaddasi's complaint of the great power of Christians and Jews in the Holy City. We have further confirmation in the Karaite Salmon ben Yeruḥim's description of the sufferings of the Jewish community there. "The uncircumcised [Christians]," he stated, "have now reached such a position of power that they beat us, and try to expel us from Jerusalem and to separate us from it. I hope that the God of Israel will not fulfill their wish." Cf. his Commentary on Ps. 30:10 in Mann, *Texts and Studies,* II, 18 f. Despite chronological difficulties, it is hard to envisage this passage as having been written when Muslim rule was firmly established in Palestine, even in the years preceding the Faṭimid conquest. The most likely date still is 972–74, during John I Tsimiskes' successful Syrian campaign, which had led to a temporary Byzantine occupation of Tiberias, Nazareth, and Acco, though not of "all of Phoenicia, Palestine and Syria" as the emperor himself boasted in a letter to Armenia. Cf. Ostrogorsky's *Geschichte,* p. 238; and M. Canard's explanation of the chronological sequence in "La Date des expéditions mésopotamiennes de Jean Tzimiscès," *Annuaire,* X, 99–108. Even if we were certain that Salmon composed his commentary about 955 and that he died before 970, as Poznanski and Mann respectively assumed, there would still remain the possibility that this passage was sharpened by a disciple or copyist writing at a time when the Byzantine hosts were knocking at the gates of the Holy City. Cf. *infra,* Chap. XXIX, n. 73; and *supra,* Chap. XVII, n. 34. Needless to say that in the early 930's probably only a few Jerusalem Jews were converted. The ensuing bitterness helps us explain the active Jewish participation in the attack on the Church of the Holy Sepulchre in 966, which, as we recall, Yaḥya ibn Sa'id was so harshly to condemn. Cf. also the meritorious, if somewhat too imaginative, study by V. Mošin, "Les Khazars et les Byzantins d'après l'Anonyme de Cambridge," *Byzantion,* VI, 309–25, and infra, n. 34.

12. "Vision of Daniel," ed. by Ginzberg in *Ginze Schechter,* I, 320; Krauss's comments thereon in *REJ,* LXXXVII, 14 ff.; those by Starr in *Byzantine Empire,* pp. 7 f., 152 ff., Nos. 93, 95; and by Ibn Shemuel in *Midreshe ge'ulah,* pp. 242 f., 250 f.; the letter from Khazaria, ed. by Schechter in *JQR,* III, 181 ff.; ed. by Kokovtsov, pp. 33 ff. (Hebrew), 113 ff. (Russian). Perhaps the description of Romanos' persecution as "merciful" merely reflected the apocalyptic author's belief in the legends which had gradually been forming about the earlier events, like that concerning the use of oil presses. Being himself closer to the period of the 930's, the visionary knew that no tortures had been applied to the Jews then, and hence contrasted favorably Romanos' procedures with those employed in the previous persecutions. The conclusion of the apocalypse is extremely obscure. Krauss is undoubtedly right in connecting the prediction of the fall of Byzantium into the hands of Great Tyre, that is Western Rome, with the Latin conquest of Constantinople of 1204. We need not, however, for this reason, date the whole apocalypse in the thirteenth century. With the lack of restraint characteristic of that type of literature, any later copyist might have altered the original tenth-century conclusion by bringing it up to date three centuries later. Perhaps because he failed to substitute an entirely new ending, but modified the existing text to suit his purposes, he created that utter confusion which has so baffled all commentators.

Understandably, general Jewish opinion loathed the memory of these "merciful" proceedings. In the Khazar correspondence, discussed below in this chapter, Romanos' name is as a rule provided with the characteristic epithet *ha-rasha'* (the evil-doer). A Byzantine-Hebrew compiler of a *Seder Malkhe Romi* (List of Roman emperors) from Julius Caesar to Nicephorus II (963–69), evidently writing in 967, departed from his usually dry enumeration of names and dates to emphasize that half a century earlier Romanos had "robbed the empire" from Constantine Porphyrogenitus. Cf. the text, ed. by Neubauer in *MCJ,* I, 186; Krauss's *Studien,* pp. 142 f.; and *infra,* Chap. XXVIII.

13. Constantine VII, *Vita Basilii,* xcv (*Theophanes continuatus,* in *PG,* CIX, 357). On the correspondence between Ḥisdai ibn Shapruṭ and the imperial couple of Byzantium, cf. *supra,* Chap. XVIII, n. 40; and *infra,* n. 41.

14. Cf. the sources cited by Starr, *Byzantine Empire,* pp. 167 f. No. 115; 173 ff. Nos. 121, 126–27; 190 No. 131; 246; esp. the text of abjuration published by V. N. Beneshevich in his "On the History of the Jews in Byzantium, 6th–10th Centuries" (Russian), *Evereiskaya Mysl,* II, pp. 308 ff.; Benjamin of Tudela, *Massa'ot,* ed. by Adler, pp. 16 (Hebrew), 14 (English). Cf. *supra,* Chap. XVI, n. 28; *infra,* n. 29; and Chaps. XXXV–XXXVI. The events which transpired during the arrival of the successive groups of Crusaders will be treated *infra,* Chapter XXI. To understand Nicon's departure from the prevailing policies of the Church, we must bear in mind that he came to Sparta fresh from his missionary exploits in Crete, where he had succeeded in converting to Christianity a large number of inhabitants whose ancestors had adopted Islam in the intervening centuries of Muslim rule. Cf. his (Nikon Metanoites) *Bios, Politeia, Eikonographia* (Life, Policies, and Iconography), ed. by M. E. Galanopoulos, pp. 72 ff., 96 f.; and the introduction thereto, pp. 22 f. (the appended plates show Nicon's persistent influence on the population of Sparta until today); its long-known Latin translation by Jacob Sirmondus, entitled *Vita Sancti Niconis Metanoitae monachi* in *Veterum Scriptorum et monumentorum historicorum amplissima collectio,* ed. by E. Martène and U. Durand, 2d ed., VI, 852 ff., 859 f. Nicon's admiring biographer himself admitted that the saint had encountered considerable resistance among the local leaders.

15. Leo III and Constantine VIII, *Eklogé,* XVII.52, in Zépos and Zépos, *Jus graecoromanum,* II, 61; the anonymous Appendix thereto in A. G. Monferratus' ed. of the *Ecloga Leonis,* pp. 64 ff., 72 f. (both in E. H. Freshfield's English trans. in his *Manual of Roman Law,* pp. 113, 130 ff., 137 ff.); Basil I's *Procheiros,* XXXIX.31–32, in *Jus graecoromanum,* II, 219; his and Leo VI's *Epanagogé,* IX.13 and XL.33–34, *ibid.,* pp. 255, 362; the latter's *Basilicorum libri LX,* ed. by G. E. Heimbach *et al.,* esp. I, 1. All these passages are summarized and annotated by Starr in *Byzantine Empire,* pp. 94 f. No. 15, 97 f. No. 19, 126 f. No. 60, 138 ff. No. 75, 144 f. No. 83 (enumerating the laws contained in the *Basilika,* and comparing them with those included in the Code of Justinian). The respective dates of these codes are given here as a rule in accordance with the authorities cited in Ostrogorsky's *Geschichte,* pp. 122 n. 5, 128 f., 175, 193 ff.; and in B. Sinogowitz's survey of "Die byzantinische Rechtsgeschichte im Spiegel der Neuerscheinungen, 1940–1952," *Saeculum,* IV, 313–33. More recently J. Scharf has suggested the less precise date of 879–86 for the *Epanagogé.* Cf. his "Photios und die Epanagogé," *BZ,* XLIX, 387 f. On Photius see also *infra,* n. 47. On Anna Comnena, cf. G. Buckler's biographical "study," pp. 306 n. 1, 331.

16. According to R. S. Lopez, Leo III not only summarized the existing customary laws, but also had at his disposal an earlier legal compilation by Heraclius. If so,

the new sanctions were a Byzantine invention, and rather exemplified the reverse influence of Byzantine law on both the Arab and the medieval Teuton laws in this area as well. Cf. Lopez's pertinent observations in his article on "Byzantine Law in the Seventh Century," *Byzantion,* XVI, 445 ff., despite the objections raised by Sinogowitz in *Saeculum,* IV, 321.

17. Cf. H. F. Schmid's careful analysis of *Die Nomokanonübersetzung des Methodius.* Even the *Epanagogé,* which apparently was never fully translated into Slavonic, became known to the Balkan as well as the northern Slavs through later summaries. The most important Byzantine law code, the *Basilika,* which almost completely superseded the earlier legislation, is unfortunately not preserved in its entirety. However, much of its content can be restored from later scholia. Cf. E. Seidl's observations on "Die Basilikenscholien im Tripukeitos," *BZ,* XLIV, 534–40. This summary of the *Basilika* was prepared in the twelfth century by a Judge Patzes. In some respects it represents, therefore, the last word on the Jewish status before the Latin conquest of 1204. Cf. the successive editions of Books I–XLVI by C. Farrini *et al.* in *Studi e testi,* Vols. XXV, LI, CVII, CLXXIX. Further light is thrown on certain points by the *Scholia* to the *Basilika* itself now in the course of publication by H. J. Scheltema and D. Holwerda (Vols. I and II give the scholia to Books I–XIV). This publication has been followed by a new critical edition of that code, of which Vol. I, ed. by Scheltema and N. Van der Wal, contains books I–VIII.

18. Appendix to the *Eklogé,* IV.6; the letter of 1166 by a Pisan resident of Constantinople, Ugone Ettoriano, ed. by G. Müller in his *Documenti sulle relazioni delle città toscane coll' Oriente cristiano e coi Turchi,* pp. 11 ff. In his introduction and excursus on Astafortis (pp. 18 f., 235 f.), Starr contends that this early Hungarian Jew had turned Christian before this particular incident. However, the Pisan writer nowhere indicates Astafortis' conversion (the term apostate, if it refers to Astafortis, certainly did not bear the connotation of conversion *to* Christianity), but merely calls him "this circumcised fellow." In any case, it is remarkable that a Hungarian Jew could so easily join the invading Byzantine army and soon attain a powerful position in the imperial capital, then under the reign of the fairly tolerant Manuel I. For this reason one need not rule out the possibility, as does Starr (*Byzantine Empire,* pp. 18, 223 f.), that the emperor employed also a Jewish soothsayer, Aaron Isaakios. Of course, we have no evidence for the latter's Jewishness other than his name. But much of our knowledge of Jewish history in other areas and periods, too, depends on records containing Jewish-sounding names. Cf. *supra,* Vol. I, p. 350 n. 25. Even if Astafortis and Aaron were professing Jews, however, they would not prove any extensive employment of Jews in public service, for a semiprivate taxgatherer and a soothsayer could hardly be considered members of an official bureaucracy.

19. Cf. *Basilika,* I.1.44, 47 (Starr, *Byzantine Empire,* pp. 144 f.); J. B. Bury, *History of the Later Roman Empire,* I, 382. Such protective laws were much needed in view of the widespread popular antagonisms so clearly alluded to by Benjamin. Although refraining from attacks on Jews and their synagogues, the populace of Constantinople and other Byzantine cities certainly required the restraining influence of the law.

20. *Basilika,* I.1.38, 46, 53, 57, etc. (Starr, *Byzantine Empire,* pp. 144 f.). All these laws were essentially renewals of older regulations, dictated by the exigencies of

legal tradition even more than by any contemporary needs. Yet it appears that at least some of them were enforced also in later periods. Cf. *supra,* Vol. II, pp. 180 ff., 259, 416 n. 35; and Chap. XVI, n. 11.

21. Cf. A. Scheiber's ed. of "A New Fragment of the 'Life of Obadiah the Norman Proselyte'" (Hebrew), *KS,* XXX, 93–98; and in the English translation (by J. L. Teicher) in "The Origins of Obadyah, the Norman Proselyte," *JJS,* V, 32–37. This translation is somewhat revised in Scheiber's "Fragment from the Chronicle of 'Obadyah, the Norman Proselyte: From the Kaufmann Geniza," *Acta Orientalia* (Budapest), IV, 280 f., followed by facsimiles of the Hebrew text. The conversion of an eleventh-century Italian archbishop to Judaism is highly questionable. It certainly would have left some imprint on the contemporary Christian or Jewish sources, as did the conversion of lesser clerics like Bodo and Vecelin. See *infra,* Chap. XX, nn. 69, 85. Moreover, the only recorded Bishop Andreas in Bari of that time was, as Scheiber himself recognized, one who officiated in the years 1062–78 and died there as a professing Christian. Johannes-Obadiah, likewise a priest, whose own conversion occurred in 1102, must have been impressed by a much-garbled tale concerning an earlier event. Cf. Mann, "Obadya, prosélyte normand converti au judaisme," *REJ,* LXXXIX, 245–59. It is likely that in the intervening years popular imagination magnified the rank of the first cleric who had embraced Judaism. Both proselytes ultimately secured peace only by finding refuge in the Muslim Near East. Cf. also S. D. Goitein's "Obadya, a Norman Proselyte," *JJS,* IV, 74–84; *supra,* Chap. XVIII, nn. 22, 56; and *infra,* Chap. XXV, n. 68. Incidentally, although a native of Oppido in southern Italy, Obadiah could describe himself in the colophon of a prayer book as a Norman (*ha-Normandus*), for he doubtless was of Norman ancestry. The Normans had occupied Bari in 1071. Obadiah's brother Roger, a warrior, typified the Norman conquerors just as he himself represented the class of studious Norman priests. Their father may well have been among the original Norman invaders of southern Italy.

22. *Basilika,* I.1.39–41, 43, 45, 47 (Starr, *loc. cit.*). It is this type of legislation, rather than the antagonistic *Novella* 55, which impressed Jewish contemporaries. We may therefore understand Aḥimaaz's assertion that Leo VI had annulled his father's anti-Jewish decree and even allowed Jewish converts to return to their former faith—a daring defiance indeed of the Church's stringent rules against any form of relapse after the indelible sacrament of baptism. Cf. *supra,* n. 7; and *infra,* n. 28.

23. Cf. the sources in Juster's *Empire romain,* II, 287 f.; Ibn Khurdadhbah's *K. al-Masalik w'al-mamalik* (Book of Routes and Kingdoms), ed. with a French trans. by M. J. de Goeje (in *Bibliotheca geographorum arabicorum,* Vol. VI), pp. 111 (Arabic), 83 (French); Constantin IX's privilege of 1049 for the monastery Nea Moné, in Zépos and Zépos, *Jus graecoromanum,* I, 633 f.; its renewal, in 1078, by Nicephoros III, *ibid.,* pp. 643 f.; A. Neubauer's "Egyptian Fragments, II," *JQR,* [o.s.] IX, 26 ff., reproduced by J. Mann in "The Messianic Movements during the First Crusades" (Hebrew), *Hatekufah,* XXIII, 253 ff.; Starr, *Byzantine Empire,* pp. 111 No. 44, 197 f. No. 143, 202 f. No. 151, 205 No. 153. On the latter source see also D. Kaufmann's German translation and comments in "Ein Brief aus dem byzantinischen Reiche über eine messianische Bewegung der Judenheit und der zehn Stämme aus dem

Jahre 1096," *BZ*, VII, 83–90; and in "Eine unbekannte messianische Bewegung unter den Juden vornehmlich Deutschlands und des byzantinischen Reiches ums Jahr 1096," reprinted in his *Gesammelte Schriften*, II, 190–202; and *infra*, Chap. XXV, n. 64. On the meaning of the term *majus* in Ibn Khurdadhbah, cf. R. Dozy's *Recherches*, II, 275 ff., Appendix xxxiv, p. lxxxii; E. Lévi-Provençal's remarks in *Byzantion*, XII, 14 ff.; and *infra*, n. 25. The problem of a special Jewish tax in Byzantium, vividly discussed in the 1930's, still is far from a definitive solution. Cf. esp. M. A. Andreades's studies, "Les Juifs et le Fisc dans l'Empire byzantin," *Mélanges Charles Diehl*, I, 7–29 (largely denying it), and "The Jews in the Byzantine Empire," *Economic History*, III, 1–23 (grudgingly admitting it); F. Dölger's *Beiträge zur byzantinischen Finanzverwaltung, besonders des 10. und 11. Jahrhunderts*, p. 50; and "Die Frage der Judensteuer in Byzanz," *VSW*, XXVI, 1–24 (arguing in favor of the existence of a moderate "entehrender Rekognitionszins"); Starr, pp. 11 ff.; and *infra*, n. 29. After reviewing anew the extant sources for the period before 1204, Starr concluded that "the Jew's tax burden during these centuries was no greater than the Christian's." This may be an overstatement; it was modified by Starr himself in his *Romania*, pp. 111 f. But there is little doubt that whatever special taxes Jews paid sporadically under one or another regime did not lay heavily upon them. Unlike their ancestors under the declining ancient Roman Empire, they rarely voiced grievances on this score. Similarly, the failure of all new law codes, other than the *Nomocanon*, to repeat the ancient provisions, indicates that Jewish taxes had made little impression on the minds of legislators, too. Cf. also H. Grégoire's review of Starr's *Jews in the Byzantine Empire*, in *Renaissance*, II–III, 481.

24. Benjamin, *Massa'ot*, pp. 15 (Hebrew), 13 (English). Cf. in general Dölger's *Beiträge*, pp. 48 ff., 62; A. M. Andréadès's brief survey of "Public Finances: Currency, Public Expenditure, Budget, Public Revenue" in Baynes and Moss, *Byzantium*, pp. 71–85; and J. Danstrup's "Indirect Taxation at Byzantium," *Classica et medievalia*, VIII, 139–67. The high customs duties applied not only to imports, but also to exports, and were supplemented by taxes on retail sales, transit dues, and other imposts. Cf. also Andréadès's estimates of *Le Montant du budget de l'empire byzantin*.

25. Cf. A. A. Vasiliev's *Byzance et les Arabes*, I, 235 ff.; Ibn Khurdadhbah, cited *supra*, n. 23. The mention of Zoroastrians (if these are meant) alongside Jews as taxpayers would otherwise be incomprehensible. We know of some Muslims in Constantinople; they were even allowed to maintain a mosque there from the days of Leo III. But we know nothing of a Zoroastrian settlement in European Byzantium, whereas the presence of some Persians along the fluctuating frontiers between the two empires in Asia Minor and Armenia is highly probable. Cf., e.g., J. Gagé's data on "Le Perses d'Antioche et les courses de hippodrome au milieu du IIIe siècle," *Bulletin de la Faculté des Lettres de Strasbourg*, XXXI, 301–24, which refers, however, only to cases in ancient times. Conceivably, Ibn Khurdadhbah merely reproduced here an antiquarian reminiscence from the days before the Muslim conquest when Jews and Magi alone were subjected to certain taxes of the kind of the Jewish *aurum coronarium*. He may have heard about this system from his informant on the conditions in the Byzantine provinces, Muslim al-Kharami, who had spent some time there before his release in the prisoners' exchange of 845–46. Cf. De Goeje's ed. of Ibn Khurdadhbah's "Book of Routes," pp. 105 (Arabic), 77 (French). The alternative sug-

gestion that he had in mind Normans (see *supra,* n. 23) is also not devoid of difficulties, since we have no record of any permanent settlement of pagan Normans in territories under Byzantine control.

26. Gregorios Asbestas in his aforementioned "Treatise," ed. by Stoop; Starr, *Byzantine Empire,* pp. 105 No. 28, 137 No. 74. See *supra,* nn. 9, 12. That there may have been some intrinsic connection between Leo III's initiative in outlawing icons, and similar measures taken several years before by Yazid II (720–24) with respect to the Caliphate's Christian churches, has long been recognized. Contemporaries called Leo "Saracen-minded." However, the persecution of images in the Caliphate was short-lived. As Vasiliev pointed out, it was John of Damascus, an officeholder under the Caliphate, who wrote the most effective polemical treatises *Adversus Iconoclastas.* Cf. his *Opera* in *PG,* XCVI, 1347–62; and Vasiliev's brief sketch of the relations between "Byzantium and Islam" in Baynes and Moss, *Byzantium,* p. 316. But there is no evidence for any direct Jewish involvement in this internal Christian controversy. That Michael II should have freed all Jews from taxation appears to be a pure invention of opponents, mouthed a century later by a chronicler writing under the supervision of the inconodulic emperor, Constantine VIII.

27. Benjamin, *Massa'ot, supra,* n. 24; and *infra,* Chap. XXII, nn. 18, 23. No full-fledged riots were recorded in any of the sources after Heraclius used by Starr. Whatever disturbances occurred doubtless were not only sporadic, but resulted in little bloodshed.

28. Cf. the texts published by V. N. Beneshevich in *Evereiskaya Mysl,* II, 308 ff.; Zépos and Zépos, *Jus graecoromanum,* I, 373 ff.; Manuel Comnenus, *Novellae Constitutiones* in *PG,* CXXXIII, 717; Starr, *Byzantine Empire,* pp. 163 f. No. 109, 173 ff. No. 121. Manuel's constitution reproduced here (*PG,* cols. 715 ff.) a lengthy statement on the Jewish oath, reputedly submitted by a Jewish convert to Christianity. The Trullan prohibitions spread also to the countries of Islam, although they had little effect there. Cf. *supra,* Chap. XVIII, n. 14. The formulas of abjuration and especially of the oath *more judaico,* on the other hand, penetrated mainly Western Christendom, where all these discriminatory provisions were greatly elaborated. They will, therefore, be more fully analyzed in connection with the general evolution of Judeo-Christian social relations in the later Middle Ages. On the *Basilika's* generally discriminatory provisions regarding the testimony of Jews and heretics in Byzantine courts, cf. A. Berger's recent "Studi sui Basilici," *IVRA Rivista internazionale di diritto romano i antico,* VI, 104–19.

29. Hai Gaon's resp. in *Teshubot ha-geonim,* ed. by Harkavy, pp. 105 f. No. 225; *infra,* Chap. XXVI, n. 29; Benjamin, *Massa'ot,* pp. 16 (Hebrew), 14 ff. (English); Petaḥiah's *Sibbub,* ed. by Grünhut, pp. 36 (Hebrew), 49 (German), in Benisch's English trans., pp. 66 f.; Starr, pp. 228 ff. No. 182, 238 No. 186. M. A. Andréadès found that the figures of Jewish population recorded in Benjamin's travelogue totaled 8,603. He realized that our traveler had not visited all Jewish communities in the Empire, but took it for granted that Benjamin recorded everywhere the number of souls, rather than families. Somewhat arbitrarily he assumed therefore that the total figure would approximate 15,000. Having reached elsewhere the conclusion that the imperial population during that period amounted to some 15,000,000, he estimated a Jewish ratio

of only 1 per thousand. Cf. his "Sur Benjamin de Tudèle," *BZ,* XXX, 458–61; "La Population de l'Empire byzantin," *Bulletin de l'Institut Archéologique Bulgare,* IX, 117–26 (more cautious); and his observations in *Mélanges Diehl,* I, 24 f., and in *Economic History,* III, 4 f. However, this low estimate of the Jewish population runs counter to all other known facts. It certainly could not be squared with such an assertion as Petaḥiah's here quoted, or with Aḥimaaz' aforementioned figure of one thousand communities affected by Basil I's hostile decree. While we need not take either assertion at its face value, both seem to indicate the presence of Jews in many more communities than happen to be recorded in our chance sources. Nor is it at all likely that Benjamin listed total population figures. Relying exclusively on information supplied him by local leaders, he must have referred to estimates based upon communal roles of taxpayers. Cf. *supra,* Chap. XVII, n. 48. Precisely because the imperial Treasury did not collect at that time any special Jewish taxes—Benjamin's silence on this score is indeed a major argument for denying such special Jewish taxation—the Jewish communities lacked the usual incentive of keeping an exact record of contributors. Although we know practically nothing about the communal revenues in Byzantium, it would seem that the communal treasuries, too, relied principally on some indirect sources. Hence only a minority of direct taxpayers would have been entered in the rolls. For this reason Benjamin's figures must be multiplied by five, the usual average for families at that time, and further increased by those relating to unrecorded members in the larger communities, and possibly many more living scattered in innumerable small settlements. We may perhaps assume, therefore, that the Empire under the Comneni, and very likely also in earlier periods, embraced as many as 100,000 Jews, or more than one half percent of the total population.

30. St. Jerome's *In Zech.* 10:11 (*PL,* XXV, 1568 f.). For the last quarter century all Hebrew documents, including the important Cambridge fragment (first published by S. Schechter in "An Unknown Khazar Document," *JQR,* III, 181–219), have been available in a fine critical edition (with some noteworthy variants and a Russian translation) by P. K. Kokovtsov in his *Evreisko-khazarskaya perepiska v X viekie* (Jewish-Khazar Correspondence in the Tenth Century). They were soon thereafter submitted to renewed careful scrutiny by S. M. Dubnow and others. Cf., in particular, Dubnow's "Latest Conclusions in the Khazar Question," *Poznanski Mem. Vol.,* Hebrew section, pp. 1–4. More recently M. Landau and A. N. Poliak have again carefully reviewed the available material, both Jewish and non-Jewish. Cf. M. Landau's *Beiträge zum Chazarenproblem;* his "Present State of the Khazar Problem" (Hebrew), *Zion,* VIII, 94–106; Poliak's "Adoption of Judaism by the Khazars" (Hebrew), *ibid.,* VI, 106–12, 160–80; and particularly his comprehensive Hebrew work, *Khazariyyah* (Khazaria: The History of a Jewish Kingdom in Europe), 3d ed. A second volume is yet to appear. In addition to using the available literary sources, Poliak made a valiant effort to utilize the epigraphic and archaeological data assembled by Firkovitch and analyzed by Chwolson and others, despite the wholly legitimate aspersions cast upon Firkovitch's reliability by Harkavy, Strack, and other critics. Much is to be gained by the further pursuit of these lines of investigation. Poliak has also advanced a number of suggestive, though not always conclusive, hypotheses. Cf., for instance, the serious reservations made by P. Friedman in his Yiddish review in *YB,* XXXVI, 294–300; by M. Landau in his Hebrew review in *KS,* XXI, 19–24; and the debate between A. Z. Aeshcoly and Poliak in their Hebrew essays in *Moznayim,*

XVIII, 298–304, 375–83; XIX, 288–91, 348–52 (here also a reply to Landau). The latest comprehensive work, *The History of the Jewish Khazars* by D. M. Dunlop, has subjected the scattered evidence to renewed examination and includes many excerpts, especially from Arabic sources in English translation, but it has by no means superseded these older writings. Of some interest is also H. Rosenkranz's recent Vienna dissertation, "Das Chazarenproblem im Lichte der historischen Entwicklung des Judaismus and Chazaro-Judaismus" (typescript). Cf. also A. N. Poliak's somewhat overdrawn critique of Dunlop's interpretation in "The Khazars and Arab Propaganda" (Hebrew), *Molad,* XIII, 377–80; H. Inalcik's pertinent data from Turkish sources in his review of Dunlop's volume in *MW,* XLV, 287–89; and *infra,* n. 52.

In view of the complexity of these problems the following monographs, old and new, are worthy of special consideration: in "Les Khazares et les Byzantins d'après l'Anonyme de Cambridge," *Byzantion,* VI, 309–25, V. Mošin has added new arguments in favor of the hypothesis that the Khazar conversion was gradual and proceeded from the royal house to the upper classes without ever including the bulk of the people. On the other hand, in "Les Khazars dans la Passion de St. Abo de Tiflis," *Analecta Bollandiana,* LII, 21–56, P. Peeters concluded from the failure of this hagiographic work, written under Harun ar-Rashid, and of other Christian sources to mention Judaism in Khazaria, that the story told by King Joseph in his letter to Ḥisdai was wholly unhistorical. But this is a much too far-reaching conclusion to be made from an *argumentum a silentio.* With the mention of the monotheistic "King of the North," especially, Peeters's arguments against Mošin (p. 55 n. 2) appear untenable. Similarly far-fetched was H. Grégoire's even more radical, though ingenious, effort to deny the historicity of the entire conversion story in "Le 'Glozel' khazare," *Byzantion,* XII, 225–66, 739–40, or his suggestion that the king of Gebalim mentioned in Ḥisdai's letter as his main channel of correspondence with King Joseph need not have been a Slavonic ruler, since *gavlim* included all Westerners. Cf. Grégoire's essay in *Mélanges Dussaud,* II, 489–93; those cited *infra,* n. 39; and S. Assaf's very plausible criticisms of the "Glozel" theory in "Rabbi Yehudah Barceloni's Statements concerning the Khazars" (Hebrew), reprinted in his *Meqorot u-meḥqarim,* pp. 91–95. That thesis has been convincingly refuted also by Landau and Poliak, although it is still upheld, in part, by A. Zajaczkowski in his *Ze studiów nad zagadnieniem chazarskim* (Etudes sur le problème des Khazars; with a French summary), pp. 6 ff. The latter's searching philological inquiry has uncovered many significant links between the Khazar and Turkish languages and the dialect spoken by the Polish Karaites. Cf. also O. Pritsak's detailed review of these "Studies" in *Der Islam,* XXIX, 96–103, referring to an unpublished, two-volume Ukrainian work on the history of the Khazars to the tenth century, completed in 1941 by A. Krymskii; and T. Lewicki's recent Polish essay "On the Studies concerning the So-Called Khazar Correspondence," in the *Bulletin* of the Żydowski Instytut Historyczny (Jewish Historical Institute in Warsaw), XI–XII, 3–16. From the anthropological angle the older work, *Die Chazaren. Historische Studie* by H. von Kutschera, has largely been superseded. But, like Kutschera, A. Baschmakoff found the authenticity of King Joseph's epistle fully borne out by his investigations of the Khazars' racial origin and the geographic position of their capitals. Cf. "Une Solution nouvelle du problème des Khazares," *Mercure de France,* CCXXIX, 39–73; and "Neues über die Chazaren," *Litterae Orientales,* LVIII, 4–6. Cf. also W. W. Ginzburg's more recent Russian study of "The Anthropological Materials on the Origin of the Khazar Khaganate" in

Sbornik of the Moscow Museum for Anthropology and Ethnography, XIII, 309–416. The testimony of the main Muslim eye-witness, Ibn Fadhlan whose observations, as Muqtadir's ambassador in the Volga Bulgarian capital in 921–22, influenced all subsequent narratives, was reedited twice in 1939: by I. Y. Krachkovskii, *et al.* (with a Russian trans. by A. P. Kovalevskii), and by A. Zeki Validi Togan (*Ibn Fadlans Reisebericht,* with a German trans.). Cf. also D. M. Dunlop's review of Zeki Validi's ed. in *Die Welt des Orients,* IV, 307–12; R. N. Frye and R. P. Blake, "Notes on the Risala of Ibn-Faḍlan," *Byzantina-Metabyzantina,* I, Part 2, pp. 7–37; and K. Czegledy's "Zur Menschheder Handschrift von Ibn Faḍlans Reisebericht," *Acta Orientalia* (Budapest) I, 17–60. Of considerable value also are J. N. Simchowitsch's dissertation, *Studien zu den Berichten arabischer Historiker über die Chazaren,* available only in typescript, but fully summarized in the *Jahrbuch der Dissertationen . . . Berlin,* 1919–20, pp. 248–52, and in the review by M. Palló in *Ungarische Jahrbücher,* II, 157–60, which cites several Hungarian writings on this subject; and A. N. Poliak's succinct review of "The Jewish-Khazar Kingdom in the Mediaeval Geographical Science" in the *Acts* of the Seventh International Congress for the History of Science, IV, 488–92. A new Muslim source, the *Akam al-Marjan* by the eleventh-century Spanish geographer Isḥaq ibn Ḥusain, has been made available by A. Codazzi's partial edition from an Ambrosiana manuscript, with an Italian translation, in the *Rendiconti* of the R. Accademia dei Lincei, 6th ser., V, 373–463; and in the supplementary notes thereon by V. Minorsky and R. N. Frye in *BSOAS,* IX, 141–50, and *JNES,* VIII, 90–94, respectively. Cf. also Minorsky's translation of a tenth-century Persian geographic work, *Ḥudud al-'Alam* (The Regions of the World), pp. 450 ff.; with his "Addenda" thereto in *BSOAS,* XVII, 250–70; J. Brutzkus's theory of "The Khazar Origin of Ancient Kiev," *Slavonic and East European Review,* XXII, 108–24; and other studies (before 1938) listed in the comprehensive bibliography compiled by A. Yarmolinsky *et al.* on "The Khazars," *Bulletin* of the New York Public Library, XLII, 695–710 (an enlarged reprint appeared in 1939). Another somewhat more up-to-date bibliography, independently prepared by A. Zajaczkowski in 1944, was burned by the Nazis. It was not fully replaced by the brief survey in the first chapter of his *Ze studiów.* A complete collection of Arabic and other non-Hebrew sources, to parallel that by Kokovtsov, though often discussed and even planned, has not yet materialized.

31. Saadiah's responsum in *Teshubot ha-geonim* (Geonic Responsa), ed. by A. E. Harkavy, p. 278 No. 557, 8; Muqaddasi, *Descriptio imperii,* ed. by De Goeje, p. 355; Ibn an-Nadim, *K. al-Fiḥrist* (Book of the List), edited by G. Flügel, p. 20 ll. 3–4; and I. Ben-Zvi's Hebrew essay "On the Jews of Khwarizm and the Khazars" in his *Nidḥe Yisrael,* pp. 211–18, reviewing recent theories advanced by Soviet archaeologists, especially S. N. Tolstov. Cf. also *infra,* n. 33. Khazar use of the Hebrew alphabet seems to be borne out by two Hebrew inscriptions in an as yet unidentified language. Cf. D. Chwolson's *Corpus inscriptionum hebraicarum,* cols. 140 f., 146 f., Nos. 35, 154; and Poliak's *Khazariyyah,* pp. 121 ff., 241 f., referring also to the indebtedness of the Cyrillic script to the Hebrew alphabet. See *infra,* n. 45. One may mention in this connection the remark of a Persian writer (Mubarak Shah), in 1246, that "the Khazars also have a script which is related to the script of the Rus." Cited by R. N. Frye in his "Notes to Islamic Sources on the Slavs and the Rus," *MW,* XL, 23. The sequence seems to indicate, however, that he thought of a script running from left to right! On Armenian Jewry, see *supra,* Vols. I, p. 169; II, pp. 165, 204, 404 n. 36; Chaps. XVI,

n. 18, and XVII, n. 44; the Jews of Khiva and Bukhara and the so-called Mountain Jews of the Caucasus, cf. also J. Marquart's *Osteuropäische und ostasiatische Streifzüge,* pp. 284 ff.; and *infra,* n. 45.

32. *Seder Eliyahu rabbah,* XXVII (XXIX), ed. by M. Friedmann, p. 146. To be sure, V. Aptowitzer's theory that this midrash is to be dated in the ninth century has been disputed by other scholars. Cf. *infra,* Chap. XXVIII, n. 7. Yet the present formulation may stem at least from a later copyist who rephrased an older homily in the light of the intervening conversion of the Khazars.

33. Cf. Dunlop, *History,* pp. x, 60 ff. The date of Bulan's conversion, and even the fact itself, have often been debated. Since Yehudah Halevi, it has been more or less generally assumed that that conversion took place approximately in 4500 A.M. (740 C.E.). However, the fact that Bulan is recorded to have attacked Ardabil in 730, has induced S. P. Tolstov to suggest that he himself had been one of the Khwarizmian leaders who, according to Al-Biruni, had been forced out of their country by the Muslims in 712. Following up his general theory of the predominantly Khwarizmian origin of Khazar Jewry, Tolstov suggested that Bulan, as well as his reputed teacher Isaac Sanjari, mentioned in Joseph's letter to Ḥisdai ibn Shapruṭ, had already been Jewish military leaders in Khwarizm. Cf. V. Altman, "Ancient Khorezmian Civilization in the Light of the Latest Archaeological Discoveries (1937–1945)," *JAOS,* LXVII, 81–85; and especially Tolstov's *Po sledam drevnekhorezmiiskoi tsivilizatsii* (On the Traces of the Ancient Khwarizmian Culture; available also in O. Mehlitz's German translation); and his and T. A. Zhdanko's *Archeologicheskiye i etnograficheskiye raboty Khorezmskoi ekspeditsii 1945–1948* (Archaeological and Ethnographic Work of the Khwarizmian Expedition of 1945–1948; the ethnographic studies, pp. 247 ff. are particularly relevant). Cf. also Ben-Zvi's comments in his *Nidḥe Yisrael,* pp. 216, 218; and A. N. Poliak's succinct observations on "Soviet Archaeology and Research in Jewish History" (Hebrew), *Molad,* VIII, 315–17. But there is no supporting evidence for Tolstov's obviously far-reaching suggestion. Even if Sanjari's name were derived from a similar-sounding Khwarizmian military title and he professed Judaism before Bulan's conversion, these assumptions would prove nothing concerning his pupil's origin or earlier faith. These are but a few of the numerous difficulties of utilizing unwritten archaeological data for historical research. See *infra,* n. 52. On the other hand, in "The Date of the Conversion of the Khazars to Judaism," *Byzantion,* XV, 76–86, G. Vernadsky has suggested 862–66 as the most likely historical juncture. However, he has placed too much reliance on Ibn al-Faqih's sweeping assertion that "all Khazars are Jews; they have but recently adopted Judaism." Cf. his *K. al-Buldan* (Liber Regionum), ed. by M. J. de Goeje (in *Bibliotheca geographorum arabicorum,* Vol. V), p. 298. This assertion is based on pure hearsay, no more historically valid than, for instance, Eldad ha-Dani's contention that the Khazars were descendants of the tribe of Simon and the half tribe of Menasseh (in his "Reports," ed. by A. Epstein, pp. 25, 30)—a genealogy already doubted by the author of the Cambridge document published by Schechter. We have, therefore, followed here the accepted date of about 740, at least until some further evidence shall be uncovered. See *infra,* n. 44.

34. Cambridge fragment, ed. by Schechter, "Document," *JQR,* III, 204 (Hebrew), 21 f. (English); Kokovtsov's *Perepiska,* pp. 33 (Hebrew), 114 (Russian). The begin-

ning of this document is unfortunately in such poor condition that the editors had to leave many lacunae. But it appears that the author referred here to arrivals from the Byzantine Empire alongside those from Armenia. True, the authenticity of this document has frequently been impugned. Kokovtsov himself, who provided it with a fine, detailed commentary, was inclined to date it from the thirteenth century. However, these critics were effectively refuted by Landau, who plausibly suggested that that letter had reached Ḥisdai before the composition of his epistle to King Joseph. Amplifying statements by several predecessors, Landau pointed out many similarities between the two letters which can best be explained by the assumption that the famous grammarian, Menaḥem ben Saruq, acting as Ḥisdai's secretary, time and again referred to passages in the Khazar communication. Cf. Landau's *Beiträge,* pp. 30 ff., 45 f. The letter may, indeed, have been brought to Spain by an earlier Byzantine visitor, although its transmission through Isaac ben Nathan, Ḥisdai's unsuccessful messenger, via Constantinople is not altogether impossible on chronological grounds. In this case we merely would have to assume that Ḥisdai's original letter, entrusted to Isaac about 944, was subsequently rewritten in the light of the fuller information about Khazaria then available in Cordova and dispatched some time later through Germany and the Slavonic countries. On the generally friendly Byzantine-Khazar relations during the crucial eighth century, see B. T. Gorianov's review article "Byzantium and the Khazars" (Russian), *Istoricheskie Zapiski,* XV, 262–77.

35. Schechter, "Document," *JQR,* III, 206 ff. (Hebrew), 216 f. (English); Kokovtsov's *Perepiska,* pp. 31, 34 f. (Hebrew), 101, 116 (Russian); Mas'udi, *K. Muruj adh-dhahab,* II, 8 f.; Abu Isḥaq al-Fárisí al-Istakhri's *K. Masalik w'al-mamalik* (Viae regnorum. Descriptio ditionis moslemicae), ed. by De Goeje (in *Bibliotheca geographorum arabicorum,* Vol. I), pp. 220 ff. On the threefold Sabbath observed by the ruler of "Khaidan," near Derbend, see Muslim ibn Abu Muslim's report, cited by J. Marquart in his *Osteuropäische und ostasiatische Streifzüge,* p. 285. According to some Arab authors, the number of superior judges was nine rather than seven. Cf. Dunlop's *History,* p. 93. On Jewish religious influences on other Caucasian and Slavonic tribes, see Poliak's *Khazariyyah,* pp. 154 ff.; and *infra,* nn. 47, 50.

36. Schechter, "Document," *JQR,* III, 206 (Hebrew), 215 (English); Kokovtsov, *Perepiska,* pp. 17, 23, 34 (Hebrew), 67, 80, 115 (Russian); Ibn Fadhlan's "Missive" in the excerpt translated and commented on by Dunlop in his *History,* pp. 109 ff. (the figure of 25 vassal kings is confirmed by a variant in Eldad's account); the inscriptions reproduced in A. Harkavy and H. L. Strack's *Catalog der hebräischen Bibelhandschriften der Kais. Oeffentlichen Bibliothek in St. Petersburg,* pp. 35 ff. No. 14, 39 ff. No. 15. Cf. Poliak, *Khazzariyyah,* pp. 161 ff. Harkavy's criticisms of the Firkovitch inscriptions are partly borne out by the "Two Letters from Abraham Firkovich," published by A. Kahana in *HUCA,* III, 359–70. Yet even in his fabrications the latter so skillfully blended genuine documentation with his forgeries that each testimony must be critically reexamined on its own merits. Characteristically, the cave as a center of Jewish worship, and its role in the conversion of Khazars, was also mentioned in the traditions recorded in Yehudah Halevi's *K. al-Khazari* (II.1). On the extensive use of caves for religious purposes by the Crimean and other Christians then and later (there were "cave monasteries" all over southern Russia throughout the Middle Ages) and the discoveries of Hebrew biblical scrolls in Near Eastern caves at that time, see the data furnished by J. Sauer in "Die christlichen Denkmäler

im Gotengebiet der Krim," *Oriens christianus,* 3d ser. VII, 188–202, and Plates II–IV, including a reproduction of the old synagogue of Tshufut-Kale; I. Stratonov in "Die Krim und ihre Bedeutung für die Christianisierung der Ostslaven," *Kyrios,* I, 386 f.; and *infra,* Chap. XXV, n. 56. On "The Bosporus Inscriptions to the Most High God," extensively debated since their publication by Latyshev in 1890, cf. now E. R. Goodenough's pertinent essay in *JQR,* XLVII, 221–44.

37. Cf. Joseph's correspondence with Ḥisdai, the Cambridge fragment, and Yehudah bar Barzillai's *Sefer ha-'Ittim* (fragment first published by S. Assaf) in Kokovtsov's *Perepiska,* pp. 34, 127 f. (Hebrew), 115, 128 f. (Russian); Petaḥiah's *Sibbub,* ed. by Grünhut, pp. 4 (Hebrew), 4 f. (German); in Benisch's English trans., pp. 6 ff.; Poliak's *Khazzariyyah,* pp. 145 f. To be sure, H. Field and E. Prostov make no mention of Jews or monotheism in their review of "Recent Excavations in Crimea: Phanagoria," *Gazette des Beaux-Arts,* 6th ser., XXIII, 129–34. But this essay is evidently too sketchy to allow for any conclusions on this score. Phanagoria, moreover, no longer appeared in the medieval sources under that name, but rather under its Turkish designation, Tmutarakan. Known from the Cambridge fragment and other sources, this name has long been debated. H. Grégoire seems to be a minority of one to postulate its Greek origin. Cf. "Le Nom de la ville de Tmutarakan," *Nouvelle Clio,* IV, 288–92. Grégoire adheres here to his general denial of the historicity of the Cambridge fragment, see *supra,* n. 30. Cf. also the impressive list of eleven predecessors during about a century and a half after the days of Obadiah, enumerated by Joseph in his letter to Ḥisdai in Kokovtsov's edition and translation, pp. 24, 80 f. All of them bore Hebrew names.

38. Kokovtsov, *Perepiska,* pp. 23 f., 80; Ibn Daud, *Sefer ha-Qabbalah* (Chronicle) ed. by Neubauer, *MJC,* I, 79. On the developments leading up to the arrangement of regular Hebrew prayer books in the ninth century, see *infra,* Chap. XXXI. One must also bear in mind the old syncretistic traditions of the entire Black Sea region, which go back to ancient times. See for instance, the characteristic magic text found in a silver talisman encased in bronze which was detected in Pontian Amisos (Samsun), in Frey, *Corpus,* II, 53 f. No. 802; and *infra,* n. 43.

39. Yaqut, *K. Mujam al-buldan* (Geographisches Wörterbuch), ed. F. Wüstenfeld, II, 440; Schechter, "Document," *JQR,* III, 210 (Hebrew), 218 f. (English); Kokovtsov, *Perepiska,* pp. 35 f. (Hebrew), 118 ff. (Russian); Poliak, *Khazariyyah,* pp. 188 ff.; Dunlop, *History,* p. 113 n. 101. The confusion between Oleg and Igor in the Cambridge fragment has given rise to several conjectures, such as that our author referred to the powerful Olga, Igor's wife, that he had in mind an otherwise unattested Tmutarakan prince by that name (Mošin, "Les Khazares," *Byzantion,* VI, 319 ff.) or that he used "Helgo" in a generic sense as the "grand-duke" of Kievan Russia. The latter suggestion is slightly supported by a Bulgarian Greek inscription of 904, in which the word *oglou* is explained by K. Menges as a derivative from the Turkish *oglu* (son). Cf. the literature listed by H. Grégoire in "L'Histoire et la légende d'Oleg prince de Kiev," *Nouvelle Clio,* IV, 281–87. But even if the name Oleg were a mere lapsus, it would certainly not invalidate the entire account. Cf. Landau, *Beiträge,* pp. 34 ff.; and *supra,* n. 30. Cf. also the doubts, in our opinion excessive, concerning the subjection of Russians to Khazar rule, voiced by B. A. Rybakov in his "Rus and Khazaria" (Russian), *Sbornik . . . Boris Dmitrievich Grekov,* pp. 76–88; and *infra,* n. 43.

40. Benjamin, *Massa'ot,* pp. 51 ff. (Hebrew), 54 ff. (English); J. Mann, "Messianic Movements during the First Crusades" (Hebrew), *Hatekufah,* XXIV, 347 f.; Poliak, *Khazariyyah,* pp. 188, 232 ff., 278 ff. The date and circumstances of David Alroy's uprising are still uncertain. On this complicated problem, cf. *infra,* Chap. XXV, n. 69. Cf. also W. J. Fischel, "Azarbaijan in Jewish History," *PAAJR,* XXII, 3; A. N. Poliak, "David Alroy" (Hebrew), *Ha-Kinnus ha-'olami* (World Congress of Jewish Studies), I, 404–6. On the "Shield of David" cf. also T. Nussenblatt's Yiddish essay (with notes by Z. Kalmanowicz) in *YB,* XIII, 460–76, 583–84; G. Scholem's succinct observations on "The Curious History of the Six-Pointed Star," *Commentary,* VIII, 243–51; P. J. Diamant's "How Has the Shield of David Turned into a Symbol of Judaism?" (Hebrew), *Reshumot,* n.s., V, 93–103 (postulating a nexus with heraldry used by the communities of Prague, Vienna and Frankfort); and H. Levy's "Origin and Significance of the Mâgên Dâvîd," *Archiv Orientalni,* XVIII, 330–65 (referring to two old Assyrian seal impressions and connecting the symbol with the cult of Shalim in Jerusalem). None of these authors makes any reference to Alroy, whose connection with the *Magen David,* postulated by Poliak, still awaits further elucidation and proof.

41. Ḥisdai's letter in Kokovtsov, *Perepiska,* pp. 16 (Hebrew), 66 (Russian); Isidore of Seville, *De fide catholica contra Judaeos,* Book I in *PL,* LXXXIII, 464; Christian Druthmar, *Expositio in Evangelium Mattei,* lvi (on Matt. 24:14), *ibid.,* CVI, 1456. The relations between the Khazars and the racially related Magyars are discussed by C. A. Macartney in *The Magyars in the Ninth Century,* pp. 96 ff., 197 ff., 219 ff., 229 ff.

42. So eager were the North African and Spanish Jews of the ninth century to hear about the fate of the Lost Ten Tribes, that they avidly swallowed the narratives of Eldad ha-Dani about the remote Jewish communities which he had allegedly visited. Only the ritualistic variations recorded by him raised questions in their minds concerning his own orthodoxy and that of these distant Jewries. See *supra,* Chap. XVII, n. 53. On the legends concerning the Ten Tribes and their messianic implications, see also *infra,* Chap. XXV, n. 69.

43. Ibn al-Faqih, *K. al-Buldan,* ed. by De Goeje, p. 271 (De Goeje's note thereon is superseded). The authenticity of the crucial Tmutarakan inscription, frequently doubted, has been effectively defended by M. Miller in his "Third Russian Center" (Ukrainian), *Naukovii Zbirnik,* I, 54 ff. A corrective to the exaggerating assertions concerning Russian domination over that duchy, indeed over all of Khazaria, is supplied by N. Banescu who, on his part, overstates the Byzantine control during the eleventh and twelfth centuries. Cf. "La Domination byzantine à Matracha (Tmutorokan), en Zichie, en Khazarie et en Russie à l'époque des Comnènes," *Bulletin* of the Rumanian Academy, Hist. Section, XXII, 57–77; and other data discussed by G. von Rauch in his "Frühe christliche Spuren in Russland," *Saeculum,* VII, 59 ff. The impact of Khazar migrations was felt in both East and West. While the influence of Khazar settlers in the Slavonic countries has often been treated, especially by scholars interested in the origins of East European Jewry, that in Asiatic lands is only now beginning to emerge from age-old obscurity. Cf. *supra,* nn. 31–32; and, more generally, A. Zajaczkowski's Polish essay "On Khazar Culture and Its Heirs," *Myśl Karaimska,* n.s., I, 5–34.

44. Frey, *Corpus,* I, 481 ff. Nos. 678, 680–81; A. Scheiber, "Jews at Intercisa in Pannonia," *JQR,* XLV, 194 (based on the recent Hungarian excavations of that ancient Roman frontier post). Cf. also the other inscriptions reproduced by Frey, pp. 487 ff. Nos. 675–94; and *infra,* n. 50. Some of those classified by Frey as stemming from either Judaizing pagans, or as "probably" Christian (pp. 576 ff., Nos. 78*–79*, 102*) may likewise be of Jewish or "God-fearing" origin, despite their obvious syncretistic traits. Cf. L. H. Feldman's "Jewish 'Sympathizers' in Classical Literature and Inscriptions," *Transactions* of the American Philological Association, LXXXI, 200–208; and *supra,* Vols. I, pp. 178 f., 375 nn. 14–15; II, 388 n. 28. In any case, they offer incontrovertible testimony for the influence of Judaism on the ancient populations of the Balkans and the Black Sea region. On the general continuity of life in the Danubian basin from Roman times, cf. A. Alföldi's *Untergang der Römerherrschaft in Pannonien.* Cf. also P. Lemerle, "Invasions et migrations dans les Balkans depuis la fin de l'époque romaine jusqu'au VIIIe siècle," *RH,* CCXI, 265–308; *supra,* n. 38; and the literature listed *supra,* Vol. II, p. 406 n. 42.

45. Eldad's "Itinerary," ed. by Epstein, p. 25. The so-called "Mountain Jews" of the Caucasus will be treated more fully in a later context. Cf. the extensive bibliography appended to R. Loewenthal's essay, "The Judeo-Tats in the Caucasus," *HJ,* XIV, 80 ff.; and C. Toumanoff's related recent study of "Christian Caucasia between Byzantium and Iran: New Light from Old Sources," *Traditio,* X, 109–89.

46. Correspondence with Nicholas I in the latter's *Epistolae et decreta,* in *PL,* CXIX, 978 ff., 1014 f. We do not possess the original Bulgarian inquiry, but its contents can be reconstructed from the papal answer. Cf. the rather meager data assembled by S. Mézan in *Les Juifs espagnoles en Bulgarie,* pp. 5 ff. In "La Date de la conversion des Bulgares," *Revue des études slaves,* XIII, 5–15, A. Vaillant and M. Lascaris contend that that conversion took place in 864, after Petronas' victory over the Muslims. On the Bogomils, see Euthymius Zigabenus, *Panoplia dogmatica,* XXVII, in *PG,* CXXX, 1289 ff. (this tract, largely devoted to polemics against Christian heresies, also contains a separate Section VIII, *In Hebraeos,* cols. 257 ff.); and D. Obolensky's analysis of *The Bogomils: a Study in Balkan Neo-Manichaeism.* The latter's impact on the Western sectarian conflicts and their relations to Jews and Judaism will be discussed *infra,* Chaps. XXI, n. 54, and XXIV, nn. 29–30.

47. The Life of St. Constantine-Cyril, ed. from a fifteenth-century MS by P. J. Šafařík in his *Památky dřevniho pisemnictví jihoslovanův* (Monuments of Old Southern Slavonic Literature), p. 8 (also ed. with a Czech translation by J. Emler in *Fontes rerum bohemicarum,* Vol. I, p. 11); Photius' letters to the Oriental patriarchs in his *Opera,* in *PG,* CII, 736 f.; and G. Tzenoff's *Geschichte der Bulgaren und der anderen Südslaven,* pp. 242 f. On Photius' likely Khazarian origin, see Dunlop's *History,* p. 194. The eleven characters of the Glagolitic alphabet frequently identified with Hebraic patterns are: A, B, V, G, E, K, P, R, S, Sch, T. The "Russian" Gospel and Psalter, which Cyril allegedly studied in Kherson, were most likely written in Syriac, rather than in the Gothic script and language of Ulfila. Cf. D. Gerhardt's "Goten, Slaven oder Syrer im alten Cherson?" *Beiträge zur Namenforschung,* IV, 78–88; and G. von Rauch's remarks in *Saeculum,* VII,

42 ff. 62 f. But the missionary may have mastered some rudiments of Hebrew already during his earlier services as professor in Constantinople, or even in his younger years in Salonica. Cf. E. H. Minns, "Saint Cyril Really Knew Hebrew" in *Mélanges . . . Paul Boyer,* pp. 94–97; R. Jakobson, "Saint Constantin et la langue syriaque," *Annuaire,* VII, 181–86; and, more generally, F. Grivec's comments on his edition of *"Vitae Constanti et Methodii"* in the *Acta* of the Belgrade Academy, XVII, 1–127, 161–277; F. Dvornik's comprehensive analysis of *Les Légendes de Constantin et de Méthode vues de Byzance;* and some more recent writings listed in M. G. Popruzhenko and S. Romanski, *Kirilometodievska bibliografia za 1934–40 god.* (Bibliography of Cyril and Methodius for the Years 1934–40), a continuation of G. A. Ilyinski's comprehensive bibliographical work to 1933, ed. by Popruzhenko. Cf. also *infra,* n. 54.

48. Cf. V. Novak's survey of "The Slavonic-Latin Symbiosis in Dalmatia during the Middle Ages," *Slavonic and East European Review,* XXXII, 1–28; Ḥisdai's letter to Joseph in Kokovtsov's *Perepiska,* pp. 16 f. (Hebrew), 65 ff. (Russian); V. Mažuranić's *Gebalim,* summarized by C. Lucerna in the appendix, "Der König der 'Gebalim'," of Mažuranić's *Südslaven im Dienste des Islams (vom X. bis ins XVI. Jahrhundert),* pp. 47 ff. The identity of that kingdom still is debatable. From the letter of the Spanish statesman we learn only that the *Gebalim* had sent to Cordova an embassy which included the two Jews. Another identification, namely with *giblim* (mountains) and hence with lands in the Alps, has been suggested by T. E. Modelski in his *Król "Gebalim" w liście Chasdaja* (The King of Gebalim in Ḥisdai's Letter). Cf. also that author's debate with I. Schipper in their Russian communications in *Evreiskaya Starina,* IV, 142–48; V, 100–7. More venturesome is the attempt to connect the name with that of the Croats, allegedly derived from the word *chorb* (mountain). Cf. H. Grégoire's repudiation of this theory in "L'Origine et le nom des Croates et des Serbes," *Byzantion,* XVII, 88–118; "L'Origine et le nom des Croates et leur pretendue patrie caucasienne," *Nouvelle Clio,* IV, 322–23 (offering the equally daring explanation that the name was derived from that of the Bulgarian king-liberator, Kuvrat); and his even more extreme views cited *supra,* n. 30. On the progressive stages of the Christianization of the Serbs, see G. S. Radojičić's analysis of "La Date de la conversion des Serbes," *Byzantion,* XXII, 253–56, placing the final conversion in 867–74, a short time after that of the Bulgarians.

49. Cf. E. Turdeanu's pertinent observations on "Les Apocryphes slaves et roumains: leur apport a la connaissance des apocryphes grecs," *Studi byzantini e neoellenici,* VIII, 47–52; and such more detailed studies as that accompanying A. Vaillant's recent edition of the Old Slavonic text, with a French translation, *Le Livre des Secrets d'Hénoch* (includes an analysis of the Judeo-Christian elements, pp. xi f.). On the historic significance of the Slavonic Josephus, cf. F. Scheidweiler's "Sind die Interpolationen im altrussischen Josephus wertlos?" *ZNW,* XLIII, 155–78; and the literature cited *supra,* Vol. II, p. 379 n. 2. As mentioned there, the Slavonic text shows considerable deviations from the Greek Josephus known to Photius and his contemporaries in the Byzantine capital. This is not necessarily proof of its much later composition, for the translator may have had at his disposal some manuscripts, current along the shores of the Black Sea, which had been brought down in an expanded and modified form by the older Christian

or Jewish settlers. On the Slavonic heritage of Byzantine liturgy and church music and the Jewish ingredients thereof, cf. *infra,* Chap. XXXI.

50. *Monumenta Hungariae Judaica,* ed. by A. Friss *et al.,* I, xxxvii; John Cinnamus, *Epitome rerum ab Joanne et Alexis Comnenis gestarum,* ed. by A. Meineke, pp. 107, 247; Constantine Porphyrogenitus, *De administrando imperio,* XXXVII–XL, ed. by G. Moravcsik with an English trans. by R. J. H. Jenkins, pp. 166 ff., 172 ff. Cf. H. Grégoire's ingenious interpretation of these passages in "Le Nom et l'origine des Hongrois," *ZDMG,* XCI, 630–42; and J. Deér's searching analysis of "Le Chapitre 38 du 'De administrando imperio'," *Annuaire,* XII, 93–121. To be sure, the historicity of the claim of the Jews of Sopron (whose German name, Ödenburg, was curiously explained by a sixteenth-century theologian as derived from the Hebrew *Eden Berekh* or *Barakh,* meaning a place blessed with a fine fragrance) has often been doubted. Cf. especially M. Pollák's *A Zsidók története Sopronban* (History of the Jews in Sopron from Ancient Times to the Present), pp. 10 f. However, more recent students of Ödenburg, founded in the days of Emperor Tiberius and endowed with a municipal statute under the Flavians (its Roman name was Scarbantia) are inclined to agree that Jewish life, too, may have originated there long before the tenth century. Cf. especially K. Mollay's careful investigation of "Scarbantia, Ödenburg, Sopron: Siedlungsgeschichte und Ortsnamenkunde," *Archivum Europae Centro-Orientalis,* IX–X, 222 ff., 264; and *supra,* n. 44.

The identity of the *Khalisioi* with the *Khvalisi* has long been debated. The latter are mentioned in connection with the Caspian Sea, which is called the *Khvaliskoye More* in the *Primary Russian Chronicle,* and hence probably were an offshoot of Khazaria. Cf. that Chronicle, long attributed to Nestor but more recently recognized as a composite work, in S. H. Cross's English translation, with Cross's note thereon; and A. Harkavy's older but still valuable study of *Ha-Yehudim u-sefat ha-Slavim* (Die Juden und die slawischen Sprachen), pp. 132 ff. The further connection of this Jewish, or Judaizing, tribe with the *Khabaroi,* the derivation of that name from the Hebrew *ḥaber,* and the origin of both groups from Khwarizm, are postulated by Tolstov in his *Po sledam.* True, in his *Nidḥe Yisrael,* p. 217, Ben-Zvi objected to the equation of Khabaroi with *ḥaberim,* because the latter term often designates in the talmudic literature Persian magi, rather than rabbinic scholars. But, after the rise of Islam, it obviously was used in both Hebrew and Arabic for such Jewish teachers as *Ka'b al-Aḥbar.* Cf. also D. M. Dunlop's *History,* p. 93 n. 21. Some scholars have interpreted Cinnamus' second statement to mean that he considered the *Khalisi* as Muslims. Cf. B. Kossanyi's analysis of "The Religion of the Khalisi" (Hungarian) *Emlékkönyv Domanovszky Sándor,* pp. 355–68. However, this obscure second passage relating to their following "Persian opinions," cannot controvert the first passage clearly stating that they adhered to "Mosaic laws." Cf. also I. Kniezsa's "Ungarns Völkerschaften im XI. Jahrhundert," *Archivum Europae Centro-Orientalis,* IV, 352 f. (does not refer to Jews, perhaps because of the prevailing antisemitic trend in 1938); and C. A. Macartney's "Studies on the Earliest Hungarian Historical Sources," *ibid.,* pp. 484 f. (especially stressing the equation of *Khalisoi* with the *Kabars*). On the ancient inscriptions, cf. *supra,* n. 44. To those reproduced by Frey one may add one dating from the second or third century from the Roman camp of Brigetium (Ó-Szóny) on the Danube northwest of Budapest. In his "Introduction to the Study of New

Vestiges of the Jewish Settlement in Pannonia," *Löw Mem. Vol.,* Hebrew section, pp. 5–14, Z. Balasz has offered few new materials. But he has advanced some additional arguments for accepting the Jewish provenance of some of these inscriptions, despite their overtly pagan or Christian ingredients. A "mons Judaeorum," two thirds of which belonged to the monastery of Saint Hippolytus, is mentioned in a document of 1113, excerpted in the *Monumenta Hungariae Judaica,* ed. by B. Mandl, II, 509.

51. Cf. G. Bondy and F. Dworsky, *Zur Geschichte der Juden in Böhmen, Mähren und Schlesien,* I, 6 No. 11; Mansi's *Collectio,* XX, 763, 773; XXI, 112 (cf. the summaries in Hefele's *Histoire,* V, 369 f., 542 ff.); and *infra,* Chap. XXI, n. 22. Of interest is J. Deér's analysis of "Der Weg zur Goldenen Bulle Andreas' II von 1222," *Schweizer Beiträge zur allgemeinen Geschichte,* X, 104–38. Although not referring directly to Jews, the author shows here the general impact of West European institutions. The sources for the early history of the Jews in Hungary were carefully assembled in the *Monumenta Hungariae Judaica,* Vols. I–IV, published by the Hungarian Jewish Literary Society. Another volume is now being prepared according to A. Scheiber's communication in his "Recent Additions to the Medieval History of Hungarian Jewry," *HJ,* XIV, 153 (the materials mentioned by Scheiber relate to the thirteenth century and after). A convenient source book in Hebrew is I. Goldberger's *Meqorot le-qorot ha-Yehudim be-Hungariah* (Sources to the History of the Jews in Hungary). There is a vast bibliography on Hungarian Jewish history in the Hungarian language, in which have also appeared such significant Jewish periodicals as the *Magyar Zsidó Szemle.* Readers unfamiliar with Hungarian will find certain data in J. Bergl's older *Geschichte der ungarischen Juden;* and Y. J. (L.) Greenwald's *Toiznt yor yidish leben in Ungarn* (Thousand Years of Jewish Life in Hungary). Perhaps because of the absence of widespread hostility toward Jews, the older Hungarian chroniclers refer to them rather infrequently. Cf. their collected writings in *Scriptores rerum Hungaricarum,* ed. by E. Szentpétery; and C. A. Macartney's succinct analytical guide thereto, entitled *The Medieval Hungarian Historians* (summarizing in part his earlier voluminous *Studies on the Earliest Hungarian Historical Sources*). Cf. also J. Deér's analysis of *Die Entstehung des ungarischen Königtums* (although denying direct conferral of rights by Otto III, he nevertheless shows how Hungary was irresistibly drawn into the German orbit, and hence also into western feudalism); and *supra,* nn. 41, 44.

52. Cf. the Russian and other surveys cited by I. Spector in *An Introduction to Russian History and Culture,* 2d ed., pp. 6 ff.; and in the review articles by T. Lehr-Spławinski, "The Present State of Investigations in the Origins of the Slavs in Soviet Science" (Polish), *Przegląd Zachodni,* IX, Part 1, 508–16 (stressing especially the abandonment of the earlier theses by N. J. Marr); and by J. Eisner, "Les Origines des Slaves d'après les préhistoriens tchèches," *Revue des études slaves,* XXIV, 129–42. After surveying some of these archaeological and prehistorical researches, W. B. Walsh came to the judicious conclusion that "as a result of the Balkan events of the fifth–seventh centuries the center of political life had evidently shifted to the west of the Dnieper, where a tribal union of the Dulebs arose which is presumed to have had the form of a primitive state. Unfortunately archaeological science is as yet unable to say anything about the Dulebs or about their archaic state, for archaeological remains along the western Bug are still waiting to be

explored." Cf. *Readings . . . in Russian History,* enlarged ed., p. 15. These difficulties are, of course, fundamental in all archaeological research, as we have noted in connection with biblical archaeology. Cf. esp. *supra,* Vol. I, p. 299. In the case of Russia, only the recent diggings in Novgorod have yielded written documents dating from the eleventh century and after. Elsewhere we are limited to the usual rather inconclusive testimony of potsherds, remains of buildings, and the like. Cf. G. Stökl's interesting twin reviews of "Russisches Mittelalter und sowjetische Mediaevistik," and "Zeitschriftenschau: Von der Entstehung des Kiewer Staates bis zum Ende der Wirren (862–1613)," *Jahrbücher für Geschichte Osteuropas,* n.s., III, 1–40, 105–22, 264–73, esp. pp. 8 f. Here Stökl also shows the diametrically divergent views on the origins of the Russian state held by such authorities as G. Vernadsky, H. Paszkiewicz, and the Soviet collaborators in a large collective work on the period of Russian feudalism in the ninth to the fifteenth centuries which was published by the Institute for the History of Material Culture of the Soviet Academy of Science as Vol. II of the *Ocherki istorii SSSR* (Outlines of the History of the USSR). Cf. also A. Vucinich's more recent critique of the theory advanced by such Soviet historians as B. D. Grekov and V. V. Mavrodno, concerning the existence in what is Volhynia today of a Slav state during the sixth century, in "The First Russian State: an Appraisal of the Soviet Theory," *Speculum,* XXVIII, 324–44; and I. Ljapushkin's "Early Slavonic Settlements on the Left Bank of the Dnieper" (Russian), *Sovietskii Archiv,* XVI, 7–41. The sparse and, for the most part, rather equivocal ancient sources up to the eighth century are assembled and analyzed in M. Plezia's Polish translation of *Najstarsze świadectwa o słowianach* (Earliest Testimonies concerning the Slavs), while the more articulate Arabic sources are discussed by T. Lewicki in "The Slavonic World in the Eyes of Arab Authors," *Slavia Antiqua,* II, 321–88. Cf. also F. Dvornik's general historical survey of *The Making of Central and Eastern Europe,* with C. Backvis's critical comments thereon in *Byzantion,* XX, 273–87; G. von Rauch's observations in *Saeculum,* VII, 40 ff.; and the interesting bibliographical data supplied by W. Leitsch *et al.* in "Bibliographie zur Geschichte des Mittelalters aus slavischen Zeitschriften," *MIOG,* LXI, 225–41, 496–501, and LXIII, 167–91 (covering Polish and Bulgarian periodicals in 1945–51 and Czechoslovakian publications in 1945–53). Evidently few recent authors, here discussed in more than usual detail because of the inaccessibility of some of their writings to many readers of this work, have evinced concern for the Jewish aspects of early Slavonic history. F. Kupfer and T. Lewicki have at least tried in several publications to analyze the general information obtainable from Hebrew sources. Cf. especially their joint work, *Źródła hebrajskie do dziejów Słowiań* (Hebrew Sources for the History of Slavs and Some Other Central and East European Peoples; was reported "in the press" in 1955).

Nevertheless, the bearing of all these researches on early Jewish history in the Slavonic countries outside the ancient Roman *limes* is obvious. Scholars have generally looked to the Khazars as the main source of early Jewish manpower in all these regions. Most outspoken in this respect have been the various studies by J. Brutzkus, including his aforementioned essay on "The Khazar Origin of Ancient Kiev," in the *Slavonic and East European Review,* XXII, 108–24. The contrary attempt by B. A. Rybakov, in his "On the Problem of the Role Played by the Khazar Khaganate in Russian History" (Russian), *Sovietskaya Arkheologiya,* XVIII, 128–50, to minimize that role is too deeply interlocked with Russian nationalist endeavors to prove the native origins of the early Russian principalities to merit unquestioning acceptance. On the other hand, in "The Decline of the Khazars and the Rise of the Varangians," *American Slavic and East European Review*, XIII, 1–10, F. I. Kaplan stressed the undermining of Khazar strength by Varangian economic competition, but admitted general Khazar mobility and hence the likelihood of deep Khazar influence on the nascent Slavonic nations. But by accepting Grégoire's doubts (*supra,* n. 30) about the authenticity of the Khazar Hebrew documents, the author has deprived himself of some valuable data in support of his thesis. Cf. also A. Zajączkowski's observations in *Myśl Karaimska,* n.s., I, 5–34. It may now be possible to find traces of Judaism in the Dnieper and Bug regions even before the conversion of the Khazars. The long-disputed Firkovitch materials, especially, may appear in a new light from the standpoint of these and the forthcoming archaeological discoveries, like those in the probably pre-Christian cemeteries at Przeworsk and Oskyw. For example, the recent protracted debate among Soviet and western scholars as to whether the difference between burning the dead and burying them—both methods were used in the early Slavonic areas—was due to the racial distinctions between Teutons who practiced burial and natives who preferred cremation, may have unduly neglected the religious factor. Certainly Jews coming from Khazaria or other lands practiced burial, and they probably taught it to some natives in the earliest stages of proselytization.

53. Gen. 9:25; Benjamin, *Massa'ot,* end, pp. 72 (Hebrew), 80 (English). The legend of the Canaanite emigration to the Slavonic lands is mentioned already by Yosephon (ed. by D. Günzburg, I, 4; on the date of this remarkable blend of history and folklore see *infra,* Chap. XXVIII). True, Yosephon mentions also the alternative of the Slavs' descent from the Dodanim, which comes closer to Saadiah's identification of Ashkenaz, Riphat, and Togarma, the sons of Gomer, the Japhetite (Gen. 10:3–4) with the Slavs, Franks, and Burgundians. Yosephon's Canaanite equation is doubly remarkable, as the Bible had clearly counted the Canaanites among the Hamitic races. Yet we find a similar equation of Canaanites with Franks or Alemans in Rashi's, Ibn Ezra's and Qimḥi's commentaries on Ob. 20. The latter clearly placed Alemannia side by side with Ascalonia, or rather Isclavonia, as countries under Canaanite control. These traditions may have had a kernel of historic truth similar to the legends current in North Africa, which made Christian inhabitants in ancient Tanger display an inscription reading, "We are Canaanites expelled from our country by Joshua, the robber," as attested by Suidas and, with some variants, by Procopius. Cf. the Jewish sources analyzed by W. Bacher in "The Supposed Inscription upon 'Joshua the Robber,'" *JQR,* [o.s.] III, 354–57; *supra,* Vol. I, p. 374 n. 13; and Chap. XVI, n. 3. See G. Flusser's Czech essay, "The Report on the Slavs in a Hebrew Chronicle of the Tenth Century," *Česky Časopis Historický,* XLVIII–XLIX, 238–41, which, however, is entirely based on the tenth-century date of Yosephon. In the light of these persistent traditions we may also understand Ḥisdai's simple identification of the King of *Gebalim* with the Slavs, while Khagan Joseph claimed Khazar descent from Togarma. Cf. Kokovtsov's *Perepiska,* pp. 16, 20, 27 (Hebrew), 65, 74, 91 (Russian); and *supra,* n. 48. Only as an afterthought have later generations, including Benjamin's informants, connected the name "Canaan" with the Slavs in their capacity as suppliers of slaves. Cf. also the non-Jewish sources (from Germany in the tenth century and from Italy in the thirteenth century and after), shedding light on "L'Origine de Sclavus-Esclave," analyzed by C. Verlinden in *Bulletin Du Cange,* XVII, 97–128. By accepting some such chron-

ological sequence we also might put to rest modern disputes arising out of this ethnological confusion. Cf. especially S. Krauss's comprehensive analysis of "Die hebräischen Benennungen der modernen Völker," *Kohut Mem. Vol.*, pp. 397 ff.; P. Rieger's interrelated notes on "Ashkenas-Deutschland," *MGWJ*, LXXX, 455–59; and "*Leshon Kenaan*—die Sprachen Deutschlands," *ibid.*, LXXXI, 299–301; and *infra*, Chaps. XX, n. 1; XXVIII, n. 92. Some interesting insights may also be obtained from the related study, "Zur Bezeichnung und Wertung fremder Völker bei den Slaven," by J. Matl in *Festschrift M. Vasmer*, pp. 293–306.

54. *The Russian Primary Chronicle, Laurentian Text*, trans. by S. H. Cross and O. P. Sherbowitz-Wetzor, pp. 96 ff.; D. Abramovich's ed. of *Kievo-Pecherskii Paterik* (Acts of Saints of the Kiev Cave Monastery), *passim*. The identity of Hilarion with Nikon is denied, however, by R. P. Casey in his "Early Russian Monasticism," *Orientalia christiana periodica*, XIX, 373 n. 2, 403 n. 5. Neither the specific circumstances, nor even the date of Vladimir's conversion (986–87, 989 or 991) are definitely known, despite the availability of many Slavonic, Byzantine, Armenian, Arabic, and western sources. Cf. the list appended to H. Koch's "Byzanz, Ochrid und Kiev 987–1037," *Kyrios*, III, 290 ff. Most of these sources are silent on the Jewish aspects of that conversion. The presence of Jewish, including Khazar, propagandists for their faith is evidenced, however, by the story reported by the biographer of Methodius, concerning that apostle's religious disputation with a Khazar, Zambrii, before many Jews and pagans at the Moravian court. Cf. the interesting passage in the Prologue to Methodius' *Vita*, cited in English translation by R. Jakobson in his "Minor Native Sources for the Early History of the Slavic Church," *Harvard Slavic Studies*, II, 65. Cf. also G. Vernadsky's pertinent remarks in "The Status of the Russian Church during the First Half Century Following Vladimir's Conversion," *Slavonic and East European Review*, XX, 294 ff.; his *Kievan Russia*, esp. pp. 60 ff., 160 f. (mentioning also a bishop of Jewish descent, Luka Zhidiata of Novgorod); and the critique of these and other theories in N. Zernov's "Vladimir and the Origin of the Russian Church," *Slavonic and East European Review*, XXIII, 123–38, 425–38. The nationalistic and political motivations of Vladimir's conversion are undeniable. It was aimed not only at the Jewish Khazars, but also at Christian Byzantium. For this reason the latter long refused to canonize Vladimir, while it speedily honored his two sons. Yaroslav's subsequent attempt at independence from Byzantine tutelage by his appointment of Hilarion to the metropolitan see was nipped in the bud. This combination of nationalism with religious orthodoxy helps explain the sudden outcropping of anti-Jewish polemics, especially in the circles around the Petcherskii Monastery. Cf. also the brief summary of M. Heppel's London dissertation, "The Kievo-Petchersky Monastery from Its Origin to the End of the Eleventh Century" in the *Bulletin* of the Institute of Historical Research, XXV, 78–80; and, more generally, G. P. Fedotov's keen analysis of *The Russian Religious Mind: Kievan Christianity*.

On the beginnings of the Jewish community in Russia, cf. the comprehensive analysis of available data in I. Berlin's *Istoricheskiia sudby evreiskago naroda* (Historic Destinies of the Jewish people in the Territories of the Russian Empire); and the collection of "Sources to the History of Jews in the Slavonic Countries" (Yiddish) by S. Huberbrand in *Bleter far Geshichte*, IV, 97–130. Compiled in the Warsaw ghetto during the dark days of 1942, this collection is far from complete and repeats much of the material long known from Harkavy's *Ha-Yehudim u-sefat ha-Slavim.* It nevertheless offers a good review especially of the western rabbinic references to East European Jews in the eleventh to the fifteenth centuries.

55. Cf. Vernadsky, *Kievan Russia,* p. 94. Although emerging from historic obscurity only in the fourteenth century, these Judaizing sects doubtless had more ancient roots in the Russian soil. Cf. the extensive literature up to 1936 listed by D. Oljancyn in his "Was ist die Häresie der 'Judaisierenden'?" *Kyrios,* I, 176–89. A more up-to-date bibliography is clearly indicated. Oljancyn is too insistent on the West European, rather than Khazar, background of that sect, which will be analyzed here in its more familiar late medieval evolution. The impact of the Hebraic, and especially the Old Testament, spirit even on the more orthodox early Russian literature, including the *Primary Chronicle,* has been elucidated in detailed Russian investigations, particularly by G. M. Baratz. Cf., e.g., those listed in Poliak, *Khazariyyah,* p. 332 n. 24.

56. Cf. Bondy and Dworsky, *Zur Geschichte der Juden in Böhmen,* I, 4 No. 6; Adam of Bremen's *Gesta Hamburgensi ecclesiae pontificum,* II.19, ed. by J. M. Lappenberg, in *MGH,* Scriptores, VII, 312 f. On the mysterious personality of Moses of Kiev, see the few data culled from medieval MSS by A. Epstein in his comments on "Das talmudische Lexikon *Yiḥuse tanna'im va-amora'im* und Jehuda b. Kalonymos aus Speier," *MGWJ,* XXXIX, 511; in his brief note, "Moses aus Kiew," *ibid.,* XL, 134; and more fully in his Hebrew essay, "R. Moses ben Jacob ben Moses of Kiev" (1898), reprinted in his *Kitbe,* pp. 301–7, all mainly based on a MS reading in Jacob Tam's *Sefer ha-Yashar,* No. 522. Moses' correspondence with Samuel ben 'Ali is not mentioned, however, in Samuel's letters, ed. by S. Assaf in *Tarbiz,* Vol. I. Cf. also A. E. Harkavy's comments ("Old and New") on the Hebrew translation of Graetz's *Dibre yeme Yisrael* (History), Vol. IV, Appendix, pp. 44 f. The career of this Kievan Jew was evidently made possible only by his emigration from his homeland to the great center of Jewish learning in France. Whatever intellectual achievements he may have had to his credit while still at home would probably never have become known to posterity if he had remained there. Similarly, a book written in 1124 by one Samuel, "the Russian," is cited only in an Italian manuscript, while some "Novellae on the Pentateuch" composed thirty years earlier were wrongly attributed to Russian authorship. Cf. Harkavy's *Ha-Yehudim u-sefat ha-Slavim,* pp. 16 f.; U. Cassuto's reference in *I Manoscritti Palatini ebraici della Biblioteca Apostolica Vaticana,* p. 144 No. 94 (in Assemani's *Codices* No. 56); and his oral communication to Poliak cited in the latter's *Khazariyyah,* pp. 18 f. Presumably there were other Jewish scholars in eastern Europe at that time who were completely obliterated from memory by the loss, during the storms of the Mongolian invasions, of all Hebrew records existing there before 1240.

Although the Podole (the lower part of Kiev often flooded by the Dnieper) seems to have been the original habitat of Jews and other foreigners (Roman coins found in that district date from the third and fourth centuries), a document of 1151 mentions a "Jewish gate" located in the northeast corner of the city. It stands to reason that this gate opened up on the Jewish quarter of that period. Cf. M. Hrouchevsky's study of "La Principauté de Kyiv (Kiev) au Moyen Age," *Bulletin* of the International Commission of Historical Sciences, XII, 9–21. There is no evidence, however, that there was anything like a formal ghetto in medieval

Kiev, or anywhere else in the Kievan principality. Probably some Jews continued to live in the Podole, and possibly also in other sections of the capital.

57. Ibrahim ibn Ya'qub's "Itinerary," fols. 1 ff., in T. Kowalski's Polish translation, pp. 48 ff. and Plates II, III (reproducing the Laleli Arabic codex). Cf. also the related Polish essays, "The Oldest Report on Poland in a New Edition" by G. Labuda in *Roczniki historyczne,* VI, 100–83; and "Some Remarks on Ibrahim ibn Ya'qub's Report concerning the Slavs" by R. Jakimowicz in *Slavia Antiqua,* I, 439–59 (with an English summary); and, more generally, Lewicki and Kupfer's study mentioned *supra,* n. 52. The results dovetail with the aforementioned researches of Soviet and Czech scholars to show the existence of a fairly advanced civilization long before the Christianization of medieval Poland. Cf. also A. Gieysztor's review of "The Genesis of the Polish State in the Light of More Recent Researches" (Polish), *Kwartalnik Historyczny,* LXI, 103–36; his and his collaborators' annual surveys of "The Direction of Researches concerning the Beginnings of the Polish State" (Polish), appearing in *Przegląd Zachodni* (e.g., that for 1952, IX, Part 1, pp. 206–54); and the more comprehensive annual *Bibliografia historii polskiej* (Bibliography of Polish History) ed. by J. Baumgart (of which two parts coverings the years 1948 and 1949 have appeared). The legends concerning the earliest Jewish arrivals may well contain a kernel of historic truth. Their subsequent elaboration was further stimulated by the self-interest of embattled Jewish communities which thus wished to prove the antiquity of their sojourn in Poland. The evidence of the various place names derived from either Jew (in Slavonic *Zhid*) or Khazar, first advanced by M. Gumplowicz in his somewhat imaginative but still basic study of *Początki religji żydowskiej w Polsce* (Beginnings of Jewish Religion in Poland); and accepted by many other scholars, has unnecessarily been doubted by J. Brutzkus in "The First Data concerning the Jews in Poland" (Yiddish), *Historische Shriften* of the Yiddish Scientific Institute, I, 55–72. Cf. especially the data assembled by Ignacy (Yiṣḥaq) Schipper in *Di Virtshaftsgehichte fun di Yidn in Poiln* (Economic History of the Jews in Poland during the Middle Ages; Yiddish translation from the Polish), pp. 36 ff. Cf. also *infra,* Chap. XXVIII, n. 87.

Unfortunately, we possess neither Jewish nor Polish literary records bearing on Polish Jewry before the end of the first millennium, since all Polish chronicles written before the middle of the thirteenth century disappeared during the Mongolian invasions. This shortcoming will but partially be remedied by the concerted effort of Polish scholars to publish new critical editions of the extant early historical records. Cf. G. Labuda's remarks in the aforementioned report for 1952 by A. Gieysztor *et al.* in *Przegląd Zachodni,* IX, 209 f. The absence of data, on the other hand, in Petaḥiah's travelogue is probably owing to the truncated shape of that itinerary as it emerged from the hands of its thirteenth-century German editors, rather than to the traveler's own lack of interest. A selection of the few extant sources was conveniently assembled for students by R. Mahler and E. Ringelblum in their *Teksty źródłowe* (Source Materials for the Teaching of the History of the Jews in Poland and Eastern Europe), Vol. I (appeared also in Yiddish).

58. M. Gumowski, "Minters and Their Role in the Period of the Piast Dynasty" (Polish), *Wiadomości numizmatyczno-archeologiczne,* I, 137. The problem of the Polish coins with Hebrew inscriptions has been much debated since their first dis-

covery two centuries ago. The most valuable studies still are those by the Polish numismatists M. Gumowski and Z. Zarkrzewski. Cf. especially the latter's Polish study "On the Bracteates with Hebrew Inscriptions," *ibid.*, Vols. I–V. On the other hand, Gumowski's more recent *Corpus nummorum Poloniae,* Vol. I, dealing with the coins of the tenth and eleventh centuries, is strangely silent with respect to the Hebrew bracteates. Perhaps the author attributed them to the period of Mieszko III, and hence relegated them to the unpublished Vol. II. In the meantime there have been many additions to the hordes of Arabic coins found in northern Russia and the Scandinavian countries. Dating particularly from the eighth to the tenth centuries, these coins have reinforced the old assumption that Khazar Jewish traders were major bearers of commerce between the Near East, espcially the regions around the Caspian Sea, and Eastern Europe. After the dissolution of the Khazar Empire this trade greatly diminished, although more Jews doubtless became permanent settlers in all these lands. Some Hebrew coins, it may be noted, were found also in thirteenth-century Germany and elsewhere. Cf. M. Szulwas's illustration in *Die Juden in Würzburg während des Mittelalters,* p. 33 (with reference to Aronius's *Regesten,* pp. 173 No. 389, 188 f. No. 425); and *infra,* Chap. XXII, n. 79. It may be noted that these Hebrew inscriptions are not adorned by such biblical motifs, largely borrowed from the New Testament, as are found on many coins struck by Christian rulers in both East and West. Cf., for instance, J. Vandervorst's illustrations of "Les Emprunts bibliques dans la numismatique de l'Empire Byzantin et du Proche-Orient," *Muséon,* LXIV, 293–304 (with a bibliography including the author's nine previous essays relating to biblical motifs on western coins).

59. Johannes Canaparius, *Vita et passio Sancti Alberti,* XII, ed. by J. Emler in *Fontes rerum bohemicarum,* I, 244 f.; Gallus Anonymus, *Cronica et gesta ducum sive principum Polonorum,* ed. by K. Maleczyński, pp. 17 ff. (on the identity of this important chronicler, apparently a twelfth-century arrival from western Europe, see also J. Zathey's Polish report, "Which Schools Did Gallus Anonymus Attend?" in *Sprawozdania* (Bulletin) of the Polish Academy of Science, LIII, 555–58). Cf. Bondy and Dworsky's *Zur Geschichte der Juden in Böhmen,* I, 3 No. 3; and Aronius's *Regesten,* p. 58 No. 137. On Jewish landowners in Silesia, see *ibid.,* p. 160 Nos. 360–61; and, more generally, *infra,* Chap. XXII n. 7. The historical value of these much-debated sources is discussed in the handy summary by P. David, *Les Sources de l'histoire de Pologne à l'èpoque des Piastes (963–1386),* pp. 35 ff., 91 ff.; in G. Labuda's *Studia nad początkami państwa polskiego* (Studies in the Beginnings of the Polish State). Bishop Adalbert's original biography refers to his difficulties in ransoming Christian slaves while he was still in Prague in 989. A new effort to reconstruct his biographical data from the Polish chronicle by Gallus was made by M. Plezia in "The Oldest Remnant of Polish Historiography" (Polish), *Przegląd Historyczny,* XLIII, 563–70. Plezia believes that Gallus had excerpted passages from a biography of the bishop written by an intimate disciple before 1025. Cf. also S. Krakowski's *Kościół a państwo polskie* (Church and State in Poland to the Beginning of the Fourteenth Century).

60. Isaac bar Moses of Vienna, *Sefer Or zaru'a* (Legal Treatise), ed. Zhitomir, I, 196 No. 694; Eliezer bar Nathan, *Sefer Eben ha-'Ezer* (Legal Treatise), ed. by S. Albeck, pp. 7 No. 8 (responsum), 150 No. 327 (on Niddah), 403 (on 'Erubin). On Yehudah ha-Kohen, see A. (V.) Aptowitzer's *Mabo le-Sefer Rabiah* (Introduction to the Book

Rabiah by R. Eliezer bar Joel ha-Levi), pp. 252, 340. Cf. also M. Schorr's *Żydzi w Przemyślu* (Jews in Przemysl); his briefer sketch, *Aus der Geschichte der Juden in Przemysl,* pp. 4 f. (unfamiliar with our document and hence referring to first Jews recorded in the fifteenth century); and other data assembled by Huberbrand in *Bleter far Geshichte,* IV, 97 ff.; and especially by Harkavy in *Ha-Yehudim u-sefat ha-Slavim, passim,* where the author lists also various borrowings from the Slavonic languages found in the eleventh-century Hebrew writings by Nathan ben Yeḥiel of Rome, Rashi, and their successors. Little has been added to the knowledge of the early history of Polish Jewry in recent years. For this reason R. Mahler's more recent *Toledot ha-Yehudim be-Polin* (History of the Jews in Poland) was able to add but a few data to S. M. Dubnow's *History of the Jews in Russia and Poland* (English trans. from the Russian); and J. Meisl's *Geschichte der Juden in Polen und Russland.* On the other hand, T. Jeske-Choinski's *Historja Żydów w Polsce* (History of the Jews in Poland) has contributed an overdose of antisemitic bias, but no new historical facts.